Political Topographies of the African State

Centralized political authority has come under ideological and political challenge almost everywhere. Nowhere have the issues been framed with more urgency than in regionally divided or multiethnic states, where state building and territorial integration are ongoing projects. How will the center govern the provinces? Will political authority at the subnational level compete with, or reinforce, power at the center? What explains variation in the autonomy of the provinces? When is the center likely to hold?

Political Topographies of the African State shows that central rulers' power, ambitions, and strategies of control have always varied across subregions of the national space, even in countries reputed to be highly centralized. Catherine Boone argues that this unevenness reflects a state-building logic that is shaped by differences in the political economy of the regions – that is, by relations of property, production, and authority that determine the political clout and economic needs of regional-level elites. Center-provincial bargaining, rather than the unilateral choices of the center, is what drives the politics of national integration and determines how institutions distribute power. When devolution occurs, will we get local democracy, decentralized despotism, or disintegration of authority? *Political Topographies* shows why and how the answer can vary across space within a single national unit.

This fresh analysis of state building in agrarian societies engages mainstream debates over the origins of political institutions and why institutions change over time. Boone's innovative analysis speaks to scholars and policy makers who want to understand geographic unevenness in the centralization and decentralization of power, in the nature of citizenship and representation, and in patterns of core-periphery integration and breakdown in many of the world's multiethnic or regionally divided states.

Catherine Boone is Associate Professor of Government at the University of Texas at Austin.

Cambridge Studies in Comparative Politics

General Editor
Margaret Levi   *University of Washington, Seattle*

Assistant General Editor
Stephen Hanson   *University of Washington, Seattle*

Associate Editors
Robert H. Bates   *Harvard University*
Peter Hall   *Harvard University*
Peter Lange   *Duke University*
Helen Milner   *Columbia University*
Frances Rosenbluth   *Yale University*
Susan Stokes   *University of Chicago*
Sidney Tarrow   *Cornell University*

Other Books in the Series

Continued on the page following the index.

Political Topographies of the African State

TERRITORIAL AUTHORITY
AND INSTITUTIONAL
CHOICE

CATHERINE BOONE

University of Texas at Austin

PUBLISHED BY THE PRESS SYNDICATE OF THE UNIVERSITY OF CAMBRIDGE
The Pitt Building, Trumpington Street, Cambridge, United Kingdom

CAMBRIDGE UNIVERSITY PRESS
The Edinburgh Building, Cambridge CB2 2RU, UK
40 West 20th Street, New York, NY 10011-4211, USA
477 Williamstown Road, Port Melbourne, VIC 3207, Australia
Ruiz de Alarcón 13, 28014 Madrid, Spain
Dock House, The Waterfront, Cape Town 8001, South Africa

http://www.cambridge.org

First published 2003

Printed in the United States of America

Typeface Janson 10/13 pt.   *System* LaTeX 2_ε [TB]

A catalog record for this book is available from the British Library.

Library of Congress Cataloging in Publication Data
Boone, Catherine.
Political topographies of the African state : territorial authority and institutional choice /
Catherine Boone.
    p.   cm. – (Cambridge studies in comparative politics)
Includes bibliographical references and index.
ISBN 0-521-82557-1 – ISBN 0-521-53264-7 (pb.)
1. Africa – Politics and government.   2. Central-local government relations – Africa.
3. Tribal government – Africa.   4. Sociology, Rural – Africa.   I. Title.   II. Series.
JQ1879.A15B66   2003
320.96 – dc21
                                                                                    2002041690

ISBN 0 521 82557 1 hardback
ISBN 0 521 53264 7 paperback

To Joshua and Alexander

When a state accustomed to live in freedom under its own laws is acquired, there are three ways of keeping it: the first is to destroy it; the second is to go live there in person; the third is to let it continue to live under its own laws, taking tribute from it, and setting up a government composed of a few men that will keep it friendly to you. Such a government, being the creature of the prince, will be aware that it cannot survive without his friendship and support, and it will do everything to maintain his authority. A city which is used to freedom is more easily controlled by means of its own citizens than by any other, provided one chooses not to destroy it.

Niccolo Machiavelli, The Prince (Donno edition)

Contents

Maps, Tables, and Figures

Maps

Tables

Figures

Preface and Acknowledgments

Barrington Moore Jr. wrote that in modernizing Europe, methods of extracting the agricultural surplus formed the core of nearly all social and political problems. In studying rural marketing circuits and land tenure politics in Senegal and Côte d'Ivoire, I gradually realized the salience of this point for Africa, where general forms of the postcolonial state and political trajectories are usually seen as largely autonomous from the main currents of constancy and change in agrarian society. Modern African states have been understood as "bureaucratic states" or "postcolonial states," but rarely as the agrarian states that they (also) are. This book adopts this perspective to rethink some key issues of state formation, territorial integration, and institutional development in modern Africa.

The main argument is that social forces have gone far in shaping and constraining patterns of state formation since the end of the nineteenth century, but that the full significance and implications of this are only revealed through development of appropriate spatial and temporal frames of analysis. We depart from much earlier work by highlighting the existence of geographically uneven patterns of state building within any given country; these uneven patterns are the "political topographies" referred to in the title. How and to what extent agrarian societies in Africa have been incorporated into the modern state are outcomes that have been determined by center-periphery struggles that are themselves shaped by local political facts. As Machiavelli pointed out in describing a different context, successful rulers devise governing strategies that take local opportunity and challenge into account. In Africa as elsewhere, structure and choice are both at work as rulers make states under circumstances not of their own choosing.

Although the errors and larger interpretations herein are solely mine, the reader will soon see that I am indebted to many others, and in this sense the work is a collective product. I owe most to those whose work is cited in the footnotes, and give special mention to the work of Paul Pélissier, Robert Brenner, and Peter Geschiere, which provided foundational ideas. For ideas offered in conversation and/or comments on earlier papers and versions of this manuscript, I would like to thank Musa Abutudu, Arun Agrawal, Anthony Appiah-Mensah, Atta Brou Noel, Gareth Austin, Joel Barkan, Robert Bates, Linda Beck, Michael Chege, Toyin Falola, Kathryn Firmin-Sellers, Joshua Forrest, Clement Henry, David Himbara, Norma Kriger, David Laitin, Barbara Lewis, Joel Migdal, Mick Moore, Martin Murray, Greg Nowell, Brett O'Bannon, Jesse Ribot, John Saul, James Scott, Ibrahima Thioub, Peter Trubowitz, Nicolas van de Walle, Leonardo Villalon, Brian Wampler, Jennifer Widner, Dwayne Woods, and Crawford Young. Kendra Bartsch provided research assistance for three years while she finished her undergraduate degree at the University of Texas at Austin. Jackie Johnson of the University of North Carolina Press drew the maps of West Africa.

The project was launched while I was an Academy Scholar at the Harvard Academy for International and Area Studies from 1990 to 1992, and I thank Henry Rosovsky for his early interest in this work. Field research was funded by the Harvard Academy of International and Area Studies, the Social Science Research Council, Fulbright, and the McNamara Fellowship of the World Bank Development Institute. During the Ivoirian part of the research I was a visiting researcher at the Centre Ivoirien de Recherche Economique et Sociale and benefited greatly from the collegial support of Assalé Kouapa and Atta Brou Noel. The Centre des Etudes Supérieures en Gestion provided an initial base for research in Senegal and connections to the Université Cheikh Anta Diop in Dakar. I would like to thank all those who made these affiliations possible. Versions of the argument have been presented at the Yale Seminar on Agrarian Studies, the Kellogg Institute at Notre Dame, the University of Florida African Studies Center, the departments of political science at Northwestern University and the University of Michigan at Ann Arbor, and annual meetings of the American Political Science Association and the African Studies Association. Early input I received from the Yale presentation added several years to the project by convincing me of the need for in-country comparisons (alongside the cross-country comparisons), and for that I thank James Scott and members of the Agrarian Studies Seminar. Thanks also to the University of Texas at Austin for a Dean's Fellowship in the Spring of 1999, which provided a research leave that allowed me to complete the Senegal portions of the manuscript, and to Jesus Velasco and the Division of International Studies at the Centro de Investigación y Docencias Económicas (CIDE) in Mexico City, where I worked as a visiting professor during the 2000–2001 academic year and completed the manuscript. I am grateful to Bob Bates, who was one of the first readers of the entire manuscript, and who was key in bringing it to finished form.

Permissions to use material that appeared, in earlier form, in journal articles were granted by *Journal of African Economic History*, *Journal of Development Studies*, *Comparative Politics*, and *Comparative Political Studies*.

My greatest thanks go to Peter Trubowitz, who traveled with me to Senegal and Côte d'Ivoire, read versions of this work in its different forms, and gave me ideas from international relations, American studies, and political geography that brought the research into focus. He had great faith in the project, and over the years sustained the hope that it would someday sit on the coffee table as a finished book. During the years I worked on this project, we were blessed with two beautiful sons, Joshua and Alexander Trubowitz, to whom this book is dedicated.

1

Introduction

Changes sweeping sub-Saharan Africa have rekindled interest in popular politics, local communities, and institutional reforms that might decentralize and democratize everyday political life. Activists and observers voice hopes for political devolution and forms of democracy that can empower ordinary citizens and producers. Yet on a continent where 50 to 70 percent of the population remains rural, such hopes are often tempered by skepticism about African rulers' willingness to empower the rural masses, and uneasiness and ambivalence about the political impulses and potential of African peasant society. Do farmers and villagers really represent the core of African political community, "the inner strength of society"?[1] Or is rural Africa reactionary and despotic, the mainspring of xenophobias and destructive subnationalisms? When we look at today's villages of farmers, traders, and chiefs, do we see the democratic antithesis of the authoritarian state or local despotisms that have been reinforced – or even created – by modern forms of rule? These are questions about power, political capacity, and state institutions in rural Africa. They have implications for how we understand African state building, for formulating and justifying strategies for institutional reform, and for envisioning Africa's economic future.

This book engages questions about power and political capacity in rural Africa. How is politics configured at the local level? How do rulers choose strategies for governing the countryside, and when do strategies change? Answers matter, for they can help explain the variation we observe in core-periphery relations within and across African countries. Answers can also

---

[1] Sithole, in Ihonvbere 1996:140. See also Adedeji (1994:126), who writes that "[b]eneath the rickety frames of crumbling postcolonial states lie historically evolved structures that rest on trust, respect, and the involvement of people in decision-making."

inform approaches to reforming and strengthening the political institutions that link city and countryside, a goal now defined by many as one of Africa's top development priorities.

The main argument is that there are significant regional (subnational) variations in the political capacities and interests of rural societies and rural notables, and that much of the variation we observe in regimes' strategies in governing the countryside is attributable to this fact. How power is distributed between center and periphery, and how these imbalances are institutionalized, are partly artifacts of the organization of power within agrarian society itself.

Much writing on African state formation has made the opposite argument. Work that tries to explain continuity, reform, or spatial variation in the political institutions that link rulers and rural subjects has typically focused on *exogenous* determinants of rulers' choices. Scholars have emphasized the "importation" of administrative ideologies and structures from colonial metropoles, nationalist politicians' political ideologies, or changes in international funding agencies' ideas about progressive or efficient rural governance. These variables have been advanced to explain cross-country differences in centralization/decentralization of the state apparatus, regimes' treatment of rural chiefs or old African aristocracies, or the amount of prerogative devolved to grassroots-level institutions and actors.

This book focuses on the same political variation, but identifies a different causal arrow. It argues that institutional differences are determined *endogenously*: spatial variations in institutional design and the extent of core-periphery powersharing are products of political struggles and bargaining that goes on within African society between rulers, their rural allies, and their provincial rivals.

It turns out that in Africa, as in most agrarian societies, there are significant spatial or regional variations in rural social organization and political capacity. This geographical unevenness helps explain why informed observers paint images of political society in rural Africa that differ so radically, and also why institution-building strategies aimed at incorporating rural societies into modern states have varied so starkly. Regional variations in agrarian sociopolitical organization, and in rural modes of production, have tended to be overlooked as a source of difference in African state-formation trajectories, considered in an asystematic manner, or analyzed in highly localized contexts. This, I submit, has led to an unwarranted emphasis on the exogenous determinants of variation in how modern state structures have been imposed and implanted in the African countryside.

2

Introduction

This study employs a political-economy approach to map out political contours and cleavages in rural Africa. A close read of histories of colonial conquest, the decolonization period, and the politics of regime consolidation since the 1950s reveals considerable variation in the capacity of peasant societies to bargain with, constrain, or challenge those at the center. I propose a political-economy model that highlights regional variation in the political capacities and interests of rural societies and rural notables, and argue that these differences have shaped the institution-building strategies chosen by governments trying to secure their own rule over the countryside. The result is striking unevenness in real patterns of centralization and decentralization of state power – that is, in the political topography of core-periphery linkage. Different configurations of rural authority have consequences for modern state-building trajectories, with enduring implications for the political autonomy of the local, the nature and accountability of rural elites, and the capacity of localities to organize for political engagement with the state. Possibilities for economic development and decentralized democracy are shaped decisively by these factors. They also shape prospects for sustaining the territorial integrity of Africa's postcolonial states.

The net product of the chapters that follow is a framework and a set of hypotheses for exploring differences in the political trajectories of rural Africa, and for tracking spatial and temporal variation in the geography of state making. In this approach, institution building and reform in the African countryside are viewed not as technical or administrative problems to be solved, but rather as highly political processes. Decisive struggles take place within rural society, and between rural interests and the state. One broad implication is that the African state is more deeply grounded in indigenous rural society than many previous accounts have suggested. Another is that the outcome of current efforts at institutional and economic reform in the countryside is highly dependent on local-level political factors that vary a great deal across space.

The research question is framed as a problem of institutional choice. This makes it possible to propose a theory or model of rural state formation in Africa that is more parsimonious than many other historical and sociological accounts, and that resonates widely with large macrosociological and choice-theoretic literatures on state formation in agrarian societies. In framing the analytic question in these terms, I seek to avoid false debates between choice-theoretic and social-structural approaches. The theory emphasizes the class, communal, and economic structures that demarcate general parameters within which narrower theories of "choice" and collective action must operate, and within which they take on substantive meaning.

I. State Institutions in the Countryside

Institutions linking state and countryside in Africa, as in virtually all developing countries, have formal mandates to promote development and national integration. They structure prices and other economic incentives, distribute political power and authority, and establish formal rules of the game to govern political process. Yet as political actors and analysts have long been aware, there is often acute disjuncture between the formal rules that define institutional structure and functions, and the real politics of how government agencies work. International planners and financial agencies who advocate reforms that will "get the institutions right" ignore this at their own risk, for the effects (and effectiveness) of reform are determined largely by broad features of the political-economic context in which reform is carried out.

This point is especially salient in rural Africa, where sweeping reform of the institutions structuring state-society relations and everyday economic life has come to be seen as the highest development priority. Yet here as in Mexico, the Philippines, and elsewhere in the last two decades, change in formal rule structures has not always produced the desired effects.[2] Decentralization does not necessarily empower local citizens, and can simply strengthen local powerbrokers or state agents instead. Freer markets can lead to retrenchment rather than expansion of export-crop production. Legalization of political opposition does not always protect a regime's opponents from reprisals or broaden the local political arena. Broad institution-building mandates are interpreted and implemented in locally specific ways, often with geographically uneven and contradictory effects. In these ways, official attempts in the 1980s and 1990s to restructure political and economic institutions in Africa's rural areas mirror those of earlier decades.[3] One lesson is that to explain, assess, and attempt to predict, analysts must take seriously the political and socioeconomic context of institutional choice. Informal power relations, communal divisions

[2] Consider for example Fox 1990; Rubin 1996; Crook and Manor 1995, 1998; Ottoway 1997; Agrawal and Ribot 1999.
[3] See Berry 1993.

or solidarities, and underlying economic arrangements can constitute real parameters of institutional change and choice.

In arguing that "institutions are created to vest the interests of the powerful," proponents of a positive theory of institutions are in perfect accord with most analysts of state-society relations in postcolonial Africa.[4] Few observers of the early postcolonial years question the idea that rulers created state institutions designed to entrench their power and enhance the state's extractive capacities. Power-consolidation strategies – originally conceived as means to higher ends – quickly became ends in themselves. State institutions in rural Africa seemed to exemplify the process. As Robert Bates has argued, scholars on the political left and right of the 1970s development debates gradually converged on the argument that rural development agencies in much of sub-Saharan Africa could be understood as institutions of rural political control and taxation.[5]

The state-society relations literature offered rich analyses of the state-centered factors shaping institutional choice in rural Africa. Official drives for administrative decentralization, centralization, political mobilization, party building, and nation building – which appeared in local variants such as *animation rurale*, *ujamaa*, and *harambee* – could be understood in terms of rulers' attempts to entrench their advantages in the political struggles that pitted states against peasants, urban against rural, and center against periphery.

Depiction of the state itself as predatory Leviathan had a powerful effect on discussions of governmental institutions in rural Africa. The state-centered approach identified a dominant, "rational" (self-serving) actor in institution-building politics – the regime itself. Rulers' interests were defined as the short-term pursuit of power and state hegemony, rather than development, poverty alleviation, or most of the other formally stated goals of state action. Little room was left for accounts that described marketing boards, official credit agencies, settlement schemes, and provincial administrations as politically neutral or as benevolent initiatives of the state.[6] Yet so compelling was the image of the state as Leviathan, and so striking were the generalizations about the exploitation and political disempowerment of

---

[4] See North 1990; Knight 1992.

[5] Bates 1991; see also Williams 1981; and Munro 1998.

[6] As Michael Bratton (1987:175) writes, "Political expediency plays a formative role in policy choice, with leaders using the distribution of resources as a device to attract political support, nullify opposition, and remain in control."

rural producers, that rural Africa was often depicted – often by default – as homogeneous and uniformly alienated from national politics, capable at best of retreating into local communities and local associational life.

The influential state-versus-society models of the 1980s tended to convey an image of much of rural society as cohesive, largely self-governing, and oppressed uniformly by the state. The countryside was often represented as the political antithesis of the ineffectual and decaying state. In "deep Africa," community was supposed to prevail over power, opportunism, and zero-sum relationships.

This view of rural life informed the sweeping calls for reform that were made in the 1980s and 1990s. North American and international development agencies, and many prominent African and European scholars and public intellectuals, justified calls for downsizing central government and for institutional decentralization on the grounds that these changes would promote local political participation and harness grassroots forms of democracy.[7] The accent was on rural Africa's democratic potential.

With some hindsight it is perhaps obvious that the "democratic decentralization" initiatives of the 1980s and 1990s were bound to produce uneven, contradictory, and often disappointing results.[8] In some cases, the reinvigoration of local despotisms, outbreaks of violence, or even outright decay of core-periphery linkages contradicted the most fundamental rationales for the state reform projects of the day. One problem was that the expectations of reform often were not premised upon concrete and nuanced analyses of the rural settings in which reform was being carried out, or of existing topographies of national integration and political control.

II. Countryside as Strategic Context

Mahmood Mamdani argued forcefully in *Citizen and Subject* (1996) that the state-versus-society approach in African studies did not focus much on political tensions and conflicts *within* the rural areas, on how state authority was imbricated in patterns of everyday village politics, or on uneven distributions of power within rural society. Mamdani is right: in fact, very little

---

[7] Work sponsored by the United States Agency for International Development, USAID (for example, Blair 1996), is often a good example.

[8] See Vengroff 1987; Crook and Manor 1998; Barkan and Chege 1989; Ribot 1999; Munro 2001.

analysis has been devoted to charting out and explaining regional and local variations in these aspects of rural life. This book is premised on the idea that such analysis could help to explain why the actual implementation and effects of broad liberalization initiatives have varied so much across regions and localities, and why they have often been so ambiguous in their effects.

Theorists and practitioners need analytic frameworks for describing difference in rural African political contexts and for hypothesizing about the sources and effects thereof. One step in this direction is a better understanding of the political forces and interests shaping actual configurations of state power at the regional and local level. That is the objective of this book.

I have framed the analytic problem as one of explaining regional variations in the design and functioning of state institutions that were built in the countryside during Africa's "first independence" period, roughly from the late 1940s through the 1980s. Institution building is viewed as a contested process, driven forward and undone by struggles between regimes, rural elites, and farming populations. I ask: What explains variation in the course and outcome of these contests? In efforts to tax and govern peasantries, why did regimes' institution-building strategies differ? The analytic task can be defined as one of developing a theory of "institutional choice" in rural Africa.

The 1950s were years of rural political mobilization and foment in much of sub-Saharan Africa. Intense renegotiations of power and privilege, both within rural society and between city and countryside, persisted into the 1960s, 1970s, and beyond. For the new governments born of the peaceful transfers of power, the immediate goal was to consolidate the political dominance of the center, and to sustain or intensify the taxation of rural producers – and to do so without provoking revolt, or driving peasants out of export-crop production. Nationalist leaders had to impose their political hegemony by demobilizing the rural populations that had been brought en masse into the anticolonial movements.

The rub was that in the regions, localities, and villages, there were established rural elites – chiefs, aristocratic families, religious authorities – who had a stake in defending and enhancing power already achieved. Ordinary farmers were interested in protecting themselves against corrupt and arbitrary rule at the local level. They also wanted to retain a larger share of the wealth they produced. New regimes sought to transfer resources *out* of agriculture in order to fund consumption and investment in the cities. So it was that two core issues of the day – central versus local authority and

7

rural taxation – created conflicts of interest both within rural societies, and between rural actors and the state. In a recent study of Ghana, Rathbone (2000:161) refers to this as "the battle for control of the countryside." Across the continent, these battles would bear decisively on the form and prospects of the postcolonial state.

In the 1960s the mobilizational politics of the nationalist era gave way to a politics of consolidation, centralization of power, and state building. Everywhere, there was steady movement toward updated forms of authoritarian rule. Colonial institutions linking state and countryside were reformed and rebuilt, and new institutions were created. To demobilize rural masses and consolidate the center, regimes sought to alter distributions of power between central authorities and rural elites.

As the chapters that follow will show, rulers adopted strategies that differed significantly across subregions within a single national territory. In some regions, nationalist politicians shared power with rural chiefs and aristocrats. In others, they sought to destroy the foundations of neotraditional power. Some zones were governed intensively, through tight, top-down control, while others were left to their own devices, granted extensive autonomy, or simply neglected and not incorporated into the national space. The chapters that follow constuct a typology of these "institutional strategies," and propose a theory about the conditions under which rulers are likely to chose each one. Cases from West Africa are used to test the propositions and sketch out their implications for development, democracy, and the cohesion of contemporary states.

Chapter 2 proposes an institutional-choice theory to explain variation in institutional outcomes. Strategic choice theorists define the most generic elements of such a theory: models of bargaining or competition over institutional choice should specify actors' choice sets, interests, resources, and relative bargaining power. State-centered analysis in African studies concentrated almost exclusively on *rulers'* interests, often implying that rural actors and interests were simply overwhelmed by regimes' coercive and bargaining power. A strategic choice model draws attention to what is underspecified in this equation: existing theories do not go far enough in specifying the *rural* interests, resources, and bargaining strengths that constrained regimes' power and strategies, and that thus played a role in shaping institutional outcomes. Studies of modern African state building have been insufficiently attentive to the fact that regimes sought to impose their rule on rural societies that differed considerably in their capacity to shape the terms of their integration into national political economies.

Introduction

There were differences in rural Africans' ability to use state power to serve local purposes and to contest the hegemonic and extractive drives of new regimes. New politicians in the cities found themselves locked in negotiations and confrontations with rural elites over the distribution of power, political prerogative and authority, and rural wealth. Rural elites, meanwhile, tried with varying degrees of success to wield power and influence over the ordinary farmers who were their followers, clients, kinsfolk, and subjects. The intensity and nature of the rural political challenge to new African regimes varied by region, shaping and constraining possibilities for collaboration between regimes and rural notables. I offer a social-structural theory of these patterns in rural politics, and argue that they have had systematic political (institutional) effects.

In defining the strategic context of choice, I propose a model that captures two social-structural sources of variation in the interests and political capacities of rural elites.[9] It predicts that variations in class and communal structure will produce different patterns of political battling and bargaining between regimes and rural elites. Regimes "choose" the institution-building strategies that maximize their advantage in particular political contexts. Different institutional configurations – different ways of distributing power and administrative prerogative – are the result.

The analytic strategy is similar to that employed by Margaret Levi (1988) and Barbara Geddes (1991, 1994), who analyze institution building as if it were a strategy of "rational" rulers seeking to tax society and to reproduce their own power. By assuming (imagining) that all rulers have similar interests, and that a regime can be taken as a unitary actor, the focus of analysis can be shifted away from the state itself. This allows for more focused analysis of the societal sources of variation in political outcomes.

An institutional choice approach is useful given the purposes of this study. We can push to the limit the argument that *state-building strategies differ because rulers face different challenges and opportunities* – rulers operate within different structural or strategic contexts. The proposition is not so improbable

---

[9] Contributors to a new literature on center-region bargaining in what Treisman (2001) calls "territorially divided states" adopt similar logics. What is needed is a definition of who the decisive regional actors are (who are the leaders?), and then some theoretical specification of (1) their willingness to challenge the center and (2) their capacity to do so. On the former Soviet Union, see Bunce 1999, Treisman 2001, and Stoner-Weiss 2001, who specify these variables in different ways. For another way of giving substance to the same logic, this one focused on explaining cross-national unevenness in patterns of decentralization in Latin America, see Willis, Garman, and Haggard 1999.

or far-fetched. It is consistent with the basic logic advanced by Charles Tilly, Barrington Moore, Robert Brenner, Perry Anderson, and Margaret Levi in explaining variation in European state-building experiences.

As a partial test of this logic, this book offers case studies of institution building in six main regions. They are Senegal's groundnut basin, the Casamance region of Senegal, southern Côte d'Ivoire, the Korhogo region of northern Côte d'Ivoire, the Senegal River Valley, and the Asante region of southern Ghana. Taken together, these regions display strong variation in rural class and communal structure. From these six case studies, distinctive patterns of institutional choice – distinct institutional outcomes – emerge. My argument is that the state-centered factors that are often invoked to explain cross-case similarities and variations fall short in explaining the patterns uncovered here. The observed institutional outcomes cannot be explained without reference to local-level configurations of power and interest.

Analysis of the cases will show that societal constraints, so conceived, explain much of the variation in the rural institution-building strategies that are described here. The empirical material also shows that we still need more refined theories of rural political capacity, of resource constraints that can force regimes to make interregional tradeoffs, of how rulers can play one region off another, and of factors that can shift regimes' assessments of the political risks of exploiting, or not exploiting, certain regions. The usefulness of this book, I submit, is that it offers a theoretical base for building more refined and extended models. Such theories can contribute to thinking about politics in Africa, and about processes of national integration, in more nuanced and empirically grounded ways.

2

Mapping Political Topography in Africa

It is necessary to appreciate, first, that there were extensive regional social organizational differences in early modern Europe, and second, that these regional differences influenced the course of the formation of modern state apparatuses. Yet these considerations have generally been ignored in the literature. The failure to take regional differences in social organization into account has led to an unwarranted emphasis on the exogenous determinants of initial state formation in Western-European history.

Hechter and Brustein 1980:1063

Rural political landscapes vary widely, even across closely neighboring regions in West Africa. Some states have sought to build a local presence that intrudes in the most intimate workings of village life, and even to "rewire the circuits of local authority" (Dunn 1975:195). Others remain aloof. To repeat Goran Hyden's (1983) evocative phrase, they remain suspended balloon-like in mid-air. In some places, the state's administrative outposts are captured by local big men and chiefs, while elsewhere state officials posted in the localities are constrained only by the directives of their superiors in capital cities like Abidjan, Accra, or Dakar. There are variations in the intrusiveness of the state at the local level, in rulers' autonomy vis-à-vis local interests, and in the capacity of rural actors to harness state prerogatives and resources to serve their own purposes. What produces these different outcomes? Who chooses the rules, and why?

All postcolonial governments have sought to extend the reach of the state into rural Africa. Most analyses of these state-building processes have focused on cross-national variation, and have employed statist or institutionalist logics to explain differences. Most accounts have focused on the ideologies of the political leaders that were brought to power by

11

African independence, or on colonial institutional inheritances (the staying power of "imported institutions"). Yet when we undertake a closer examination of state building on the ground, and then survey a broader sweep of African institutional landscape, the received analyses look less and less satisfying.

This chapter argues that as general theory these statist and institutionalist explanations carry a congenital flaw that runs through a large family of New Institutional theory in political science. Like most other explanations of institutional origins that hinge on arguments about state autonomy or path dependency, they tend to offer no theoretical explanation for the preferences of key actors, to stumble over the inconvenient facts of institutional change (path switching) or failure, and to downplay or ignore variations across cases that are supposed to be governed by the same actor preferences or to be following the same path. Limitations of the New Institutionalism through the 1990s – in both its rational choice and historical variants – pointed to the need to go beyond institutionalist logic to develop better accounts of institutional origins and change. Institutional theory had to be grounded in more macro- and/or more microscopic analyses of human context and behavior.

Existing accounts of rural institutional variation in Africa embody the limitations of statist, institutional theory. This book shows that they tell only part of a story that is, in fact, more deeply political – and more shaped by structured political relations within rural African society – than the existing accounts suggest. This finding has implications for how we understand state power in general, for it shows that even in what are conventionally viewed as the modern world's most top-heavy and "artificial" states, the political authority of government is conditioned by micro-level political economies of property relations, personal dependency, and social control. The argument also has practical implications for Africa, for it helps identify and explain the geographically uneven effects of the crises and reforms that are now remaking political landscapes across the continent.

This chapter provides building blocks for an endogenous theory of state building in rural Africa. Part I considers existing descriptions and explanations of differences in how African governments have sought to incorporate rural populations, especially export-producing peasantries, into the modern state. It shows that most analysts have located the source of rural institutional variation in forces that lie outside the rural areas, and indeed, often in forces that lie outside of African society and politics.

Part II makes the case that to explain institutional choice – not only in Africa, but in general – we must theorize macrosociological context. Attempts to do otherwise inevitably fall short of the goal of explaining variation across time and space. Macrosociological theories of the kind historical- and rational-choice institutionalists have sought to avoid offer theoretical specification of the groups/actors that are party to bargaining over institutional design, their interests, their relative bargaining power, and how these variables can change over time. These are necessary ingredients in a theory of institutional choice.

Part III proposes a way to think theoretically about how rural social contexts differ in contemporary Africa. I draw upon literatures on state building in other agrarian societies to propose a model of politically salient social-structural variation in the African countryside. It focuses on differences in rural leaders' interests and bargaining power in their dealings with central rulers.

In order to make the argument that these differences have systematic political-institutional effects, we need a way of describing variation in institutional design and process ("institutional outcome"). Part IV does this by modifying descriptive schema proposed by public administration scholars. Here we incorporate factors that are prominent in political scientists' and historians' more contextualized and usually more politically frank descriptions of institutional structure and process. This yields a matrix that describes four different "institutional configurations." In spite of its roughness, this matrix captures cross-case variations in state-building strategy that have been recognized by scholars since Machiavelli (1966:24). The differences are clearly recognizable in modern Africa: although they are dramatic, they have been overlooked or untheorized in nearly all of the work on African state building since the 1960s. Similar patterns of variation can be observed in the different reform trajectories of the 1990s.

With these elements in place, Part V of this chapter lays out the theory of societal cause and institutional effect that will be examined in the case studies.

One result, I hope, is new and suggestive hypotheses about the nature, sources, and effects of political variation in rural Africa. The ultimate goal is a better understanding of the "deep politics" of institutional choices that shape the fate and fortunes of African populations, including those in some of the continent's most densely populated, most productive, and most heavily commercialized zones of agricultural production.

13

I. Institutional Variation in Africa: External Determinants?

This study is interested in variations in center-local relations and in how they have been institutionalized in postcolonial states. How have earlier analysts described these variations? How have the differences been explained?

From existing studies it is possible to distill two models of variation in the institution-building strategies adopted by African regimes in their efforts to govern the countryside. One model contrasts statist, aggressively interventionist, or transformative institution-building strategies with more conservative, moderate, and less interventionist strategies. The pivotal distinction in Mahmood Mamdani's *Citizen and Subject* (1996) is between radical and conservative regime ideologies.[1] A second model contrasts institutional structures in terms of their degree of political centralization or decentralization; that is, in terms of the degree of political autonomy they afforded to local-level political authorities and government agencies. This model emphasizes continuities that span the colonial and postcolonial periods. It stresses the imported origins of the modern African state and the enduring institutional legacies of European colonialism. Miles's *Hausaland Divided* (1994) is an example. There is little systematic overlap in these two descriptions of the design and operation of postcolonial states, and so far, analysts have tended to explain the differences almost exclusively in terms of state-centered variables. I hope to show that these formulations are underdetermining, and that we can move forward by bringing the alternative conceptions of state design into alignment and pursuing a more political theory of institutional choice.

The first model, which contrasts radical and conservative models of rural development and institution building, focuses attention on differences in the political character of regimes that came to power in the 1960s. In many accounts of this kind, regimes that pursued interventionist strategies are said to have done so because they were guided by Marxist or socialist logics. They built state agencies to constrain the role of capital and the market in the rural economy, sweep away colonial administrative legacies, and radicalize the consciousness of rural populations. Those with a pro-capitalist and neocolonial character, by contrast, were moderate and status-quo oriented in their approach to rural governance. Although Mamdani does not seek out the sources of this difference, many accounts resting on this distinction

---

[1] For an early statement, see Lombard 1967:272.

trace it to postindependence leaders' political ideologies – that is, to their political educations or backgrounds in metropolitan politics, and to the influence of powerful European or Soviet-bloc patron states.

Models that hinge on regimes' ideologies do identify a political variable that differentiated regimes in striking ways, especially in the decolonization years of the 1950s and 1960s. They leave much unexplained, however. From the perspective of the present analysis they are not wrong but underdetermining. Could not politically strategic actors use ideological rationales to justify strategies chosen for other reasons? What historical and political circumstances constrained the practical realization of ideological visions? Ideological explanations also do not explain regional variations within one country (or colony): Why would the strategies of an ideologically charged regime like Kwame Nkrumah's vary across regions *within Ghana?* Analysis of ideology can provide clues about moves or postures in political games, but in itself it is too blunt an instrument for explaining institutional choice.

In the second model, which focuses on institutional legacies of colonialism, the pivotal distinction is between French and British rule. It is said that the state in French colonies was a highly centralized institution which governed the countryside through forms of "direct rule" that conceded very little autonomy to provincial agents of the colonial government, be they French or African. This strategy of rule is seen as the extension of governing philosophies and practices prevailing in metropolitan France (that is, of the so-called prefectoral system). The character of British rule in Africa was very different: The British established forms of "indirect rule" wherein indigenous African authorities would exercise considerable power and autonomy on the local level (the so-called Westminister system), and wherein indigenous forms of government would be hardened and reinforced, rather than dismantled or pushed aside. By this argument, the institutional legacies of colonialism produced more decentralized forms of rule in postcolonial anglophone Africa, and more centralized administrative structures in francophone Africa.[2] Miles (1994) develops this longstanding argument in a new and compelling account of the division of Hausaland into French-governed and British-governed colonial territory.

---

[2] For an introduction to these long-running discussions and debates, see Lugard 1926; Akpan 1956; Deschamps 1963; Crowder 1964; Kiwanuka 1970; Miles 1987, 1994: especially 9–12; Mamdani 1996; and Firmin-Sellers 2000.

15

The institutional legacy argument is important but not completely satisfactory, as Mamdani and earlier analysts have insisted. Obviously it cannot account for variation among or within territories colonized by the same European power. The theory of indirect rule was masterminded by Lord Lugard in the 1920s and implemented in textbook form in Northern Nigeria. The same theory produced very different administrative and political institutions in Eastern and Western Nigeria. Institutions linking state and countryside in Senegal and Côte d'Ivoire differ dramatically, even though both were colonized by France.

Much of the rethinking of colonial politics and administrative practice since the 1960s has stressed the extent to which expediency drove both Britain and France to rely on improvised versions of indirect rule whenever they could. By these accounts, what determined the directness of rule was less preconceived administrative doctrine than the success of European colonizers in finding cooperative African leaders and authority figures (intermediaries and *interlocateurs valables*) through whom they would effectively govern the regions and localities. This suggests that the explanation of administrative and institutional difference must take more systematic account of the political realities that rulers confronted in the countryside.

In the cases selected for analysis here, explanations of institutional choice that rest heavily on state-centered factors prove to be either underdetermining (ideology) or overdetermining (colonial institutional legacy). Regimes sometimes developed institution-building strategies that broke dramatically with colonial administrative legacies. They also adopted strategies that varied considerably across regions within their own national jurisdictions.

Existing explanations of institutional variation in Africa display weaknesses or limitations that have serious practical consequences. The received wisdom suggests that colonial regimes and African states forged institutional arrangements in accordance with their own ideologies and visions of social transformation. There is a presupposition of virtually unbridled state autonomy. When carried over into prescriptive work, this can produce widely exaggerated expectations about outside reformers' capacity to make and remake political and administrative process at the local level. When it comes to theory, presuppositions about rulers' autonomy can make for voluntaristic and strangely apolitical theories of the origins and structure of state institutions. As suggested above, these problems are generic to a large and theoretically explicit political science literature on institutional choice. My argument is that systematic conceptualization of the *strategic contexts* of institutional choice helps resolve these problems.

II. Institutional Choice as a Macroanalytic Problem

What does institutional theory in political science tell us about explaining institutional choice? The issue of institutional choice or "origins" actually emerged as a second-generation research problem in this literature. New Institutionalism's original innovation was the argument that humanly devised rules of the game go far in explaining political process and outcomes. In most of the empirical work done in both the historical and the microanalytic variants of this approach, the problem of institutional origin was not an issue: rules or institutional configurations were taken as given, as "independent variables." Comparative work was devoted to showing that differences in the institutional rules or parameters that shape individual choices, or group interaction, account for cross-case differences in outcomes. In longitudinal analysis, stable outcomes were attributed to the persistence of institutional structures that shape actors' preferences and choices (path dependency).[3]

Institutionalists set their work in opposition to the macrosocial modes of explanation that dominated earlier schools of structuralist thought, and in contrast to the atomized, institutionless world of behavioral analysis. Yet over the course of the 1990s, as the challenge of explaining institutional origins posed itself more and more insistently, proponents of the new institutionalism were pushed back toward behaviorialism and macrosociology.

Historical and rational-choice institutionalism ran into trouble when it came to dealing with questions that were not only about institutional origins, but also about change and failure. Analysis that started from a given set of institutional parameters was hard pressed to explain where the parameters came from in the first place. In models that specified no source of actors' preferences other than institutional structures themselves, where did actors find the incentive to alter institutions, or create new ones? With no underlying theory of conditions or forces that reproduced institutional structure, it was also impossible to explain why institutions collapse.

In studies of the making and unmaking of governmental institutions, the matter of direct concern in this analysis, Historical Institutionalists experimented with one solution to these problems. They resorted to theories of state autonomy. The argument was that new ideas, theories, preferences, or visions – factors exogenous to institutionalism's explanatory equation – could explain change over time in leaders' or bureaucrats' preferences for

[3] See the contributions to Steinmo, Thelen, and Longstreth, eds., 1992.

particular institutional configurations. This is the analytic strategy we see in explanations of cross-case institutional variation in Africa. Differences in the structure of territorial administration, for example, are seen as the product of contrasting colonial administrative ideologies, or of the different, Western-inspired visions of the developmentalist project that African rulers brought with them to State House. The problem with state autonomy theories is that they leave Historical Institutionalism, like the Africa-centered theories, open to the charge of voluntarism. What is missing is some logically prior theory of the more pervasive systems of constraint and incentive within which rulers are forced to operate.

Institutional theorists have found two ways to solve this problem. One lies in probing at the micro level to explore the inner worlds of individual and group psychology. Analysts from both the historical and the rational choice schools have turned to behavioral or cultural analysis to theorize "soft" ideational variables – values, norms, trust, and so on – that can answer the question: "What are actors' preferences?"[4] A second approach to dealing with the problem of institutional choice is to return to the macroscopic world of sociological theory.

In 1992 a critic of the New Institutionalism, Paul Cammack (1992:426), argued that institutionalist theory could not stand on its own – it had to operate within a broader sociological framework that it was itself unable to produce. In practice, most institutionalists do just this. Many writers simply make assumptions about social organization and structure, or take key features of a broader social context as given in order to isolate the effect of institutions on particular outcomes. Much of Historical Institutionalism tackled institutional choice problems via comparative analyses in which social structure could be held constant, or invariant, across cases. Rational-choice institutionalists devised micro-analytic theories of institutional choice that *began* with assumptions about power inequalities, social conflicts, and actors' material and economic interests in particular settings.[5] Douglass North (1990) and Jack Knight (1992), for example, showed that it is possible to develop deductive theories of institutional choice once the parties to decision-making conflicts are defined, the distribution of power

---

[4] See Bates 1988; Bates and Bianco 1990.

[5] For North (1990:73), parties to conflicts over institutional design are constituted "as a function of income." Outcomes are determined by the "relative bargaining strength" of competing groups. Jack Knight (1992) provides context for his model of institutional choice by offering theoretically agnostic descriptions of concrete situations of distributional conflict among groups of unequal power.

between them is fixed and known, constraints on choice are specified, and the substance of their goals and preferences is known. Other practitioners of the New Institutional Economics have confronted the issue of sociological constraints in a more empirical manner. Elinor Ostrom (1990:21, 193 *inter alia*) calls for an approach in which key social-structural variables, or "informal institutional structures," are identified on the basis of direct observation of concrete micro-situations. Close field study allows the analyst to set values for situational variables such as "imbalances in power relations among individuals."[6] As her analysis suggests, structure is important in determining outcomes, but institutionalist theory cannot tell you how to discover the structure of the situation in order to conduct the analysis.

Another way to solve this problem is to employ macrosociological theory in an *explicit* manner to specify features of social context that define the parameters and players in institutional choice. This happens to be the strategy of choice in a large, choice-theoretic literature on state formation in agrarian societies.[7] In *Rule and Revenue*, Margaret Levi shows that as modes of production vary, so too do rulers' transaction costs and bargaining power when devising strategies to tax their subjects.[8] Hechter and Brustein (1980) argued that as rural modes of production varied in fourteenth-century Western Europe, so too did the individual calculus of rural elites who contemplated the costs and benefits of surrendering autonomy to a centralized state. These choice-theoretic explanations of variation in state structure are firmly grounded in classic macrosociological definitions of variation in agrarian social organization and modes of production: sociological parameters of institutional choice are defined in terms of class structure, communal structure, and modes of production.[9] This is the theoretical strategy pursued here.

---

[6] Ostrom also calls for close field study to discover the factors that affect the internal world of individual preference formation.

[7] The turn to macrosociological theories of social constraint is also a strategy for transcending the limits of institutionalist explanations in other contexts. See for example Pontussen 1995.

[8] "There seemed to be no reason why an appreciation of the role of structural factors in social life could not be combined with a concern for individual action.... Structure first determines the constraints within which individuals act [but is] insufficient to determine his or her behavior" (Hechter 1983:8). Levi (1988:203) writes that "[r]ational choice theorists are both methodologically individualist (as the term implies) and structuralist (which the term does not connote). Structures – that is, a collection of social relations, institutions, extant organizations, and rules of the game – are a crucial aspect of the analysis."

[9] This is exemplified by the work of Barrington Moore Jr. 1966; Perry Anderson 1974; Robert Brenner 1976, 1982; and Charles Tilly 1964, 1990.

III. An Endogenous Model of Institutional Choice

Institutional choice – in this case, variation in state-making patterns – is the outcome to be explained. Following Levi (1988) and Hechter and Brustein (1980), institutional outcomes are viewed as the product of political bargaining and conflict amongst social groups with differing bargaining power (resources and capacity for coordinated political action) and interests. As institutionalists have been saying, these elements in the explanatory equation are traceable in part to formal political institutions themselves. Yet as Levi, Hechter and Brustein, and a long tradition of historical macrosociologists have argued, they are also traceable to more deeply embedded social arrangements. The focus here is on the role of these embedded patterns of social organization in shaping rulers' institutional choices in Africa.

What is needed at this point is hypotheses about politically salient variation in rural social structure in Africa. We need a theory of how power and politics are configured at the local level, and of the macropolitical consequences of these differences. Macro- and microsociological literatures on state formation in agrarian societies suggest two lines of inquiry, one focused on communal structure and the other focused on class relations.[10]

A. Rural Social Structure and Its Political Effects

The first line of inquiry has to do with the effects of communal structure on rural society's engagement with the state. Communal structure consists of the microscopic matrixes of social organization and control that define politics at the local level.[11] Key variables here are settlement patterns, land tenure and inheritance regimes, and relations of cooperation, dependency,

---

[10] Barrington Moore (1966:468, 475) argued that three aspects of the organization of peasant society are particularly important politically: (1) the character of the link between the peasant community and the overlord [or state]; (2) property and class divisions within the peasantry; and (3) the degree of solidarity or cohesiveness displayed by the peasant community. In the greatly simplified analytic equation proposed here, the first of Moore's "three aspects" is, in effect, our dependent variable, and the other two are hypothesized as independent variables. This formulation does not do justice to the complexity of the issues at stake, but it does shed some new light on the matter. Most studies of the modern African state have taken all three aspects of "the organization of peasant society" as invariant (or without theorizing variation) within and even across African countries.

[11] See Paige 1975; Popkin 1979: especially 48–9 on patron-client relations; Hechter and Brustein 1980; Bates 1981; Hechter 1983:25, 50; Hechter 1987:10; Levi 1988; Brustein 1989; Magagna 1991; Massey 1994; Lichbach 1994, 1995.

and coercion in the organization of production. In agrarian society these elements intertwine intimately with rules and institutions that distribute political power at the local level, govern access to land and other productive resources, and enforce social cohesion. Class structure is an element in the equation, but communal structure does not reduce to this; it can vary across time and space even when class structure, roughly defined, does not. "Peasant," for example, can be used as a class-analytic term, but peasants can settle in "frontier zones" where social and political organization above the household level is weak or nonexistent; they can be members of tightly structured or loosely structured village communities; villages can be autonomous or subsumed within larger sociopolitical entities. Communal structure plays a role in determining the political interests, strength, and options of individuals and groups.

Communal structure is a key variable in the macro- and micro-analytic literature focused on state formation, peasant revolutions, and rural rebellion in Europe, Latin America, and Asia. Variations are associated with differences in the autonomy of rural communities, their capacity for collective action, and the control capacity of dominant groups or social strata.[12] Barrington Moore (1966:475) and James Scott (1976) showed that strong communal structure is a precondition for sustained, coordinated political engagement with outside political forces, including the state. Weak communal structure is associated with low social coherence, low "group solidarity," and low political capacity vis-à-vis the state. Karl Marx's (1852) image of the French peasantry of the 1800s as "a sack of potatoes" captured this argument: Marx attributed the peasantry's political inertness to economic atomization, competition among producers, and social fragmentation, and to its related lack of collective consciousness.

Communal structures in different settings (or times) can be compared according to the extent to which they concentrate or disperse control over persons and resources.[13] Control over persons, resources, and access to markets are *political assets* in rural settings (as elsewhere). Landlords who mediate their tenants' or sharecroppers' access to land have often been able to leverage this relationship into one of broad political domination over the farmers whose livelihoods are so vulnerable to their discretion. Heaven

[12] For explicitly comparative work, see for example Moore Jr. 1966: especially 468–77; Anderson 1974; Brenner 1976, 1982; and much of the work cited in the preceding footnote.
[13] Here I follow Hechter (1983, 1987) who defines "group solidarity" in terms of coercive and compliance mechanisms.

help the farmer who must also depend upon the landlord for credit. By contrast, where we find freeholding peasantries who gain access to land, labor, and other farming inputs via more or less competitive markets (or web-like networks of interpersonal relationships), control over persons, resources, and market access is more dispersed.[14] (Yet as analysts of gender relations and patriarchy in peasant households insist, control over persons and resources is a political asset even within the most microscopic social unit.) The distinction between dispersed and concentrated control over persons and resources is what interests us here: concentration pools political resources in the hands of a narrow set of actors.[15] It creates a rural elite that has more political clout – more clout in dealing with the state – than a dispersed set of small asset holders would have.[16]

As Hechter and Brustein argue (1980:1076–8), more concentration is associated with an increase in the geographic and demographic size of the political unit, the existence of administrative machinery, a material and ideological framework for political cohesiveness, and thus stronger territorial political units than those found in zones characterized by more dispersed control over persons, productive assets, and markets. In Europe, pyramids of feudal economic and political authority empowered nobles vis-à-vis kings. The rise of free peasant communities, and thus a more dispersed distribution of power over persons and resources, empowered the state (Anderson 1974; Root 1987).

Here, we extract the proposition that concentrated control over persons, resources, and markets produces and defines hierarchy in agrarian communal structure, and that this pooling of political assets in rural social and

---

[14] This is exactly the point that Bates (1981) and Hyden (1980) have stressed in their arguments about rural social structure in Africa and its macropolitical implications.

[15] Hechter measures social cohesion in terms of the capacity of the group to control the behavior of its members: communal ties are a matrix for social control. The most powerful members of the community ("leaders") are those who control benefits valued by others: dependency relations are the essence of social hierarchy (Hechter 1983:25, 50). As he writes, patron-client relations in peasant societies have long been analyzed in these terms. See also Hechter 2000:21–4, 38–40.

[16] Communal cohesion can come from vertical relationships of dependency and control (concentrated control over mechanisms of social compliance). This kind of cohesion – hierarchical cohesion – is the only type of social cohesion that I consider systematically in this book. However, it is also true that communal cohesion can come from horizontal ties (interdependencies, cooperation, dispersed or decentralized social controls) – that is, from "web-like" relationships between members of a community. A full analysis would have to investigate the larger political effects of both kinds of rural social cohesion. This issue arises in the analysis of Casamance that is presented in Chapter 3.

productive relations is what can empower a rural elite vis-à-vis the state.[17] The *legitimacy* of communal hierarchy remains a factor in the equation: legitimate authority and legitimate communal institutions lower the costs of social control (incentives, coercion, enforcement, and monitoring). In a hierarchical peasant society, rural leaders are political actors whom the center must engage, either as allies or as rivals. The working hypothesis will be that the extent of rural social hierarchy determines rural elites' bargaining power vis-à-vis the state: the more hierarchy, the greater the rural elites' bargaining power.

To what ends will this power be used? The answer will depend largely upon the interests of the rural elite. Here we turn to class relations.

Agrarian property relations shape the political needs and interests of provincial elites. This is a major theme in studies of Latin American politics and state formation, and of the rise of modern Europe. Charles Tilly (1975, 1990), Barrington Moore (1966), Robert Brenner (1976, 1982), and Jeffrey Paige (1975) are among those who have pursued this theme. A key variable is the extent to which rural elites depend on the coercive and legal powers of the central state to control labor and to appropriate their share of the rural surplus. Where European landed classes depended upon the state to shore up labor-repressive modes of agricultural production, collusive relationships between central and local authorities often emerged. Where landholders relied more on markets (or local coercion) to control labor, they often enjoyed more political autonomy vis-à-vis central state authorities. This contrast is drawn starkly in Brenner's comparisons of landed elites in Eastern and Western Europe in the seventeenth century. Barrington Moore draws the same contrast between the French and English nobilities during the period of the rise of commercialized agriculture. The proposition can be boiled down to this: the greater rural elites' reliance on the market as a mechanism of surplus extraction and labor control, the greater their potential for political independence vis-à-vis the state and thus for confrontation with regimes bent on centralizing power. Greater dependence upon the state creates structural conditions conducive to collaboration between rural elites and the center.

---

[17] For a similar approach, see Magagna 1991. This point is the logical corollary of Bates's, and indeed Hyden's, arguments about how the dispersion of political and economic power in African peasant society weakens the capacity of African farmers to act collectively in the national political arena. Hyden stresses the fact that even farmers who are politically weak in this sense are still "free enough" to exercise the exit option in their dealings with the state.

These are general propositions about the political implications of variation in rural communal and class structure. They can be used to explore political variation across a set of West African cases.

B. Variation in West African Peasant Societies

American political scientists have, for the most part, looked at "African peasantry" as a single system of social organization; more nuanced accounts have tended to differentiate only by national context. As Alan Issacman (1990) points out, the tendency has been to say, for example, that "the Kenyan peasantry" differs from "the Mozambiquan peasantry" without acknowledging how artificial these constructions are given the realities of uneven development within countries, differences in indigenous forms of social organization, and variation in local systems of land use, labor use, and production. Due attention has been paid to the critical distinction between peasant and capitalist farmers, but this does not offer much leverage on variation within the category "peasant," or "African smallholder agriculture." As for cross-regional variations in communal or local-level political institutions, this has received almost no systematic attention from anglophone political scientists since the early 1970s.

In fact, class and communal organization in rural Africa varies considerably by region (and sometimes by locality), and this has always been so. Considering the period since, say, the 1940s, we can say that many of the starkest differences are rooted in factors that include ecological constraints, differences in the geographic scope and salience of political organizations that preexisted or were external to the modern state, the political impact of colonial rule, the uneven commercialization of agriculture, and the extent of class formation. Local elites – chiefs, marabouts, big planters, big merchants, and other notables – occupied different positions in the social relations of production, appropriated rural surpluses in different ways and degrees, and relied on different social processes to reproduce their local status and power.[18] Their bargaining power and economic autonomy (or dependence) vis-à-vis the state are key variables in explaining politics of the nationalist and state-building eras.

---

[18] Mafeje (1991) shows how these factors shaped patterns of precolonial state formation (sixteenth to nineteenth centuries) in the Great Lakes region of central Africa, and extends his argument to the postcolonial period (p. 135 *inter alia*).

In going down this path of analysis, do we run the risk of overemphasizing the relatively stable and structured aspects of rural social organization in Africa? Yes, we do. It is very true that in rural Africa in the twentieth century communal and class relations have been sites and targets of complex social struggles and renegotiations. Communal structures have been extensively manipulated by states, mutated by broader socioeconomic processes, and contested at the grassroots. Rural economic and social decay, an undeniable feature of parts of the African countryside in the 1980s and 1990s, can revolutionize local power relations, as can economic development.[19] It would be an equally serious mistake, however, to look at the forces of change or disarray and draw the opposite conclusion – that configurations of economic and political authority are or have been completely fluid, ethereal, or lacking in structure. During the period of postcolonial state building, social inequalities and communal hierarchies in rural Africa were often maintained or even reinforced. This analysis focuses on the relatively structured aspects of such relations in order to highlight cross-regional variation that existed during the main time period under study, from about the 1940s to the 1980s, and shows that these variations have long-term institutional effects that are visible in the 1990s and beyond. Where state building institutionalizes preexisting social hierarchies, this in itself becomes very important in explaining the stability of hierarchy in local political life.

Communal Structure. Since about 1970, this factor has been more or less systematically neglected in the study of postcolonial African politics. This outcome, I believe, is traceable to the confluence of a few different factors. The first, paradoxically, has to do with the great deal of attention that modernization theorists paid to "traditional polities," ethnicity, and what some called tribal structure.

Political scientists of the 1950s and 1960s were very interested in coalition building in the nationalist era, including regional coalition building within Africa's emergent states. They devoted considerable analysis to the political relationships between new politicians and rural aristocrats, emirs, and chiefs. Many drew upon anthropological notions of variation in indigenous African communal and political structures (e.g., state vs. stateless or "acephalous" societies) to explain different patterns of incorporation of the rural areas into national-level politics. To explain differences in the organization and dynamics of "mass mobilizational" versus "brokered" (or elite)

---

[19] See Berry 1985.

political parties of the nationalist era, for example, analysts such as Zolberg (1964), Apter (1968), and Lemarchand (1977) pointed to differences in the status, legitimacy, and scope of authority of neotraditional rulers in the rural areas. These writers tended to see the main sources of sociological cohesion and division in rural Africa as rooted in primordial and cultural factors. Ethnic identity was understood mostly in these terms.

Writers in the 1960s seemed most interested in the effects of neotraditional elites on the conservatism or radicalism of new African governments, the prospects for successful national integration, and the prospects for democracy. Many took for granted that the center's gains in political power would come at the expense of the localities. As consolidation of the center progressed, the political clout of neotraditional elites was expected to dissipate. With the end of formal political competition and the rise of one-party states, usually by 1970, most observers of African politics seemed to assume that this process – the dissipation of rural authority – was virtually complete.

Interest in African studies then moved away from analysis of formal political process and institutions and toward broader structural generalizations. As this happened, much of the earlier work on the political importance of the chiefs, princes, and ruling houses of old Africa came to be seen as predicated upon disproven assumptions about the stability, legitimacy, and authenticity of "traditional culture," as overly focused on reified notions of ethnicity and ethnic groups, and as too fixated on ideational factors to see the role of material constraints and coercion in African political life.

Political economists since the 1970s have stressed the extent to which colonial conquest and rule weakened or destroyed, bastardized, and corrupted indigenous African political institutions and political authority; they have emphasized the relentlessness of regimes' attempts to suffocate all competing loci of political power. Many African regimes did announce early on that chieftaincy had been dismantled and that traditional rulers had been stripped of all vestiges of precolonial prerogative and authority. Modernity had arrived! Peasants were freed from the reactionary grip of old elites! Progressive reform or not, it was clear to all that exclusion of African peasants and farmers from the political arena was near absolute. Many political economists thus concluded that variations in local social organization and indigenous political structure had little enduring relevance to contemporary African politics. Inherent in this conclusion was, I argue, a bias that had also existed in modernization theory: analysts were downplaying the material foundations – and thus the staying power and high political-economic stakes – of communal cohesion, hierarchy, and political power in agrarian society.

The colonial chieftaincy was one source of coercive hierarchy at the local level common to virtually all export-producing peasantries, and this institution was indeed targeted for reform by almost all postcolonial regimes. Focusing on these similarities has obscured the fact that there were important *variations* in the functional and territorial scope, legitimacy, and embeddedness of the colonial chieftaincy itself. These differences are attributable in very large part to preexisting forms of political authority and other factors external to the colonial state, such as lineage structure, land tenure relations, and religion. Regional contrast in the embeddedness of chieftaincy was stark in Nigeria, for example. In northern Nigeria, the British gave chieftaincy titles to kings, emirs, and aristocrats, and thus grafted a colonial institution onto a preexisting sociopolitical apparatus. Colonial rule rigidified social hierarchy in this region and concentrated political power in the hands of a narrower and more autocratic stratum. In southeastern Nigeria, by contrast, the British could not find a secure political foothold. Colonial chieftaincy was created of whole cloth; the British named "warrant chiefs" who remained vulnerable because they could appeal to no source of authority other than colonial rule itself. There is no state-centric explanation of this contrast. It is entirely attributable to facts the British encountered on the ground.

What did variation in communal structure mean for center-periphery relations from about the 1940s onward? I will put forward the argument that cross-regional variations in the extent of communal hierarchy determined rural notables' political clout in their dealings with governments. Hierarchical authority that was broad in its functional scope, broad in geographic extent, and concentrated in the hands of a small number of individuals gave rural leaders maximum political leverage. If rural hierarchy and authority were anchored in shared beliefs about community and tradition, so much the better: rural notables' capacities for collective control or mobilization would be enhanced.

Class Relations. Agrarian class structure also mattered. The analytic leverage of this variable is underexploited in work on African politics that conflates large landholders, rich peasants, and capitalist farmers. The same holds for work that generalizes about "peasants" without distinguishing between truly independent household producers, households whose land rights are an entitlement of community membership, sharecroppers, and tenants or others with tenuous land-use rights. These distinctions matter because they defined the modes by which rural elites appropriated agricultural surpluses and the extent to which they were able to do so.[20] How did provincial elites reproduce the material, rural foundations of their privilege? This was key in defining their political needs and interests vis-à-vis the state.

Under colonialism, leading social actors in rural Africa became more dependent upon agricultural sources of wealth than African rulers had been in the eighteenth and nineteenth centuries. They also became dependent in varying ways, and to varying degrees, on the colonial state. European conquest and rule suppressed many other sources of wealth, including taxing the long-distance trade, taxing European traders, and the slave trade, along with conquest, raiding, and some forms of tribute. Some accounts have suggested that the economic bases of the old elites were undercut completely: they were reduced to dependency on salaries paid by the colonial state, or to the status of ordinary farmers, eking out whatever living they could from subsistence and cash-crop farming. These accounts obscure many of the mechanisms by which economic power was produced and reproduced in rural Africa. As Bayart (1985) has emphasized, the old African elite proved to be very resourceful.

In zones of extensive export-crop production, many African elites went directly into cash-cropping, but this did not exactly put them on par with their subjects. Many used new or old political powers to mobilize land and labor for this purpose. In parts of Senegambia, Ghana, Uganda, and Nigeria, rural political authorities set up large estates to produce crops destined for Europe. Elsewhere, rural bigwigs were able to tap agricultural surpluses by investing in the trading-and-transport circuit. Meanwhile, control over access to arable land remained an important political resource; sometimes it also generated income in the form of rents or other payments. The question here is: From the 1940s onward, how much did wealth generated in agriculture contribute to the material clout and status of rural political authorities? If agriculture played an important role, did rural elites have direct access to rural land and labor and agricultural surpluses, or was their access mediated by the state? The answers have to do with rural elites' economic autonomy (or dependency) vis-à-vis the state.

The analysis that follows shows that in Africa's zones of peasant export-crop production, regionally specific configurations of class and communal

[20] Mafeje (1991:85–92, 102–3) reviews the "modes of production debate" in African studies.

28

structure had patterned effects on the interests and bargaining power of rural elites, making them more or less powerful, threatening, and useful to the new African regimes that came to power around 1960. The effects can be summarized as follows.

Hierarchical communal solidarity gave rural elites bargaining power, for it made more credible their threats/promises to control peasants and mobilize collective action (through the use of persuasion or coercion). Where there was little solidarity (i.e., absence of hierarchy), rural notables had less bargaining power vis-à-vis the center.

The bargaining power of rural elites could be harnessed to the new regimes' advantage, or it could represent a threat to them. That would depend upon the *interests* of the rural elites who wielded bargaining power. Here, I predict that rural elites who did not appropriate their own share of the rural surplus directly, relying instead on state intermediation, would be interested in aligning with new regimes. Those able to appropriate directly a share of the rural surplus were more likely to position themselves as antagonists or even competitors to new regimes. They would be positioned for a fight with the center over the division of the rural surplus.

These contrasts are summarized in Table 2.1.

In the African countryside, as in agrarian societies at other times, regional differences in the communal and class structures produced variation in the political interests of rural notables and in their capacity to advance their interests vis-à-vis those of rulers bent on centralizing power. I will argue that these differences structured the strategic contexts in which new African

Table 2.1. *How Rural Elites Are Positioned vis-à-vis the Center*

	Economic Autonomy of Rural Elite	
	Low	High
Social Hierarchy		
Low	Rural elites want to collaborate with the center, but have low bargaining power. **Weak allies**	Rural elites may position themselves as rivals to the center, but they have low bargaining power. **Weak rivals**
High	Rural elites want to collaborate with the center, and they have high bargaining power. **Strong allies**	Rural elites are positioned as rivals to the center. They have high bargaining power. **Strong rivals**

regimes sought to consolidate their power, constraining and shaping the rural institution-building strategies they chose.

C. Variation in Institutional Structure and Process

The outcome we try to explain here is variation in the institutional arrangements linking core and rural periphery in postcolonial Africa. The writers discussed at the beginning of this chapter conceptualized variation in unidimensional terms as either "radicalism versus conservatism" or "centralization versus decentralization." This analysis proposes a two-dimensional comparison that taps both these notions of difference and that can serve as a more discriminating schema for measuring (describing) cross-case variation.

The schema employed here borrows from Cohen and Peterson (1996, 1997, 1999). Following these authors, institutions linking core and periphery can be compared along two dimensions. The first is spatial: it has to do with the physical placement on state agencies and institutions within the national space. The second is processural: it has to do with de facto distributions of authority between central and local actors. In analyzing process, Cohen and Peterson focus on formal *and informal* relations between governmental *and nongovernmental* entities.[21]

In this study, the spatial dimension of institutional variation is understood in terms of concentration and deconcentration of the governmental apparatus. Are localities administered from agencies based in the capital city, or from rural outposts of the state? Where are administrative and allocative tasks carried out – in a few agencies sited in the capital city or a few provincial centers? Or is there a deconcentrated network of state agencies and outposts that is spread across the villages and small towns?[22] The spatial dimension of comparison taps variations in the density of the state apparatus on the ground. Where there is spatial concentration of the state apparatus, links in the administrative chain that connect core and periphery are few, state agents govern from the center rather than from localities, and the presence of the state in the localities is minimal. Where there is spatial deconcentration of the state apparatus, many institutional layers of the

---

[21] Cohen and Peterson 1997:21, 33 *inter alia*. These are significant departures from convention in the public administration literature.

[22] It is possible to talk about both horizontal and vertical de/concentration of the state apparatus.

national party-state are interposed between rural locality and capital city. In localities, the presence of the state is visible and multifaceted: village cells of the ruling party or state-run producer cooperatives are important organizational structures in the local political arena. There are multiple points of access to state resources and administrative prerogative.

The second dimension of variation is processural: Cohen and Peterson call it a "roles and authority" dimension. It measures de facto devolution of political authority. At one end of the continuum, the central regime monopolizes roles and authority; there is no devolution of authority to political players based in the rural areas. (This can also be referred to as "centralized authority.") At the opposite end of the continuum, agents of the center establish partnerships and brokerage relations with rural authorities; this produces various forms of devolution of state authority and discretion, including devolution of control over the local use of state resources, devolution of administrative discretion, and devolution of political gatekeeping prerogatives.[23] This dimension captures variation in the extent to which regimes opted for "indirect rule" in governing the localities.

The established indigenous authorities we are talking about are those whose power derives in part from sources that lie beyond direct and immediate state control. Land ownership or personal wealth, land rights commanded by corporate entities such as lineages or royal families, social status and legitimacy, religious powers, and heredity are the kinds of nonstate sources of authority that could give local elites a powerbase not completely controlled by political leaders in capitals such as Abidjan, Dakar, or Accra. Where the institutional arrangements were designed to shore up and reinforce the political, administrative, and even economic prerogatives of local-level notables of this kind, regimes were delegating or devolving authority. The opposite strategy aimed at the centralization of authority; that is, enhancing the power, prerogatives, and resources of direct state agents. A direct state agent is a functionary sent directly from national headquarters to a locality not in his native region, a bureaucrat working in the capital city, or a local boss or party hack who is a sheer creation of the center without any autonomous power or authority of his or her own.

---

[23] Cohen and Peterson 1997:5, 21. For them, the essence of delegation is the conceding of discretion to subordinates. The less specific the task, the greater the amount of discretion (authority) delegated. Binder (1978), in an analysis of relations between governmental and neotraditional authorities in Egypt, argues that discretion is the key resource that local authorities seek to capture and retain.

Although we are borrowing terms that have long pedigree in the public administration literature, there are three important departures from standard use in that field. The first is a focus on substantive patterns of political interaction and real distributions of power and prerogative. Formal-legal mandates for local government, or published laws defining administrative structure and procedure, are only important when they have substantive effects.[24] The second departure is that there is no assumption that "local government" is participatory or democratic. On the contrary, I am arguing that local-level government in Africa has been geared to controlling and taxing peasants. Third, the local-level political authorities who appear here are not necessarily democratically elected officials, or bureaucrats. Many of those locked in de facto powersharing relationships with the central rulers are local notables who derive power from hereditary or spiritual authority, land tenure relations, and their willingness to serve the center.

We now have a device for describing variations in patterns of rural governance. Each institutional configuration, or institution-building strategy, can be described in terms of two separate dimensions: spatial concentration versus deconcentration, and centralization versus devolution of authority. This scheme yields four hypothetical institutional configurations, or institution-building strategies.

  A. Deconcentrated institutional structure; devolved authority. A dense network of state institutions in the rural areas provides political infrastructure for de facto or de jure devolution of authority to indigenous elites. This strategy is named "powersharing."
  B. Deconcentrated institutional structure; centralized authority. A dense network of state institutions in the countryside provides infrastructure for state agents to "rewire the circuits of local authority" and micromanage local political process. This is "usurpation."
  C. Concentrated institutional structure; centralized authority. State institutions seem suspended balloon-like over the rural localities. State

---

[24] Here we follow political scientists developing a positive theory of institutions, such as Knight (1992) and Weingast (1995), who focus on the origins and effects of de facto rules and institutions, whether these rules are enshrined in formal-legal texts or not. This analytic strategy is also the norm in the disciplinary subfield of comparative politics, where a government would not be considered democratic, for example, just because its constitution declared it to be so.

agents govern the localities from a few strategic outposts of the state, and act with great autonomy from local influences and pressures. This strategy looks a lot like military occupation. We will thus call it "administrative occupation."

D. Concentrated institutional structure; devolution of authority. State institutions seem suspended balloon-like over the rural localities, but state agents do not seek to exercise authority in the local arena. Localities are left to their own devices: the regime seems to abdicate authority. The center does not seek to engage or impose. This is "non-incorporation." We should not expect to see this strategy in a zone of commercial agriculture, especially in an area of export-crop production, because the state will have an interest in taxing producers and in monitoring the accumulation of wealth in private hands.

This matrix is presented in Table 2.2.

In this book we show that these different institutional configurations or strategies can be found in West Africa, and establish this variation as the object of explanation. When do central rulers choose one strategy over another? That is the question of institutional choice.

IV. The Argument

Regardless of their ideological stripes, new African regimes – like colonial administrators before them – pursued institution-building strategies that

Table 2.2. *How Rulers' Institutional Strategies Vary*

	Who Wields Authority at the Local Level?	
	Rural Elites (Devolved Authority)	State Agents (Centralized Authority)
Spatial Configuration of State Apparatus		
State institutions created at village level (Deconcentration)	POWERSHARING A.	USURPATION B.
State institutions "suspended above" localities (Concentration)	NON-INCORPORATION D.	ADMINISTRATIVE OCCUPATION C.

were designed in response to situations they confronted on the ground. Regional variation in the bargaining power and interests of rural notables produced predictable differences in patterns of spatial deconcentration of the state apparatus and in the extent of devolution of authority to chiefs, aristocrats, marabouts, and other rural elites. This argument should hold regardless of colonial administrative doctrine (France's formal commitment to direct rule, and Britain's to indirect rule), and even across regions within a single postcolonial state.

A. Social Hierarchy and the Spatial Ordering of the State Apparatus

Hierarchical communal structures increased the bargaining power of rural elites in their dealings with new regimes. Variations herein are expected to shape new regimes' rural state-building strategies in systematic ways. Where rural notables and leaders could credibly broker the votes, political cooperation, and acquiescence of large groups of dependents and followers, their bargaining power in their dealings with urban-based politicians was high. The hypothesis is that in attempts to extend state control in such areas, new rulers would undertake intensive state-building efforts at the local level aimed at harnessing and manipulating local-level power relations. Regimes would pursue strategies aimed at building spatially deconcentrated institutional apparatuses in the rural areas. This could provide institutional infrastructure for either powersharing or usurpation.

We find support for this idea in an older state-formation literature. Anderson (1974) and Hechter and Brustein (1980) link the parcellized sovereignty associated with feudalism to more deconcentrated state structures: as a consequence of parcellized sovereignty, "functions of the state were disintegrated in a vertical allocation downwards, at each level of which political and economic relations were, on the other hand, integrated."[25] Hierarchical authority produces more layering of the state apparatus and more embedded state structures.

Where hierarchy is absent, we have the counterfactual situation. Established rural elites do not control local populations and are therefore neither very threatening nor very useful to the regime. The regime will attempt to govern from the center rather than build dense networks of state outposts in the rural areas. The regime avoids institution building at the local level either because it does not want to create new frameworks for the congealing

---

[25] Anderson 1974:148–9, as quoted by Hechter and Brustein 1980:1075.

of political influence or authority at that level (in this case the ruler choses administrative occupation),[26] or simply because it is forsaking state building in this region (here the choice is non-incorporation).[27] Non-incorporation would be the stategy of choice in regions that pose neither threat nor benefit to the center. We do not expect non-incorporation in zones of commercial agriculture, for reasons noted above.

B. Rural Interests and the Possibility of Powersharing

Where rural elites had bargaining power, would new regimes seek to co-opt them or displace them? For the new rulers of the 1960s, established agrarian elites could be either allies or antagonists. It is reasonable to expect that, as in other agrarian societies, African rural elites' mode of surplus appropriation would shape their interests, their political strategies, and the nature and extent of their collaboration with the state. Where rural notables' economic privileges and prerogatives depended upon the direct and continuous exercise of state prerogative, rural notables did not have much autonomy vis-à-vis the regime. Dependency upon the state would seem to have a predictable effect – it would probably make rural elites want to align themselves politically with new regimes. They would be regime allies. Economic dependency on the government would enhance the rural notables' reliability as rural agents of the regime. I thus expect to find powersharing alliances – devolution of de facto administrative authority – where rural elites were economically dependent upon the state.[28]

---

[26] As Gourevitch explained in *Paris and the Provinces* (1980:29, sa. 44–53), local governments, even weak ones, can be threatening to the center. They can provide local actors with an organizational base...even with limited powers, local structures afford at least some opportunities to attract a clientele via patronage of various kinds.... For those in opposition, local government is an arena in which to prepare the terrain for gaining power at the center." As Gourevitch (1980:46) argues, "(i)n explaining reform [of administrative/political structure], we must look to factors which shape politicians' evaluation of the costs and benefits different schemes would bring." See also Frye 1997. On direct rule in Europe, see Tilly 1990:115; Hechter 2000.

[27] On non-incorporation as political strategy, see Herbst 2000:170.

[28] From the perspective of the principal (the ruler, in this case), delegation or devolution of authority (powersharing or subcontracting) can work well if the agent can be trusted to do a good job, and to *not* subvert or capture the center. If the agent is too untrustworthy, the principal is expected to opt for a strategy of vertical integration (direct rule), which entails higher transaction costs up front, but may ward off costly disasters down the road. To judge the efficiency of one strategy over another, we need (1) to know what, exactly, both the principal and the agent are trying to maximize, and (2) a broad sense of the cost-benefit

By contrast, where rural notables accumulated wealth via means largely independent of direct state intervention, relative economic autonomy vis-à-vis the regime would enhance their political autonomy. The potential for direct competition between regimes and rural elites over rural wealth and political authority is much higher in these cases. As a result, rural elites would be less reliable agents of the central authorities. Here, regimes were most likely to pursue state-building strategies aimed at taking power away from the rural elite. This is usurpation.

V. Institutional Choice Scenarios

Four causal scenarios can be deduced from this logic. In the first, we encounter a hierarchical rural society in which elites are in a tributary position vis-à-vis the state (that is, they are economically dependent upon the state). This is when we expect the center to choose powersharing. Institution building aims at cementing and organizing a powersharing relationship between the center and rural elites.

Second, we find hierarchical rural societies in which rural elites appropriate their share of the rural surplus directly, without relying on the state's intermediation. Here, rural elites are more autonomous from the center and thus more powerful and threatening to the center. We expect usurpation: the center will choose to usurp the power and position of its powerful rivals, aiming to undercut or even destroy them.

Third is a scenario that emerges where peasant society is not hierarchical. There is an absence of hierarchical cohesion; this means that there is no rural economic elite that appropriates a surplus from subordinate social groups. If this is a zone of commercial agriculture, and the regime therefore has an interest in incorporating the region into the national political economy, we expect that they will choose the strategy of administrative occupation. The regime will attempt to govern from the center rather than building dense networks of state outposts in the rural areas, and will not devolve power to rural actors. The regime avoids institution-building strategies that could create new possibilities for the congealing of political power at the local level.

equation in which the transactions are embedded. One question is, What is the real balance of power between the principal and the agent? See Epstein and O'Halloran 1999:7–9 and Sandler 2001:99, 108.

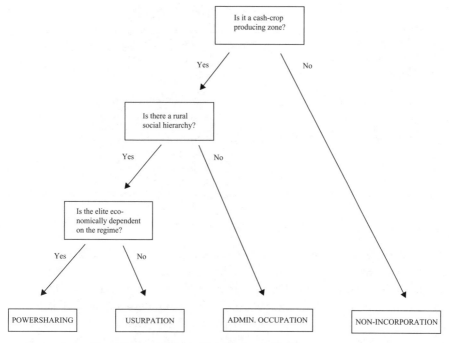

Figure 2.1. Rural Determinants of Institutional Choice

Fourth is a scenario wherein peasant society is neither threatening to the center nor, from the rulers' perspective, worth trying to exploit. The regime is not interested in incorporating the region into the national political space. Farmers are not engaged in much commercial agriculture, and surely not in the highly taxable activity of export-crop production. Zones occupied by nomadic groups engaged mostly in subsistence activity would fit this description.[29] French colonialists referred to areas like these as *Afrique inutile*. A strategy of non-incorporation is expected here: the regime will not build a deconcentrated institutional apparatus in this region and will, for the most part, leave local populations to govern themselves.

These arguments are summarized in Figure 2.1.

---

[29] However, nomadic societies have endured appropriation by the state (or by groups supported by the state) of access to their range lands, their water rights, and their right to simply carry on. See for example Schoonmaker-Freudenberger 1991. Ribot (1996) describes changes that can ensue when rulers begin to see forested rangeland as a resource to manage and control. See also Agrawal (forthcoming).

Table 2.3. *Uneven Institutional Topography: Cases*

POWERSHARING	USURPATION
Wolof Groundnut Basin	Asante
Senegal R. Valley, 1970+	
Korhogo 1970+	
[Dagomba, N. Ghana]	
NON-INCORPORATION	ADMINISTRATIVE OCCUPATION
Senegal R. Valley, 1940–1960s	Southern Côte d'Ivoire
	Lower Casamance
	Korhogo, 1952–1960s
	[Sine]

VI. Research Design and Outline

This book's core chapters describe and explain patterns of institutional choice across rural zones of West Africa. (See Table 2.3 and Map 2.1.) The main timeframe is the 1940s through the early 1980s, which in most African countries was the high-water mark of state building under consolidating, developmentalist regimes. Core chapters and the conclusion look forward into the 1980s and 1990s to identify trajectories that continue beyond the year 2000. Readers who do not know much about West Africa may be surprised to see such wide variation in rural class and communal structure. Others may not have realized that the real workings of state institutions in the countryside have varied so widely across space, even within a single country, and across countries forged within the same colonial administrative tradition. The studies document unevenness in both social and institutional landscapes in rural West Africa.

Cases perform three functions. First, they show that the social causes and institutional effects (choices) that have been modeled as ideal types in the preceding pages are indeed recognizable in the real world. Second, they make it possible to ask whether, and to what extent, social causes produce the expected political and institutional effects in these cases. Third, the cases were selected and paired to challenge rival theories of institutional variance in postcolonial Africa. The rivals considered here are explanations that center on regime ideology, colonial administrative doctrine, and ecological/agronomic determinants. If the institution-building strategies of a single regime vary over time or across regions within one country, if strategies vary across countries colonized by the same European power, or if they vary across regions with the same ecological/agronomic profile, then

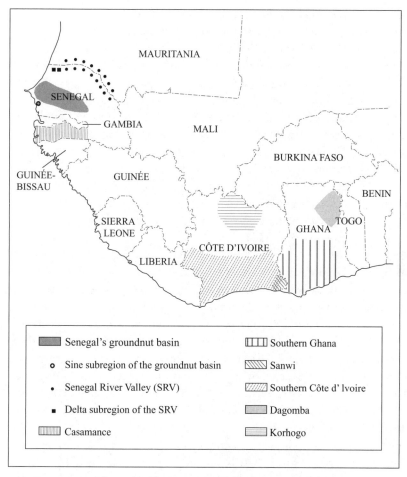

Map 2.1. Main and Secondary Case Studies Located on Map of West Africa

none of the rivals is a satisfying explanation of institutional choice.[30] All these patterns of variation are found in the cross-sectional and logitudinal analyses that follow.

In each case, I gauged spatial deconcentration of state institutions and centralization/devolution of authority in two time periods. The first is the

---

[30] See Snyder 2001b:93 on subnational comparison as a method of analysis that mitigates some characteristic limitations of small-N research, allows for controlled comparisons, and makes it possible to "track the spatially uneven effects of processes of economic and political transformation." See also George and McKeown 1985.

late colonial period from the mid-1940s to the time of independence (about 1960). The second is the era of postcolonial consolidation and state building, approximately 1960 to the mid-1980s. In each period we gauge institutional deconcentration and devolution across three functional domains of state action in the countryside – territorial administration, rural development, and organization of export-crop marketing. This generates about six observations of the institutional outcomes we are interested in for each case.[31] When cause and the predicted effect appear together, in the predicted patterns, we gain confidence in the theory. When government action produces the same institutional effect consistently – that is, across time and in different substantive domains of state regulation – we assume that there is some intentionality to what state actors are doing (choosing).

The chapters also attempt to reconstruct the historical chains of events that link cause and effect. This is process tracing, or the construction of analytic narratives. The smoking gun in each case is evidence that central rulers' institution-building strategies were forged ("chosen") *in reaction to* regional and provincial political threats that had already manifested themselves, or to already proven possibilities for alliance building with a well-grounded and stable rural elite. This places a special premium on a close reading of the internal political dramas of the nationalist era (approximately 1945 to 1960). In a few instances, African regimes make institutional choices that diverge from those predicted by the theory: these represent "counterfactual" episodes, or instances of off-the-path behavior.[32] Under these conditions, the expected effect is regional political instability or breakdown of regime hegemony in the countryside.

Chapter 3 is an in-country comparison. It focuses on two regions of Senegal: the Wolof groundnut basin and Lower Casamance. Here, in an archetypically "overcentralized" African state, a regime wedded as tightly as any to French institutional inheritance chose to govern its core export-producing region indirectly, via an institutional strategy of powersharing. Structures of the party-state were designed to devolve power to a trusted rural elite of aristocrats and Islamic marabouts. The contrasting case of Lower Casamance shows that Senegal's rulers were perfectly capable of building strongly concentrated and centralized institutions. In Lower Casamance, they chose to govern via administrative occupation when they feared that

---

[31] See Appendix: Note on Sources, Data, and Measurement, which includes a brief discussion of operationalizing the dependent variable.

[32] See Tetlock and Belkin 1996. See also Bates, Levi, Rosenthal, and Weingast 1998.

decentralization would empower rural actors who might challenge the center. Here we see one regime pursuing two different institutional strategies. National-level factors like regime ideology cannot account for this outcome. A subnational focus on the different political threats and opportunities postcolonial rulers confronted in the provinces can.

Chapter 4 compares rulers' institutional choices in two wealthy export-producing regions of the West African forest zone: southern Côte d'Ivoire and southern Ghana. The same crop, cocoa, was produced on both sides of the Ghana-Côte d'Ivoire border. (Southern Côte d'Ivoire produces coffee, too.) Yet postcolonial governments sought to tax and govern export producers in very different ways. Ivoirian rulers governed the south through a strategy of administrative occupation. In Ghana, the regime of Nkrumah was bent on usurpation: it dismantled the inherited institutions of British indirect rule and sought to build a state apparatus that would usurp the local power and authority of the old cocoa elite. Do rulers' contrasting ideologies explain this outcome, as so many writers have argued? The answer offered here is that ideology is just as plausibly endogenized in a theory that explains rulers' choices in terms of rural threats and challenges: rulers selected ideologies, as it were, to fit with strategies formulated in response to local challenges. Rural power constellations were decisive in producing very different institution-building trajectories in these two regions of West Africa.

Chapter 5 pairs two cases in which institution-building strategies change over time. The Senegal River Valley and the Korhogo region of northern Côte d'Ivoire are peripheral zones in two former French colonies. The chapters show that in the 1970s, in order to secure their political hold on these regions, rulers were forced to revise institutional strategies chosen in the 1960s. These are cases of path switching. In the Korhogo case, the strategy of the 1960s was not the one predicted by the theory. The "off-the-path choice" produced political instability; rulers sought to remedy it in the 1970s via an institutional strategy much closer to what the model would predict. In the Senegal River Valley case, shifts in rural social structure (cast in stark relief by the crisis of the Sahelian drought) threatened old modes of governing this region. Senegal's rulers made institutional innovations that addressed the crisis in ways that shored up the authority of their long-standing rural allies. In both peripheral regions, powersharing was the institutional strategy for promoting rural development in the 1970s. Closing of the nationalist era did not do away with the incentives that led rulers to seek powersharing arrangements with old provincial notabilities.

Postcolonial Senegal and Côte d'Ivoire have both been portrayed as paragons of statism and overcentralization, the result of administrative habits carried over from the era of French rule. Overcentralization and statism in Ghana is blamed on the socialist ideology of the nationalist regime. The cases presented here underscore the need to reconsider characterizations of core-periphery linkage that are so very apolitical. There is a politics of institution-building in the countryside – involving bargaining and compromise between central rulers and regional elites – that shapes the structures of the state itself, along with possibilities for using state power to promote economic transformation and liberal visions of citizenship.

Chapters that follow offer an account of the regional geopolitics of state building in Senegal, Côte d'Ivoire, and Ghana. What is surprising here, given received wisdom about the overcentralization and autonomy of the postcolonial African state, is the decisive role of rural political forces in determining how rulers sought to project state power into the countryside.

To focus on the founding crises of the postcolonial state is not to retell stories just to set the record straight, or to place African trajectories in broader comparative context (although these are worthy goals). The more urgent objective is to point out that these matters of state formation, national integration, and political authority are far from resolved. In fact they surfaced with a vengeance after 1990 with the reigniting of territorial politics and the reopening of questions about the form and purposes (and in some cases, the viability) of the state itself.

3

Uneven Institutional Topography within One State

Institutions that project state power into rural Africa distribute political and administrative authority between central and local elites. This chapter traces this institutional topography in Senegal and reveals a political landscape marked by striking geographic variation. This variation has virtually no basis in legal text and goes largely unnoticed in studies that generalize from findings from the groundnut basin, Senegal's export-producing core. The unevenness is an artifact of the periphery's ability to shape the choices of institution builders at the center.

A conventional wisdom holds that postcolonial African states are so centralized and bureaucratic, and African rulers so heavy handed in their dealings with the countryside, that significant regional variations in state structure and process have not been allowed to develop. Postcolonial Senegal is often depicted in these terms. It is often presented as the archetype of the overcentralized, bureaucratic state. In Wunch and Owolu's *Failure of the Centralized State* (1990), the Senegalese government is described as driven by a passion for territorial administrative uniformity and top-down control.[1] These excesses are said to reflect the modernizing instincts of the nationalist elite, the heavy imprint of French administrative law and tradition, and the legacies of French direct rule.

Centralizing impulses have indeed been ever present, and accounts that stress this must be taken seriously in an African country with a history of administrative continuity and political stability as long as Senegal's. This makes Senegal a good test of our central argument, which is that rulers' institutional choices are determined as much by balances of power on the

---

[1] See also Gellar 1990:133, 141.

ground as by the formal "rules of the game" laid down in the capital city and in administrative texts. If we uncover significant regional variation in state structure in Senegal, then the argument that the same kinds of variation will be found elsewhere, where administrators are less obsessed with uniformity, becomes more plausible.

Here we examine two regions of Senegal, the Wolof groundnut basin and Lower Casamance. The comparisons reveal differences in rural social organization that are almost as stark as any found in sub-Saharan Africa. Yet not many studies of politics in Senegal have focused on this difference, or explored its implications for forming and reforming the institutions of the modern state.[2]

There is a large, superb literature on the Wolof groundnut basin, but much of it has stressed what is sui generis in this region, rather than broad features of rural social organization – or basic dynamics of core-periphery relations – that can also be found in other parts of Africa and the agrarian world. For present purposes, what is general is most important. The groundnut basin serves as a model, or archetype, of a particular kind of hierarchical rural society – one in which elites are powerful in their relations with the peasantry but politically constrained by their economic dependence on the modern state. I argue that this configuration of rural society had a predictable effect on state building: colonial and postcolonial rulers chose to *share power* with the rural notability. To do so, they built a deconcentrated state apparatus and grafted local-level networks of party-state institutions onto preexisting political and economic hierarchies. Wide authority in running the local state was devolved to provincial elites.[3]

The argument finds support by way of counterfactual in the study of Casamance. Rural society in Lower Casamance was configured along very different lines. It lacked institutionalized hierarchy. Political authority was highly decentralized and dispersed throughout society. Colonial and post-colonial rulers found it difficult and risky to establish local-level political institutions in this setting. *They therefore avoided doing so.* To govern this region, Dakar did not attempt powersharing, and central rulers avoided

---

[2] Studies that compare explicitly across regions of Senegal are Pélissier 1966; Balans, Coulon, and Gastellu 1975; and Beck 1996.

[3] In the Sine (Siin) subregion of Senegal's groundnut basin, a distinctive social configuration generates a different institutional outcome. This subcase is discussed briefly below.

initiatives that would involve intensive state building at the local level. Linkages between core and rural periphery were few and far between. Local actors had few points of access to a state apparatus that was closed (insulated from local pressure), compact, and "suspended above" rural society. In Lower Casamance, Dakar built a state apparatus that was spatially concentrated in the regional capital of Ziguinchor and in which authority was centralized in the hand of Dakar's direct agents and appointees. This case provides an archetype of the *administrative occupation* institution-building strategy. We see this strategy not only in Lower Casamance but also in parts of Côte d'Ivoire where the absence of rural social hierarchy deprived state builders of reliable local interlocateurs and thus made them eager to avoid doing anything that would incite grassroots political mobilization in rural localities.

Two patterns of state building are thus found within a single African state. These outcomes are traceable to regional specificity in rulers' strategies for taxing and governing the rural areas. For better and worse, the rural alliances and exclusions underpinning Senegal's government are literally institutionalized in the structures and processes of the state. Rulers made choices that were designed to deliver on compromises made with rural leaders in some regions and to lock in their advantages vis-à-vis provincial actors in others. There have been enduring consequences for the autonomy of the center, its responsiveness to local interests, and possibilities for using the state to promote development. Institutional choices made by the regime have also shaped local actors' possibilities and strategies for gathering political power at the local level and for engaging the regime in subsequent rounds of state reform.

This chapter shows that divergent state-building strategies emerged within one African state. Attributes of the center alone or of the national unit as a whole – rulers' ideologies, colonial administrative legacy – cannot explain this in-country variation. The fact that these variations in core-periphery institutional linkage exist does much to move the analysis forward: it forces a search for explanatory factors that are subnational. Chapters 4 and 5, read together, present another in-country contrast, this time in the comparison between southern and northern Côte d'Ivoire. Given conventional understandings of African state building, subnational variation in the Ivoirian case is just as unexpected as it is in Senegal, perhaps even more so. The Houphouet regime was far more effectively centralized and bureaucratized than its counterpart in Senegal.

Subsequent chapters extend these arguments. Powersharing also emerges as rulers' institutional strategy in northern Côte d'Ivoire and in the Senegal River Basin. These two regions lack the charismatic, regal notabilities that have attracted so much academic attention to rural politics in the Wolof groundnut basin, and to politicians' highly visible alliances with the rural elites in that region. However, these cases do share the basic features of rural social organization that underwrote powersharing in central Senegal. Similar state-building strategies emerged in all three places.

Administrative occupation was the state-building strategy in Casamance, and this outcome is encountered again in southern Côte d'Ivoire. This is surprising: in terms of the political and economic variables that have attracted most analysts' attention, these regions could hardly be more different. Southern Côte d'Ivoire is more important as an export-crop-producing zone. And whereas Lower Casamance has been a political thorn in Dakar's side for most of this century, southern Côte d'Ivoire has been an electoral stronghold of the postcolonial regime. The two regions are similar, however, in the absence of strong hierarchy in rural society – the absence of sure political footholds for postcolonial state building. Administrative occupation turns out to have been the rulers' choice in both places (with similar contemporary implications in the two regions).

Part One: Powersharing in Senegal's Groundnut Basin

The new alignment became possible when the southern conservative[s] ... decided that they were willing to abandon their ambitions to win power nationally in return for undisputed control over the South.

> Schattschneider 1960:77 on the powersharing deal that underpinned the partisan realignment of 1896 in the United States

A powerful patron can be viewed as a substitute for the state.

> Alston and Ferrie 1999:8

I. Hierarchy and Rural Authority in Central Senegal

The groundnut basin is modern Senegal's center of gravity. It is the country's main export-producing zone and home to over half the population. In the 1950s, 75 percent of the colony's exports were grown here, mostly on small peasant holdings. It is a dry, sandy Sahelian zone, with a harsh climate, short growing season, and fickle rains. Groundnuts have been cultivated for export in the northern reaches of the groundnut basin since the 1830s, and land degradation was already extensive in this area by the 1920s and 1930s. Soil erosion, land degradation, and population growth pushed the settlement frontier steadily eastward into "new lands" in the semidesert expanses of the Ferlo and along the Dakar-Niger railway.[4]

What is now the northern groundnut basin – demarcated by the triangle formed by the cities of Thies, Diourbel, and Saint-Louis – is the site of Wolof (Djolof) kingdoms dating to the thirteenth century. (See Map 3.1.) It is the cradle of an old and complexly structured society that has been shaped by centuries of integration into the world economy, first by way of the trans-Atlantic slave trade, then through the production of groundnuts for export, and then by French conquest and colonial overrule. Through these long processes of socioeconomic transformation, political upheaval, and southward and eastward expansion, Wolof society remained remarkably hierarchical and stratified.

Precolonial Wolof society was described by French geographer Paul Pélissier as hyper-developed politically (1966:108). There was a large population of noncultivators that included a political aristocracy, an Islamic religious nobility, a warrior caste, and artisans. Rich political-military traditions reached back to the era of the Djolof Empire.[5] Social organization followed the lines of "sharp and closed hierarchies" characterized by "intimate articulation of political and social structure." Like many other Senegambian societies, Wolof society was organized into endogamous castes separating nobility and freemen from casted occupations and slaves. These divisions have not been erased by the political upheavals of the last few centuries. Old social structures that many have described as "feudal" are still visible in the oldest zones of settlement, where dense networks of villages are organized hierarchically around leading families, some of whom trace their land rights and political privileges back six or seven centuries.

---

[4] "Nowhere in Senegal are the climatic conditions so severe and agricultural activity so precarious [as in the old zone of Wolof settlement, the northern groundnut basin]. . . . Each planting season is a gamble, each harvest in defiance of climatic insecurity. . . . Given the vulnerability of any agricultural activity around Louga, one is less surprised by the degradation of the landscape and relatively low population densities and the rates of emigration than by the continuousness of human settlement, stability of the villages, and the people's attachment to lands that are so unyielding [aussi ingrats]. The situation is not so bad as you go down toward Tivaouane" (Pélissier 1966:98).
[5] It lasted from the thirteenth to the sixteenth centuries.

Map 3.1. Senegal

A. Revolution and Conquest

Over the course of the 1700s and 1800s, violence linked to the slave trade
and the predations of the Wolof warrior aristocracy shook the old order.
Society was rent along the lines of both caste and class-like divisions. Political authority fractured along the lines of long-standing tensions between
the aristocracy and the Islamic nobles who held privileged places in the
royal courts. Deepening French and British influence in the region further
destabilized the situation. In the midst of these multiple and overlapping
crises, a cohort of charismatic Islamic leaders arose and positioned themselves as a revolutionary counterelite. They contested the legitimacy of

48

the old princely elite, and they raised armies to defend peasant communities against the rapaciousness of the old warrior castes. Muslim leaders established spheres of territorial control, often within the boundaries of feudal-like land grants their families had received from Wolof monarchs in preceding centuries.

France entered the fray decisively in the 1850s and 1860s, when the revolution of the Islamic reformers was nearly won. France defeated the last Wolof state of Cayor in the 1880s, stealing victory from the Islamic revolutionaries.[6]

The job of the colonial commandants and governors in Senegal was to put together some kind of rudimentary governing apparatus that would secure their military conquest and enable them to tax the people of this region. French administrators embarked on a process of state building that was iterative and experimental. Its eventual shape would be determined as much by political structures and currents in African society as by any doctrine imported from Paris.

From the start, the intention of French commanders in West Africa was to rule this region *indirectly* – through intermediation of indigenous political elites and within preexisting political units. Yet in faraway Paris, the architects of imperial France would eventually embrace direct rule as a formal administrative doctrine, and so declare their ambition to sweep away the old and erect a modern bureaucratic state run by direct agents of the empire. As things turned out, the practical politics of colonization in this part of Senegal dictated the outcome. In *pays Wolof*, France imposed itself upon an old, hierarchical society that had possessed state structures of its own. France's de facto strategy, pursued with striking consistency, was "to take all possible advantage from the existing order"[7] by collaborating with indigenous elites. The challenge for the Europeans in central Senegal was to figure out who the indigenous authorities really were. In a society racked by revolution and war, who controlled the peasantry?

---

[6] Lat Dior, the last Damel of Cayor, is a national hero in Senegal who is remembered for leading a heroic resistance to the French.

[7] Faidherbe, governor of Senegal from 1854 to 1864, "was convinced that a small group of alien officers could control an African population by confirming and manipulating traditional chiefs.... Until 1920, most of Senegal was at least in theory ruled under a series of protectorate treaties." In the 1920s and 1930s the strategy of respecting "traditional authorities" was confirmed by official mandate. "Martial Merlin suggested in 1920 that 'where there still exist native organisms capable of functioning well, we should reenforce them in order to take from them all possible advantages'" (Klein 1968b:194, 196, 200–1).

In the first round of colonial state building, colonial administrators placed their bets on the old Wolof princes. Wolof states of Cayor, Baol, and Djolof were carved up and aristocrats were invited to govern on a diminished scale, subject to French extractions and overrule. Zucarrelli (1973: 224) described the old kingdoms as organized on "decentralized, feudal bases," and wrote that "the French were most interested in the components of the old kingdoms that appeared to them to be the most solid – the cantons." Outlines of royal provinces were indeed discernible in the division of central Senegal into cantons, French colonialism's basic administrative units. Cantons were grouped into "provinces," which generally followed the lines of traditional kingdoms (or half a kingdom).[8]

Many analysts have stressed the extent to which France destroyed the old political jurisdictions by breaking them up. Preservation of territorial dominions was also a part of this game, however. Family dynasties and land domains of the Wolof elite were written into the basic units of the colonial state.

Colonial policy was to choose nobles of "great influence" from the aristocratic families and name them as provincial chiefs (*chefs supérieurs*) and cantonal chiefs.[9] As Rathbone (2000:9) noted in a study of central Ghana, the term "chief" rhetorically diminished the old aristocrats and denied any claims to state power they might have harbored.

Power over the lives and livelihoods of local populations was concentrated in the hands of cantonal chiefs. This gave rise to a cadre of provincial strongmen who wielded autocratic power virtually unmatched in any precolonial setting.[10] French governors had neither the will nor the means to supervise the chiefs closely.[11] Canton chiefs developed into *caciques* who

---

[8] Klein 1968b:200. Delimiting of cantons began in 1898. See Pélissier 1966:102, 136–8 (for *pays Wolof*), 186–8 (*pays Serer*). Klein (1968b: 199–200 n. 11) elaborates: "[m]ost Senegalese kingdoms contained smaller units, some with hereditary ruling families, some under chiefs appointed by the king. These smaller units often were the basis of the canton. In some areas conquered by the Moslems [in the nineteenth century], the canton was often similar in size or extent to the area controlled by one of the marabout chiefs."

[9] Selection criteria were general enough to create a large candidate pool, creating "a sort of chiefly caste." France appointed those who could be trusted or manipulated to promote France's cause (Zucarelli 1973:224).

[10] See for example Klein 1968b:198.

[11] About 400 French administrators ruled all of French West Africa, a territory 8 times the size of France, with a population of 15 million in the 1940s. At the zenith of the colonial occupation in the late 1930s, about a dozen French administrators were responsible for governing all of central Senegal (not including the four coastal municipalities). Four *commandants de cercle*, each one assisted by two to three French subdivision heads, were responsible for

carried out France's dirty work, abusively extracted taxes and labor from their rural subjects, and consolidated their own personal dominions and wealth in the process. They rounded up forced laborers, exercised local police powers (including to fine and imprison), and gathered military recruits. Their large entourages and bands of thuggish retainers became symbols of decadence and intimidation. France invoked a de facto doctrine of indirect rule to justify this form of rural government: according to colonial authorities, cantonal chiefs were enforcing their "customary rights." Few rural subjects were taken in by this argument. Canton chiefs had been drawn from a social stratum whose legitimacy had been in a state of advanced decay even before the French conquest. Their thuggishness, corruption, and venality eventually proved to be more of a liability than an asset for France.[12]

By about the 1910s and 1920s it had become clear to French administrators in Senegal that governing the Wolof through the old aristocracies was not working very well. The ground had shifted in Wolof society – Wolof aristocrats did not control the hearts and minds of the population – and the colonial administrators gradually came to recognize this fact. To govern and exploit Senegal effectively, France was again forced to adapt its administrative strategies to realities on the ground.

B. Rise of the Sufi Brotherhoods

Wolof populations since the mid-1800s had been turning to the Islamic counterelite for protection and leadership. Final defeat of the Wolof states had created a leadership vacuum, and charismatic Muslim leaders stepped into it. Conquest by France had led to the "massive and unanimous" adherence of the Wolof people, including most of the nobility, to Islam.[13]

---

all of rural Senegal until the early 1950s: in central Senegal their jurisdictions would have covered 200,000 to 300,000 persons. Cantonal chiefs were below the subdivision heads on the official ladder of command. Cantonal chiefs' autonomy enhanced French officers' ignorance of local affairs. Personnel rotated frequently; officers rarely stayed in their posts for more than two years (Cohen 1971).

[12] France commissioned an inspection into abuses of power in the 1930s. A French inspector found "chefs de canton and chefs de village in Baol and Sine-Saloum living 'a sumptuous life,' largely based on the exploitation of the local population, who were too intimidated to raise a complaining voice. . . . In comparing the chiefs of Baol to those of Sine-Saloum, the inspector wrote: 'Their cupidity is as great and their appetites as voracious'" (Tignor 1987:108).

[13] Pélissier 1966:116, 301–63. See also A.-B. Diop 1981:247–62, and Cruise O'Brien 1971a.

With the imposition of France's *pax coloniale*, two main Sufi orders coalesced in *pays Wolof*. These organizations would provide the framework for the reintegration and reconstruction of Wolof society. Eminent Muslim leaders, or marabouts, attracted ambitious and entrepreneurial disciples – including unemployed princes and warriors of the *ancien régime*. The holiest marabouts and their most important disciples gathered large followings made up of freed slaves, displaced artisans and courtiers, and peasants. Everyone was seeking protection, land, and new opportunity, and this is precisely what the Sufi clerics offered.

At the center of this social movement was the Sufi *confrérie* (brotherhood) of the Mourides, which gathered around the mystical and pious Amadou Bamba, a marabout descended from a line of renowned Islamic teachers.[14] Amadou Bamba's leading disciples began to organize the displaced of Wolof society into religious communities that cleared forests, established new farming communities, and devoted themselves to prayer and production of groundnuts. Between 1900 and the 1910s a mass movement of agrarian settlement gained momentum, largely on margins of French authority. The other Sufi order, the Tidjane brotherhood, was older and deeply implanted in the more ancient zones of Wolof settlement.

Social organization within the Sufi orders owed much to older Wolof forms. Like precolonial Wolof society, the orders were tightly built hierarchies that defined social position, and hence personal relations of authority and obligation, with precision. Pélissier (1966:321) observed that in the Mouride order, old modes of political structuration "were largely transposed from the political to the religious realm." Paralleling the forms of the Wolof states, the Sufi brotherhoods took shape under the kingly authority of Grand Khalifs. Family dynasties organized and legitimated authority, as in the monarchies, and gave the Sufi orders their basic political structure. The Grand Khalifs' eldest sons, most important disciples, and key lieutenants made up a stratum of *grands marabouts* who reigned over their own territorially defined fiefdoms and amassed large personal followings of their own. In both the Mouride and Tidjane orders, well-defined maraboutic hierarchies reached all the way down to the village level.

Under Mouride leadership, vast new expanses of central Senegal were opened to export-crop production. After the 1880s, energetic and

---

[14] Amadou Bamba had worldly charisma too, thanks to his close personal association with Lat Dior, the last king of Cayor, in his final stand against the French. See A.-B. Diop 1981:249–50.

prestigious Mouride marabouts began to gather young male followers, often unemployed warriors and freed slaves, into *dara* (schools) devoted to serving the founder of the order, Amadou Bamba. These disciples devoted themselves to prayer and unpaid agricultural labor in the service of the Sufi saints. They carved groundnut estates from central Senegal's dense underbrush, cultivated the marabout's fields for a decade, and turned all estate proceeds over to him. After ten years of servile work for the marabout, disciples received land of their own: the large estates were divided up among the laborers. Disciples got married, built village communities that remained united in devotion to their founding marabout, and continued to turn a share of their agricultural output over to their spiritual guide. Marabouts acted as the patrons, benefactors, and political leaders of agricultural communities they had founded. Part of their job was to provide a social safety net for disciples in times of worldly need.

Groundnuts thus became "the foundation of the fortunes of Mouride officials, as well as the basic resource of the order." Pélissier (1966:334) explains:

From the Khalif Général to the most modest cheikh, each marabout has his own personal groundnut fields which vary in size with his influence, and are cultivated directly by his dara. The most notable have pioneering dara throughout the Terres Neuves, all the output of which goes to them. Beyond this, each Mouride village collectively cultivates a groundnut field, the harvest of which goes directly to the marabout. These [collective fields] vary in size with that of the village; they often cover several tens of hectares. The income of lower-level marabouts makes it way back up the hierarchy... each official in the chain taking some, in proportion with his influence and standing.

Some observers have characterized this mode of export-crop production as a form of semi-slavery, for establishing and cultivating the large estates was the work of unpaid laborers who placed themselves in subservience to their marabout. For Mouride disciples, it apparently did not feel that way: agricultural work for a marabout was an investment in a good afterlife; it also produced worldly dividends in the form of a land grant, a community, and a political-economic patron.[15] Donal Cruise O'Brien (1984) once

---

[15] Alston and Ferrie studied dependent labor relations in the postbellum U.S. South. Before the mechanization of southern agriculture after World War II, labor control hinged on a kind of paternalism in which landowners protected workers from social and political violence and covered some basic needs in exchange (so to speak) for cheap and subservient labor. The southern elite maintained control over local social and political life. These powerful patrons "substitute[d] for the state" (1998:8).

described the Mouride system as one in which the meek really did inherit the earth, and this does capture the fundamental political economy of the matter.[16] The material base of Mouridism was a process of land pioneering that created villages of peasant farmers organized under the authority of marabout-chiefs.

C. France's Powersharing with the Marabouts

Colonial administrators, at first suspicious and even hostile toward the Sufi brotherhoods, soon recognized this social movement as a force that could create political and social order and produce rapid increases in export-crop production. The Muslim leaders were in many ways colonialism's perfect intermediaries: they were less discredited and more listened to than the Wolof aristocrats who had been appointed as cantonal chiefs, they made groundnut cultivation a religious duty for the peasants of central Senegal (and were large producers themselves), *and* they sought accommodation with French rule. "Taking all possible advantage from the existing order" took on new meaning in central Senegal.

From about the 1920s on, France moved to forge alliances with the Islamic leaders and to fuel Mouride-led waves of agrarian settlement. This maturing of the purposes of French power in Senegal involved new state-building initiatives. France undertook to deconcentrate the state apparatus – that is, to create new state institutions in the rural areas – in order to give colonial authorities operational bases at the front lines of the peasant economy. At the same time, France undertook to anchor this new, denser administrative machinery in the political order created by the marabouts. Power to distribute state resources on the local level, to regulate land access, and to administer local justice would be invested in these indigenous rural leaders. Like the powersharing strategy that had centered on the cantonal chiefs, it was aimed at "naturalizing" the powers of an alien colonial state.

By the early 1930s input and intervention from the colonial state was required to sustain the momentum of Mouride agrarian settlement.[17] Soil

---

[16] See also Pélissier (1966:335), who writes that "one needs to see that . . . the [Mouride] order assures social security functions that no other institution can provide. . . . For the farmer in Cayor, watching with anguish rain clouds that refuse to burst open, for the pioneer lost in the hostile immensity of the Ferlo, for the *chef de famille* seized by fever just at planting time, the guarantees that come with integration into the brotherhood have no price."

[17] From about 1910 to the death of Amadou Bamba in 1927, most expansion occurred north of Diourbel, along the rail line leading north from Thiès to Saint-Louis (completed in

erosion had diminished the productivity of estates created in the first phase of expansion, the costs of creating new estates began to rise, and new lands were less easily accessible. Mouride leaders needed capital and infrastructural support. Colonial authorities, eager to expand export-crop production, designed institutions to funnel credit and inputs to the rural areas.

Groundnut "cooperatives" – the Sociétés Indigènes de Prévoyance, or SIPs – were imposed in some parts of central Senegal in the 1910s to stock seeds.[18] In the 1930s this network and its functions were expanded: virtually all peasant households in the region were forced to pay dues to an SIP, contribute to a communal seed stock, and, at the end of the growing season, repay (with 25 percent interest!) seeds obtained from the SIP at planting time. SIPs became mechanisms for direct state taxation of Senegalese peasants; they also were a source of agricultural inputs and loans for large groundnut producers. France created two institutions to funnel loans to groundnut producers, both directly and via the SIPs, in the 1930s: first a Crédit Agricole Mutuel, and then a Fonds Commun des SIP. These institutions "worked in harness with leading Murid cultivators and hence supported the advance of Wolof groundnut cultivators into new lands."[19] Mostly they provided loans and agricultural equipment to the Mouride elite. So it was that so-called cooperatives became mechanisms for channeling loans, tools, and fertilizers to rural heavyweights, mostly to subsidize production on the big maraboutic estates.

By the 1930s pioneering marabouts also needed France's military clout to appropriate land from Peul pastoralists in the eastern forests of Senegal's Ferlo. France eagerly sponsored a concerted expropriation of Peul lands. So rapid and successful was this process that by 1936 the administration felt compelled to delimit classified forests "to canalize the colonization wave and protect some domain for the pastoral Peul."[20] France cut roads and

---

1885) and along the new lines running eastward toward Kaolack and Kaffrine (Pélissier 1966:304–12).

[18] SIP were France's first direct intervention in peanut production. First created in Sine-Saloum in 1910, SIPs stocked and distributed selected groundnut seeds. They charged dues and interest on groundnut seed advances. In 1915 membership was made compulsory for all farmers and herders in a *cercle*. French commandants were placed in direct charge of the SIPs (a role lost in 1919 but reassumed in 1923). During the depression, the cooperative experiment was extended throughout French West Africa.

[19] Tignor 1987:107. The Fonds Commun was created in 1936. See also Cruise O'Brien 1971a:218.

[20] Pélissier 1966:308, 311. On expropriation of the Peul, see Schoonmaker-Freudenberger 1991.

dug wells in Senegal's Ferlo to prepare the way for pioneer colonies. The Mourides supplied the pioneers: they mobilized "a veritable population wave" going straight east from Diourbel.[21] Descendants and lieutenants of Amadou Bamba oriented their followers toward different zones, carving out fiefdoms deep in eastern Senegal. The Terres Neuves (new lands) were almost exclusively Mouride.

By the time of World War II the French authorities and the leaders of the Sufi brotherhoods were locked in partnership. Sufi leaders collaborated closely with colonial governors and instructed their disciples to accept colonial rule, pay taxes, cultivate groundnuts, and submit to forced labor and military conscription.[22] Colonial administrators, in turn, supported the Islamic brotherhoods economically with agricultural loans, land concessions, roads and wells in zones of Mouride settlement, and cash grants.

Institutional pillars of this partnership were the chieftaincies, especially village chieftaincies, and the SIPs. Rather than define either as a direct emanation of European presence or authority, France insisted that the entire "administrative-SIP network," as Jonathan Barker (1971:52) called it, was an excrescence of traditional society. It is true that this stood in total contradiction to formal administrative texts, which defined chiefs as direct agents of a modern, bureaucratic state. As we have seen, in central Senegal France found it convenient to exploit political possibilities that existed in the indigenous order. The ideology of traditionalism prevailed.

French policy at the village level was to "preserve the status quo" (Diop and Diouf 1992a:69). In practice, this involved trying to uphold (or help create) mechanisms of community coherence, patriarchal authority, and chiefly authority.[23] To this end, France made official "village chieftaincies" the most deconcentrated instance of the state apparatus. Holders of this office were invested with land prerogatives, authority to adjudicate civil disputes, and power to collect taxes on behalf of the state. In the Wolof groundnut basin, these posts fell under firm maraboutic control. Pélissier described village

---

[21] Pélissier 1966:306. See also Tignor 1987:104.

[22] During World War I, even the mystical Amadou Bamba saw advantage in advising his disciples to enlist in French ranks (Klein 1968b:205).

[23] A 1920 circular from the governor general reads: "[T]he emancipation of the individual, which our own concepts incline us towards, risks a profound disturbance of the indigenous order.... I do not need to remind you that it is this paternal authority, and by extension, the authority of the village and canton chiefs which we recently drew upon to recruit military contingents destined for European battlefields" (from the French colonial archives, quoted by Guyer 1981:107).

chieftaincy in the 1950s as "basically an extension of maraboutic author-ity."[24] Marabouts themselves sometimes served as chiefs. In old zones of Wolof settlement, leading marabouts usually chose members of local aris-tocratic families (dominant lineages) to fill this job. In new zones, where villages had been created by the parceling out of the maraboutic estates, marabouts chose *dara* leaders drawn from the old warrior castes to serve as chiefs.[25] This means that at the grassroots level France anchored the state apparatus in a symbiosis of aristocratic and maraboutic authority, and in social hierarchies defined by lineage and control over land.

France also defined the groundnut cooperatives (the SIPs) as outgrowths of natural solidarities in traditional society. It was therefore "natural" that the job of running the SIPs be devolved to "traditional communal authori-ties" – that is, to members of the local chiefly and maraboutic elite.[26] Chiefs and marabouts were named as SIP officials and mandated to collect dues, requisition seeds, distribute seeds (on credit), make loans to farmers, and manage storage and marketing of the groundnut crop. Powers and prerog-atives so devolved by the state greatly expanded the patronage resources available to the rural elite, especially the marabouts, and magnified ordi-nary peasants' economic dependency on the local notables.

This turned out to be a very effective mechanism for reinforcing the hi-erarchical authority relations that were already embedded in land tenure re-lations, the Islamic brotherhoods, and Wolof society in general. Dominique Gentil (1986:31) characterized the SIPs as means "to reinforce the domi-nance of local notables and as a means of political control." As René Dumont put it: "Let us repeat that these cooperatives were inserted into a society that was already *very hierarchical*, where leading families kept tight control of the villages. French colonization had maintained and even developed the existing, quasi-feudal system, adding to it new privileges."[27]

By the 1950s, the political and social hegemony of the rural elite that had coalesced under colonialism was virtually unchallenged. Individuals most directly associated with the cantonal chieftaincy, it is true, had lost their claim to legitimate leadership. There were about fifty cantonal chiefs in the groundnut basin in the 1950s, most drawn from princely lineages,

---

[24] Pélissier 1966:338. When the office of village chief was made elective around 1945, subor-dination of the chiefs to the marabouts became even more obvious: the village chiefs "were essentially chosen by the marabout" (Cruise O'Brien 1971a:266).

[25] See Pélissier 1966:346.

[26] French colonial administrators did not relinquish formal control over these institutions.

[27] Dumont 1972:193, emphasis in original.

and as a class they were very unpopular.[28] As Martin Klein (1968b:206) noted, in Senegal, the colonial chieftaincy – including the abolition thereof – was not a major political issue in the late 1950s. Most cantonal chiefs had already been marginalized or redeployed by the end of the decade, when the cantonal chieftaincy was finally assimilated fully into Senegal's civil service.[29]

The summary fate of the cantonal chiefs should not be taken as evidence that French colonialism had destroyed the dominant lineages of central Senegal, or reduced the old aristocrats to mere cogs in France's administrative machine, or indeed that nationalist/socialist modernizers swept away the last vestiges of precolonial authority in Senegalese peasant society. All three arguments have been advanced in the literature on Senegal to demonstrate the autonomy of the modern state, and to suggest a stark disconnect (temporal and structural) between the "imported" authority of the modern state and indigenous sociopolitical institutions. Dismantling the cantonal chieftaincy, however, was not the deathblow to Senegal's neotraditional elite; it did not put an end to their collaboration in modern state building or to their power as rural political leaders.

The privileges of the groundnut basin's leading families were not tied to the cantonal chieftaincy and had not come to rest completely on the dispensations of the French. From the mid-1800s, as power shifted on the ground, Wolof nobility sought to associate themselves with the up-and-coming Islamic reformers. Leading marabouts in the twentieth century, for their part, broadened the bases of their own legitimacy by associating themselves with the royal lineages, and thus with the memory of Wolof statehood.[30] Ruth Morganthau wrote that "over the generations, through intermarriage and conversion to Islam, almost a single social category concentrating rural religious and secular power and wealth had emerged out

---

[28] As Cruise O'Brien (1975:98–100) explained, they "no longer performed any function valued by the mass of their subjects."

[29] Cantonal chiefs who were still politically viable were given new jobs as *chefs d'arrondissement*. Of the eighty-four *chefs d'arrondissement* appointed in 1960, forty-nine were *chefs de canton* and sixteen were assistant chiefs prior to the reform. In 1965, half of the eighty-six *chefs d'arrondissement* were former cantonal chiefs (Cohen 1971:42, 198, 245 n. 9).

[30] El Hadj Malik Sy, founder and Grand Khalif of the main Tidjane botherhood, is an example. His second wife was Safiétou Niang, niece of the king of Jolof (Djolof), Albury Ndiaye. She is the one who settled with Malik Sy in Tivaouane. She died in 1946. Their son Abdoul Aziz Sy inherited the Khalifat in 1957 and remained its leader until 1997 (McLaughlin 1997:4 *inter alia*). Abdoul Aziz Sy was, in this sense, both a grand marabout *and* a prince. See Coulon 1981.

of the maraboutic, trading, and traditional chiefly families."[31] Wolof royals still claimed birthrights to political roles, and they did indeed establish privileged places in the postcolonial state. Aristocratic lineages' land rights were still in force in the old zones of Wolof settlement.[32] What Dumont calls the *grandes familles* of the Wolof groundnut basin remained a decisive presence in the groundnut basin.

When it came to the ability to rally Wolof populations, power clearly lay with a narrower stratum: the Sufi saints. France institutionalized a partnership with these rural heavyweights. Through this process, the Islamic leaders had grown economically dependent on the state. They needed state-provided land, wells, loans, purchased inputs, and equipment to reap profits from their own estates, to sustain the process of groundnut pioneering (and thus establish new followings), and to reproduce the relations of economic dependency that tied peasants to the maraboutic elite.

Even as political and religious organizations, the Sufi orders consumed far more than groundnuts alone could finance. Cash grants and "loans" from the French to the Grands Khalifs had become routine by the end of the 1940s. Government money helped marabouts maintain their courts and entourages, the yearly cycle of religious display and ritual, Islamic libraries, mosques, and charitable agencies. France helped to finance the construction of Africa's largest mosque in Touba, the Mouride capital, and a spectacular mosque in Dakar that was named after El Hadj Malik Sy, founder of the Tidjane order.

Colonial authorities also had a hand in maintaining cohesion and discipline within both orders. Upon the deaths of the founders, colonial administrators took sides in succession conflicts, recognized only one supreme leader of each order, and dispensed state largesse in a way that reinforced centralized command. Through political intrigue and the manipulation of state patronage, the French authorities also helped marginalize dissidents and splinter movements (Behrman 1970:42–50).

In the 1940s and 1950s the Sufi hierarchies were well defined and disciplined enough, especially in the case of the Mourides, to provide effective structures for collective action in the political arena. The Grand Khalif of the Mouride order was Falilou Mbacké, son of Amadou Bamba. Under him

---

[31] Morganthau 1964:147. There was also some tension between the maraboutic and chiefly elements over land. See Pélissier 1966:339.

[32] Within old feudal domains, aristocratic families tried with varying degrees of success to enforce their rights to regulate land access and collect dues (Pélissier 1966:128).

were about a dozen *grands marabouts*, each with a territorial fiefdom of his own. About two hundred lesser Mouride marabouts made up the next rung on the Mouride hierarchy: each had a personal following large enough to give him political clout in the groundnut basin. The Mourides dominated the newer zones of groundnut settlement and, thanks to their organizational coherence and discipline, had a capacity for collective action that would enhance their weight in the national political arena. The Tidjane order was the major political force in the northern groundnut basin. It was similar in structure to the Mourides, but was looser, less disciplined, and more factionalized. Its following was more urban and literate, and less imbricated in the peasant groundnut economy.

With the enfranchisement of Senegal's rural populations between 1946 and 1956, the Sufi leaders became kingmakers.

II. Senghor Gathers Power via "Fusion of Elites"

In Senegal, democracy preceded universal franchise, as it did in the United States and Britain. As a result, the Senegalese elite was able to organize its political hegemony in the rural areas before the floodgates of politics opened. This is surely a factor in explaining the stability of the political configuration that crystallized during the decolonization era. Over the course of nine elections held between 1946 and 1959, Senegalese political leaders forged a sprawling and inclusive coalition of elites. The strategy that propelled Léopold Senghor to political preeminence was to offer to share power with established rural powerbrokers – that is, to guarantee them political power and autonomy within their own fiefdoms. His choice was dictated largely by the realities of power in central Senegal: in the groundnut basin, no political party has ever adopted a different strategy for mobilizing electoral support.

A national political elite in Senegal was consolidated during a period of rapid expansion of the state apparatus. This facilitated the process; cooptation is easier with a growing pie. After World War II France launched wide-ranging reforms of colonial institutions. There was an extensive deconcentration of the state apparatus, coupled with a "democratization" process by which authority was devolved to elected African leaders. The rural development apparatus in the groundnut basin stretched farther and deeper into the localities, and it swelled as more state resources were pumped into the rural economy. Deconcentration and devolution provided urban-based Senegalese politicians with resources to build political parties of wide territorial scope.

Voting rights, hitherto held exclusively by citizens of the Quatre Communes, Senegal's four coastal municipalities, were extended to rural populations in an incremental manner. In 1946 all Senegalese were made French citizens, but voting in the countryside was restricted to holders of school certificates, veterans, civil servants, chiefs, and licensed traders. Widening of the electorate in 1951 produced a decisive shift in the voting majority away from the coastal towns and to the rural provinces. Universal suffrage came in 1956, four years before Senegal gained formal political independence from France.

The ruling party of the Quatre Communes, the French Socialist Party (SFIO), was rooted in the "assimilated" coastal elite of lawyers, politicians, professionals, and traders. The party had long, informal ties with the rural areas, and especially the maraboutic and chiefly notables of the groundnut basin.[33] It began organizing SFIO units headed by rural notables in the 1930s and 1940s, and used state resources flowing through the groundnut cooperatives to incorporate cantonal chiefs and SIP agents into the SFIO political machine. As the rural electorate began to expand, however, the SFIO became vulnerable to two heavy charges. One was that it remained a tool of the old, Dakar-based elite of the Quatre Communes. The other was that to extend its reach into the rural areas in the 1940s, the SFIO had done little more than crawl into bed with cantonal chiefs, the most corrupt and resented members of the rural notability.

With the initial enfranchisement of rural voters in 1946, party leader Lamine Guèye chose Léopold Senghor to be the SFIO "deputy for the provinces." In 1948 Senghor broke with the SFIO and set out to exploit in full the opportunities created by the enfranchisement of rural populations. Like his nationalist-era counterparts in Côte d'Ivoire and Ghana, Senghor used the political and demographic weight of the rural masses to counter-balance and thus enhance his own political autonomy vis-à-vis the lawyerly and professional African elite that had coalesced around the colonial state.

With his right-hand man, the progressive economist Mamadou Dia, Senghor set out to mobilize a "rural bloc" against the old Dakar elite. The

---

[33] Urban politicians had long ties to provincial powerbrokers. The first campaign of Blaise Diagne, who served as Senegal's deputy to the French National Assembly from 1914 to 1934, was financed in large part by Mouride marabouts. On this era, see Johnson 1971.

centerpiece of this strategy was alliance with the Muslim leaders of the groundnut basin, who would carry most of the rural electorate with them. Alliances with powerbrokers and political leaders in Senegal's peripheral zones – the Senegal River Valley and the Casamance – would also be decisive in bringing Senghor to power.

Senghor and Dia "toured the provinces continuously"[34] to put together the party they called the Bloc Démocratique Sénégalais (BDS). They campaigned, bargained, and negotiated to win support of established elites who could deliver the votes of their own personal followings, clans, and constituencies. Party leaders sought out "favorite sons" and recruited them to stand as BDS candidates in their constituencies.

In the groundnut basin, the BDS and the SFIO tried to outdo each other in courting Mouride and Tidjane leaders. "The most effective means employed by the political leaders in their efforts to win the marabouts' favors is direct economic assistance."[35] Sufi leaders, for their part, were eager to use their clout as electoral brokers to nail down alliances with the nationalist politicians destined to assume control of the postcolonial state. Donal Cruise O'Brien (1971a:262) wrote that they became "the political agents" of the major parties after the enfranchisement of the countryside. Patronage-driven electoral politics turned out to be a boon for the confréries, and it became a factor in itself in reinforcing the status and influence of the Sufi elite. "The flow of money from political sources in the 1950s made it possible for certain marabouts to acquire wealth on a scale hitherto unimaginable. In the 1950s, politics became by far the greatest source of revenue for the Mouride elite" (ibid.).

Nationalist leaders offered the elite of central Senegal more than cash, for this alone would have been insufficient to guarantee their future in a Senegal under African rule. In approaching the marabouts as vote brokers and as intermediaries between the urban politicians and the peasants, the nationalists implicitly, and perhaps explicitly as well, recognized existing structures of political hierarchy and indirect rule in the central groundnut basin. The politicians showed how the rural status quo could provide the basis for a political order that served both their interests and those of the established rural elite. Political alignments forged at this moment provided the basis for the powersharing deal between the Sufi elite and Léopold Senghor, and thus defined the structure of nationalist-era contests in Senegal. The

---

[34] Morganthau 1964:146 *inter alia*.
[35] Cruise O'Brien 1971:262. He and Morganthau (1964) offer rich accounts of this era.

provincial notables surely bargained for something akin to what E. E. Schattschneider, in describing U.S. politics in 1896, called southern conservatives' demand for "undisputed control over the South."

With the backing of the Sufi leaders, the BDS scored early and spectacular electoral victories. By 1952, Senghor's party had achieved territory-wide dominance. Only Dakar and Saint-Louis remained strongholds of SFIO support. The BDS took control of Senegal's Territorial Assembly and with it, wide authority over the day-to-day running of government and territorial administration in Senegal. The party had won an overwhelming institutional advantage: it was able to gather power as "party in government" for almost eight years *before* the transition to formal political independence in 1960.[36]

A. Reappropriation of the State

Electoral victories of the 1950s gave the BDS control over a vast pool of governmental resources that it could deploy to make friends, co-opt skeptics and rivals, build alliances, and seal deals. The BDS was able to appoint personnel at all levels of government, including grassroots and regional levels of provincial administration, in a rapidly expanding state apparatus. In the groundnut basin, the BDS gave positions to favorite sons and influential local figures, thus helping to anchor provincial administration in the already established agrarian elite. SIPs were thoroughly colonized by chiefs and marabouts, and the BDS relied on these institutions as vehicles to co-opt local influentials and harness the votes of their disciples and dependents. Senghor's party sponsored the creation of new producer cooperatives in localities around the rim of the groundnut basin, further deconcentrating the party-state machine and extending its territorial reach. Public works projects, the chance to take sides in electoral contests over chieftaincy posts, and the licensing of private groundnut buyers were also opportunities for party building that were skillfully exploited by Senghor, his lieutenants in Dakar, and his rural allies.[37] The

---

[36] French officials gradually stepped aside. Many receded into supervisory or "advisory" posts, or positions within the higher administration (foreign affairs, international trade, constitutional affairs) that France would not fully relinquish until many years after independence.

[37] After the 1952 victory, *chefs de canton* were drawn into the BDS orbit. Senghor argued that "the maintenance of traditional chiefs is in conformity with the spirit of scientific socialism." The chiefs, meanwhile, "were not unresponsive to the BDS suggestion of higher salaries

BDS easily constructed territory-wide electoral victories in 1952, 1953, and 1956.

Institution building during this period also involved a reconfiguration of the party itself. In the wake of Senghor's decisive win in 1952, party sections that had grown from preexisting caste, ethnic, or religious associations were replaced by BDS cells that were organized exclusively on the basis of *locality*. Cells were pulled together into a hierarchy of territorially based subdivisions that followed the lines of existing maps of electoral representation and provincial administration. Senghor created new, executive organs of the party at the regional level, and these were taken over by provincial heavyweights and vote brokers. They were perfect institutional bases for the Sufi brotherhoods that dominated central Senegal. The BDS gave local dignitaries wide autonomy to run party affairs, dominate civic life, and distribute party resources within their own fiefdoms. Regional notables made decisions about candidate recruitment, campaign financing, and appointments to local posts within their own domains. It was "grassroots democracy" BDS style, and it produced a party structure that was widely perceived in the hinterland as more democratic and inclusive than that of the SFIO.

About a decade later, Jonathan Barker (1971:53) wrote that "[i]t is possible to say that the pattern of political support represented by the [ruling party] in the peanut-growing region accurately reflects the pattern of social stratification. The persons in the upper strata who are dominant in terms of prestige, wealth, and religious reputation have key positions in the political network that supports the government of Senghor."

In 1956 the BDS co-opted its partisan rival, the SFIO. The ruling party was renamed the Union Progressiste Sénégalaise (UPS). Fusion confirmed the basic logics by which Senghor had consolidated power: patronage politics, supporting local strongmen, and encouraging local autonomy over constituent elements of the political machine. The most important political barons – those with the largest political followings – got the most important political posts, the largest fiefdoms, and the most latitude over the deployment of state prerogative and resources. This was powersharing, and by definition it limited the autonomy of the center. Many observers of Senegal's ruling party have argued that the decentralized, loosely structured coalition character of the BDS machine "placed severe constraints

and secure status" (Morganthau 1964:149). Expansion of the institutional apparatus of the state created new positions to which chiefs could be "promoted."

on the degree of authority the national party leadership could wield over constituent elements of the movement they led."[38]

B. Attempted Co-optation of the Left: An Off-the-Path Initiative

Senghor's party also undertook to co-opt the vocal and mobilized urban elements – trade union and youth movement leaders, university students and well-educated professionals, and small parties of leftist intellectuals – whose support would be needed to govern Senegal successfully, but who still lay outside the party fold. By its very nature, however, the party would have difficulty absorbing those who envisioned decolonization as a chance for a progressive break with the colonial and feudal past. Senghor's most important alliance was with the very "feudals" the progressives denounced.

Some of the leftist intellectuals and trade unionists were co-opted into the BDS in 1956. Some received important posts in the BDS executive. Through this process of co-optation, the party led by Senghor acquired a left wing whose outspoken and articulate leaders challenged the old party barons and criticized the party for its conservatism, especially in the rural areas. Leftist leaders also pushed for a clean break with France, but perhaps more critical in understanding political choices in Senegal was their agenda in the rural areas, especially the groundnut basin. Their goal was to mobilize the masses, challenge local bosses, and free the peasantry from the exploitation and domination of religious notables. This agenda introduced considerable ideological incoherence, even dissonance, into the ruling party's rhetoric and official posturing. As Schumacher shows (1975:xviii–xxi, 86–93), the progressive intellectuals who were helping to write party platform papers and policy studies were basically calling for a direct attack on the economic bases of maraboutic privilege and authority.

This turn of events was sufficient to galvanize the Mouride and Tidjane religious leaders into concerted political action. In a brief but decisive moment in the decolonization process, the Sufi elite attempted to form a unified front outside (not within) Senghor's party, which they must have perceived as flirting dangerously with the urban left, and perhaps even wavering in its commitment to them.[39] In 1957 the rural elite formed the Conseil Supérieur des Chefs Réligieux. It first met in 1958 to oppose the Left's call for immediate independence and to endorse de Gaulle's proposals

---

[38] Schumacher 1975:17. See also Diop and Diouf 1992a.
[39] On this episode, see Behrman 1970:81–3; Boone 1992:87–95.

for Franco-African community. At this critical juncture, the ruling party's newly acquired left wing got frustrated, walked out (was pushed out?) of Senghor's party, and regrouped within two new opposition parties.[40] They pledged to "arouse the peasantry" and campaigned for a "no" vote in the 1958 referendum on the Franco-African community.

The peasants of central Senegal voted massively with the religious leaders in the 1958 referendum. The Council of Religious Chiefs soon fell apart. Its political energies were reabsorbed into the ruling party, and the UPS soared toward the electoral finish line. For our purposes, this episode is significant for two reasons. First, the Sufi leaders had demonstrated some capacity for collective action – this could not have been lost on the Dakar politicians who depended on them for electoral success. Cohesive hierarchy in rural society empowered rural leaders to collectively distance themselves from the UPS, the party built upon their support, and to veto what appeared to be a reformist shift in the ruling party's agenda. Second, in this episode we see a glimmer of "off-the-path behavior" (counterfactual behavior)[41] on the part of Senegal's rulers – that is, the Senghor regime appeared willing to listen to those calling for a "revolution from above" that would usurp the power of provincial notables in the ground-nut basin. The mere possibility of such a shift in strategy on the part of the rulers destablized the powersharing deal institutionalized within the ruling party. When this happened, the Senghor regime immediately cut ties with the reformers and reaffirmed its primary alliance with the rural leaders.[42]

---

[40] One, the Parti du Regroupement Africain-Sénégal (PRA-Senegal), was cofounded by Abdoulaye Ly and Assane Seck upon their defection from the UPS. It favored the Nkrumahist variety of African socialism. It had an urban following and also an electoral majority in one region, the Casamance (a point to which we shall return). The other was the Parti Africain de l'Indépendance (PAI), led by Majhmout Diop, who had founded the party in 1957. It adopted Marxist-Leninism and had followings in Saint-Louis and the secondary towns, and "hoped to be able to arouse the peasantry." Both campaigned for immediate independence from France. On these parties, see Cruise O'Brien 1967:558–62, who also writes of their destruction and the UPS's co-optation of their leaders in the 1960s. See also Schumacher 1975:18–19.

[41] It is counterfactual in the sense that it does not conform to what our theory leads us to expect. If the Senghor regime had pursued the reform-oriented (usurpationist) course, then this would be a case that did not support ("disconfirmed") the predictions, so to speak, of our theory.

[42] The matter was not settled definitively in 1962. Some of the same issues reemerged in the 1990s.

With independence in 1960s the UPS government declared socialism to be the guiding philosophy of the state, yet this ideological posture said little about how politics would proceed on the ground. Senghor's government used all means at its disposal to institutionalize the conservative coalition of notables upon which it rested. René Dumont (1972:193) put it most strongly: "independence gave the ruling party, which was dominated by the *grandes familles*, a monopoly over political power."

It is an irony of Senegal's political history that Senghor, the urbane and scholarly embodiment of France's assimilationist ideal, cast his lot with a provincial elite that traced its lineages to the old Senegambian civilizations. It proved to be a winning political formula, and it would go far in defining the institutional architecture of the postcolonial state.

III. *Institutional Choice in the Groundnut Basin: Powersharing*

Mouride and Tidjane leaders sought alliance with the nationalists in the 1950s, and their strategy paid off handsomely. The maraboutic elite was granted wide latitude in running the political system at the regional level:

The marabouts, given their role in constituting the political networks that underpin the regime in the groundnut basin, are in a position to name Deputies to the National Assembly, choose mayors (who must seek their backing), and establish direct links with the Head of State or his closest collaborators, thus by-passing the administrative authorities at the regional and departmental level. Local administrative authorities are forced to profess their allegiance [to the maraboutic elite] in order to keep their jobs.... Functionaries in the regions seek out the marabouts' patronage at the expense of application of administrative directives. (Diop and Diouf 1992a:76)

Lucy Behrman argued in the 1960s that in the region of Diourbel, the center of the Mouride brotherhood, the marabouts were more powerful than the regional administration. "At times it almost seems as if the local and regional administration has become an appendage of the powerful organization, the Murid brotherhood" (1970:109). Mouride and Tidjane marabouts in the administrative regions of Sine-Saloum, Thiès, and Diourbel – which together comprised the groundnut basin – exert pressure in the selection of candidates for office in the local, regional, and national government. The most powerful marabouts also "exercised a great deal of influence" over administrative appointments at the village, arrondissement, and regional level.[43] Many have described the Mouride capital of Touba, some forty-five kilometers north of Diourbel, as a "state within a state." Others have used this expression loosely to characterize the groundnut basin in general. In postcolonial Senegal's groundnut basin, the interests and political clout of the Sufi brotherhoods were decisive. They systematically overrode the centralizing, statist, and developmentalist drives that emanated from some parts of the central administration.

As for the Wolof aristocrats, they too were granted a share of the post-colonial state. They remained prominent as representatives of secular political authority in central Senegal and ensconced themselves in official positions – both elected and appointed – from the village level to the National Assembly. As a political caste, they "never completely vanished"; instead they assumed the role of secular "middlemen between the marabouts and the state."[44] Marabouts retained the upper hand: they "designated the representatives of temporal authority, or tipped the balance in competitions between Wolof notables for political positions in the PS-state [party-state]."[45] Modern state making continued to provide avenues for the symbiosis of aristocratic and maraboutic authority that defined political order in this part of the Senegalese countryside.

Some accounts have depicted the arrangements that guaranteed the influence of the rural notability as "informal" – as existing outside, or parallel to, the formal structures and rules of the state. The argument here, by contrast, is that the urban-rural alliance was institutionalized deeply in state structures and processes in central Senegal. The Senghor regime worked assiduously to build formal rules and organizations that would cement and routinize powersharing with rural notables at both the village level and the level of the administrative regions (the top rung of provincial government).

Independence's first two decades were marked by a truly extensive deconcentration of the state apparatus in the countryside of central Senegal. Spatial deconcentration was accompanied by rules and norms that devolved control over these governmental outposts to indigenous elites. Nearly every level and subunit of this political system became a site for devolving official administrative and spending prerogatives to rural heavyweights. So

---

[43] For example, the Gouverneur of Diourbel appointed in 1963, Médoune Fall, "was widely regarded as a protégé of the Mouride Khalif... later Fall was named to the important post of Ambassador to France. Similarly, at lower levels of administration... the Mouride Khalif and his subordinates influence appointments... (Behrman 1970:112).

[44] Beck 1996a:173–4, sa. 54, 92 *inter alia*.

[45] Beck 1996a:174 n. 18.

extensive was the surrender of central prerogative to the local elite that government presence in this region has been characterized as "almost totally lacking in centralized control and direction."[46]

The discussion of institutional choice is organized into four parts. First is a look at deconcentration and devolution at the village level. The second part focuses on deconcentration and devolution at the level of the administrative regions (provinces) that made up the groundnut basin in the 1960s, 1970s, and 1980s. At both levels, we look at rural administration (including demarcation of political/administrative units and principal-agent questions), rural development institutions (i.e., rules governing access to factors of production – land, labor, purchased inputs, and credit), and arrangements governing commercialization of the export crop. Part three reinforces the main argument by underscoring the weakness of Dakar's direct agents vis-à-vis the indigenous rural authorities in the Wolof groundnut basin. The fourth part discusses these arrangements as a powersharing alliance between center and rural periphery, and points to some implications for rural development and possibilities for democracy in this region.

A. Deconcentration and Devolution: Building State Outposts in the Villages

At the molecular level of the villages, Dakar leaders built an administrative/political machine of tremendous weight and density to tax export-crop producers, embed the party-state in the existing rural collectivities, and regulate access to productive resources (purchased agricultural inputs and land). These are the functional domains of state action that we will consider in all the case studies presented in this book. In this part of Senegal, the local state consisted of an interlocking network made up of groundnut cooperatives run by elected officials, local cells of the ruling party, village chieftaincies, and from the 1970s on, elected Rural Councils. The sections that follow consider each of these institutions in turn. We look first at spatial deconcentration of the state apparatus (creating new layers of the state apparatus at the local and regional levels and/or expanding the functions of existing provincial institutions) and then at the devolution of authority (delegating political and administrative prerogative to rural elites) within each institutional domain.

This institutional complex was paralleled by, and supposedly overseen by, an administrative corps of state agents who were appointed by and

---

[46] See Foltz 1977:245. This is also Schumacher's (1975) main point.

(nominally) directly answerable to the center. Dakar's direct agents were headquartered in newly created *arrondissements*, each one born of the fusion of about three colonial cantons. It turns out that the state's direct agents were not able to interfere much with the local political logics and purposes that animated the state's rural outposts in this region of Senegal. If anything, the prefectorial administration aided and abetted the capture of these state outputs by the rural leaders.

Producer Cooperatives. Cooperatives, as the regime euphemistically called them, were the building blocks of the postcolonial state in the groundnut basin. Building upon the institutional inheritance of the SIP, Dakar constructed a denser, better-funded, and far more deconcentrated cooperative network. A system that had counted about 525 local units in 1960 grew to over 1,060 by 1973.[47] There was, on average, one cooperative per every twelve villages in the groundnut basin.[48] Membership was compulsory for household heads – as it had been in the 1930s and 1940s.

Like the SIPs, postcolonial cooperatives served as outlets for distributing farming inputs – seeders, seeds, fertilizers, and credit. Externally funded rural development programs came online in the 1960s, mostly to enhance soil productivity by promoting the use of chemical fertilizers. These resources were pumped into rural communities via the cooperative system. By the mid-1960s, virtually every farming household in the groundnut basin was bound by relations of debt and economic dependency to one of the village-level cooperatives. Meanwhile, between 1960 and 1967, the center imposed monopoly control over the entire groundnut marketing circuit. Functions of the village cooperatives were expanded and upgraded to handle the job of purchasing Senegal's entire groundnut output. In addition to their distributive tasks, the co-ops became the grassroots-level buying stations of the state marketing board. Cooperative officials also handled the trucking of sacked groundnuts to "cooperative unions," called Centres Régionaux d'Assistance au Développement (CRADS), that were sited at the regional level.

Viewed from below, governing the village cooperatives was a huge responsibility, for it involved deciding who would receive loans and inputs

---

[47] The figure for the 1964 harvest was 979 official cooperatives in Senegal's groundnut basin; they handled 65 percent of the crop. The 1967–8 harvest was supposed to be completely commercialized through the cooperatives. Licensed traders were eliminated from the circuit in that year. See van chi Bonnardel 1973:570, 627 n. 116, 628 n. 132; Diarassouba, 1968:216–17.

[48] There was one per every seventeen in Sine-Saloum; one per nine in Diourbel (ibid.).

(and on what terms), grading and weighing each farmer's crop, and deciding what deductions to make before the peasant family received payment for their year of labor. So acute was the farmer's dependency on every-day decisions made by cooperative officials, and so vulnerable were ordinary households to the officials' discretion, that to be a co-op leader was to have tremendous clout, leverage, and influence within the small universe of the village and its neighboring communities.

Rather than appointing state agents to handle this job, as was a common state-building tactic in postcolonial Africa, Dakar delegated control over the village cooperatives to indigenous leaders in each locality. Even the choice of these leaders was devolved to the locality: all the members of each cooperative cast a vote for the cooperative president, who then chose the "weigher." In this region, marabouts took over most of the postcolonial cooperatives directly or by way of their close relatives and/or disciples. Diop and Diouf (1992a:76) wrote that "for the first time, and indirectly, they [the marabouts] assumed modern administrative functions." A study of the Thiès region around 1970 found that in an "overwhelming number" of cases the marabout is linked to the president of the cooperative and the village chief by family ties. These arrangements permitted "a single family-based clan to exercise a grip on the political and economic affairs of the village. . . . The role of the imams [marabouts] in tightly integrated villages is to reinforce the position of the chief, especially when the chief is president of the cooperative and a relative of the imam" (Bergmann 1974:313, 319).

Cooperatives were sited in "leading villages," thus institutionalizing relations of hierarchy and subordination between villages at this cellular level of rural society. Control over cooperatives also worked to formalize (and perhaps widen) the influence of those who controlled these local outputs of the party-state. *Grands marabouts* did not hesitate to preside directly over some of the richest cooperatives. Groundnut cooperatives in Mbacké and Diourbel were presided over by *grands marabouts* of the Mbacké family, both of whom were very close to the Khalifat. Ibrahima Niasse, one of the most important Tidjane marabouts, was president of a large cooperative in the Kaolack area.[49]

The elite of the new groundnut cooperatives naturally included much of old and experienced personnel of the SIPs. In addition to the marabout, this included chiefs who had a long history of using cooperatives for their

---

[49] Diop and Diouf 1992a:80; they also cite Tignor 1987:122 n. 1.

own political and economic ends.[50] Postcolonial expansion of the cooperative system also created much-needed opportunities for co-opting the Senegalese groundnut traders whose businesses had been effectively expropriated by the state. In the mid-1960s these important supporters of the Senghoriste parties of the 1950s were displaced. Those who remained faithful to the party were, however, compensated: many were co-opted into the new statist system as licensed buyers, weighers in the cooperatives, or marketing board employees.[51]

Ruling Party Structure, Village Chieftaincies.   As Schumacher explains, the 1960 reforms that deconcentrated and "Africanized" provincial administration sought no change in village and community organization. Post-independence deconcentration was marked by "striking continuity in the structure and personnel of local politics and administration, and in the way in which tasks were carried out" (1975:88). In the Wolof groundnut basin, this meant that party-state institutions were grafted onto preexisting social hierarchies, and thus became an organic part of a rural social order dominated by marabouts and the old Wolof aristocracy.

In Wolof-Mouride areas, village chiefs continued to be marabouts, or selected by them, thus ensuring a fusing of the most deconcentrated instances of both state and indigenous authority. After independence, party cells were systematically added to this institutional complex. Senghor left little to chance in this electorally strategic region: like good communists, central rulers chose to organize the smallest constituent units of rural society – extended households under the rule of patriarchs, compounds and *quartiers* within large villages, religious schools and dara – into UPS cells of fifty to one hundred card-carrying party members. The authority of the party was thus married to that of village patriarchs and elders, who were responsible for political order and getting out the vote in their own micro-cosmic domains.

These same local notables named the local UPS men charged with constituting village-level cells of the ruling party. In much of the Wolof groundnut basin, the roles of UPS man, marabout, and chief melded together to form a system of village government that was focused on family patriarchs

---

[50] Dumont and Diarrasouba argue that reform of the marketing circuit after 1960 "had the contrary effect of maintaining the old system, shoring up some of its weak links, and politicizing it" (Dumont 1972:192, citing Diarrasouba 1968).

[51] See Barker 1971:52–4; Amin 1969:60–3.

and that reinforced communal cohesion and order. Like marabouts and chiefs, UPS cell leaders cultivated their legitimacy as local leaders by acting as community patrons. They helped villagers pay school tuition, buy medicine, and even pay taxes. Like marabouts and chiefs, UPS men contributed money for local ceremonies such as baptisms and burials, and they intervened with prefects and *sous-préfets* to secure places in school, vaccination certificates, and identity papers (Beck 1996a:218–9). All this required continuous outlays of cash, most of which came from above. As in the 1940s and 1950s, the downward flow of resources from Dakar helped sustain the patron-client relationships that tied peasants to marabouts and leading families in the groundnut basin. Connections to the state also amplified preexisting forms of authority. For example, connections to the party-state are what gave Mouride marabouts secular authority over even the non-Mouride families in their villages. Accounts of local politics in the Wolof groundnut basin in the 1990s underscore how stable these arrangements have proven to be in this region of Senegal.[52]

Land Law and Rural Councils. Senegal's 1964 tenure law laid another stone in the foundation of the postcolonial state. With the 1964 Loi sur le Domaine National, the state formally appropriated all powers and prerogatives to distribute land throughout the entire national territory.[53] It was a dramatically statist and radical move; it is widely known as Senegal's 1964 "land reform." The law was supposed to eradicate all traditional, customary, aristocratic, and feudal land dues, rents, and tithes, and thereby liberate peasants from the oppressive overrule of the old elite. Inheritable rights to farmland would henceforth be granted to whoever established "user's rights" by cultivating the land for three consecutive years, on the condition that the farmer resided in the community and farmed the parcel personally, with the aid of family members. The law had an explicit developmentalist thrust, for it was supposed to remove social barriers to bringing new land into productive use. By some accounts, the 1964 National Domain Law dealt the final blow to the old Senegambian aristocracies and placed Senegal in the vanguard of African socialism.

Under the 1964 land law the state's powers as manager of the national domain were to be devolved to elected Rural Councils (Conseils Ruraux,

---

[52] See for example Diop and Diouf 1992a; Beck 1998; Patterson 1996, 1999; Blundo 1995, 1998a, 1998b. On Sine (Siin), which is different, see Galvan 1995, 1996, forthcoming.

[53] Land held under private proprietorship was excluded.

or CR).[54] These were to preside over new jurisdictions called Commu-nautés Rurales, or Rural Communities, comprising between ten and fifty villages (depending on the region), and located below the *arrondissements* on the provincial administrative hierarchy.[55] Rural Communities were to serve as deconcentrated political and administrative centers. Like the agricul-tural cooperatives, these new jurisdictions were carved out along the lines of what state builders called "natural sociological groupings": the Rural Communities were supposed to take account of traditional solidarities, shared interests based on proximity, and the existence of local notabilities.

Councils were empowered to manage the distribution and redistribu-tion of land within the territory under their jurisdiction and to settle land disputes.[56] This included the right to revoke the land-use rights of anyone who did not farm the land continuously or who otherwise failed to exploit adequately his/her land terrain. These rules were supposed to "restore the communal aspect of customary tenure."

Each twelve-to-twenty-one-member Rural Council also received a broad mandate to provide local infrastructure, social assistance, and "civil protec-tion and public tranquility," and to manage communal resources (forests, wells, land).[57] To this end, each council was given a budget of about USD $20,000 (in the 1970s and 1980s) that was supposed to be devoted to com-munal projects – such as well digging and constructing health clinics.[58] These budgets amplified the distributive powers of the Rural Councils: they had powers over not only land, but also jobs, cash, and contracts.

Rural Councils were duly assembled in the groundnut basin in the early 1970s, adding another layer to an already deconcentrated state apparatus.

Senegal's 1964 National Domain Law has been the subject of much anal-ysis: was it progressive, conservative, reactionary, or profoundly statist in

[54] Two-thirds of the members of each Rural Council were elected by inhabitants of the Rural Community; one-third of the members were appointed by the cooperatives located within each Rural Community.

[55] Early on, Birame Ndiaye (1979:547–8) noted that the Rural Councils were, contradictorily, instances of both administrative deconcentration and political devolution. The *sous-préfet* was given a "double role" vis-à-vis the council: he is "both principal and agent." This ambiguity was resolved differently in Senegal's different regions.

[56] On the 1964 law and the CRs, see Niang 1975, 1983:219 *inter alia*; Hesseling 1994:250; Verdier 1971; Gastellu 1983:277–8; Niang, 1983:219–22; and Pélissier, 1966:123 n. 1. Schumacher pointed out that provisions for rural communities or "democratic decentral-ized collectivities" were contained within the 1956 Loi Cadre (1975:92).

[57] See Ndiaye 1979. The size of the Rural Council depended on the population of the Rural Community.

[58] Vengroff and Johnson (1989:109) report that the average budget was $20,000 in 1980.

intent and effect?[59] It turns out that the answer depends on which region of Senegal you visit. In the Wolof groundnut basin, the 1964 land law and creation of Rural Councils transferred critically important state competencies to the provincial elite. These reforms ratified and institutionalized their control over land, the primordial source of power and political identity in agrarian society. A handful of Rural Councils was created in the 1960s, but this political-administrative reform was not generalized throughout the groundnut basin until the mid-1970s.[60] Control over these deconcentrated instances of the party-state was straightforwardly devolved to the local political and maraboutic elite. Darbon (1988:173) described it this way:

It is unthinkable that the leader of the Communauté Rurale would not be a traditional chief or his representative ["emanation"].... In general, the members of the rural council are delegates of local authorities.... The CR is thus, in a way, a *mandataire* [the tool, agent] of the traditional structure. The feudals' take-over of the communal institutions is explained by the important powers wielded by the rural council in ... land matters, and also by the pecuniary advantages that can be gained by holding the office of President of the council.

Rural Communities in the groundnut basin were substantial administrative units. They usually contained thirty-five to fifty villages, about five groundnut cooperatives, and populations of ten thousand to twenty-five thousand.[61] The Rural Councils empowered to govern these jurisdictions were supposed to be elected democratically, but in practice this meant that villagers ratified lists of local notables that were drawn up by none other than the local notables. What we have seen at other levels of the party-state apparatus held true in the case of the Rural Councils: Dakar invited the

[59] On the basis of an analysis of the Sine (Siin) subregion of the groundnut basin, Galvan (1996) writes that the 1964 land law completely reformulated land-tenure relations and disempowered customary aristocratic lineages. In Sine, he found that the CRs displaced customary rural authority. He thus sees the 1960s reforms as radically statist in intent. However, in the Wolof groundnut basin, the land law and the CRs did not have these effects. More on this below.

[60] Senegal's National Domain Law was "not applied" and virtually ignored by the government and the elite of central Senegal during the first decade of independence. "In 1971, seven years after the promulgation of the law, for about 10,000 villages only six elected Rural Councils actually functioned" (Dumont 1972:222). Communautés Rurales were phased in by region between 1972 and 1982. In the groundnut basin, Rural Councils were created between 1972 and 1976. The government would eventually create about 3 to 4 Rural Communities per arrondissement, for a total of 314 between 1974 and 1982 (Gellar 1987:146).

[61] These figures are for the 1970s (Vengroff and Johnson 1989:26–8). See also Sow 1988:81, 97.

local notability to govern within their fiefdoms; the center did not seek to supplant established rural leaders with its own lackeys or agents. Candidates for Rural Councils were elected collectively, off of one party list, in a winner-take-all contest. "The landowning elite in the peanut basin . . . held a monopoly on nominations to the . . . party list, which, in a majority-take-all electoral system controlled by the party-state, was assured victory."[62] Council presidents were supposed to be elected by council members – that was stipulated by law – but some observers report matter-of-factly that presidents were in fact chosen by the Minister of the Interior "on the basis of their traditional standing."[63] The center endorsed what Darbon called "the feudals' take-over of these institutions." Even as the electoral hegemony of Senegal's ruling party cracked in the 1980s and 1990s, the old elite of the Wolof groundnut basin retained a near iron grip on the Rural Councils (Beck 2001).

Inner workings of the Rural Councils not only reproduced but also surely accentuated political hierarchy in the countryside. Power was devolved directly to council presidents and vice-presidents. Writing twenty years apart, Diarrasouba (1968) and Darbon (1988:170) both reported that in the groundnut basin, decision-making powers were concentrated ("individualized") in the hands of council presidents, who made their decisions, including land tenure decisions, on the basis of consultation with "village elders." Blundo reported in the 1990s that the councils in the southeastern groundnut basin were run by cliques of "local bosses" who "made all decisions" and kept the other council members in the dark.[64] *Sous-préfets*, the government's top administrators at the *arrondissement* level, were indeed supposed to supervise the Rural Councils, but in this region they were more often partners and co-conspirators with the provincial bigmen. By several accounts, council presidents, vice-presidents, and *sous-préfets* constituted a triumvirate that ran the Rural Councils in their own interests and in response to pressures from religious and political notables. It seems that

---

[62] Beck 1996a:187–8, 256–7. Meanwhile it seems clear that the regime did not pack the CR's with cadres: Hesseling (1994:256, 256 n. 19) wrote that "in 1993, one of my students observed that 80 percent of the counselors in a Rural Community near Thiès were illiterate." Niang (1991:2) and Vengroff and Johnson (1989:37) make similar observations; the latter report that 60 percent of a "representative sample" of 114 council members had attended Koranic school only.

[63] Darbon 1988:173; see also Diarassouba 1968:240.

[64] This is not inconsistent with Vengroff and Johnson's (1989:58) finding that the president and vice-president of the CR are central in "local influence networks," while the other councilors are marginal.

council operations were characterized by "all manner of enrichment, embezzlement, [and] private use of communal resources on part of chairman and vice-chairman of CR."[65]

As progressive and modernizing as the 1964 Loi sur Le Domain National may have sounded at first, in this region of Senegal its effects were deeply conservative in at least three ways. First, by devolving land tenure authority to Rural Councils, the law effectively empowered the existing village-level elite to allocate and reallocate land in the name of both the community and the state. As Dumont (1972:224) said: "The results of the [1964 land tenure] law depend on who is applying it; thus, on the real powerholders." Niang offered this specification: "The law is subverted for the benefit of traditional authorities who profit from their social standing to attribute land to themselves."[66] Second, in seeking to "defend and protect the solidarity of farmers, on the basis of base communities," the law reinforced the hierarchical collectivities that were already fundamental sociopolitical units in this region. The law named the "community," rather than the individual, as rural society's basic agent and legal entity. No legal provision existed for individual landholding as such: individuals were supposed to gain access to land by right of membership in the collectivity.[67] Third, it ratified a "very unequal" distribution of land holding in the groundnut basin. The largest marabouts had landholdings of tens of thousands of hectares, while most households cultivated about three.[68] The 1964 law passed in silence over marabouts' land appropriation and exploitation privileges, central as these had been to state-supported efforts to increase export crop production in

---

[65] Blundo 1998a:15–17 *inter alia*, all referring to the 1990s. Abuses of land-attribution powers by council presidents were so widespread and flagrant in the 1970s that legislation to curb their autonomy and enhance the supervisory powers of the *sous-préfets* was passed in 1980 (Darbon 1988:170). Blundo's report suggests that this action did not have much effect.

[66] Niang 1991:2. See also Dumont 1972:221; Darbon 1988:170. Pélissier (1966:902–3) saw the 1964 law as conservative and, he added, as leaving completely open the whole question of land policy in Senegal.

[67] Caverivière and Debene (1988:70–1, 183) make this point and ask, "Who is a member of the community? Who is a stranger?"

[68] Dumont 1972:223. In the late 1960s, 58 percent of the households in the groundnut basin cultivated less than 3 hectares (accounting for only 22 percent of cultivated land), 6.4 percent of the households had holdings of 3–10 hectares (26 percent of the cultivated land); 2.8% of all households had holdings over 15 hectares (14.3 percent of cultivated land) (Diarrasouba 1968:115). On large holdings, Behrman (1970:137, see also 143–4) notes for example that "Falilou Mbacké, one of the largest producers of peanuts in Senegal, had enormous fields at Touba-Bogo, including 7,000 hectares under cultivation." See also Cruise O'Brien 1975:126, 143 n. 17.

Senegal since the 1920s.[69] Maraboutic land-use practices continued to have no legal basis in Senegal.

Darbon (1988) emphasizes that the creation of these institutions reinforced the influence of the "traditional notables" because land distribution was a political resource used to win political support. For the average farming household in the groundnut basin, however, perhaps what was really crucial was the council's power to *revoke* land-use rights. Such an act by the council president was legally justified in two circumstances, both very broadly defined: in the case of insufficient *mise en valeur* (insufficient development) or poor maintenance of the parcel, and when a farmer ceased to farm the land himself (notably when he ceased to reside on the land) (Diarassouba 1968:240). As Dumont suggested in the 1970s and Galvan stressed in the 1990s, the fear of losing land rights under the terms of Senegal's land-use law could be very real.[70] Farming households in the groundnut basin revealed themselves to be less ignorant of the law than some observers have suspected. There was a noticeable decline in land-use practices such as fallowing and pawning that could be construed by a hostile party as "abandonment," insufficient development, or failure on the part of the use-right holder to cultivate a parcel continuously.

In the groundnut basin, the 1964 land law did not simply preserve and perpetuate preexisting land tenure patterns. In Senegal, "dominant strata – bureaucratic and maraboutic – *modify* land tenure logic to their own advantage," and the land law and Rural Councils were certainly used in this manner.[71] Provincial notables used the Rural Councils to appropriate land for themselves. The Peul of the western and then the eastern Ferlo thus found themselves victims of the new rules that were ostensibly promulgated to protect "customary users": appropriation of Peul lands, justified by opportunistic invocation of the 1964 National Domain Law, helped Mouride marabouts sustain their old land-pioneering practices (and also old strategies of disciple recruitment) well into the 1990s, when the groundnut economy in older parts of the central basin was in a state of advanced decline.[72]

---

[69] Cruise O'Brien (1975:69) mentions forest concessions of forty-two thousand hectares given to six leading Mouride marabouts in 1962 and 1966. Some declassified forest concessions attributed to influential marabouts in the early 1970s were two thousand hectares in size.

[70] See Dumont 1972:222–3; Galvan 1996:380.

[71] Caverivière and Debene 1988:71.

[72] Schoonmaker-Freudenberger (1991) explains that the *mis en valeur* clause has been used to dispossess Peul herders and justify the appropriation of their lands by groundnut pioneers:

Land also became a resource for greasing alliances between rural authorities and members of the Dakar-based political class. Land attributions and land gifts from Rural Councils to Dakar politicians were not uncommon (notwithstanding legal provisions that forbade absentee farming and reserved land-use rights for residents of rural communities).[73]

The village chieftaincy, UPS cells, groundnut cooperatives, and Rural Councils were all run by rural elites as extensions of their birthright and God-given authority. Each of these institutions represented a channel for the downward flow of resources from center to periphery. Control of the local state allowed the indigenous elite to tap this flow for their own purposes and also to mediate the access of their subordinates, followers, subjects, and dependents to resources offered by the state. This system functioned to reaffirm – and perhaps, for peasants, to deepen – existing relationships of authority and dependence.

B. Deconcentration and Devolution at the Provincial Level

Rural powerbrokers in central Senegal played on political stages that were much larger than the multi-village groupings of the groundnut cooperatives or Rural Councils that embraced as many as fifty villages. Deconcentration of the state apparatus in the early-postcolonial years created new sites for gathering and exercising power at "departmental" and "regional" levels, and these too became political arenas dominated by central Senegal's provincial elite. As we shall see later in this book, this was the highly particular outcome

---

livestock raising seems not to be the "productive land use" that confers use rights under the 1964 law. "Declassification" of forest of "sylvo-pastoral reserves" was basically the only source of new land available for the expansion of groundnut cultivation in the western Ferlo in the 1960s (Cruise O'Brien 1975:69; Dumont 1972:221). This continued eastward into the 1990s. A 1991 Presidential Decree gave 45,000 hectares of forest to the Mouride Khalif. Promptly thereafter, "173 square miles were clearcut in one of the last remaining wooded areas in Senegal's degraded heartland. More than 6,000 pastoralists and 10,000 animals were evicted.... The clearcutting operation actually began in a village which served as a site in a World Bank forestry-conservation resource management project.... [This pattern underscores the] virtually unchallenged political strength" of the Mouride elite within the groundnut basin (Schoonmaker-Freudenberg 1991:7, 10), as well as dependence of the Mouride elite (and indeed, of the system of agricultural pioneering that was Mouridism's original material base), upon resources allocated by the state, including land. The state drilled the wells in the Ferlo that made groundnut pioneering possible (Pélissier 1966:312–17).

[73] As we shall see, this became a major political issue in Casamance. It also became a political issue in the Senegal River Valley.

of a secure powersharing arrangement between central and rural elites. In Casamance and in southern Côte d'Ivoire, central rulers feared nothing more than the coalescing of provincial power in these larger institutional arenas of the postcolonial party-state.

Around the time of independence, the territorial grid of provincial administration in the groundnut basin was reorganized in a way that better reflected power distributions on the ground. Senegal's twelve colonial *cercles* – the administrative domains of the French commandants – were replaced by seven official "regions." Regions were defined on the basis of underlying "social and economic homogeneity"; they were supposed to represent Senegal's largest natural political units. Although the regions were conceived as administrative units, they were also designated as Senegal's main electoral districts. The most deconcentrated structures were implanted in the populous groundnut basin: three of the seven new regions were created here.[74]

Central Senegal was divided into the administrative regions of Sine-Saloum, Thiès, and Diourbel. These divisions retraced the jurisdictional lines of the colonial *cercles* and the old Councils of Notables that had been appointed to advise the French commandants. Postcolonial map-making logic was expressly political (as it was in the earlier period); the lines drawn in 1960 allowed for the efficient and direct incorporation of distinctive electoral fiefdoms into the ruling party.[75] The UPS reaped the full political potential of this by reinforcing "regional UPS unions" in each of the official regions. Party infrastructure at the regional level thus institutionalized the political fiefdoms of the largest provincial notables.

UPS regional unions in the Wolof groundnut basin served as sites for organizing coalitions of provincial notables – thus enhancing their capacity for collective political action – and for forwarding candidates to national office. UPS regional union bureaus were the political bases of "big politicians with political support among municipal and departmental clan

---

[74] Three regions made up the heart of the groundnut basin – Sine-Saloum, Diourbel, and Thiès. The Region of Louga covered the oldest zone of groundnut cultivation in Senegal. Louga was less dynamic economically but remained a politically strategic zone and a provincial base of the Tidjane confrérie.

[75] It is possible that one reason that Diourbel was broken off as a separate administrative region was that the city of Diourbel was a electoral base/stronghold of Mamadou Dia (Schumacher 1975:91).

leaders, prestigious marabouts, and national party officeholders."[76] They nominated candidates for UPS lists for the National Assembly.

In an extraordinary act of powersharing and concession to this provincial elite, the party-state apparatuses at the regional level were endowed with a material base of their own. No single fact stands in starker contradiction to the claim that the Senghor regime was obsessed with centralized control. In central Senegal, regions were the sites of CRADs (Centres Régionaux d'Assistance au Développement).[77] CRADs functioned as halfway houses between the Dakar headquarters of the groundnut marketing board and the village-level producer cooperatives. CRADs were also positioned right in between the national development bank and the cooperatives. Virtually all resources that passed up and down the groundnut circuit passed through the CRADs: these agencies were responsible for managing seed stocks, distributing food credits, collecting the crop from the cooperatives, retrieving cooperative debts for the national bank, and running the input-distribution programs ("integrated rural development programs") targeted at the groundnut basin.

From the start, the CRADs were "highly politicized" (Diop and Diouf 1992a). The majority of CRAD personnel had worked before independence in the SIPs.[78] In the early 1960s these veterans were joined by *bons militants* of the ruling party who "ensconced themselves in the administration of the CRAD."[79] Rural notables quickly asserted control over these institutions. CRADs in the groundnut basin became notorious in Senegal as provincial hotbeds of political intrigue, corruption, and cronyism. Sheldon Gellar (1987:129) wrote that CRAD "very quickly acquired a reputation for corruption and subservience to the wishes of powerful politicians, rural notables, and religious chiefs who sought to divert credit and other resources their way." Like the village cooperatives, the CRADs short-changed

---

[76] See Schumacher 1975:41, 42.
[77] On CRADs, see van chi Bonnardel 1978:569, 627 n. 122. Fusions of CRADs and the OCA created ONCAD in 1966, which took over all internal commercialization of the crop and, after 1971, all external commercialization. Between 1975 and 1980 a new parastatal, SONACOS (Société Nationale de Commercialisation des Oléaginaux du Sénégal) took over transport of the crop to the processing factories, the factories themselves, and the organization of groundnut exports, thus completing the state's takeover of all activities downstream from the producers. In 1980, ONCAD was dissolved and replaced by a lighter structure, SONAR (Société Nationale d'Approvisionnement Rurale). See Casswell 1984.
[78] The groundnut cooperatives changed names a few times in the 1950s, but the basic logic, structure, and personnel of the institutions stayed the same.
[79] van chi Bonnardel 1978:624 n. 99.

peasants and embezzled cooperative funds, which were used to finance the economic and political projects of rural powerbrokers. In three short years, the seven CRADs had accumulated a total deficit of FCFA 1 billion (about US $3 million), when

> 1963 inspections revealed the very considerable extent to which CRAD resources, services, and personnel policies remained in the grip of regional and local clan politics. Even the UPS political bureau found it necessary in 1964 to invoke sanctions against incumbent party office holders in the towns of Kaolack and Nioro-du-Rip following the "Kaolack CRAD affair" in which several prominent politicians were discovered to have used CRAD funds to finance personal campaigns for party nomination to municipal office. (Schumacher 1975:117)

CRAD authorities were positioned as economic intermediaries between the peasants and the state and they skimmed tribute from the upward and the downward flow of resources. The pattern established early on persisted for the life of the groundnut marketing board. Dakar used the marketing monopoly to tax the groundnut producers, but CRAD personnel were positioned to milk profits from this trade even before Dakar got its share. CRAD officials also took a hefty cut of the downward flow of inputs. Much of the credit and fertilizer that had been officially earmarked for small producers never made its way to the farmers. Renamed ONCAD (Office Nationale de Coopération et d'Assistance pour le Développement) in 1966, this deconcentrated and decentralized marketing board grew into what Nim Casswell (1984) called "an obese parasite" that drained resources from Senegal's groundnut economy for the benefit of its own officials and nearly 2,000 agents. Casswell wrote that ONCAD was hijacked by provincial elites and commandeered outside the scope of central control. By the time it was disbanded in 1980 at the insistence of Senegal's external creditors, ONCAD was draining as much out of state coffers as it contributed in the form of taxes appropriated from the farmers. Capture of the groundnut marketing board by the provincial elite represented the ultimate – and for the center, most debilitating – form of power devolution.

For the rural elite of central Senegal, regional- and local-level franchises of the ruling party and marketing board were not the only games in town. When Dakar abolished the old colonial *cercles* at the end of the 1950s, *cercle* subdivisions – many of which were reincarnated provinces of the independent Wolof states – were renamed "departments."[80] These became the main

---

[80] There were originally twenty-four departments, created out of the twenty-four *cercle* subdivisions. The top administrator in each department was a prefect. (The new departments

arenas of provincial politics and administration. Each departmental capital became a full *commune* with an elected mayor and municipal council. This dual upgrading of the old colonial subdivisions – both administrative and political – translated into a major deconcentration of state agencies that were purveyors of jobs, governmental and social services, and agricultural inputs. So it was that on the eve of independence twenty new *communes* were added to Senegal's original four. More towns of the interior were upgraded to commune status in the 1970s and 1980s, bringing the total to thirty-seven. A new round of decentralizing reforms brought the total to forty-eight in 1990.

Politics at the department level emerged as a major focal point of electoral politics and factional competition among members of the provincial elite. This was especially true of the highly politicized municipal government structures. "The enhanced patronage resources afforded by the new municipal governments in the interior constituted a long-sought prize for local party elites" (Schumacher 1975:90). Jobs, contracts, and municipal budgets were deployed to consolidate the political bases of some of the groundnut basin's biggest political barons. One of the boldest of these was Babacar Ba, a one-time minister of the economy who, "with strong support from local religious leaders and Senegalese businessmen, and certain powerful Lebanese traders, built up a 'state within a state' in the region around Kaolack."[81] In municipal governments throughout the groundnut basin, party clans struggled for control over the "scarce but politically decisive central resources" allocated through the party structure, the municipal council, and the provincial administration.[82]

C. The Weakness of the State's Direct Agents

Where regional UPS barons were strong, the state's direct agents were weak. Field agents of the central administration were indeed stationed throughout all of Senegal: every region had a governor, every department had a prefect, every *arrondissement* had a *sous-préfet*. In the groundnut-producing region an army of field representatives of the central government was supposed to supervise and regulate the cooperatives, rural development

were confusingly named "cantons" until 1964.) Below the departments were the 135 old colonial cantons, which were regrouped into 85 *arrondissements*. In the 1960s the government also created one official tribunal for each department.

[81] *Africa Confidential*, 20, no. 12 (6 June 1979).

[82] This is Cottingham's (1970:104–5, see also 106–12) description of Kebemer in 1967–8.

programs, and the Rural Councils. These administrators, technocrats, and extension agents were appointed directly by Dakar ministries: they were not elected by, or answerable to, anyone in the provinces. Analysts who have criticized Senegal's government for "statism" and "overcentralized rule" have devoted much attention to documenting these agents' heavy presence in the countryside.

The prefectorial administration was the arm of the Interior Ministry. In command structure, agents' comportment, and the supposedly apolitical nature of its mandate, it was modeled along military lines. It was supposed to be Dakar's instrument of "direct rule." (One writer captured the analogy by calling the *sous-préfets* modern incarnations of the French Commandants de Cercle.) *Sous-préfets* were Dakar's men-on-the-spot: they were supposed to keep a grip on the cooperatives and Rural Councils.

Within the prefects' jurisdictions, Dakar ministries stationed a large corps of state agents to implement rural development programs aimed mainly at enhancing production and productivity in the export sector. *Arrondissement*-level agencies called Centres d'Expansion Rurale (CERs) were created around 1960 to base and coordinate all technical and extension personnel sent out to the rural areas by central government ministries.[83] Developmentalists in Senegal invested tremendous hopes in these agencies: they were supposed to be the vanguard force that would bring modernization and innovation to central Senegal. Vengroff and Johnson (1989:143) registered the vigor of this effort in Senegal: "Senegal, perhaps more than any other Francophone African country, has put an enormous number of personnel into the rural areas to help stimulate and support production efforts."

CERs were the provincial outposts of Senegal's Cooperation Service. In 1960 and 1961, this subagency of the Ministry of Development was charged with realizing a developmentalist, reformist vision of rural transformation known as Animation Rurale. Animation Rurale was the brainchild of progressive planners, developmentalists, and agricultural experts in Dakar and France who had established themselves in Senegal's new rural development and planning agencies at the end of the 1950s. They dreamed of state-led investment and education (consciousness-raising) programs that would free the peasantry (and all Senegal) from risky dependence on the

---

[83] See Diarassouba (1968:89, 201) for the origins of the CER idea in the mid-1950s. Their original mandate was "to be responsible for virtually all aspects of local-level development."

groundnut and the oppressive hold of Wolof marabouts and feudal aristocrats. Attached to the Cooperation Service were the young activist field workers of Animation Rurale. These reformists rallied around Prime Minister Mamadou Dia from 1958 to 1961; with his support they succeeded in fielding Animation Rurale as an integrated rural development program in the groundnut-producing zone.

Young activist field workers attached to the Cooperation Service were sent out into the rural areas. Their job was to encourage peasants to break out of the undemocratic, feudal mentalities that kept them illiterate and poor, invest in crop diversification, try new production technologies to raise productivity and protect soil fertility, join cooperatives and ensure that these served the ordinary farmers' interests, and "overcome their mistrust of the state" (Gellar 1987).

Animation Rurale was the agenda for grassroots reform first articulated on the national stage in 1958. By 1961 it had taken form as a concrete attempt to bring "revolution from above" to the groundnut basin by usurping the positions and prerogatives of the rural elite. It is another episode of counterfactual behavior on the regime's part, for it is the opposite of what the theory would predict. What happened?

The Demise of Animation Rurale.   Part of what happened is well known: stakeholders in the status quo in the groundnut basin, led by the Mouride marabouts, were violently opposed to Animation Rurale and all it represented. They turned against Mamadou Dia, Animation's sponsor and patron in Dakar. In the rural areas they obstructed the Animation service in every possible way. In Senegal's National Assembly, members of parliament from the groundnut basin openly criticized the Prime Minister and his attempts to assert top-down control over the provincial outposts of the newly independent state. These events were background to Senegal's political crisis of December 1962, which culminated in Mamadou Dia's removal from office and imprisonment, followed by the thorough purging of his supporters from every level of the ruling party and governmental administration.[84] The year 1962 represented a turning point for Senegal, for it

---

[84] Dia's broad vision of reform was laid out in the famous "Circulaire 32" of May 1962 (Gellar 1987). This program also called for making the cooperatives "multifunctional" by using them as a network for the retail distibution of consumer goods (Boone 1992:92–3). Aspects of Dia's agenda that were viewed as particularly objectionable by the rural elite were his "insistence on the repayment of governmental loans" and his determination to curtail the autonomy of village and regional agencies of the state (Schumacher 1975:66, 105). This

marked the final and definitive victory of the old provincial elite over the idealists, socialists, reformers, and progressives who had, since the mid- to late-1950s, found places in the rural development bureaucracies of the central government.[85] Any central government impulse to govern the groundnut basin "directly" via usurpation was extinguished. Under the determined leadership of Senghor, rulers in Dakar surrendered to a powersharing deal that handed political initiative and prerogative in central Senegal over to the old, indigenous elite. "This is the price the political system has had to pay in order to exist" (Diop and Diouf 1992a:87).

Death of Animation Rurale was followed by the introduction of a new rural development strategy, the Programme Agicole, in 1964. As we have seen, it played into the hands of the established rural elite by strengthening their positions as large producers and by reinforcing their control over peasants' access to productive inputs. The Programme Agricole was a capital- and technology-intensive ("green revolution") solution to the grave problems threatening the sustainability of export-crop production in this zone – declining soil fertility and erosion. It centered on the distribution of chemical fertilizers (and herbicides and treated seeds) via the cooperatives, village-level institutions already in the firm grip of marabouts, chiefs, and Wolof society's leading families. Introduction of the Programme Agricole marked the definitive turn away from agricultural strategies that threatened elite interests in central Senegal – land reform, crop diversification, the promotion of fallowing, and conservation plans that would limit land pioneering in the ecologically fragile Ferlo.[86]

story may also have a geopolitical dimension. Dia's family roots were in the Senegal River Valley; he was a Tidjane, not a Mouride; his most famous speech against "corruption" in independent Senegal was delivered in Podor, in the Senegal River Valley, and "was taken as threatening by Falilou Mbacké" (Behrman 1970:101–2). Dia was attempting to solidify his own political base by pushing the "unity" of Islam in Senegal. Meanwhile, his electoral base was in the city of Diourbel and, it seems, parts of the Petite Côte. Was Dia – like Nkrumah in Ghana – playing the rimland against the heartland in Senegal, attempting to rein in the marabouts of the groundnut basin (and loosen their grip on the Senegalese budget) by mobilizing support among constituencies in politically peripheral regions?

[85] Mamadou Dia and a few of his closest associates remained in prison in Eastern Senegal until March 1974. Dia was not allowed to organize a legal political party under the new "pluralistic system" inaugurated by Senghor in 1974, so he organized an unofficial grouping called the Coordination de l'Opposition Sénégalaise Unie (COSU), which called among other things for the dismantling of ONCAD (see below) and more farmer participation in a revitalized cooperative network (*Africa Confidential*, 21, no. 10, 7 May 1980; *Africa South of the Sahara*, 1982–83: 687–8).

[86] Some have engaged in thought experiments: What would rural development in Senegal have looked like under the leadership of Mamadou Dia, had he been able to pursue policies

First and foremost, village leaders and large marabouts used the agricultural inputs and extension services offered by the state to develop their own holdings. By the early 1970s use of state-supplied fertilizers and tractors on large maraboutic holdings was widespread. The new inputs did help compensate for declining soil fertility, and possibly also for declines in the availability of free labor as fewer disciples accepted the "virtual enslavement" implied by years of servitude on maraboutic estates. Judged against a larger backdrop, however, the input-distribution programs clearly failed in their macroeconomic objectives: the groundnut marketing board never paid peasant farmers enough to cover the costs of inputs and credit they accepted from the cooperatives. By the end of the 1960s a pattern was clear: farmers accepted the credit, refused the fertilizers, began to prioritize food-crop production, and sold their groundnuts illegally on the parallel market. As Jonathan Barker (1985:64) put it: "There was never any evidence that the main aims of the policy [the Programme Agricole] were being achieved."

Yet is was clear that the Programme Agricole served political functions that were integral to consolidation of the postcolonial regime. State resources that flowed through the cooperatives beefed up the distributive capacity of rural political brokers, thus bolstering their acceptability and perhaps legitimacy in the eyes of their subjects and dependents. Meanwhile, relations of hierarchy and dependency were affirmed; even when peasants declined to use purchased inputs they were tied to the cooperatives as debtors, and in the hope of receiving of new loans. Surely these political logics help explain Dakar's commitment to the groundnut program, which came at the cost of real reform of established social relations and modes of production in central Senegal, and probably also at the cost of serious state commitment to developing commercial agriculture in other, more promising regions of the country (like Lower Casamance).

State builders in Dakar accepted the economic dysfunctionalities of the Programme Agricole. In this region, they ran provincial administration and

aimed at ending the powersharing alliance with the groundnut-basin notables? Was this ever really in the cards? They have responded by pointing out that Dia's vision was unacceptable to the political class, the Mouride marabouts and Wolof aristocrats, the largest producers and political brokers in Senegal's export-producing region, the grand commercial families of Saint-Louis who were linked to parliamentarians and French interests, most of the urban bourgeoisie, European business, and France. Cruise O'Brien (1975:128) summarized by saying that Dia's downfall "was a victory for the already dominant elements of Senegalese society." Gentil (1986:153–4) concludes that given the balance of political forces, "Dia's vision could not be realized."

rural development programs in a way that guaranteed wide autonomy for the provincial elites.[87] One of the clearest signs of this was the center's failure to back or support CER staff who were supposed to "oversee all aspects of rural development": their mandates included the protection of classified forests, extension work on peasant farms, and providing technical support in the cooperatives and Rural Councils.[88] From the beginning, CERs were starved of resources; this paralyzed the professionals, reformers, and progress monitors who were often perceived as a nuisance by the rural elite. Observers' universal assessment is that CERs in central Senegal were "totally ineffective" and isolated.[89]

The striking fact of government in this region was that the authority of the center's direct agents – regional governors, prefectorial officers, and the agents of the central ministries – was trumped by that of grands marabouts, Wolof aristocrats, and regional UPS barons. The regional governors were party militants loyal only to Senghor. They could have been perfect agents of centralized, top-down control. In the groundnut basin, however, the governors were systematically marginalized as political actors, and this despite the attempts of some Dakar reformers to give the holders of this office wide authority over all state agents in the provinces.[90] (The opposite was the case

---

[87] All this has echoes in recent United States history. Alston and Ferrie (1999) recount how in the South in the 1920s to 1950s Southern elites blocked the implementation of New Deal legislation that compromised their control over dependent agricultural laborers, gained control over programs they could not veto in order to blunt their local effects, and sought to limit appropriations for federal social welfare programs that would threaten existing "paternalistic" mechanisms of control over rural labor.

[88] In the groundnut basin, CERs role in "modernizing production" was supplanted by the Société d'Assistance Technique et de la Coopération (SATEC) from 1964 to 1967, and the Société de Vulgarisation et de Développement Agricole (SODEVA) from 1967 to 1980. These externally funded parastatals were heavily dependent on expatriate personnel, but they appear to have played no role in the cooperatives' business. See Schumacher 1975:115–19.

[89] CERs in 1963 were described as a "total failure" by van chi Bonnardel (1978:625 n. 101). In 1988 and 1989 two reports document that CERs lacked "the most rudimentary necessities required by local agents to execute their work," including fuel, vehicles, and notebooks. In many offices, "agents seemed to have little if anything to do" (Vengroff and Johnson 1989:144, 175, 178, 203; Sow 1988:98). Vengroff and Johnson (1989:5) showed that in the mid-1980s agents of Senegal's approximately ninety CERs were frequently rotated from one post to another. Nearly two-thirds were posted outside their home regions.

[90] The first seven gouverneurs, appointed in 1960, were all civil servants or intellectuals personally loyal to Dia and Senghor, not UPS barons (Schumacher 1975:92; Cohen 1971:199). Legislation was passed in 1961 and 1964 to strengthen them by placing all provincial functionaries under their direct authority (Gellar 1990:138) but in the groundnut basin, control over prefectural administration and developmental agencies never passed to

in Lower Casamance, where a very different local state was constructed to govern the peasantry.)

Meanwhile, in central Senegal, prefectoral agents and rural development officers had little room to act when their official mandates ran counter to the interests of powerful rural brokers. More often than not, prefects and *sous-préfets* were drawn into departmental- and local-level political arenas as players, rather than as referees or aloof bystanders. As Schumacher (1975:90) wrote, "few found it possible to remain aloof from intraparty clan struggles." Prefects and *sous-préfets* were highly politicized actors: they cultivated the patronage and favor of the Wolof notables, rather than vice versa, and deferred to the most powerful marabouts and aristocrats. Many shared in rural notables' corrupt pilfering of the state's rural outposts: the willingness of the *sous-préfets* to conspire with rural notables to milk the cooperatives and Rural Councils was legendary.[91] "Supervisory authorities (prefect, governor) intervened seldom and superficially [in the affairs of the Rural Councils].... The central authority, despite its interest in reform, seems strangely disconnected from the affairs of the CR."[92]

Governing the groundnut basin in powersharing alliance with rural barons made central control almost impossible. As Foltz (1977:245) said, discipline is nearly nonexistent, and "[r]eform measures which may threaten individual power bases are regularly blocked by local politicians, while the money appropriated for such purposes often finds its way into private pockets." The resistance of provincial authorities not only squelched Animation Rurale, but also successfully limited the extension of state-sponsored schooling and modern health care, land tenure reform, implementation of pastoral land management plans, and the deepening of the cooperative movement.[93] In general, the weakness of centralized control over how the

governors. Ndéné Ndiaye wrote that the 1961 decree "passed unnoticed in our legislative history" (cited by Diop and Diouf 1992a:74). Later legislation to strengthen regional governors also appears to have had no substantial effect in this region. See for example Dione 1992:7.

[91] See Blundo 1998; Gellar 1990:145 n. 12.

[92] "A generalized absence of administrative accounts that justify budget expenditure seems to be regarded as normal... the representatives as well as the public servants are hardly touched by sanctions (Blundo 1998a:19–20). Meanwhile, the embeddedness of the "local bosses" protects them: "To denounce somebody within [one's] own circle to the State is regarded as a shameful act because of the destructive effects on the local fabric in a face-to-face and close society like that of the rural areas" (Blundo 1998a:20–1, citing J.-P. Olivier de Sardan).

[93] Behrman (1970:143, 147–50) noted that in 1961, only 6 percent of Diourbel's male school-age children were in French-language (i.e., state-sponsored) schools. As for modern health

powers, resources, and prerogatives of the state were used was reflected in bureaucratic incoherence and "indiscipline," the appearance of "purpose-lessness" and paralysis of central administration, and the pervasive subor-dination of the bureaucratic logic to the local politics of party and clan alliance.

Although provincial leaders were allowed wide latitude in running their own fiefdoms, the fact remained that they were economically dependent upon the regime's top leaders in Dakar, as they had been since the 1940s. Access to the central government remained an indispensable political and economic resource for the maraboutic and aristocratic elite of central Senegal. To maintain their own estates and sponsor the creation of new communities, they needed land, credit, water, roads, inputs, and producer-price subsi-dies that only the central state could provide. The wealth and beneficence of rural elite was sustained by their connection to the state, not by profit or tribute extracted directly from the groundnut economy. Economic de-pendence on the regime made the rural elite, as Donal Cruise O'Brien (1975:132) put it, "very much the subordinate partner in the governing alliance with urban politicians and bureaucrats."[94] This enabled regime leaders in Dakar to manage and manipulate the "coalition of notables" that comprised the UPS. Senghor was a master at directing the downward flow of state resources to structure local-level competition, balance factional in-terests, temper rivalries, and make sure that provincial notables' political ambitions did not exceed the scope of their own fiefdoms.[95]

Decay of the groundnut economy over the course of the 1980s and 1990s did not overturn this powersharing system. Yet it did render the old polit-ical arrangements considerably less reliable in terms of the government's electoral interests. Decay attenuated the marabouts' political hold on the peasantry, thereby assuring that they would not dominate Senegal's po-litical stage quite as decisively or conspiciously as they had from 1950 to

care, "the Mouride Khalif does not approve of doctors and prefers that his disciples seek healing through prayers" (145). See also Diop and Diouf 1992a:28.

[94] On the debate over whether the marabouts constituted an independent accumulating class, and the emergence of a consensus in the literature that in fact they did not (at least as long as they depended on groundnut production to reproduce their sociopolitical power), see also Copans 1988:228–32; Coulon 1981; Diop and Diouf 1992a:72.

[95] For example, Senghor could force rival clan leaders to institutionalize factional represen-tation in the allocation of municipal posts or on UPS party lists. An example is the case of Kebemer in 1968, as described by Cottingham (1970:104–12).

1985.[96] Decline of the groundnut economy forced rural dwellers to turn to commercial and/or urban livelihoods that allow people more room for maneuver vis-à-vis leading families in their villages and more range of choice in choosing their marabout. In rural localities, however, the political and economic hold of the old elite remains powerful: recent studies from the groundnut basin suggest that when it comes to village politics, not much has changed in this regard since the 1960s.[97]

The economic engine of the Mouride order shifted from groundnut production to commerce after the mid- to late-1970s. As this happened, key structural attributes of the old powersharing relationship between the regime and the Islamic order were preserved, even if the marabouts gained some autonomy vis-à-vis the regime. Hierarchically structured Mouride commercial networks, in which the rank-and-file members were employed by prestigious patrons/leaders, developed in the import and export circuits. To the extent that large profits were to be had, they were made mostly in extra- or quasi-legal import dealings. In the 1970s and 1980s, state loans helped finance the operations of some of the biggest marabout-traders, and traders linked closely to leading marabouts. The regime's tacit complicity in helping the marabout traders to circumvent Senegal's trade laws was also clearly evident.[98] So it is that even after the groundnut era the regime has continued to invest in sustaining the material bases of the Mouride order, and thus to provide the economic linkages by which religious prestige and legitimacy were transformed into worldly political clout. Senegal's opposition politicians in the 1990s courted the marabouts almost as assiduously as Lamine Guèye and Léopold Senghor did in the 1950s.

Postcolonial structures of provincial politics and administration had confirmed the positions and authority of an existing elite within a society that remained extraordinarily stratified and hierarchical, right down to the molecular level of the village and household. In this case, there was no rewiring of the circuits of local authority after independence. On the contrary, the postcolonial state confirmed, reinforced, and anchored itself in the preexisting circuits of rural authority. It is hard to imagine a starker case of postcolonial indirect rule, or a modern African state that is more deeply rooted in indigenous authority structures in the countryside.

[96] See Villalón 1995; Beck 2001.

[97] Diop and Diouf (1992a) discuss 1980s reforms of the groundnut marketing circuit and the cooperatives. On political decentralization in the 1990s, see for example Blundo 1995, 1998; Patterson 1996, 1999; Ribot 1999; Beck 2001. We return to this in the conclusion.

[98] See for example M.C. Diop 1981; Boone 1992, 1994; Thioub, Diop, and Boone 1997.

There have been consequences for rural development and rural democratization. Early on, there was widespread perception in administrative circles in Dakar (and by outsiders) that rural government was run in pervasive defiance of laws and formal directives emanating from the center, that rural notables used their influence within state agencies to obstruct the formal directives of the center, and that there was far-reaching corruption including illicit enrichment of local bosses and diversion of state funds. The system looked wasteful and inefficient from the developmental perspective, but it has worked very well as a system for organizing parcellized sovereignty and powersharing between central and peripheral elites. It was also obvious that all plans and programs for more serious structural reform of a clearly ailing groundnut economy had been shelved in deference to the rural elite of this region.

Participatory democracy also remains illusive in this region, for even with widening of partisan competition in the last fifteen years, rival factions of the long-standing rural elite continue to monopolize the political stage.

Postscript: Sine (Siin) as a Counterfactual

The analysis here focuses on the Wolof groundnut basin. Variation within this region helps advance our argument by way of counterfactual, but we do not have space to explore it systematically here. We can note briefly, however, the exception of Sine (Siin), which lies on the southwestern periphery of the groundnut basin.[99] Sine is a sociocultural, political, and geographic territory that traces its origins to one of the precolonial Serer kingdoms (Pélissier 1966; Klein 1968a, 1972; Balans, Coulon, and Gastellu 1975:106; Galvan 1996, forthcoming). After Senegal's independence, Sine became part of the administrative region of Sine-Saloum.

Sine is a non-Mouride, non-Wolof zone. Rural social organization differs from that of the Wolof zone, and we do in fact see differences in institutional choice. The Sereer of Sine have a long-settled agrarian society

---

[99] Most writers in French and English have written "Sine" to refer to the precolonial state and to this region of Senegal, which was incorporated into the modern administrative region of Sine-Saloum (see for example Pélissier 1966; Klein 1968a; and A.-B. Diop 1981). More recently, Galvan (1996) uses "Siin" to refer to this region *and* to the precolonial polity.

without steep social hierarchy of its own. In the generations before French conquest, the Sereer were subjected to the overrule of a foreign, conquering aristocracy. The monarchs were never viewed as indigenous by the Sereer, and their governing/administrative structures never penetrated Sereer society deeply at the molecular level of village organization or land tenure relations. France signed treaties with the aristocrats, but the African elite were never very useful as governing intermediaries because of their basic lack of legitimacy and because of the lack of much indigenous administrative infrastructure – in fact, many Sereer looked to France to liberate them from their oppressive overrulers. Meanwhile, Mouridism did not penetrate the Sereer zone, especially Sine, as deeply and completely as in the Wolof areas. To the extent that Sufi Islam did come to the Sereer, it was not in the form of the pioneering (marabout-dominated) agricultural communities found in the newly settled parts of the groundnut basin. Mouride marabouts did not emerge as a landholding elite in Sine.

In governing the Sereer of Sine, both France and the postcolonial regime confronted a society less hierarchical and more egalitarian than Wolof society. In this regard, the Sereer were more like Diola in the Casamance than their Wolof neighbors. (Pélissier 1966 draws this analogy.) Central rulers did not find an elite in the Sine region that was both cooperative and politically useful: as predicted by the theory advanced here, there was less powersharing in Sine. The mode of colonial and postcolonial rule in Sine was more direct than indirect – the governing strategy was similar to what I have called administrative occupation. *Sous-préfets* ruled Sine with a heavy hand and were unconstrained by indigenous rural authorities. When Rural Councils were created, they were dominated by the state's own agents: in this zone, the state itself took direct control of land tenure. For these contrasts, see Pélissier (1966) and Klein (1968a, 1968b). On provincial administration in Sine, see Galvan (1996, forthcoming). Galvan (1996:378) observed, for example, that "the factions that dominate most Rural Councils are directly linked to important PS barons, usually deputies in the National Assembly or [*arrondissement*-level] 'section-chiefs,' leaders of the party's regional units." Galvan's analysis of implementation of the 1964 land law in the Sine subregion also supports the argument advanced here. Local powerwielders in Sine, including those who came to exercise authority over land, were creations of the modern state – they derived their power from the state itself. Galvan stresses their disconnect from Sereer society.

Part Two: Administrative Occupation in Lower Casamance

[Of all the people of Senegal], none in the final analysis is more open to the play of democratic competition [than the Diola,] and more ready for it.

Pélissier 1966:679

State building in Lower Casamance proceeded along a very different trajectory. Here, the Dakar regime found no rural leaders with whom to broker a stable and secure political alliance. There was neither the political opportunity nor the immediate threat that a politically dominant indigenous strata would have represented. Rather, for Dakar the challenge in Lower Casamance was to govern an egalitarian and politically fragmented society without doing anything that would facilitate the organization or mobilization of what was already, in the 1950s and 1960s, a diffuse undercurrent of resistance to the center. These circumstances gave rise to political relations with the center that differed from those that linked the Wolof groundnut basin to Dakar. A different politics and process of state building was the consequence.

Casamance has always been recognized as a distinctive region of Senegal, but this distinctiveness has often been attributed to nonpolitical causes. Most accounts portray this region as one that has remained marginal in national context – in spite of the center's heavy-handed efforts at national integration – because of its awkward geographic separation from the rest of Senegal and because of cultural difference. The argument here is that a more political analysis is warranted, both for understanding the politics of institutional reform in Senegal and for theorizing state building in agrarian societies in general. A close look at this case shows that Lower Casamance's marginality must also be understood as an artifact of politically driven institutional choices made by the center. Dakar did everything possible to ensure that no local state machinery, and no state resources, would be captured by political communities in Casamance that the center could neither harness nor discipline.

Casamance is territory that is mostly noncontiguous with the rest of Senegal. Except for its most eastern reaches, Casamance is divided from the rest of Senegal much as Alaska is separated from the rest of the United States, as Cabinda is cut off from the rest of Angola, or as the sea divides the islands that make up the Indonesian archipelago. In Senegal, this inconvenient fact is an artifact of colonial history. The Gambia River cuts across Senegambia from the eastern highlands of the Fouta Jallon to the Atlantic coast. Although territory to the north of the river (comprising most of Senegal) and to the south of the river (the Casamance) fell under French rule, the Gambia River itself and its immediate environs remained under British control. The British colony of Gambia was a finger jutting into French-controlled Senegal. Today, this former British territory separates Lower Casamance from the rest of Senegal. A trans-Gambia highway that was opened in 1953 links the city of Ziguinchor, the administrative and economic capital of the Casamance region, to Dakar.

While the Gambia's unfortunate location separates most of the Casamance from the rest of Senegal, it is only Casamance's western quadrant, the region known as Lower Casamance, that possesses the cultural and ecological attributes that many point to as the main source of the region's distinctiveness. Lower Casamance is the region that concerns us here: it is the area lying west of the town of Sédhiou and west of the Soungrougrou River (see Map 3.2), and is home to almost half of the

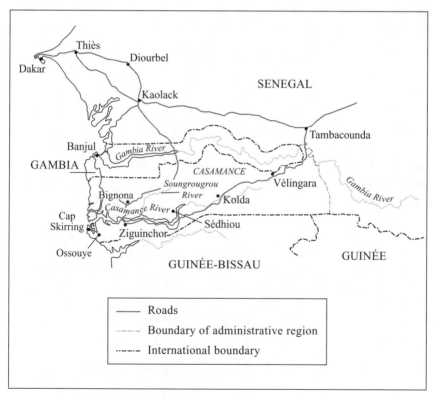

Map 3.2.   Casamance Region of Senegal

total Casamance population. It is not part of the Sahel and was never incorporated into the hierarchical states and empires that dominated the Senegambia region. Lower Casamance is upland sub-Guinea forest criss-crossed by mangrove channels and estuaries of the Casamance River. Here, green countrysides and relatively abundant rainfall allow farmers to grow rice, groundnuts, and fruit. Diola people constitute the overwhelming majority of the population of Lower Casamance and 10 percent of the population of Senegal. Among the Diola and smaller groups of Lower Casamance, most notably the Balant, there are no castes, no monarchies or aristocracies, and no hierarchical or bureaucratic state structures. Islam came late to this region, less uniformly and less hegemonically than in the North, and not in the form of the centralized brotherhoods that so dominate central Senegal.

As you travel east of Soungrougrou River, things begin to look much more like the groundnut basin in sociological, political, and economic terms. The Manding people of Middle and Upper Casamance – like the Wolof and Toucouleur people to the north – belong to an Islamic, hierarchical, patriarchal, ex-slave-owning, and casted society (and, we shall see, institutional connections to Dakar resemble those of the groundnut basin).[100]

That Lower Casamance has posed a challenge of "national integration" to rulers in Dakar is perhaps not surprising, given the geographic and cultural facts. For the last forty years, Lower Casamance has indeed been a politically disenfranchised and restive part of Senegal's rural periphery, a neglected region, and an economic backwater. At issue here is why this is so: what exactly is the source of the problem, and what is Dakar's role therein? Most analysts suggest that Dakar's failure to fully incorporate Lower Casamance is the unfortunate by-product of a statist and overcentralized mode of postcolonial (and colonial) rule. Dakar has been too centralized, and too obsessed with national administrative uniformity and top-down control, to fully take account of the particularities of Lower Casamance. Yet as we have seen, this view assumes too much about the standard operating procedures of Senegalese state builders. In the Wolof groundnut basin, Senegal's political core, we do not find a

---

[100] Indigenous Manding political institutions are less centralized than those of the Wolof or Toucouleur. Since the breakup of the Manding Empire, Manding political forms have been "lineage based," rather than the "aristocratic" forms found, for example, among the Wolof (Girard 1963; Linarès 1992; Hesseling 1994:248–9).

regime hell-bent on statism and centralization. On the contrary, the regime cultivated alliances by sharing power with an indigenous rural elite. If there was overcentralization of state power in Lower Casamance, then this cannot be attributed to a simple carry-over of administrative habits formed in the groundnut basin, or to statist ideologies inherited from the French.

From the start, it was clear that Dakar viewed Casamance as a serious political problem that required distinctive institutional solutions. And this is how things developed: the state institutions linking the Lower Casamance to Dakar were markedly different from those built in the Wolof groundnut basin. Here, the institutions of the party-state were spatially concentrated: they were suspended above village society, offering peasant communities few possibilities of access to state agencies and institutions. Within these institutions, authority was centralized in the hands of direct agents of the central regime, producing "state autonomy" in Lower Casamance when this appeared to be totally lacking in the Wolof groundnut basin. Lower Casamance was governed under a system of direct rule that empowered the center while stifling political life in the localities. It was a system of administrative occupation that created distance between rulers and ruled, and enforced subjects' exclusion from access to the state.

Deliberate institutional choices made by the center, and tailored for Lower Casamance, produced this outcome. In Lower Casamance, the regional governor, a direct agent of the center, was powerful and acted autonomously from local political influences: governors in the groundnut basin were weak, even marginal, actors. In Lower Casamance, *sous-préfets* were also autonomous agents of centralized control; in the Wolof groundnut basin, they were the politicized co-conspirators and allies of local notables. In Lower Casamance, Dakar never built a deep-reaching party-state apparatus. No five-tiered institutional apparatus was made available for colonization by local political notables, and no provincial or local political arenas were created to help indigenous elites gather and organize their own electoral constituencies. Departments and villages in Lower Casamance were not linked to the party apparatus, not irrigated with resources supplied by the center, and in general simply not allowed to emerge as sites for building clientelist networks or foci of political activity. And groundnut producers were left to their own devices – the regime chose not to create a statist commercial circuit in Lower Casamance, even though it was a groundnut-producing region with considerable potential for further development in this direction. Had "standard procedures" conceived by statists

Table 3.1. *Institutional Choice in Senegal: Powersharing versus Administrative Occupation*

	Functional Domain		
	Provincial Administration: Party-State Apparatus	Export Marketing: Marketing Board, Co-ops	Allocating Factors of Production: Co-ops, Rural Councils (CRs)
Wolof Groundnut Basin	Spatial deconcentration Devolution of authority Powersharing	Spatial deconcentration Devolution of authority Powersharing	Spatial deconcentration Devolution of authority Powersharing
Lower Casamance	Spatial concentration Centralization of authority Administrative occupation	No export institutions Market forces govern export circut Market forces	No institutions until post-1979 land allocation Administrative occupation

in Dakar, or administrative habits hammered out in the political heartland of central Senegal, simply been applied in this region, the institutional structure of the local state in Casamance would have looked very different. The contrasts are summarized in Table 3.1.

Someone looking at Lower Casamance today might counter this book's argument with a purely economic explanation of the observed institutional differences. Lower Casamance is economically marginal to the rest of Senegal today, they could say: perhaps we can reason backward and argue that Dakar declined to build a deeply penetrating state apparatus here because Lower Casamance was not worth exploiting. With a longer time frame, we see that this is an unjustified rewrite of history. French colonialists regarded the Lower Casamance as a region that could become the "jewel" of Senegal. It was so rich in fertile land, rainfall, and underexploited agricultural potential that French development planners in 1960 identified it as a potential breadbasket for the rest of Senegal.[101] Lower Casamance in the 1960s produced groundnuts, rice, and fruit. Casamance also occupied a significant place in the national export economy: in the 1960s, it produced about 12 to 15 percent of Senegal's groundnut exports, and perhaps half of

---

[101] Compagnie d'Etudes Industrielles et d'Aménagement du Territoire (CINAM) and Société d'Etudes et de Réalisations Economique et Sociales dans l'Agriculture (SERESA) 1960.

this came from Lower Casamance. The farmers were prosperous: Regine van chi Bonnardel (1978:447) wrote that in the 1960s, the Lower Casamancais lived in better houses and ate better than farmers anywhere else in Senegal. Van der Klei (1978:30, 36) described Lower Casamance as one of the most fertile areas in Senegal and even in all of former French West Africa; per-capital income, he noted, was regarded as the highest in Senegal. Literacy rates in Lower Casamance were higher than in the groundnut basin, thanks to mission education. And there were districts around Bignona, just south of the Casamance River, with some of the highest rural population densities in all of West Africa (Pélissier 1966:645).

In the early 1960s, at a time when agricultural experts were pessimistic about the sustainability of commercial agriculture in the groundnut basin, why was so much invested in that dry and declining region?[102] Why did Dakar do so little to mobilize the demonstrated agricultural potential of the Lower Casamance and to harness it to Senegal's national market? The answers have to be political, at least in part. It is obvious that rural development in the groundnut basin provided the means for alliance consolidation and intensive state building. By the same token, the economic neglect of Lower Casamance in the 1960s and 1970s surely reflected political calculations. The argument here is that Dakar sacrificed the economic gains to be had from more serious efforts to develop this region because the political risks of more intensive state building in Lower Casamance were high.

The challenge of governing Lower Casamance was that Dakar could not find interlocateurs who were trusted enough, and powerful enough, to package local populations into secure and acquiescent electoral blocs that could be offered up to the ruling party. As Linda Beck (1996a:196) argued, Lower Casamance's "egalitarian society offered no infrastructure for a [clientelist] mode of national integration." Lower Casamance's "uncaptured peasantry" was politically unorganized and under no one's centralized command. Dakar's strategy was to sustain this status quo and to keep this rural population politically unorganized. Dakar provided no resources – institutional or financial – that would help local political entrepreneurs harness existing collectivities and social networks, or overcome the collective action problems built into the fragmented nature of rural social organization in this region. Dakar built a postcolonial party-state apparatus in

---

[102] Concern about agricultural decline (soil erosion and exhaustion) in the groundnut basin dates to the 1920s. See for example Portères 1952; Pélissier 1966; and Boone 1992:86–92.

Lower Casamance that was designed to limit political activity on the local level.

It turns out that similar institutional choices were made in other parts of West Africa, where regimes confronted similar configurations of rural authority and similar challenges in governing the peasantry. Southern Côte d'Ivoire, the second case presented in Chapter 4, was similar to Lower Casamance in these ways.

I. Rural Social Organization: "A Society without Political Cement"

Like the French colonialists before them, Dakar politicians in the 1950s and 1960s found rural society in Lower Casamance difficult and risky to organize politically. Pélissier described the Diola, who constitute the main ethnic group of Lower Casamance, as "a society without political cement."[103] Among the Diola and Balant peoples of this region, indigenous socioeconomic and political organization provided no secure or reliable foothold for the modern state. For at least the last century, analysts and observers have described Diola social and political organization as egalitarian, territorially fragmented, and lacking in any customary administrative infrastructure, including chieftaincy. Political structure has been described as "acephalous" or "gerontocratic." There has never been slavery, there is no caste system, and, in contrast to the Wolof and Tucouleur, there is an "absence of land rights of the feudal kind" (Pélissier 1966:688).

Although the peoples of Lower Casamance have a long history of sedentary villages and agriculture, there is a "quasi-general absence of supra-village social structuration" (Darbon 1988:165). Village communities are largely independent. Many villages lived in "extreme isolation" for long centuries; even after fifty years of colonial rule, villages in Lower Casamance, with a few exceptions, recognized no common authority. Linguistic heterogeneity within the Diola group itself bears testimony to a history of sociopolitical segmentation, isolation, or fragmentation.[104]

---

[103] Pélissier 1966:671; see also 710 n. 1. Pélissier describes the Diola (also written as Jola, Joola, Jula) as the northernmost of the populations stretched out along the Rivières du Sud coast. These societies developed civilizations based on rice in the context of egalitarianism and weak political institutions. This group includes the Diola, Balant, Papel, Mandjak, and the societies of Guinée Bissau.

[104] Pélissier 1966:677, sa. 661 *inter alia*; Linarès 1992:5; Darbon 1988. The term Diola itself "did not come into widespread use until after World War I." Before that time, "the speakers

The basic socioeconomic unit is the extended family, consisting of a group of close patrilineal relatives of four or five generations, with a family elder as leader. Extended families cluster into descent groups centered around a patriarch. Descent groups make up village "wards"; two or more wards linked by marriage ties make up Diola villages. Even in precolonial times villages could be quite large, but they were free of any unified, village-wide political structure. The first Frenchmen to visit this region regarded the agglomerations of wards as "groups of villages," not integrated political units.[105]

The main authority figures are the patriarchs who represent Diola descent groups. In an analysis of Diola society in the 1980s, Linarès (1992:76) stressed the limited geographic and functional scope of their power. Lineages per se do not play a dominant role in Diola life, and patriarchs do not control access to land or labor.[106] Elders' control over youth in general was also more attenuated than it was among the Diola's neighbors east of the Soungrougrou River, the Manding people of Middle Casamance, or in the Sahelian societies to the north.[107] The social standing of the Diola patriarchs came mostly from their role as intermediaries for the spirit shrines that are the centerpiece in customary modes of regulating land, agricultural production, social life, and common space.[108] Since there are numerous spirit shrines within a community, some more powerful than others, socioreligious authority is dispersed.

"Riziculture techniques [that] were among the most advanced in Africa" were the material foundation of precolonial Diola society.[109] Van der Klei (1985:75) writes that

Portuguese travelers who visited the region around 1450 noted the intensive and ingenious nature of their farming methods. The Diola grow rice on the gently sloping banks of the many tributaries of the Casamance River. The clearing of these fields required a great deal of work. The most favorably situated fields have been cultivated for centuries. A system of small dikes catches the rainwater during the rainy season (July–October), so that every year rice can be grown on the same fields.

of nearly a dozen dialects of what is now called the Jula language had little sense of belonging to a common cultural or ethnic group" (Mark, de Jong, and Chupin 1998:37).

[105] See van der Klei 1985:76.

[106] See Linarès 1992:25, 28, 77–8.

[107] Hesseling 1994:248–9. She draws on Linares.

[108] On spirit shrines, see also Pélissier 1966:699–702; Darbon 1988; Linarès 1992:25.

[109] See Girard 1963.

The mechanisms that worked to disperse authority within and among lineages were embedded in economic relations. Basic modes of control over land and labor affirmed the autonomy of the family unit and thus contributed to the dispersion of political authority. Here there was no land-controlling elite. In Diola society, extended families control the rice fields they have obtained via inheritance or have claimed from the forest and cleared themselves. Each nuclear unit (headed by a married male) had control over its own share of family land.[110] All men were entitled to a share of family land upon initiation and marriage. Upon death of a land holder, cultivated fields passed from fathers to sons in a rigid inheritance system. These land-tenure arrangements foreclosed most possibilities for gathering power via the manipulation or accumulation of land tenure rights.

Meanwhile, nuclear families did not use political authority, relations of economic dependency, or markets to mobilize agricultural labor or extract surpluses from non–family members. Agricultural labor was organized within families on the basis of a highly developed, gender-based division of work. There were, however, ways of mobilizing labor for large, occasional tasks (e.g. land clearing) or at peak moments of the agricultural cycle. Horizontal labor-pooling and labor-sharing relationships existed among households, within wards, and at the village level. In extended families, households took turns helping in each other's fields. At the ward and village levels, unmarried men and women were organized into "age groups" that performed collective farm labor.

The templates for social cooperation that appeared in agriculture-centered norms and institutions were also visible in other arenas of village-centered associational life, including circumcision societies and other socio-religious groupings, the keeping of sacred forests, and the organization and performance of village-wide initiation ceremonies that occurred once a generation.

Diola modes of production and social organization were successful and were sustained over long centuries, well into the current era.

---

[110] van der Klei 1985:77. Pélissier writes that the land tenure system "is a rigid one based on inheritance by sons, which over time can lead to great disequilbrium within villages. One family can end up with so little land that it is forced to move, while another can end up with much more arable land than it has family labor to cultivate. Arable land can thus go unused." There do not seem to be mechanisms for the reallocation of land (Pélissier 1966:688).

Within extended families, rice surpluses could be substantial. Powerful redistributive norms and levelling mechanisms limited the accumulation of wealth over generations, however. In precolonial times, rice surpluses were turned over to patriarchs (extended family heads) who accumulated rice as a form of savings that was devoted mostly to the purchase of prestige goods – cattle – from the itinerant Manding traders who traveled around Lower Casamance. Rice wealth converted to cattle wealth was consumed completely at periodic intervals: cattle were slaughtered in large numbers upon the death of the family patriarch, and at the initiation cremonies. Initiation ceremonies were followed immediately by the marriage of all members of an entire age group, more cattle slaughtering, and the allocation of rice fields to the heads of these new nuclear households. These events served as an ostentatious form of display of wealth and family prestige, as a means of redistributing wealth and land within and among the lineages or descent groups (wards) that made up village agglomerations, and to affirm group solidarity.[111]

Interlacing of age groups, extended families, and descent groups within sedentary and often isolated villages made for a remarkably coherent if decentralized form of social organization. Many observers of Diola society, past and present, have been struck by its cultural coherence and "capacity for self-regulation" at the ward and village level.[112] Pélissier, Darbon, and Linarès attribute this to the paradoxical combination of "solidarity and individualism" within families and villages.

This capacity for "decentralized self-regulation" was and is manifest in the remarkable proliferation of self-help associations in Diola villages. Many of these have long historical lineages: the most obvious examples are the agricultural work societies based on age groups. In Diola villages, these intertwine with other self-help associations based on age groupings or other horizontal linkages between individuals – ties of friendship, residential proximity, family relations, or simple common interest. Self-help cooperatives or associations select leaders from among their own members, serve functional needs, and work on the basis of "strict reciprocity." Examples are rotating savings associations, childcare cooperatives, and groups organized around planning and saving for a particular event, celebration, or village project. Around 1975, Francis Snyder (1978) counted 25 different,

---

[111] van der Klei 1985. On initiation ceremonies in the 1990s, see Mark et al. 1998.
[112] See for example Darbon 1988:185, 174–5; Pélissier 1966:680–6; Linarès 1992.

sometimes overlapping, work associations in a Diola village with a population of 350, located about 25 kilometers from Ossouye. A distinctive and noteworthy form of Diola association is the communal militia, made up of male youth. Pélissier (1966:698) writes that these also have long pedigree in Diola society; he found in the 1950s and 1960s that they were typical of large villages throughout the Diola zone. In the mid-1970s, Snyder described the militias as a "kind of village police whose mandate is to ensure respect for collective discipline and the obligations and taboos of tradition."[113]

Lack of hierarchy in rural social organization weakened the capacity of Diola leaders to engage and bargain with rulers in Dakar, and goes far in explaining the state-building strategies rulers chose to pursue in Lower Casamance. At the same time, as we have seen, there is more to Diola social organization than "lack of hierarchy." Relations of production dispersed authority, but they also gave rise to supra-familial forms of economic cooperation that carried over into other spheres of social and political life. Diola villages organized *cooperation in the absence of hierarchy* or coercion. This kind of rural political capacity is not anticipated in the analytic framework laid out in Chapter 2, but as we shall see, in this case it is impossible to ignore. In Lower Casamance, it is difficult to explain the collective political action that *has* emerged among peasants in the last one hundred years, and especially in the recent period, without reference to these long-standing, decentralized mechanisms of social cooperation. This kind of social structure is not unique to the Diola: some analysts have identified cooperation in the absence of sociopolitical hierarchy as one of Africa's original contributions to the full array of human sociopolitical forms.

Governing Lower Casamance: Colonial Precedents

Senegal's governments faced state-building challenges in Lower Casamance that are altogether different from those encountered north of the Gambia River. Diola social structure did not offer Dakar secure footholds, or possibilities for alliances with local elites that could have magnified the authority and influence of the state. On the contrary, the center faced extreme sociopolitical segmentation and a mode of political organization that grew out of, and worked to reproduce, atomization of authority and social egalitarianism within village society. These are the social-structural

---

[113] The militias are called *étendoukaye*. Snyder observed that some were flexing their muscles at the expense of the elders. See also Darbon 1988:174.

and institutional concomitants of a political culture described by Pélissier (1966:28):

[The Diola and Balant of Casamance] have manifest over the entire course of their history an extraordinary faithfulness to their refusal of all political infrastructure, along with an irrepressible commitment to [volunté] individual independence and social equality.... They have maintained this personality by isolating themselves, either by taking shelter in defensive social practices or by rendering their territory inaccessible to foreign influences.

Authority and associational life in Diola society were not configured in ways that were very useful for those bent on imposing a centralized form of political overrule in Lower Casamance. More than that, in *pays Diola*, governments confronted rural populations who happened to be resistant to the *idea* of overrule. Rural populations in this zone also happened to be equipped with village-level political institutions that *counteracted* the concentration of authority.

Diola sociopolitical organization made for a process of colonial conquest quite different from what took place in Senegal's monarchies to the north. As in southern Côte d'Ivoire, conquest was a long and drawn-out process that began around 1836 and was not declared complete until after World War I. Colonial administrators described social and political organization in Lower Casamance (and southern Côte d'Ivoire) as "total anarchy," "total confusion."[114] Pacification of *pays Diola* and *Balant* was "marked by an incredible number of treaties, each important village requiring its own particular convention, sometimes several, preceded by an armed intervention.... The affairs of one village do not concern its neighbors, each military operation is carried out in the context of indifference on the part of neighboring populations."[115] Revolts continued through the 1910s. In November 1917, Governor General of French West Africa Van Vollenhoven declared: "We are not in control of Lower Casamance.... We need to make sure that the Casamance does not become the wart [*verrue*] of this colony when it should be the jewel" (Diaw and Diouf 1992:20).

---

[114] Diaw and Diouf 1992:20; Zucarelli 1973:214. Taxes were imposed in 1901, even though populations of Lower Casamance were still not under France's political control.

[115] Pélissier 1966:675–6. The French installed themselves at Carabane in 1836. Ziguinchor, the main Portuguese port of Lower Casamance, was ceded to France in 1886. A permanent military post was established at Ossouye in 1901. "It takes seventy-five years, from 1836 to eve of World War I, for the French to achieve complete military, administrative, and commercial penetration of Lower Casamance" (ibid.).

Establishment of a colonial administrative apparatus in Lower Casamance was late and difficult. As Darbon (1988:62–6) shows, the process itself, and the institutional configurations it produced, differed from those in Senegal's other regions. Darbon attributes this mostly to "distance [from Dakar] and the hostility of local populations" (ibid.:62). It is also clear that indigenous social-structural factors forced France to resort to different state-building strategies. Unlike what happened in the Wolof groundnut basin, in Lower Casamance France drew administrative districts (cantons, subdivisions) that had "no customary significance and only rarely the kind of geographical value that one can see in regions where territorial demarcations are based on some preexisting organization of chieftaincy."[116] These demarcations were subject to an "incessant" and "apparently anarchic" pattern of changes that accompanied France's attempts to pacify the region.[117] Pélissier explains that

[i]t took several decades and permanent pressure on the part of the administration to impose notions as simple as "chef de village" or "chef de canton" and to give some substance to their authority which was not based on any customary institution. . . . [As an administrator in residence at Ziguinchor in 1906 complained,] "[w]e have to try to increase the authority of the village chiefs. Their subjects do not listen to them. . . ." The [higher-ranking chiefs] are no better respected; they are regarded as spies, thieves; the people threaten and sometimes abuse them. . . . It was hard for the colonial administration to get "volunteers" to take these positions. One former military man was pressed into service only after a stay in prison legitimated him in the eyes of his future subjects. (1966: 678–9)

Pélissier takes these problems as evidence of the weakness of the administration in face of the Diola "institutional vacuum," and he is right. Lack of hierarchical political authority – that is, the absence of a preexisting machinery for social control – deprived the French of a foothold in Diola society and led them to apply military (and military-style) solutions to the problem of governing Lower Casamance.

Compounding France's problems was the fact that colonial administrators did not like or trust the *interlocateurs* they *did* find in this region. "The only authorities who could effectively play the role of intermediaries were [Catholic] missionaries; the problem was that they acted more in the

---

[116] See Pélissier 1966:646.
[117] Darbon 1988:66; see also 63–5.

interests of the population than the administration."[118] Dakar has never been able to solve this problem in Lower Casamance.

To govern Lower Casamance, Senegal's colonial government departed from many of the institution-building practices followed in the Wolof groundnut basin. At the bottom of the administrative hierarchy, the French appointed their own direct agents – usually retired soldiers or "northern-ers" (Senegalese from north of the Gambia River) – as village chiefs. This was a pure example of French direct rule. As we have seen, in Senegal the French resorted to such strategies only when they had to: it is in this sense that France's institutional choices were determined endogenously, by po-litical realities at the local level, rather than in offices in Dakar or Paris. For villagers in Lower Casamance, it meant that the local, day-to-day represen-tative of state authority was a foreigner who probably did not even speak their language.

In the 1910s, during the period of military pacification, the colonial regime constructed a highly deconcentrated field administration in Lower Casamance. As one administrator pleaded in 1910, "[We need] to find bet-ter administrative adaptation for this region, one that would be closer to the ethnic reality of the area. In truth it would be necessary to make each group or party its own circumscription."[119] A very large number of *cercles* and cantons was created to take account of "the disarticulation of the social structure, compared to Upper and Middle Casamance."[120] Once pacifica-tion was complete, many of these subdivisions were eliminated, making for a streamlined and more tightly concentrated state structure. It was a direct-rule system with administrative authority centralized in the hands of French officials and their employees.

Once a political apparatus was in place, in the early 1920s, France turned to the colonial *mise en valeur* of the region. Expansion of groundnut

---

[118] Darbon (1988:125), citing a 1937 report of Casamance's Administrateur Supérieur.

[119] Cited by Darbon 1988:63.

[120] Darbon 1988:62, 67. The number of *commandants de cercle* in Casamance peaked at five between 1917 and 1922, close to the total for all of the rest of rural Senegal at that time. Stationed above the commandants was an *Administrateur Supérieur*, a sort of "deputy" colonial governor for Casamance and the only official in Senegal with this title. Over the course of the 1920s through 1940s, many of the administrative subdivisions (*cercles* and cantons) were eliminated. On *cercles*, the numbers by year went like this: one to two in 1890–1907, three in 1912, five in 1917–22, three to four in 1923–38, two in 1939, one in 1944. The number of cantons in Lower Casamance fell from forty-six in 1930 to eighteen in 1960. The post of Administrator Supérieur was eliminated in 1932. See Pélissier 1960:647; Darbon 1988:64–6.

production was the centerpiece of this strategy, as it was in central Senegal. Soon after the French authorities had imposed an administrative grid and official chiefs in the area around Bignona (in 1924), they undertook "a huge effort to create a network of roads and trails making it possible for vehicles to reach most of the important villages of Basse Casamance."[121] Pélissier writes that this was a decisive factor in permitting the expansion of ground-nut production in Lower Casamance. Simultaneously, the authorities un-dertook a massive propaganda campaign in favor of this crop. Not wanting to rely on persuasion alone, France also applied force: they doubled head taxes. Household heads who did not produce enough groundnuts to sell, and were therefore unable to pay the tax, were beaten and humiliated.[122]

France's efforts were largely successful, and in the 1930s there was rapid take-off of groundnut production north of the Casamance River and west of the Soungrougrou River in the zones around the administrative capi-tal of Ziguinchor. Development centered around Bignona.[123] Large parts of the forest were cleared for groundnut cultivation, and as early as about 1935 French authorities began creating classified forests in this region to prevent the stripping off of forest cover. In the 1950s the Sociétés In-digènes de Prévoyance (SIP) of Ziguinchor *cercle* were distributing about 10 percent of all groundnut seeds allocated by SIPs in Senegal.[124] By the

---

[121] See Pélissier 1966:809, 781.

[122] Hamer 1981:190. She describes the severity of local tax collection in the villages around Bignona in the 1920s: "There is the frequent report, for example, of how payment refusal ended in the male head of household being tied nude in the blazing sun in shame before his family and neighbors" (ibid.).

[123] Pélissier 1966:671. For van der Klei (1985:71–3), a decisive factor in this take-off was the skills and knowledge acquired by Diola youth who worked as seasonal migrant la-borers in the groundnut-producing regions of Gambia and Middle Casamance, starting in the 1920s. The timing of this migratory current is explained by France's successful military campaign to "pacify" Lower Casamance in 1917. Pacification allowed France to restrict internal (inter-African) trade in this region. Meanwhile, as the Manding of Middle Casamance became big producers of groundnuts destined for export, they became con-sumers of Indochinese rice imported by French traders. According to van der Klei, this undermined Manding demand for Diola rice, forcing the Diola to find ways to earn cash to buy the Manding cattle that they wanted as a form of savings and a prestige good. The need for cash, coupled with the fact that pacification made travel within Lower Casamance less dangerous than it had been, explains the rapidly increasing numbers of Diola labor migrants in the 1920s. Migration was seasonal and lasted for a few months only. Returning migrants brought knowledge about, and interest in, groundnut production back to Lower Casamance.

[124] However, they distributed only 2 percent of the national total of chemical fertilizer, and no mechanical seeders (Ly 1958:47–51). On groundnut production around Bignona in the 1930s to 1960, see Pélissier 1966:782, 789, 808–9.

early 1960s, "with the exception of certain isolated villages or in the estuaries, the groundnut [was] present everywhere in Basse Casamance and form[ed] an integral part of Diola agriculture. Only the region south of the river participat[ed] only modestly in groundnut production."[125]

Islam came to Lower Casamance along with the spread of the monetary economy and export crop production. Its influence, however, was uneven. South of the Casamance River, Christianity was widespread and coexisted with, and even tended to help conserve, traditional Diola religion.[126] Pélissier described the Department of Ossouye as the last bastion of traditional Diola civilization: this area escaped the penetration of the groundnut and Islam until the 1950s.

North of the Casamance River the influence of Islam was (and is) more pronounced. Along the eastern and northern facades of Lower Casamance, and especially in the valley of the Soungrougrou River, Diola populations converted to Islam in the period between 1925 and 1935. The process took only one generation; as of the early 1960s about 75 percent of this population was Muslim. Islam did not come to this region in its dominant Senegalese (Wolof) forms, however. Here there was less unity and organizational coherence, the marabouts' power and scope of influence was far more limited than it was in the North, and there was no maraboutic hierarchy. Both of Senegal's main Sufi orders were present in the region, but they came without the political infrastructure forged in the North. Girard (1963:154) refers to a village in the late 1950s where Mouride and Tidjane prayed together at one mosque under the leadership of an elected *imam*. In most of this zone, Islam, like Christianity, fused with Diola ways: "it assimilated into the general structures of traditional Diola social and economic life."[127]

Although Diola social and economic life changed a great deal during Senegal's late-colonial period, general features most relevant here – the

---

[125] See Pélissier 1966:782.

[126] See Pélissier 1966:808, 811–13; on Ossouye, ibid.:782, 791. On Islamization, ibid.:798; Darbon 1988:128–30.

[127] Pélissier 1966:812. There is however a nuance. When Islamization occurred within the context of heavy Manding influence – that is, where "Manding Islam" was a powerful force – Diola social and economic life tended to become "Mandingized." See also Linarès 1992; and Hesseling 1994:248–9. In parts of Lower Casamance where Christianity, Islam, and the spread of the monetary economic *preceded* Manding influence, however, Manding influence was restrained (Pélissier 1966:805–8). Most of the region around Bignona was, as Pélissier says, "sheltered from" Manding influence.

lack of internal political hierarchy, the vitality of horizontal ties and associations – remained constant, and were in some ways accentuated. Groundnut production, seasonal labor migration of Diola youth, and the general spread and opening up of the monetary economy were all forces that challenged the centrality of riziculture in Diola society.[128] They promoted the economic emancipation of the individual in general and of youth in particular, and thereby worked to attenuate the authority of elders. At the same time, Diola modes of association and collective action proved to be highly resilient, supple, and adaptive.

Such changes were evident in the rise of village-based work associations devoted to all sorts of new economic opportunities (e.g., groundnut cultivation, building schools and mosques, and later *tourisme integré* projects) and new social projects, such as the formation of soccer teams, cultural and dance societies, and village hometown associations formed by urban migrants.[129] Associations also adapted to exert village-level authority and social control in new ways. In 1963 Girard mentioned as "a recent innovation" *koumpo* youth associations that acted as a kind of internal village police aiming mostly at enforcing elders' authority over youth. Girard saw these associations as an example of adaptation of old customs in the effort to preserve Diola cultural coherence and tradition.[130] Ten or fifteen years later, when Snyder studied a Diola youth militia, he detected considerable *conflict* between youth and elders. The police functions of the youth association were expanding: young men organized armed patrols to control the roaming of domestic animals and imposed sanctions on offenders. In so doing they "partially displac[ed] the locus of authority for taking decisions and coercive action in a critical sphere of rural activity . . . provoking severe conflicts between youth, elders, and adults."[131] These observations point to the progressive attenuation of elders' authority and the growing role of male youth in the exertion of social control in the villages. They suggest possible links between indigenous modes of social organization in

---

[128] On the seasonal out-migration of Diola youth (to other cash-cropping regions in Casamance and Gambia in the 1920s, and later to big cities like Dakar), see van der Klei 1985 and Girard 1963. Rice production declined in Lower Casamance in the twentieth century, some rice fields have been abandoned, and in some parts of northern *pays Diola*, rice has been left to women as men devote themselves to the groundnut. See van der Klei 1985:75; Pélissier 1966:789.

[129] See Girard 1963:157–9.

[130] See Girard 1963:152.

[131] Snyder 1978:238, 243; see also van der Klei 1985.

pays Diola, local capacity for decentralized collective action, and the emergence in the 1980s of a guerilla militia mobilized around the regionalist cause.

Diola society lacked the social hierarchies that can provide ready-made infrastructure for indirect rule, but it did possess highly decentralized and functionally specific mechanisms for organizing cooperation, and monitoring and enforcing rules. Pélissier (1966:679) thought that this made Diola society particularly well suited to take advantage of possibilities for democratic competition. And that is just the point. In 1960 it was not genuine grassroots democracy that Dakar was seeking, but rather reliable mechanisms for securing rural political order and enforcing the political hegemony of the regime.

II. Decolonization Politics in an "Uncaptured" Region

Lower Casamance was pulled into national Senegalese politics at the end of the 1940s as a peripheral region in which the dominant parties could not establish secure electoral bases. The problem had a dual nature: first, there was an absence of strong local intermediaries who could control/deliver stable electoral clienteles; second, a diffuse yet palpable regionalist and oppositional sentiment existed in *pays Diola*. Under these circumstances, modes of political incorporation that were relied upon up north – the attempts to ground state authority in indigenous, communal authority structures – could produce results just as likely to *threaten* the regime as to shore it up. All the problems posed by Lower Casamance came into sharp relief in the 1950s with the dominant party's attempts to control opposition and secure an electoral clientele in this region.

In Lower Casamance, only about five years separated the last of the colonial-era uprisings against French authority and the beginning of decolonization-era politics. In 1942 there was a major revolt at Effock. It ended with the deportation and disappearance of the Diola prophetesse Alinsitoué Diatta, who led the uprising.[132] The electoral openings that would lead to Senegal's independence started just a few years later with the political reforms of 1946. Casamance electoral politics began in

---

[132] She worked as a maid for a European family in Dakar. She "saw a vision in 1940, and returned to Basse Casamance where she instructed the Diola not to pay taxes, to refuse to fight for France, supply the French with rice, or cultivate the peanut cash crop.... [She] was exiled to Timbuktu in 1943" (Beck 1996a:238).

Sédhiou in 1947 when two school teachers, Emile Badiane and Ibou Diallo, and 121 "literate notables" signed the manifesto of the Mouvement des Forces Démocratiques de la Casamance (MFDC) to "agitate for the political disenclavement of the region."[133] Government clerks, teachers, and other professionals were prominent in this group. The MFDC wanted to be able to send locally elected representatives to Senegal's territory-wide political institutions and called for local development programs and broader educational initiatives in Casamance. It denounced excessive centralization and corruption in the colonial bureaucracy.

In 1947 the SFIO was Senegal's leading political party. At that moment, Léopold Senghor was carving out his own political domain within the party by forming alliances with political leaders from newly enfranchised regions – most notably Emile Badiane from Casamance and leaders from the Senegal River Basin – to pressure the SFIO old-guard to decentralize the party to allow the "equitable, democratic participation" of all major regional, ethnic, and economic interests. Senghor knew all about regional tensions within Senegal and how to use them to build electoral coalitions. In 1948 Senghor led the dissidents out of the SFIO and set about organizing the BDS. BDS strategy at that time was to "federate" with existing ethnic and regional associations, and Casamance's MFDC was a key element in the party's base.[134] It was one of the first truly provincial constituencies to line up behind the BDS.

This makes sense, for Lower Casamance had not been co-opted into the SFIO machine. The MFDC electorate was a kind of free-floating political asset in Senegal, available for capture by a political entrepreneur at the center. In the late 1940s, that politician was Senghor. As we shall see, this "uncaptured" quality has been a permanent attribute of the Lower

---

[133] Diop and Diouf (1990:49) and Diaw and Diouf (1992) describe this as a Diola initiative and suggest that MFDC leaders opted for a regionalist banner in an attempt to harness a wider sentiment of political marginality. See Linarès 1992:240 n. 20; Darbon 1988:183–4. The name MFDC resurfaces in 1982, under leadership of Augustin Diamacoune Senghor, with pamphlets advocating the separation of Casamance from Senegal.

[134] These included the Union Générale des Originaires de la Vallée du Fleuve (UGOVF), the Fédération des Originaires et Natifs du Oulao, Union des Toucouleurs, Association des Toucouleurs du Fouta Toro, and the MFDC. Migrants from the Senegal River Valley who lived in Senegal's urban areas made up a large constituency of the northern regional associations (Morganthau 1964:151; A.-B. Diop 1965; Schumacher 1975:9).

Casamance electorate. What was an asset for Senghor in the late 1940s became a liability when his party took power in the 1960s.

In 1954, having established control over Senegal's Territorial Assembly, Senghor moved to consolidate his party by suppressing the regional associations federated with the BDS. Henceforth all constituencies would be integrated into the party directly. Casamance politician Emile Badiane accepted these terms and became a BDS official, and the MFDC was dissolved.[135] Badiane's alliance with Senghor remained one of the most stable features of Casamance politics for the next decade. This, however, did not assure Senghor control of Lower Casamance, for Badiane failed to deliver the MFDC constituency to the ruling party.

With the co-optation of Badiane, a faction of MFDC politicians led by Dakar university professor Assane Seck broke away to form the Mouvement Autonome Casamançais (MAC).[136] Seck was a Casamançais, but his roots in the region were shallow: his father was a Wolof northerner who had served as the cantonal chief of Adéane, near Ziguinchor. Assane Seck himself had spent most of his adult life in "northern Senegal" and France. In contrast to most politicians in the Wolof groundnut basin, Seck had no claims to historical, religious, or land-based political legitimacy, and no economic powers over his constituents (such as control over access to land or credit). Casamance's two leading politicians of the decolonization era, Assane Seck and Emile Badiane, were similar in this way: they did not exercise reliable control over electoral constituencies. This would remain characteristic of the politicians who emerged to represent Lower Casamance in the national political arena.

---

[135] Morganthau (1964:150) writes that after "long negotiations," BDS leaders constituted a 1956 regional executive committee for Casamance that was "widely representative": Of the thirty-one members, ten were Diola, five were Fulani (Peul), five were Manding, and four were Wolof. Of the total, twenty were teachers or government clerks, and three were agricultural or veterinary officers. One was a farmer. Twenty-nine of them had received formal education in French schools. Emile Badiane served as a minister in Senghor's government until he died in 1972.

[136] Assane Seck was born in Inor, in what is now the Middle Casamance Department of Sédhiou. He had served as director of studies at the Ecole Normale William-Ponty. Veteran status helped him continue his studies in Paris. He returned from France after World War II, and in the mid-1950s was one of the few Africans on the staff of the University of Dakar. On the basis of interviews with Seck in the 1960s, Johnson (1971:86) reported that Seck "made his debut in politics on a ticket sponsored by Lamine Guèye in Rufisque."

Both BDS and the SFIO tried to mobilize electoral constituencies in the Casamance in the mid-1950s.[137] For the SFIO, this region became ever more important as the populous groundnut basin slipped from its grasp. In January 1956, Assane Seck allied formally with Lamine Guèye and the SFIO. So valuable were the Casamance votes that in the January 1956 National Assembly elections Seck was placed second on the SFIO candidate list headed by Lamine Guèye.[138] The BDS won the elections and became the party running the territorial government. Even in this position, Senghor's party failed to establish electoral control of Lower Casamance and resorted to strong-arm tactics to impose its own political agents. Zucarelli (1973:225) recounts the case of the 1957 elections for the chieftaincy of Pata (Ziguinchor): the SFIO candidate won the elections by a wide margin; "[h]owever the BDS candidate was named to the post."

Assane Seck followed the SFIO when it fused with Senghor's party in 1957, and he was compensated with a prominent place on the new UPS party platform committees. The next year he was among the leaders of the group of leftist intellectuals who walked out of the ruling party. Seck cofounded the opposition party PRA-Senegal, which campaigned for a "no" vote in the 1958 referendum on de Gaulle's proposal for a neocolonial Franco-African community.[139] The PRA and the other leftist parties were roundly defeated in this, but they won in Lower Casamance. Senghor and the ruling party still did not have control of this region: 20 percent of all "no" votes in the country as a whole came from the Casamance capital of Ziguinchor. Linarès wrote that "the Jola [Diola] voted for immediate termination of the French presence."[140]

From 1958 to its banning in 1966, the PRA remained the most important opposition party in Senegal. Virtually all observers describe the party as the voice of Senegal's ideological left,[141] but the key fact here is that the PRA had

---

[137] Senghor reportedly traveled extensively in this region.

[138] Morganthau 1964:154–5. In joining with the SFIO, Seck did not surrender his organizational autonomy: he was listed "not as an SFIO candidate, but as a candidate for [the MAC]." The relationship between Guèye and Seck may have preceded the formation of the MAC. In placing Seck on the ballot, Guèye was probably also trying to bring in the Dakar intellectuals.

[139] The PRA favored pan-Africanism and socialism, called for "Africanization," and warned against "the poisoned cake of French technical assistance" (Cruise O'Brien 1967:558).

[140] Linarès 1992:220–1; Darbon 1988:183–4.

[141] See for example Morganthau 1964. The historian Abdoulaye Ly, who was second in command at IFAN (Institute Fondamentale d'Afrique Noire) in the 1950s, was cofounder

a starkly *regional* electoral base. In 1959, 85.5 percent of all PRA votes came from Casamance. The party had an *electoral majority* in this region (Darbon 1988:183–4). This means that the only significant electoral opposition to the Senghor regime at the end of the 1950s was regionally based, and its locus was Lower Casamance.

When Senegal became independent, a large proportion of younger men and educated youth in Lower Casamance were members of the PRA. The hold of Senghor's ruling party, the UPS, was "extremely weak" in this region.[142] In the 1963 national elections, the most important unified opposition to the Senghor regime once again came from the Casamance-based PRA, which was "widely believed to have been much more successful than official results showed."[143] Ten PRA protestors were killed around Ziguinchor on election day.

For the Senghor regime, this state of affairs was intolerable. The PRA and the minor opposition parties were outlawed in 1966, and Senegal became a one-party state. Former opposition leaders were co-opted into attractive government posts: Assane Seck became minister of culture (and then minister of foreign affairs in 1973). The number of UPS party cards sold in Casamance climbed from 2,500 in 1961 to about 42,000 in 1963, to an impressive-sounding 84,000 in 1967.[144] At that point, Linarès (1992:221) writes, the Diola lost interest in electoral politics.

From the mid-1950s on, the goal of impeding the development of Casamance-based partisan opposition appears to have driven Dakar's state-building choices in Lower Casamance. This concern was present in BDS thinking early on. According to Morganthau (1964:151), "[l]imiting separatist inclinations of these regional groups [like the MFDC in Casamance] . . . became a major preoccupation of the party's territorial leaders after 1953, when they had already defeated the SFIO in elections." The threat in Casamance was not embodied in a powerful local elite of chiefs and aristocrats who challenged the center directly. Rather, it was diffuse, highly localized, and without overarching political structure – but, as the

and secretary general of the PRA-Senegal. In his *Les regroupements politiques au Senegal, 1956–1970* (1992), he has almost nothing to say about the Casamance.

[142] Schumacher 1975:30; sa. Linarès 1992:220–1.

[143] Cruise O'Brien 1967:562. The ruling party co-opted a dissident faction of the PRA in 1963 – "its leaders accepted two ministerial portfolios as reward" – and the ruling party made some electoral headway in Casamance (ibid.:564).

[144] Schumacher 1975:30. The 1961 number can be compared to the 66,000 UPS party cards sold in 1961 in another peripheral region, the Fleuve, in 1961.

stories of the prophetess Alinsitoué Diatta, Emile Badiane, and Assane Seck show, it could be activated (if not reliably harnessed) by individuals in the right circumstances. Political leaders emerged, but they were not able to establish a lock on local constituencies or deliver disciplined electoral blocs to the ruling party.

Analysts from Paul Pélissier (1966) to Linda Beck (1996a) have observed that these political dynamics are related to structural attributes of rural society in this region. Diola society is characterized by political fragmentation, the absence of social hierarchy, and a lack of customary administrative infrastructure. Pélissier wrote that

[i]t is easy to see the persistence of these features in contemporary Senegalese politics. Here, no customary political class intervenes to restrain the influence of elected politicians. By the same token, no population is more eager/ardent than the Diola to contest the decisions of the central or regional administration, none is more receptive to and welcoming of the ideas and initiatives of various forms of opposition to established authorities, none in the final analysis is more open to the play of democratic competition and, at the political level, more ready (*disponible*) for it. (1966:679)

III. Institutional Choice in Lower Casamance

How did the regime proceed? As Darbon (1988:131) argued, it attempted to avoid the development of localized and independent partisan organizations in Casamance. Legal coercion was one means to this end, and that is how the parties that coalesced between 1947 and 1960 were finally eliminated. More systematic and proactive strategies required institution building.

A. Implantation of Party-State Apparatus

Implantation of the party-state followed a defensive strategy aimed at preempting the kind of local "reappropriation of the state" that was the hallmark of state building in the Wolof groundnut basin. In Lower Casamance, there were fewer layers in the administrative hierarchy and no rural outposts that could be used by local politicians to organize electoral followings (even in support of the ruling party). Less state presence and less state activity (spending) meant fewer targets and incentives for organizing political activity. The government apparatus was insulated from local influences and pressures: control over the compact and closed machinery of state was centralized in the hands of administrators from "northern Senegal" (*nordistes*) who had no political ambitions or vested interests in Lower Casamance. Casamançais had few points of access to administrative and patronage resources that could be used to play party politics. In this region, there was a distinctive resistance to administrative deconcentration that Darbon characterizes as "deliberate non-utilization" of legal provisions for deconcentration, a choice he attributes to "bad faith on the part of the central administrative authorities" (1988:77, 83).

The distinctiveness of the regime's state-building strategies in Casamance was explicit from the start. In 1960 the National Assembly redrew the structures of territorial administration and created seven "natural regions" that were supposedly based on sociological homogeneity. By this decision rule, Lower Casamance would have been split off from Middle and Upper Casamance. The government considered this option, and then rejected it:

Division was debated within the commission of finances of the National Assembly, and then in the Assembly. This discussion laid out the economic and democratic advantages that would result from this split. However the question was buried – given the risk of accentuating local particularisms, notably Diola, which it risked reinforcing – in the name of "solidarity and national cohesion." (Darbon 1988:69)

In the Wolof groundnut basin, accentuating local particularisms was an efficient and politically reliable mode of organizing electoral constituencies. In Lower Casamance, this strategy was *politically risky*. The regime opted to perpetuate the "non-correspondence" between administrative jurisdiction and ethnoregional collectivities that had characterized colonial rule in this region. What Darbon and Pélissier called the "inappropriateness of jurisdictions" in Casamance allowed the center to use its relatively stronger political standing in Middle and Upper Casamance to counterbalance the political threats it confronted in Diola territory. In the same stroke, Dakar avoided creating a single administrative unit that would unite the Diola population within its boundaries. Dakar did not want to enhance the sense of collective destiny among populations in Lower Casamance – it did not want to "invent a tribe" in this region.[145] On the contrary, the goal was to avoid accentuating what the regime called Diola particularism. So it

[145] See Vail 1989.

117

was that the colonial *cercle* of Casamance became Casamance Region, and Casamance's new governor became postcolonial Senegal's only direct heir to a French *commandant*.[146]

Within Casamance, regional-level administration was a main locus of administrative prerogative. This stands in clear contrast to the groundnut basin, where regional governors were marginalized because local hierarchies of notables were connected more or less directly to the center. Casamance governors were drawn from the ranks of the Senegalese military, and were thus wholly loyal to the center. Darbon characterizes them as professionals with considerable and effective administrative authority, noting that they weilded more control over the prefectorial administration than their counterparts in the groundnut basin (1988:74–6). In the first two decades of independence, the military men who served as the highest-ranking state agents in the region also governed the largest municipality in Casamance – Ziguinchor, with over 50 percent of the urban population of the entire region – directly. This institutional arrangement effectively pre-empted deconcentration of the party administrative apparatus to the municipal level.[147] All this produced spatial concentration of the party-state apparatus that was unusual compared to the rest of Senegal, along with an extraordinary centralization of authority in the hands of the regional governor.

Control over the regional antennae and activities of government ministries that undertook economic projects in Casamance – the Ministries of Public Works and Rural Development, and the parastatals – was also centralized in the hands of Dakar appointees.[148] Crucial administrative services, such as those responsible for "rural equipment" and water, concentrated their presence and activities in Ziguinchor, "thus depriving the quasi-totality of the region of any administrative structure whatsoever," except for the corps of *sous-préfets* stationed in the localities.[149] Major spending and

---

[146] This decision was reversed in 1983.

[147] Casamance's regional governor even had wide authority over *development* spending in Ziguinchor (Darbon 1988:69–70, 88).

[148] Externally financed parastatal development agencies – Société pour la Mise en Valeur de la Casamance (SOMIVAC), Société pour le Developpement des Fibres Textiles (SODIFI-TEX), and the Projet Rizicole de Sédhiou (PRS) – came late, focused mostly on the Upper and Middle Casamance, and were more insulated politically than the massively politicized *programme agricole* implemented by the parastatal SODEVA groundnut basin. See Darbon 1988:47, 188, 200–1. SATEC ran rice-farming programs in Middle and Upper Casamance in the 1960s (Schumacher 1975:213).

[149] See Darbon 1988:82.

investment projects were run directly from Dakar without input from even the Zuguinchor-based administrative authorities, and without interference or input from local intermediaries, politicians, or businesses. "Contracts [went] to firms having no link to the Casamance."[150] Ziguinchor offices of some central ministries received no funds at all from Dakar, and most were handicapped by frequent rotation of personnel and by large numbers of abandoned or vacant posts. The region appeared "underadministered" and suffered from low levels of state spending.

Central rulers appeared intent on insulating the state apparatus from the Casamançais themselves. One indication of this was Dakar's insistence on staffing administrative and prefectorial agencies in Lower Casamance with functionaries not indigenous to the region. Local populations viewed state agents as "foreigners from Senegal." From 1960, functionaries native to Casamance were posted elsewhere in Senegal. "Some have affirmed that to prevent the [opposition] PRA from getting wrapped up with Casamançais cadres, these cadres were until 1966 systematically posted outside their region."[151] Meanwhile, as the state began recruiting Senegalese to fill government posts vacated by the French, "the highly educated Joola [Diola], who were typically teachers, were refused positions in the administration allegedly to avoid depriving the schools of trained teachers" (Beck 1996a:241 n. 24). Twenty and thirty years later this was still largely the case: government administration in Lower Casamance was still dominated by cadres not native to the region. Locals perceived postcolonial state building in their region as a process of *colonisation nordiste*.

This was a major factor in reinforcing the administrative autonomy of the state in the region. It also restricted the access of would-be political entrepreneurs to state resources that could have been used to build political clientele. One observable consequence was that the political phenomena of patron-clientelism, cronyism, and corruption appeared to be far less pronounced in Lower Casamance than they were in the groundnut basin (and, as Darbon notes, even less important in *zone Diola* than in other parts of Casamance). "Neo-patrimonial practices seem less important than elsewhere [in Senegal], they are less formalized and structured. As a result the private appropriation of state resources does not permit the weaving together of integrative clientele networks: the population of the local society

---

[150] Darbon 1988:76, see also 74–7, 82–4.
[151] Darbon 1988:132 n. 29 *inter alia*; Beck 1996a; Hesseling 1994.

is not the one that constitutes the administration. Clientelism occurs among 'nordistes.'"[152]

Formal institutional structure provided very little by way of infrastructure for organizing clientelist networks or electoral constituencies among local populations in the towns and villages. Party structures and elective government institutions were not implanted at the departmental or local levels: the deconcentration of ruling-party structure that Dakar pushed so systematically in the Wolof-Mouride zone was simply not undertaken in Lower Casamance in the 1960s and 1970s. De facto direct rule preempted the development of real municipal government in Ziguinchor and shut down the city as a locus of provincial political organizing. In the groundnut basin, by contrast, Dakar stoked municipal-level government, pumped in resources, and devolved administrative prerogative that local politicians could employ to organize their own followings. Municipal government in central Senegal was a hotbed of provincial machine politics and a staging area for local notables destined for the National Assembly. In Casamance, Dakar sought to prevent the emergence of political machines centered around the region's capital city, the other towns, or even the largest village agglomerations. There was no place in the formal structures of the party-state to build or institutionalize such constituencies.

Although the ruling party monopolized electoral politics in Casamance from 1966 to 1976, and continued to dominate in the multiparty contests of the 1980s (though in the face of significant electoral challenge), its institutional presence and influence in this region was shallow and superficial. The ruling party never built a deconcentrated network of patronage-dispensing outposts at the local level. Instead, in the 1950s and 1960s the regime sought the support of political personalities in Casamance, airlifted them out of Casamance, and parachuted them into the political world of Dakar. They were, literally and figuratively, removed from Casamance.[153] The alliance between Emile Badiane and Senghor in the 1950s, and the co-optation of Assane Seck into the ruling party in 1966, are notable examples.

After outlawing the Casamance-based PRA in 1966, the regime made a place for Casamançais within the party, but elected politicians from this

---

[152] Darbon 1988:163–4. He stresses the fact that *sous-préfets* in Casamance are well known for corruption and diversion of funds: "As the Minister of the Interior has noted, to be *sous-préfet* is synonymous with enrichment" (1988:92–4, 98).

[153] Darbon 1988:131, 133–5; Diop and Diouf 1990; Cruise O'Brien 1967:564.

region were weak and nonrepresentative. In 1983, P. Biarnes wrote that in Lower Casamance, "Dakar has practically never found support other than that of tame or contested personalities from Toucouleur, Wolof, or Lebou [i.e., northern] families."[154] Darbon (1988:136–7, 188) qualifies this as a caricature, but one that does underscore the point that "party elites of Casamance are . . . not very effective in representing the interests of their region and above all, they do not represent local populations and notably the Diola." Until grave political troubles erupted in the early 1980s, the ruling party's regional electoral lists in Casamance often included many candidates who were not born in the region.[155]

The social base of the party in this region was the civil service itself. In the Ossouye region, "the quasi-totality of PS cadres . . . are working for the government (teachers, nurses, functionaries, etc.)."[156] As we have seen, most agents of the central administration working in Casamance were not indigenous to the region. Linda Beck (1996a:246) writes that in Lower Casamance the party's patron-client networks "can only attach themselves to an educated elite of Casamançais politicians whose authority is based solely on their position in the party-state, and local communal leaders whose authority is highly atomized."

To govern the rural areas, the post-1940 division of Lower Casamance into three main subunits was retained. These became the departments of Ossouye, Ziguinchor, and Bignona.[157] Yet as we have noted in the case of Ziguinchor, real municipal governments and party institutions were not created at the departmental level: the political deconcentrations carried out in the groundnut basin were not implemented in Lower Casamance. This deprived the Casamançais of what were, in the groundnut basin, critical arenas – indeed hotbeds – of provincial politics and launching pads for regional notables interested in national-level office. In Lower Casamance the regime avoided creating institutional infrastructure for this. Diola peasants, local authorities, and would-be politicians had "very feeble possibilities for access to the apparatuses of the state" (Darbon 1988:190).

---

[154] *Le Monde*, 4 janvier 1983, as cited by Darbon 1988:136.

[155] The regime confronted the problem of "nonrepresentativeness" of elected politicians in the early 1980s, and in 1983 "100 percent of the candidates for the PS regional list were born in Casamance." The sidelining of Assane Seck in 1983 also suggests the regime's sensitivity to this problem (Darbon 1988:133–4).

[156] See Darbon 1988:132–3.

[157] These did reflect the ethnic and religious distinctions within Lower Casamance. Each department was supervised by a prefect.

Towering over the flat political landscapes of Lower Casamance were the *sous-préfets*, Dakar's agents mandated to perform the law-and-order functions of the modern state. Their jurisdictions were *arrondissements* drawn without any customary or social signification. *Sous-préfets'* authority in this region was undiluted and unmediated: they ruled without any systematic or institutionalized participation from local elders, chiefs, associational groups, or politicians. *Sous-préfets* themselves rotated often, which helped ensure that they remained agents of the center and did not become entangled in local affairs.[158] As Peter Geschiere (1986:323, 326) said of the *sous-préfets* in Makaland, in the forest area of southeastern Cameroon where local society is organized around small autonomous kinship groups, "the impressive authority of the state [in the person of the *sous-préfet*] seemed more or less suspended in air."

In Lower Casamance, *sous-préfets'* jurisdictions were smaller geographically and contained fewer villages than they did in Upper and Middle Casamance.[159] This reflects in part a demographic fact: in Lower Casamance population densities are higher and villages are larger than they are in Middle and Upper Casamance and indeed in the rest of rural Senegal. Senegal's largest village in the 1970s was Thionk Essil (population 6,000), located in the department of Bignona. Demography and institutional choice gave Dakar's men-on-the-spot, the *sous-préfets*, a palpable presence. The prefectorial network was the only part of the state apparatus in this region that was relatively deconcentrated.

No part of the party-state apparatus in this region served as a site for incorporation of local constituencies into political networks connected to the center, or for powersharing with local leaders or notables. Even village chiefs in Lower Casamance were direct agents of the center: they conformed to the stereotype of cogs in the wheels of direct rule. Linarès (1992:43) writes that "[i]n general they enjoyed no autonomous standing in the villages. By and large the chief is a civil servant and not a local authority in internal matters. He cannot demand special services by virtue of his chiefly post." They were appointed by administrative authorities and "were supposed to pass on information, collect taxes, . . . coordinate the occasional regional

---

[158] In Lower Casamance, "the *sous-préfets* are rotated often, with terms varying from only a couple of months to a maximum, in exceptional cases, of five years" (Hesseling 1986a:129). There were eight *sous-préfectures* in 1960.

[159] In the 1980s there were 80 villages in the Department of Ziguinchor and 82 in the Department of Ossouye, compared to 808 in the Department of Sédhiou and 942 in Kolda. See Darbon 1988:69–70.

services provided by government agencies, see to it that villagers inscribe their children in school, . . . [and] if there is a particularly violent fight in the community, the chief might call the police." Pélissier (1966:679) argued that they were bureaucrats executing orders from above and "not 'chiefs' in the sense that this term is understood in the rest of Senegal. . . . It is still hard for the administration to get volunteers to accept this job, whereas elsewhere in Senegal it is the object of heated competition."

There were real networks of social cohesion and status within Diola villages, but these were not connected to the official chieftaincy. In the 1960s Girard underscored this disconnect in these terms: "Effective authority in villages is held not by the official chief – the mandated intermediaries with government authorities – but rather by the *chef de l'ékafa*, the head of an association composed of all the small voluntary associations existing within a given rural community" (1963:152).

In the absence of partnership with credible indigenous authorities, the government had few political options when it came to problem solving in the localities. This reinforced the blunt, authoritarian character of local rule. A 1961 incident illustrates the point. A local property dispute degenerated into a violent conflict. Dakar turned to none other than the regional governor, who responded by deploying the full coercive powers of the state:

In May 1961, three villages [in the *cercle* of Sédhiou] fell into stark conflict over control of some ricefields. The *chef d'arrondissement*'s attempt at reconciliation failed. Arming themselves with clubs and machetes [*coupes-coupes*], the warring parties attempted to take control of the disputed territory. The *chef d'arrondisement* called the *commandant de cercle*, who failed to make reason prevail. An attempt to disarm the antagonists ended in the flight of the authorities and the four guards accompanying them; all were stoned copiously. The Governor sent reinforcements who penetrated the villages and arrested thirty-two persons. (Zucarelli 1966:273)

Official chiefs were weak; supra-village mechanisms of dispute resolution were lacking; the local administrative authorities had limited local credibility or connections. To govern, Dakar resorted to centralized, militarized controls. Not much was done in the first two decades of independence to alter this status quo. Indeed, Dakar even made some choices that reinforced it.

A net effect of institutional centralization and concentration in Lower Casamance was the distinctive autonomy of government administration vis-à-vis local social forces and interests. Writing in the 1980s, Darbon underscored the "apparent autonomy of administration in Casamance compared to Mouride North." He attributes this to the fact that in Casamance, the administration is free from the control of maraboutic pressure groups,

123

local brokers, and local political personalities. Administration in Lower Casamance is "barely integrated" into local society; there is a "total absence of penetration."[160] He contrasts this to the pattern observed in Upper and Middle Casamance: "Administrative penetration in Upper and Middle Casamance follows the indirect rule model of cooptation of notables sitting atop relatively rigid hierarchical social systems. . . . However, in Basse Casamance the military origins of the form of domination have never been transcended" (Darbon 1988:124).

One consequence of this strategy for the regime was real limits on the efficacy of government: the state was too aloof, too distant, and too lacking in local grounding to communicate with the rural population. The ongoing dilemma for the regime was that it wanted and needed local notables to approve and legitimate its actions, but did not want to deconcentrate the party-state apparatus or devolve authority in ways that might "jeopardize political unity." Snyder (1978:237) reported that near Ossouye in the late 1960s, a village-level youth association was beginning to play the role of informal intermediary between villagers and administrative authorities such as the *sous-préfet*. By the 1980s, Darbon observed precisely this kind of arrangement on a wider and more routinized basis. Darbon stresses the point that in Lower Casamance the regime was pressured to find *interlocateurs valables* – effective intermediaries at the village level – in order to achieve a modicum of administrative effectiveness. There is no indication, however, that such village-level social institutions ever became conduits of state patronage or were invested with administrative prerogative.

Rural Communities were finally created in 1979, and part of the official rationale for this was to give the regime a foothold in the villages. Casamance was one of the last regions of Senegal to see the implementation of this decentralizing reform.[161] The move produced a spatial deconcentration of the state apparatus: Dakar created a new layer of state administration that was closer to the villages than the preexisting *arrondissements*. In contrast to what we saw in the central groundnut basin, however, in Lower Casamance the reform did not entail a devolution of state power to local actors. Instead, in the Diola zone the Rural Communities functioned as direct eminations of central authority – that is, of the region's eight *sous-préfets*. The reform extended the power of the *sous-préfets* deeper into the rural localities, and

---

[160] See Darbon 1988:130, 190, 165.
[161] Casamance was divided into sixty-eight Communautés Rurales, of which twenty-six were in Lower Casamance.

thus drew the state's agents into more intimate involvement with, and even entanglement in, micro-level social and economic relationships.

Rural Councils (Conseils Ruraux, CR) were duly elected to run the new Rural Communities, but the new councilors were not respected local notables, landed elites, or influential brokers. In the 1979 CR elections in Lower Casamance, candidates chosen by the political parties to run on the council lists "were often inexperienced youths with national-level political ambitions, who were incompetent in land tenure issues, not peasants known in the local community for wise and fair decisions in land tenure matters."[162] This trend persisted in the 1980s. The elected councils were weak and unrepresentative. Most fell easily under the direct control of the *sous-préfets*, who wielded uncontested authority ("power without competition or control").[163]

Land allocation was the main responsibility of the new elected bodies. In the Rural Councils of Lower Casamance, however, *sous-préfets* usually handled land questions in more-or-less unilateral fashion, "often according to the *sous-préfets*'s personnel political and economic interests."[164] Darbon (1988:170) wrote that in Lower Casamance, rural council presidents and members "don't say anything [in land matters], leaving control over outcomes to administrative authorities who do not understand local realities." The story of one typical case was recounted by Gerti Hesseling (1994:253):

In a dispute over the loan of a land parcel, the SP, who was present at the meeting of the rural council, summarized the discussion in this fashion:

"I am of the same opinion as all those who have spoken on this point.... H. has worked this parcel for a long time and is thus in conformance with the National Domain Law. I think that you can give the parcel to H."

---

[162] Hesseling 1994:94. She writes that local issues were absent from the local election contests in Lower Casamance in 1979. "Implementation of the land reform [which was to be the most important responsibility of the newly invested rural council] was scarcely mentioned, even though it was expected that this would confront serious obstacles." Of the councilors elected in the 1984 round of elections, Hesseling reported that all were indigenous to the communities they represented, most were active farmers, and as a group, their rate of literacy was higher than that of some of the Rural Councils in the groundnut basin. Literacy rates (in French) of rural councilors in Lower Casamance in 1983 was 44 percent (council members) and 60 percent (council presidents), compared to 20 percent for rural councilors in a CR near Thiès (Hesseling 1994:94, 250, 256 n. 19; Hesseling 1986a:123–5).

[163] Darbon 1988:98.

[164] Hesseling 1986a:128–9.

Sous-préfets also controlled council budgets without local input or inter-ference. These were far smaller than CR budgets in the groundnut basin,[165] and it seems that state agents often designed projects that were guaran-teed – indeed deliberately designed – to elicit no local interest, distributional conflict, or participation. Hesseling (1986a:126, 128–9) describes how CR budgets were used in Lower Casamance: "Throughout Lower Casamance *sous-préfets* used the money to construct *maisons communautaires* to house the Rural Council itself, rather than to follow the preference of the members of the Rural Council to construct dispensaries, maternity clinics, classrooms, or marketplaces." Hesseling continues: "In these cases, the SP had made it understood, in his role as *tuteur* of the CR, that the only thing the council funds would be invested in was the construction of a *maison communautaire*. One single SP was willing to confirm this rendition of the facts, saying that he had received directives from Dakar to this effect."

By contrast, in the groundnut basin, about 75 percent of all CR spend-ing in Thiès and Sine-Saloum was devoted to water projects, health and hygiene, "development actions," youth and sports, and commercial infras-tructure, with less than 1 percent of the total going to the construction of buildings.[166] In Middle Casamance (Sédhiou), the pattern of CR invest-ment is close to that observed in the groundnut basin.[167] Lower Casamance is the exception: here, there was little in Rural Council spending that could offer incentives for community-level organization or politicking, and lit-tle to fuel or promote the ambitions of someone who aspired to political entrepreneurship.

The drawing of CR boundaries contributed to the political hollowness of these institutions. In this part of the country, Communautés Rurales were arbitrary administrative units "artificially imposed on villages."[168] In the Oussouye area, a zone where ancient solidarities are very much in force, rival

---

[165] CR budgets in Lower Casamance in the 1980s totaled about FCFA 600,000 (only about USD $2,000), compared to about USD $20,000 in central Senegal in the 1970s. Rural Communities were on average smaller here (average population about 10,000) than in the groundnut basin. Any given Rural Council president in Lower Casamance did have much less cash to play with than his counterpart in central Senegal.

[166] Ndiaye 1979:556–7. Figures are for the regions of Thiès and Sine-Saloum between 1972 and 1975. Vengroff (1987:287) confirms this argument for CRs in the groundnut basin (Kaolack and Fatick), finding CR spending "generally responding to the spending priorities expressed by rural councilors."

[167] On Sedhiou, see Darbon 1988:211, Table 8.

[168] See Hesseling 1994:256.

or enemy villages were grouped within the same Communautés Rurales, "provoking institutional weakness."[169]

Two government-certified political opposition parties were legalized in 1974, and one of the them – the PDS, Parti Democratique Sénégalais – was immediately able to gather support in Lower Casamance. The return to multipartism and creation of the new Rural Councils were two innovations of the 1970s that did create some institutional openings and opportunities for political actors in Casamance: they offered access to the formal political sphere, political focal points for organizers, and institutional mechanisms for interest aggregation. Taking advantage of these opportunities, Lower Casamance's uncaptured and unstructured electorate once again challenged the regime. In the first local council elections in this region in 1979, the PDS won three of Lower Casamance's twenty-seven Rural Councils. An opposition slate also won the commune of Ziguinchor, a jurisdiction hitherto managed directly by northern administrators appointed by Dakar. This made Ziguinchor the only municipality in Senegal to elect an opposition party slate. The PDS boycotted elections in 1983 and the ruling party reestablished its electoral monopoly. Yet by this time entire districts in Lower Casamance had switched to the PDS.

In the meantime, however, Lower Casamance had fallen into wider political turmoil, punctuated by a series of revolts from 1980 to 1983 and the emergence of a secessionist guerrilla movement. The regional capital of Ziguinchor was occupied by Senegalese army troops in 1982. Military-style governance of Lower Casamance had been taken to its logical extreme.

B. Control over Markets and Productive Resources

Lower Casamance was a groundnut-producing region, just like Senegal's central basin, so the regional variation in state-building choices that we have observed so far cannot be attributed simply to Dakar's lack of economic incentive to get involved. There were some groundnut cooperatives in Lower Casamance, but here these institutions did not function as deconcentrated strongholds of Senegal's ruling party, allocators of factors of production to the peasantry, or institutions that could help manufacture syncretic blends of state and indigenous authority. In Lower Casamance, the cooperatives were too small, weak, and geographically dispersed to produce a

---

[169] Darbon (1988:172) provides examples.

political or economic effect.[170] They had little by way of credit, equipment, or seeds to distribute, and therefore were not insinuated into the processes by which productive resources were allocated in the villages. Membership was not compulsory or enforced, and was therefore very limited. According to Darbon (1988:167–8), even members "are not interested in the functioning of these organizations." It follows that groundnut cooperatives were less politicized than they were in the North: dealings were more transparent, and there was less diversion of funds and better debt repayment.[171]

Why were cooperatives in Lower Casamance poor, politically insulated, and detached from UPS machine politics? In the 1970s and 1980s, leading observers said that cooperatives were marginal in the political economy of Lower Casamance because the region was less commercialized than the groundnut-producing areas to the North, and because the local population was disinterested in cooperatives (Darbon 1988; van chi Bonnardel 1978).

This state of affairs, however, may partly be an *effect* of the regime's institutional choices, rather than the cause. In localities of Lower Casamance, state builders did their best to create a landscape devoid of resource-purveying institutions that could be captured by local political entrepreneurs whom Dakar might not be able to master. Cooperatives would surely have been just such a source of political risk; it is plausible that Dakar chose to ensure that in this region, these institutions would be of little political value. Perhaps the best evidence in support of such an interpretation is the fact that in the 1960s, when the Senghor regime first confronted the matter, Lower Casamance populations demonstrated considerable interest in groundnuts and in state-sponsored cooperatives.

Although Casamance lies outside the groundnut basin, the presence of the groundnut is ubiquitous. It is the region's main export crop and the main source of cash for farming families, generating about 30 to 40 percent of rural incomes in this region in the 1970s.[172] As we have seen, by the 1940s and 1950s groundnut production was central to the economy of the zones all around Ziguinchor and Bignona (indeed, the entire area north of the Casamance River). By the 1950s and 1960s, even most farming households

---

[170] The entire network was hampered by the great dispersion and small size of the buying stations. Most stations operated below the profitability threshold of four hundred tons per year (van chi Bonnardel 1978:571). See also Diaw and Diouf 1992:21.

[171] See Darbon 1988:106–9.

[172] Hamer 1980:195. Groundnuts generated about 60 percent of rural income in the groundnut basin in the 1970s.

around Ossouye, south of the river, produced groundnuts for cash and to pay taxes. Lower Casamance's total groundnut production for the 1959–60 harvest appears to have been about 40,000 tons.[173] This amount increased significantly in the next few years, a fact that Regine van chi Bonnardel (1978:446) attributed to "the existence of reliable commercial outlets provided by the OCA [the national marketing board]."

By 1970 Casamance as a whole was producing about 12 percent of national output. Perhaps as much as half of that came from Lower Casamance.[174] At the end of the first decade of independence, 32 percent of all cultivated land in Casamance was planted in groundnuts, compared to an average for all Senegalese groundnut-producing regions of 46 percent.[175] Yields per acre in Casamance were slightly better than the national average. Compared to the arid and declining central basin, this was a pretty good place to grow groundnuts.

There was a rapid increase in the number of cooperatives in Casamance between 1960 and 1965 (from 74 to 302), as in other export-producing regions of Senegal. Local politicians throughout Casamance had officially registered 330 "pre-cooperatives."[176] In those days, Senegalese law provided for the spontaneous, grassroots creation of pre-cooperatives called Associations d'Intérêt Rural (AIRs), which entitled members to access to credit services provided by the central government. After a few years of operation, AIRs could graduate to "official cooperative" status. In the Diola zone, local leaders (and aspiring local leaders) seized this opportunity.

Girard wrote in 1963 that "the Diola experience with mutual help associations explains how they adapted very quickly to the cooperative system Senegal has implanted since Independence.... Without any sort of rupture, communal Diola society naturally possesses the spirit of solidarity that is the base of the entire cooperative system." State-sponsored cooperatives, he wrote, conformed easily to "juridical models" indigenous to Diola society (1963:161, 165). Villages in this zone used official cooperatives as an institutional framework for organizing a range of collective economic

---

[173] See Pélissier 1966:34–5.

[174] Casamance produced 69,000 tons of a total of 580,000 tons (van chi Bonnardel 1978: 134–5). Lower Casamance's share is based on the 1960 data provided by Pélissier.

[175] van chi Bonnardel 1978:134–5. Profitability in Casamance was, however, uneven. Hamer (1981:195) wrote that "it is good in the Mandinguized northeastern subregion, but south of the Casamance River, gains are minimal." Keep in mind that this was also true of much of the groundnut basin, especially after 1968.

[176] van chi Bonnardel 1978:627–8 n. 123; see also Schumacher 1975:150.

projects that went far beyond what was envisioned by the government of Senegal:

In Tandième [Bignona department], seven teachers took the initiative to form a cooperative with two hundred members. In 1961, the adherents voluntarily decided to market their palm nuts cooperatively, thereby extending cooperative business beyond the limit of activities controlled by the OCA [Office de Commercialization Agricole]. . . . Most cooperatives in Bignona Cercle have cooperative fields, palm nut groves, and fruit trees. Labor is provided by traditional work associations. (Girard 1963:163–4)

The cooperative movement had a fast take-off in Casamance, propelled at least partly from below. Like opposition party victories in Rural Council elections in Lower Casamance in 1979 and thereafter, the mushrooming of pre-cooperatives in the 1960s showed that when Dakar provided a few institutional resources from above, communities seized the opportunity to organize for engagement with the state and to act collectively in the formal political sphere. In these circumstances, Dakar could not easily control agenda setting. This, I suggest, was precisely the kind of thing that made institution building in Lower Casamance (spatial deconcentration, and even more so authority devolution) risky for central rulers.

How did the locally powered cooperative movement in Lower Casamance degenerate into what Darbon described in the 1980s as a "lack of dynamism" and the population's general "disinterest in cooperatives"? Institutional choices made by central rulers played a role. In 1967 Dakar dissolved all the 330 AIRs in Casamance on the grounds that they were unviable.[177]

We need to contrast this with the regime's strategies in the groundnut basin, where the Dakar displayed no such concerns about the economic viability of cooperatives or pre-cooperatives. During the same time period, Schumacher found a "general lack of concern" on the part of state officials about the economic viability of groundnut basin AIRs, or even about the distinction between pre-cooperatives and full-fledged cooperatives.[178] In central Senegal, plans for clean-up of the AIRs and consolidation of the cooperative network were discussed in 1966, but these "remained shelved." In Lower Casamance, by contrast, all AIRs were summarily wiped off the institutional map. It is hard to explain this decision without reference to the regime's worries about political organizing in this region.

[177] See van chi Bonnardel 1978:627–8, 123.
[178] Schumacher 1975:152–3, 175, 260 n. 8.

Economic factors played a role in Dakar's calculations. France withdrew its buying subsidy for Senegalese groundnuts in 1967. Senegal's government passed this loss on to peasants, who were hit with a 20 percent fall in producer prices. Farmers throughout Senegal responded by selling their groundnuts illegally in the Gambia, where they could evade Senegalese taxes and thus get a better price for their crop. Retreat into the parallel market was fastest and most complete in Lower Casamance, however, given the proximity of the Gambia and the existence of already established commercial networks linking Lower Casamance to the former British colony. In Lower Casamance, Dakar obviously concluded that the political costs of coercive efforts to crack down on the parallel groundnut trade were too high. Parallel markets developed as a major phenomenon in the groundnut basin as well, especially as the 1970s wore on. There too, the regime chose the politically easy option of turning a blind eye to the contraband trade, and thus forewent the tax revenues that coercive enforcement of its groundnut-buying monopoly might have yielded (Boone 1992). One difference between the two regions was that in central Senegal the rural cooperatives were too useful to the center to simply dismantle, whereas in Lower Casamance a grassroots cooperative network was more likely to be a political liability – a political resource possibly available to untrusted local activists and entrepreneurs – than a political asset to state builders in Dakar.

The state-sponsored cooperative network had withered away almost completely in Lower Casamance by the early 1970s. Francis Snyder (1978:239) found that in 1974 in Gasumay, a village of 350 persons located near Ossouye, only 9 peasants sold peanuts to the local groundnut cooperative.

In this politically risky zone, Dakar opted to leave commercialization of the export crop to the market. Price competition, and market competition among traders and transporters, defined the terms of market access and allocated values. These arrangements worked to depoliticize peasants' role as export-crop producers and atomize (rather than collectivize) farmers' relationship to groundnut buyers and the commercial circuit. The political effect was consistent with the Senghor's general state-building strategy in Lower Casamance, which was to avoid catalysts to political organization and activity.

It was the fight for control over *land* that proved to be Dakar's undoing in Lower Casamance. Before 1979 Dakar had not intervened in rural land-tenure relations in this region. Land prerogatives were confirmed by elders and lineage heads who enjoyed respect (but diminishing authority)

131

in the villages. Dakar ignored these leaders completely during the first two decades of independence, choosing instead to intervene minimally in local social and economic processes and to govern the villages through the center's own direct agents – *sous-préfets* and appointed chiefs who wielded little indigenous power or legitimacy. In Lower Casamance, where indigenous authority was dispersed and fragmented, Dakar chose a strategy of "administrative occupation."

Yet with the creation of Rural Councils in 1979, Senghor's last year as Senegal's president, the regime launched a riskier state-building initiative in this region. With this spatial deconcentration of the state apparatus, the scope of authority of *sous-préfets* was extended right into the heart of village affairs, and land prerogatives hitherto sanctioned by elders and lineage heads were appropriated by the state. This is the opposite of what we saw in the groundnut basin, where Rural Councils were vehicles for *devolving* the state's National Domain rights to neotraditional elites.

Counterfactual Choices. The theory outlined in Chapter 2 does not predict the risky deconcentration of the state apparatus that happened in Lower Casamance after 1979. Creation of Rural Communities and Councils in Lower Casamance can be seen as an instance of off-the-path behavior: the theory of institutional choice proposed here identifies such a move as fraught with political risk and thus likely to produce a bad outcome for rulers at the center. Why did Dakar undertake such a significant spatial deconcentration of state institutions in 1979? How did things work out?

We argued above that in the first decades of independence, "development" in Lower Casamance was an opportunity foregone by the regime in Dakar because of the high political risks it entailed. The costs of this strategy mounted over time, however. It may be possible to explain Dakar's risky state-building moves in Lower Casamance in terms of this changing balance.

Long droughts in the 1970s and the decay of the groundnut economy in central Senegal pressured the regime to look for new arable land to offer Muslim marabouts and Dakar investors, and new ways to earn foreign exchange. Near the end of the 1970s Senegal's leaders – along with their international financial backers (France, the European Union, and the World Bank) – began to search for more aggressive ways to take advantage of Casamance's underexploited agricultural potential (as well as ways to promote commercial agriculture in Senegal's northernmost periphery,

the long-ignored Senegal River Valley). It is clear that these pressures conspired to pressure Dakar to depart from the administrative and economic
strategies adopted in the Casamance in the 1960s and 1970s: virtually all
explanations of the post-1979 "land rush" in Lower Casamance focus on
pressure on Dakar to open a new land frontier and to capture new forms of
foreign and domestic investment.

The argument about institutional choice advanced here does not predict
that rulers will adopt politically risky economic development strategies.
Regimes are supposed to prefer political gain (or to avert political risk) over
economic gain.[179] It is possible, however, to envision a refinement that
theorizes conditions under which politically risky economic strategies will
be chosen. This could happen, for example, when the center is forced to
weigh different political risks against each other, as would have happened
when Senegal's rulers had to confront the dwindling of alternative sources
of patronage and the need to open a new frontier to satisfy the land hunger
of their most important allies. It is possible to see how the problem could be
conceptualized in dynamic terms, and in terms of interregional cost-benefit
calculations.

Central authorities anticipated that their move to exploit Lower
Casamance more aggressively, including the move to assert more direct
control over land tenure, would confront serious obstacles and even local
resistance. This is often cited as a factor in explaining the delay in enacting
the 1964 National Domain Law in this region. Once the Rural Councils
were created in Lower Casamance, however, there was little evidence of
caution or risk-averse behavior. Outsiders used the newly created Rural
Councils, which usually operated under the direct control of *sous-préfets*, as
mechanisms to appropriate land.[180]

Around Ziguinchor and Cap Skirring, the Rural Councils were instruments by which Casamançais from other localities, functionaries native
to other regions of Senegal, marabouts from the groundnut basin and
their peasant followers, Dakarois, and even French firms acquired land for

---

[179] The preference ranking would be, from best to worst, political gain and economic gain
(or economic gain without political risk); political gain only, or even at an economic cost;
economic gain with significant political risk.
[180] Hesseling writes that in isolated villages, the reforms had little effect except to encourage
some villages to come up with counter strategies to ensure that they would not lose land.
Villages found ways to create the impression that land was cultivated regularly when in
fact it was not, or to shorten the period of land loans to only one year (1994:251, 254).
Galvan (1996) observed the same effects in the groundnut basin.

groundnut production, orchards, touristic encampments, or fishing rights. These same actors lined up to get a piece of the action in new irrigation and land reclamation projects, many of them financed in part by international lenders such as the World Bank. In the commune of Ziquinchor, "by 1982 there were over 2,000 cases of land parcels expropriated and attributed to non-autochthons."[181] These land expropriations clearly ran counter to the spirit of Senegal's 1964 land law, which obliged Rural Councils to allocate land to residents of the community, who were supposed to develop the parcel so obtained themselves.[182] Although there were cases of such violations all over Senegal, nowhere were they as common and extensive as in Lower Casamance, where locals experienced what they perceived as an invasion and systematic land expropriation by *nordistes*. Linda Beck writes that "initiation of decentralization [i.e., the creation of Rural Communities and Rural Councils] threatened to jeopardize the land tenure of the Casamance population. . . . [L]ocal politicians were more interested in profiting from land speculation than protecting the interests of their supposed constituents."[183] Kickbacks to *sous-préfets* and Rural Council members for favorable land decisions were common.

Application of Senegal's land law in Lower Casamance from 1979 onward met with "ferocious opposition" in the Diola and Balant zones:

These populations did not hesitate to destroy infrastructure under construction, and to use all means at their disposal to obstruct the establishment of new public facilities (such as new housing projects and the road-transport station [*gare routière*] in Ziguinchor). Extended household heads in the region of Baïla [near Bignona] refused to submit to the law . . . and are ready to oppose, by resorting to force or sorcery, its application. (Darbon 1988:169)

In the commune of Ziguinchor, land conflicts were so intense that the government of Senegal created a novel institution – a Council of Notables – to participate in land-use decisions.[184] In the rural areas, however, administrative authorities made few such concessions.

---

[181] Beck 1996a:260. See also Hesseling 1994:252–3.
[182] Hesseling 1994:251–2. Meanwhile, Hesseling points out that the "land invasion" of Lower Casamance predated 1979. In the 1960s Wolof and Lebou fishing communities immigrated to Casamance's coastal region, and Mouride marabouts began coming down with their followers to establish groundnut estates. This met with Diola resistance and "revolt" against the demands and impositions of these foreigners.
[183] Beck 1996a:256–9. See also Hesseling 1994:255–7.
[184] See Hesseling 1986b.

It is certain that land conflicts were a root cause and catalyst of the violence that broke out in Casamance in 1981 and persists to this day. Linda Beck (1996a:227) and others directly attribute the emergence of a guerrilla secessionist movement in Lower Casamance in 1982 to the application of Senegal's administrative and land reforms in 1979. The regime's worst fears about its inability to control Lower Casamance were realized. It responded with an outright military occupation of the zone.

These sad events led the regime, in 1983, to reverse its 1960 decision to incorporate all of Casamance into a single administrative region. In a move that paralleled the administrative deconcentrations that accompanied military pacification in the 1910s and 1920s, the Diola zone was hived off from the rest of Casamance in 1983, making for two administrative regions – Ziguinchor and Kolda – in order to "get a better hold on *pays Diola*" and "contain the rebellion in lower Casamance."[185]

Other authors who have taken Lower Casamance on its own terms rather than as a footnote in the larger story of modern Senegal – especially Pélissier (1966), Darbon (1988), and Beck (1996a) – have observed that state-society linkages in Lower Casamance differ from those established in the central groundnut basin. They have attributed the difference to social structure in Lower Casamance: individualism of social mores, absence of village-level and supra-village political hierarchy, and absence of a class of neotraditional notables who can broker relationships between this regional constituency and the state. The analysis here aims to generalize this insight, draw out its implications for rural political capacity, and specify its impact on state building and institutional choice in both the political and economic domains. Absence of rural social hierarchy among the Diola was not only an inconvenience for Dakar, as Darbon and Beck insist, or a social fact that increased the cost of governing this territory, as Hechter (2000) would argue. It was also a source of political risk: rural communities were available for mobilization by upstart political entrepreneurs who were independent of the center's control, and once mobilized they could be particularly threatening because they were difficult to co-opt or otherwise contain.

Here I argue that Dakar responded to these risks with a particular state-building strategy. The regime chose to construct a spatially concentrated party-state apparatus that remained "suspended above" rural localities, and

[185] Darbon 1988:70; Beck 1996a:227.

in which power was centralized in the hands of direct agents of Dakar. The regime chose to build institutions in Lower Casamance that capitalized on the existing political weaknesses of Diola society, chief of which was the lack of preexisting political infrastructure. Dakar remained aloof and withheld the kinds of political resources (institutions) and spending initiatives that could stimulate local political activity. Houphouet-Boigny was confronted with a similar rural challenge in southern Côte d'Ivoire and made the same institutional choices.

In Lower Casamance, the economic cost of this was "development fore-gone" in a region that was rich in agricultural potential and that had a relatively well-educated population. Like Houphouet in southern Côte d'Ivoire, Senghor did not dare to build economic institutions – such as a deconcentrated cooperative network or departmental- or municipal-level agencies with prerogatives to design or implement spending projects – that could be captured by, and thus politically empower, untrusted local actors. In these regions lacking in indigenous social hierarchy, both regimes chose to let market forces do the work of "rural development." It so happened that this strategy produced a larger economic payoff in southern Côte d'Ivoire than in Lower Casamance.

In Lower Casamance, administrative occupation and the center's attempt to "stifle local political life" resulted in an exclusionary form of statist authoritarianism.[186] Yet for Dakar, political hegemony remained illusive. Although the regime in Dakar prevented the consolidation of a political party that could challenge the center via formal-legal means, it did not stop local political resentment from coalescing in other forms. State-society relations eventually degenerated into violent state repression of a grassroots guerrilla movement that first demanded regional autonomy and then demanded independence. By constructing an institutional edifice for "administrative occupation," Dakar rulers may have protected themselves against political risk in the early-postcolonial years, but they forfeited any chance of building institutions that could harness, organize, co-opt, or channel political life in this region. With the outbreak of armed struggle in the 1980s, Dakar had few political tools, almost no *interlocateurs*, and little on-the-ground political infrastructure to use in search of a negotiated and enforceable solution. When confronted with outbreaks of *indigène*-stranger

---

[186] This is how Stryker (1971a) described the effect of provincial administration on local political life in southern Côte d'Ivoire.

136

violence in southern Côte d'Ivoire in the 1990s, the regime in Abidjan found itself similarly bereft of mediating institutions.

There is an outstanding political puzzle in the Lower Casamance case: How did a "politically unorganized rural society" give rise to a sustained guerrilla movement?

We began with the hypothesis that absence of hierarchy in rural society implied a low level of political capacity. Diola society conforms partly, but not completely, with this characterization. Absence of social hierarchy did imply an absence of rural strongmen who could negotiate powersharing deals or win institutionalized access to the formal political sphere. Yet egalitarianism in Diola society coexists with capacities for collective action. As noted above, these are manifest in the intensity of associational life, including self-help associations, spirit shrines, agricultural work associations, and village-level militias. The horizontal solidarities that structured these village-level forms of association surely help explain the cooperation that sustains the guerrilla movement (as well as the movement's politically fragmented character, which makes coming to a negotiated settlement with Dakar more difficult). In a study of politics among the Balanta, on just the other side of the Senegal–Guinée Bissau border, Joshua Forrest (1998, 2002) makes explicit connections between village-level horizontal solidarities and local capacity for guerrilla mobilization. Political capacity can thus emerge at different scales of social organization and from horizontal as well as vertical solidarities. More thinking on this point could lead to a more complete (more complex) theory of political capacity within communities and nations, and a better understanding of collective action and state building in Africa, where many societies have long histories of developing and adapting "stateless" forms of political organization.

Conclusion

Colonial Senegal is often referred to as a model of French direct rule, and contemporary Senegal is often said never to have overcome the debilitating legacies of overcentralization and top-down control. From the rural localities, however, things can look quite different. And as Peter Geschiere (1986) has emphasized, there are regional variations in modes of state penetration of rural society in Africa. The political topography varies: what you see can depend on where you are standing.

This chapter has shown that Dakar's institutional choices, including the building of economic institutions, varied across regions within Senegal, and that these choices were shaped by political opportunities and threats that the regime perceived in the rural areas. There have been enduring consequences for the modern state. Politically, the regime cast its lot with a conservative social stratum in the Wolof groundnut basin, the maraboutic patrons and leaders of this groundnut-producing peasantry. This choice gave Senegal its distinctive combination of overall political stability and rural economic decline. Dakar invested heavily in agricultural inputs and institution building in a region that was politically strategic, but that also happened to be marked by falling agricultural productivity, extensive soil erosion, and producers' gradual turn away from export-crop production. Limits to the sustainability of groundnut production in central Senegal had been clear to all since the early 1950s, if not before.

The regime eschewed institution building, and thus "rural development," in Lower Casamance, a more generously endowed but politically risky zone. The strategy of administrative occupation also meant that when confronted with an insurgency in this zone, Dakar did not have political tools or mechanisms to forge a negotiated solution.

In *Containing Nationalism*, Michael Hechter (2000) presents direct and indirect rule as two alternative modes of state building. They are two strategies for incorporating peripheral "local states" and nations into larger territorial units controlled from the center. In his model, the technologies of control available to the center play an important role in determining whether rulers will choose direct or indirect rule. Rulers at the center tend to chose indirect rule for remote provinces where distance makes governing directly costly and inefficient, and direct rule where and when technologies of control exist to make it cost effective to do so. As modernization shrinks space and increases the power-projection capacities of the center, rulers tend to adopt more and more direct forms of rule. This can provoke nationalist backlash. Indirect rule, therefore, may be the less ambitious but more politically sustainable form of government for multinational states. The two cases from Senegal that are presented in this chapter offer some leverage on Hechter's arguments.

Hechter's insight that large, hierarchical, and solidary groups (nations) can be governed more or less effectively, and at low cost, through indirect rule (p. 41) resonates with the story of political incorporation of the groundnut basin into the Senegalese state. The reverse argument, that it is less efficient (more costly) to govern many small groups, also seems to find support, this time in the case of Lower Casamance. And the intensification of direct rule in Lower Casamance, as what had been a minimalist administrative occupation in the 1960s became more interventionist and extractive in the 1980s, did indeed provoke a subnationalist backlash, as Hechter's theory predicts. Yet the Senegal cases also shows where Hechter's model is underdeveloped, and where any explanation of institutional choice that rests on technological determinism or functionalist logic comes up short. In Senegal, distance from the center and technological constraints do not explain the variation we see in the center's modes of governing the periphery. The groundnut basin, which is near Dakar, was governed indirectly, and remote Lower Casamance was governed directly. This is the opposite of what we would expect if governing strategy were determined by distance and the technical capacities of the center.

The more general form of this problem arises in any depiction of modes of national integration, or institutional choices in general, as technically constrained but *politically unconstrained* choices of the center. This kind of voluntarism would be implied in the argument that rulers who succumb to the temptations of power and modernity will opt for direct rule and thereby stoke subnationalist resistance, while modern rulers who are wiser and less power hungry will opt to defuse subnationalisms by choosing indirect rule. In the African cases studied here, it is the *political* determinants of institutional choice that stand out, and that produce a plausible, consistent, and non-voluntaristic explanation of observed variation in patterns of institutional choice. The cases here show rulers sometimes find indirect rule to be a wise and cost-effective choice, but this is only true when and where they know that the region or "local state" has agreed to subordinate itself to the center. This was the case in the central groundnut basin of Senegal, but it was not the case in Lower Casamance, which was never a reliable ally of central rulers. Indirect rule is an expedient mode of incorporation only in the presence of a logically prior agreement between central rulers and the local state about constitutional rules that cede preeminence to the center. But getting there is precisely the problem, or the state-building challenge. In the case of Senegal's groundnut basin (or the American South after the Civil War), indirect rule became possible only after the decisive military defeat of the local state.

The origins of the state contract and the forces that shape the modes of "national integration" must be sought not only in the interests and capabilities of the center, but also in power balances between center and region, and in the interests of regions that may well have incentives to go-it-alone (or take over the center). To propose indirect rule as a solution to the problem of rebellious subnationalism in Lower Casamance today is a constructive move, but it raises many of the same stakes and dilemmas that led Senegal's ruling coalition to eschew this governing strategy in Lower Casamance in the first place. As is true for many of the other subnationalist movements that have surfaced around the world in the last two decades, regional leaders in Casamance may not be willing to accept the preeminence of the center, they may not be able to credibly commit to the constitutional contract, and/or they may demand a price for it that the center will not or cannot pay. Inherent in the political topography of the local state and the region itself are factors that shape the structure and process of national integration.

4

Taxing Rich Peasants: Regime Ideology as Strategy

Southern Côte d'Ivoire and southwestern Ghana lie in a tropical rainforest zone, separated only by a boundary drawn by Europeans in the nineteenth century. Major rivers cross these regions on their way to the Atlantic – the Comoé, the Banadama, the Sassandra, and the Volta. In Côte d'Ivoire, an extensive lagoon system shelters much of the coast from the sea. The terrain is mostly flat, except in the far-western parts of Côte d'Ivoire that border Guinée, and the air is humid. In Ghana, a long coastline of white beaches is dotted with decaying castles and forts that remain from the trans-Atlantic slave trade. Coastal lowlands give way to the gentle slopes and hills of the Asante uplands, which mark the northern limit of the forest zone in these parts. Since about the 1940s and 1950s, farmers in this broad, forested swath of West Africa have been the world's leading producers of cocoa. Southern Côte d'Ivoire is also one of the largest producers of coffee.

Postcolonial rulers in these two regions faced the challenge of governing and taxing export-producing peasantries that have been among the most prosperous in modern Africa.[1] This chapter explains why they chose such different strategies to do so. At the household level, the dynamics of export-crop production in the two regions is similar. And in both zones, the cash crop economy emerged from grassroots dynamics of innovation that involved little direct state intervention. What differed were the larger social, political, and economic "superstructures" of peasant export-crop production in the two regions. The postcolonial governments of Houphouet-Boigny in Côte d'Ivoire and Kwame Nkrumah in Ghana confronted very different rural political challenges in their quests to tax and govern the producers.

---

[1] The phrase "rich peasants" comes from Gastellu 1989.

To govern Asante, the region of southwestern Ghana that concerns us here, Nkrumah pursued as clear a strategy of usurpation as we have in sub-Saharan Africa. It was a statist, aggressively interventionist approach that aimed at asserting direct state control over rural markets, displacing a local elite, redefining micro-level relations of production and authority, and incorporating peasants directly into the ruling party's political machine. In southern Côte d'Ivoire, Houphouet chose a strategy of administrative occupation in pure form. The regime *avoided* politics and state spending in the rural areas, discouraged the formation of political organizations at the local level, and left the commodity-buying circuit in private hands. No political machine mobilized rural votes into the service of the ruling party.

Much has been made of the ideological determinants of these differences. Nkrumah was a socialist with a "radical" and statist bent: he was suspicious of capitalism and the market, as well as of traditionalism and the chiefs, and believed in the promise of state-led reengineering of African society. Houphouet was Nkrumah's ideological alter ego and nemesis: the Ivoirian regime was moderate, "liberal," and pro-capitalist, and therefore adopted a more hands-off strategy in governing the rural areas of the South. Legend has it that in 1956 Houphouet dared Nkrumah to a wager over which strategy would pay off best for postcolonial Africa.[2]

The present analysis shows that the ideology explanation, by itself, is too idiosyncratic and voluntarist: it reveals little about the more deeply rooted political constraints that shaped institutional choice in these two settings, and it is not consistent enough with the facts of the cases at hand. In the Ghanaian case, the decisive institutional choices predated the ideological ones: all the elements of Nkrumah's statist, interventionist approach to governing and taxing the cocoa belt were established before his "turn to socialism" ("turn against capitalism") in 1961. As we shall see, major strategies of the Convention People's Party (CPP) that centralized control over state power while extending the state's presence in the localities were implemented in the 1950s. Meanwhile, in both countries, neither regime was particularly faithful to its formal ideological commitments

---

[2] See for example Woronoff's *West African Wager* (1972). Even Mamdani (1996) attributes the statism of Nkrumah to a basically ideological impulse. Meanwhile, the contrast between French and British administrative ideology does not explain the difference; this contrast would lead us to anticipate the opposite outcome (i.e., a more "statist" solution in Côte d'Ivoire and a more hands-off, pro-business solution that would favor the old elite of "indirect rule" in Ghana).

when it came to institutional choice in other, less challenging regions. We see this contrast here in a side glance at the Dagomba region of northern Ghana, where Nkrumah was far more ready to build institutions that shared power with indigenous aristocrats. A similar contrast emerges in the Korhogo region of northern Côte d'Ivoire, which is a focus of Chapter 5. In Korhogo, the Houphouet regime built powersharing institutions that were more statist, more economically interventionist, and more imbricated in local-level authority relations than the "liberal" arrangements that developed in the South. State building in Korhogo followed a strategy analogous to that observed in Senegal's Wolof groundnut basin. The general point is not to completely discard the ideology variable; rather, it is to show that the ideologies themselves were forged in response to social struggles and challenges that were unfolding in these West African states. There was a strong element of pragmatism in the ideologies, and when the two conflicted, pragmatism tended to trump ideology in predictable ways.

Here we compare the politics of institution building in the forest zones of Ghana and Côte d'Ivoire. The analysis shows that Nkrumah's radicalism in reorganizing the cocoa economy, like Houphouet's liberalism in adopting a strategy of minimal state intervention in the cocoa-coffee belt, was a strategic response to the political risks and dangers rulers faced in taxing farmers. Both leaders strategized to subordinate and control the export-crop producers who would generate a tax base to sustain the postcolonial state. What differed was the capacity of wealthy producers in the two regions to demand political inclusion as a counterpart to this arrangement, or even to resist state extractions outright. In southern Ghana, central rulers confronted a politically powerful and economically autonomous rural elite that not only resisted state appropriation of cocoa surpluses, but also contested the regime's claims to state power. Nkrumah centralized authority while deepening state regulation of daily life in the localities because he sought to neutralize the power of these rural elites. Houphouet faced no such challenge. On the contrary, Houphouet (like Senghor in dealing with Lower Casamance) wanted to ensure that his regime did not bequeath to a decentralized and relatively egalitarian rural society the very political (institutional) resources that farmers would need to organize themselves politically to advance claims and complaints on the center. Under Houphouet, authority was centralized, and state institutions remained "suspended above" rural society.

In the 1950s and 1960s Ghana and Côte d'Ivoire were widely regarded as among the continent's most promising and prosperous states. Time, however, has not been so generous. The downfall of Nkrumah came in 1966. This was followed in the 1970s by the virtual collapse of the cocoa sector in Ghana, an outcome due in part to institutional strategies that were pursued under Nkrumah (and not reversed by his successors), and to the enduring stand-off between large cocoa growers and the state. The Ivoirian economy experienced booms and busts, but by the late 1980s and early 1990s both the economy and the political order built over the preceding four decades were in a clear state of decline. This culminated in the implosion of the party-state after 1999. Even in these prosperous zones, it is clear that there were limits to the staying power of institutional arrangements built during the first decades of independence in terms of their capacity to generate legitimacy for postcolonial rulers, contribution to "national integration," and impact on possibilities for enhancing rural production and productivity. Given the stakes, it is important to know why the nature of the links between state and countryside differed across these cases and from those observed in, for example, central Senegal, and to know more about the societal forces that facilitated or resisted the congealing of state power.

Part One: Usurping "Rightful Rulers": Asante in Ghana

"We are the rightful rulers," said one [Gold Coast chief], stating a fact of nature as he saw it.

Apter 1968:18

In trying to secure deference to the regime and acquiescence to taxation in Ghana's main export-producing zone, the Nkrumah government could not afford to place its bets on a skeleton crew of prefects and *sous-préfets* in the localities. Nkrumah found himself in confrontation with provincial rivals whose political and economic authority was grounded in rural social structure and nourished by the flourishing cocoa economy of the South. Powerful chiefs of Asante were positioned as competitors to the nationalists: they argued that they were sovereign powers, and therefore both withheld their full subordination to the central state and resisted taxation that would transfer their wealth to the center.[3] Faced with these circumstances, Nkrumah undertook to create new authority structures – *parallel* authority structures – that would compete against and, he hoped, eventually

---

[3] See Rathbone 2000:32 *inter alia*.

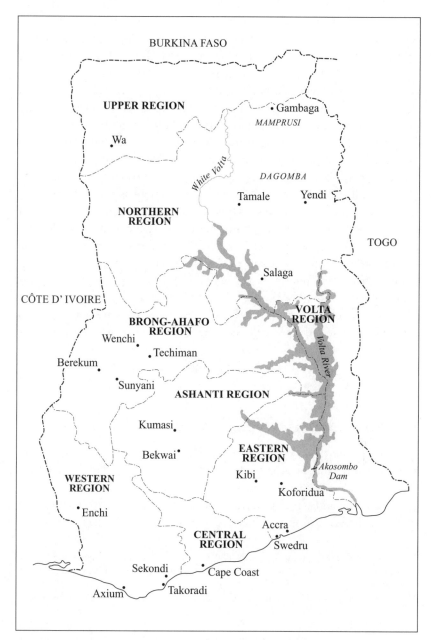

Map 4.1. Ghana

undermine the institutions and networks controlled by the planter-chiefs. This required an activist strategy of institution building that was aimed at usurping the power of the established rural elite and micromanaging local social and political process in their stead. It was truly the antithesis of Houphouet's choice of a strategy of administrative occupation to govern the localities of the Ivoirian south, and also stands in stark contrast with the powersharing of the Senghor regime in the Wolof groundnut basin.

Some have portrayed these institutional choices as the product of an anti-chief ideology on Nkrumah's part. His regime has been portrayed as bent on "the neutralization of traditional authority"; Rouveroy van Nieuwall (1987:17–18) wrote that the Nkrumah government issued "an unremitting stream of legal measures pointed unmistakably at the elimination of chiefly power." As we shall see, however, this overgeneralizes from the case of Asante. The topography of Nkrumah's radicalism was uneven, as side glances at the counterfactual case of Dagomba in northern Ghana will show. Where chiefs were politically influential in the rural areas and economically dependent upon the central state, and therefore willing to collaborate, Nkrumah built rural institutions that harnessed chiefly power and used it to extend the reach of the postcolonial state. In those circumstances, he made choices that resembled those of his more conservative Francophone counterparts – Senghor in the Wolof groundnut basin and the Senegal River Valley, and Houphouet in northern Côte d'Ivoire.

I. A Planter Elite Poised to Contest the Hegemony of the State

To conquer the territory that became Ghana,[4] the British signed protectorate treaties with chiefs and kings in the coastal zone and in the northern savannah. In the center, the British fought the armies of one of West Africa's most powerful and centralized states, Asante (Ashanti),[5] in three wars that ended with Asante's final military defeat in 1901. The well-elaborated

---

[4] In March 1957 the British colony of Gold Coast changed its name to Ghana and became formally independent. For simplicity's sake I will refer to the colony as "Ghana," even though this is anachronistic.

[5] "Asante" is the preferred term for the historical confederacy that controlled much or most of present-day Ghana in the two centuries that preceded colonial conquest, and for its core subjects. In the colonial period the British delimited a formal administrative region called "Ashanti," and this designation was retained by the postcolonial state. I use the spelling Asante except when referring specifically to the colonial or postcolonial administrative region, or when quoting sources that use Ashanti. See Berry 2001:xxxiii. I have used Asante whenever it was possible to do so in order to enhance readability.

political/administrative hierarchies of Asante and the neighboring Akan states provided perfect infrastructure for British-style indirect rule.

The Asante Confederacy was a federal grouping of Asante states under the control of a king (*asantehene*). It was, as Apter (1972:23) described it, "an elaborate military hierarchy with powerful armies, a bureaucracy, and a taste for imperialism which brought them into immediate conflict with the British, often to the latter's temporary demise. The Confederacy was a re-markable [political] achievement." Power was exercised by the paramount ruler and his counselors "through a fine spun web of subordinate authorities held together by kinship and bonds of fealty between the paramount chief, divisional (or 'wing') chiefs, and village heads."[6] As a military and com-mercial force, Asante before the mid-1800s had a sphere of influence that reached far beyond the forest zone. The savannah kingdom of Dagomba in present-day northern Ghana, for example, paid annual tribute to Asante in the form of court "hostages" and slaves. In regions just beyond Asante's reach, histories of population movement and state building have much to do with defensive maneuvers and retreats from its extractions and imperial thrusts. This is the story for much of what is now Côte d'Ivoire west of the Comoé River, including the Agni areas (including Aboisso and Abengourou) that we examine in Part II of this chapter. Once the British broke the in-dependence of the Asante and neighboring Akan kingdoms, the colonizers found it useful to govern through the existing political units and adminis-trative hierarchies.

In 1924 the Asante king, Asantehene Prempeh II, returned from exile. Nine years later the British recognized an Asante Confederacy that they themselves had reintegrated and strengthened. These were dramatic moves in a colonial strategy of trying to shore up the indigenous polities and to use them to govern the cocoa-producing peasantry of southern Ghana. In the 1930s Britain constructed Native Authorities that recognized precolonial political jurisdictions (including states), centralized power in paramount chieftaincies, cemented chains of command between chiefs and their polit-ical subordinates, made Native Tribunals compulsory courts of first instance (and strengthened their powers over time), and gave Native Authorities extensive powers of local taxation. Meanwhile the colonial authorities en-shrined in law chiefly claims over land and chiefs' right to demand land

---

[6] Austin 1964:18. As Mikell (1989a:47) recounts, Asante was weakened and in much disarray at the end of the 1800s; divisional chiefs' autonomy from Kumasi was high and some established separate treaties with the British.

tribute from subjects.[7] As we shall see, the chiefs were major cocoa producers and traders in their own right. One net effect of the legal and institutional innovations of the 1930s was to enhance chiefs' ability to appropriate agricultural wealth not only indirectly in the form of political tribute, but also directly in the form of rent, interest, and profit from their cocoa-growing subjects, the peasants.[8]

Chiefs also had a place in the political superstructure of the colony. From the 1920s they sat in colonial legislative councils and provincial councils in each of the colony's three main administrative regions: Ashanti (the region comprising the Asante Confederacy), the territory first claimed by the British and known as "The Colony" (the strip along the Atlantic coast), and the Northern Territories (a province made up of the entire northern half of what is now Ghana).[9] There were administrative and political reforms in the late 1940s that further advantaged the chiefs via devolutions of central powers to reformed and modernized Native Authorities (appropriately renamed "local governments") and provincial councils.[10]

Many analysts of colonial Ghana have stressed the fact that indirect rule in southern Ghana was always less stable and coherent than Britain's idea of "traditionalism" implied. Even so, it is also true that Asante and some of the other Akan polities did provide the indigenous political infrastructure that was the sine qua non for this kind of colonial state building. Asante government was fairly extensive in geographical scope and was structured by well-developed bureaucracy and internal hierarchy. It was also a material reality that enjoyed considerable legitimacy for most rural subjects.[11] No

---

[7] See Berry 2001.
[8] See Rathbone 1993:60–2 *inter alia* on Akim Abuakwa. See also Luckham 1978; Mikell 1989a:152.
[9] See for example Lombard 1967:222–7.
[10] See Owusu 1970:200; Crook 1986:81–4; Apter 1972:133–41. See Lombard 1967:224–5 for brief discussions of the 1948 Watson Commission, the 1949 Coussey Commission ("which also aimed at conserving the maximum amount of chiefly power"), and the 1950 Constitution which "stacked the decks in favor of the neotraditional elites." Firmin-Sellers (1992:15–17; 1996:92–109) argues that the Coussey Commission and the 1950 constitution furthered the interests of the UGCC and the paramount chiefs by concentrating power at the national level at the expense of the local. At that point in the struggle for political supremacy, Nkrumah and the CPP cultivated the support of subchiefs in opposition to these groups.
[11] In this regard, we have to take seriously Rathbone's (1993) reading of the political history of Akim Abuakwa under colonial rule. Rathbone sees Nana Ofori Atta I's systematic accumulation of nontraditional and noncustomary powers under British rule as the "modernization" and centralization of the state of Akim Abuakwa – that is, as state building. Most authors

similar political infrastructure for governing the rural areas was available to the French who colonized southern Côte d'Ivoire. For France to have created "Native Authorities" with the power and influence of those constructed in southern Ghana, French colonizers would have faced the Herculean task of fabricating African polities and bureaucracies from whole cloth: beyond the tattered remnants of the Baoulé kingdom and the series of tiny, weakly integrated Agni polities, established state hierarchies and centralized political authority did not exist in the Ivoirian forest zone.

Rise of the Cocoa Economy in Ghana

The rise of a peasant-based export economy in what is now Ghana predated the colonial era. Ghana exported significant quantities of cocoa by the mid-1890s, and by 1911 the territory was the world's leading cocoa supplier. The administrative strategies adopted by the British in the 1930s and 1940s would play an important role in defining the socioeconomic and political effects of the spread of cocoa production. Indirect rule reinforced the ability of Britain's rural allies, the chiefs, to cash in on the economic changes that were transforming Akan society. In this sense the political order built by Britain helped ensure that the development of "rural capitalism" in southern Ghana would do much to accentuate indigenous social and political hierarchy.

Cocoa farms were first established in Akwapim, where chiefs in Akim Abuakwa sold large tracts of land to companies of migrant farmers, who subdivided their holdings into individual farms. While the "company land" system took hold in some parts of Akim Abuakwa, in other parts families purchased land. Under both systems, farm labor was mobilized through wage contracts. These new land and labor relations promoted the rise of a nascent rural capitalism.[12] Production spread through southern Asante.

Around the 1930s a shift occurred: a version of the *abusa* sharecropping system became increasingly prevalent in both the Asante region and the original cocoa-producing areas.[13] This represented a move *away* from

have emphasized a different point – the corrosion and corruption of traditional authority under colonial rule. Many have focused on abuses of authority by individual chiefs, which were reflected in an increasing number of "destoolments" of chiefs which, from the 1920s on, were often provoked by popular protest and anger. See for example Mikell 1989a:88–9.

[12] Polly Hill, as reported by Southall 1978:193. See also Hill 1963; Mikell 1989a:71; Berry 1993:107, 111.

[13] Allman (1993:37), along with many others, argues that this shift to the *abusa* system was one symptom of forces that were "reversing the trend toward a more capitalist class structure,"

market-based controls over land in the most dynamic cocoa zones of southern Ghana. Under the *abusa* system, migrant farmers did not purchase land; the *abusa* farmer in southern Ghana asked local chiefs for permission to cultivate stool lands (Akan "crown lands"). This is important because it meant that in this part of the West African forest, land pioneering was a social process that fueled chiefly power.

Stool lands in the traditional Akan polities were defined as communal lands that lay under the jurisdiction of the paramount chiefs, who were supposed to administer them in trusteeship for the nation. This institution, stool land, emerged as a linchpin of British indirect rule in Ghana and a critical lever in chiefs' own strategies for amassing political and economic power. As early as 1903 British authorities had codified Asante chiefs' power "to allocate, control, and dispose of land" within territorial jurisdictions confirmed by the colonial state.[14] Restraining the development of land markets was the name of the game, for the commercialization of land would have gone far in eroding chiefly power and producing the result the European administrators feared the most – the freeing of ordinary farmers from the political control of chiefs.

Sara Berry (1993:107, 111) describes how the British, eager to restrain the commercialization of land and labor in cocoa-producing regions, enacted policies that gave chiefs wide powers to collect land tribute, or rents, from migrant farmers.

[Colonial authorities] persuaded the chiefs in Asante and Brong Ahafo to prohibit the sale of land in their domains.... They endorsed the chiefs' right to demand

---

and that this trend probably continued into the 1950s. There is considerable discussion as to why this happened. Gareth Austin (1987), who focuses on the eclipse of wage-labor relationships by sharecropping in the southern Ashanti Region in the 1930s, sees the rise of sharecropping as a reflection of northern migrants' growing power vis-à-vis southern landlords. This argument represents an important departure from the one advanced by Phillips (1989) and Kay (1972), who attribute the rollback to the political needs of the colonial state (see below). It could be that both arguments are true.

[14] "In the Gold Coast, the Ashanti Concessions Ordinance, 1903, expressly recognized the power of the Ashanti chiefs to allocate, control and dispose of land at just a time when these powers were being eroded.... In the Gold Coast, land sales had commenced at the turn of the century and had been given judicial recognition [by the colonial state]. The West African Lands Committee, however, in 1912 took the view that the sales of land were inconsistent with African customs which should be enforced. The report was officially circulated in 1917, but only published in the 1950s. After 1917 neither the administration nor the judiciary would enforce sales by Africans" (Noronha 1985:27, 31). On the colonial administration's attempts to restrain the commercialization of land and labor, see Grier 1987; Crook 1986:87–92; Phillips 1989.

tribute from "strangers" who sought permission to cultivate [stool] land. . . . [C]hiefs in Asante and neighboring states demanded one-third of the cocoa crop as tribute from stranger farmers. . . . In southern Ghana, even migrants who bought land were expected to pay tribute to the local chief, just like "tenant" farmers in Asante and Brong Ahafo.[15]

All or part of the land tribute collected by local chiefs was claimed by the national (paramount) stool treasuries. In Asante, the paramount chief received all revenues and then remitted a share to subordinate chiefs.[16]

"Stranger" or migrants farmers were a major presence in Asante in the 1950s (over 30 percent of all farmers), and they were a population that was highly sensitive and vulnerable to chiefly authority. "Citizens" of particular stools enjoyed more secure land rights, but they too felt the weight of chiefly land prerogatives. Citizens enjoyed lineal rights to land and, unlike migrants, could cultivate stool lands without paying tribute. They could hold long-term usufruct that "can and did become tantamount to freehold," and such rights were bought and sold among citizens.[17] Yet citizens' earnings and proceeds from land sales were also subject to financial claims by the chiefs to whom they pledged their political allegiance, and it seems that chiefs worked with some success to retain authority-based economic prerogatives over citizens' land. Chiefs in Asante and Akim Abuakwa tried to tax citizens who had migrated away from their homelands in search of economic opportunity.[18] Meanwhile, in attempts to stem the tide of land commercialization (and the demise of royal land rights that this would imply), stools sought to impose absolute or reversionary rights over "freehold" land within their jurisdictions.[19]

The expansion of the cocoa economy in general and the *abusa* system in particular enriched the chiefs and the stools, enforced hierarchy within chieftaincy institutions, and gave chiefs a firm political grip on migrant

---

[15] See also Rathbone's (1993:59) description of Akim Abuakwa. It seems that over time, tribute tended to become a more direct tax or "rent." Mikell (1989a:154) reported that the Asante doubled the rate of cocoa tribute for the 1950–1 cocoa season from one-half farthing to one farthing per tree. On rates of cocoa rent/tribute over the period from 1913 to the 1930s, see Austin 1987:268.

[16] On Akyem [Akim] Abuakwa, see Rathbone 1993:57, 59.

[17] Rathbone 1993:56. On usufructary rights under Ghana's communal land tenure system, see Ninsin 1989:165.

[18] Apter 1972:257–63. See also Mikell 1989a:162.

[19] See Crook 1986:89. He cites Akyem [Akim] Abuakwa as an example; see also Rathbone 1993.

communities that had settled within their domains.[20] This is in direct contrast to the pattern observed in southeastern Côte d'Ivoire, where land pioneering and sharecropping worked to disperse economic authority within precolonial political units, enrich lineage heads at the expense of the high-ranking chiefs, and turn "migrants" into free farmers within a short time span. The contrast between Asante and *southwestern* Côte d'Ivoire, where the traditions and institutions of political hierarchy had always been absent, is even more dramatic.

In Asante and the other Akan states, the small-scale peasant producers who were the backbone of the cocoa economy lived in a world dominated by what Richard Crook called "the elite network of agro-commercial interests so powerfully represented by the chieftaincy."[21] This is the social stratum that would so decisively shape the territory's future. The traditional political elite – chiefs, other office holders, and elders – had entered cocoa production early and with all the political and economic advantages their positions conferred. In the Brong-Ashanti area the political elite began producing cocoa in the 1910s and 1920s. Gwendolyn Mikell (1989a:93–4) writes that they "had a head start. They were able to select extensive and contiguous tracts of well-situated, fertile land." Chiefs and other office holders were able to invest capital not only in the development of their landholdings, but also in transport and trade (and in their own advancement within the political hierarchy).[22] Many rich planters became cocoa merchants in the 1920s, and a powerful stratum of chiefly planter-traders and absentee landholders developed in the South.

Debt emerged as a key marker of the political and economic subordination of the ordinary peasant to the planter-trader elite. Debt was also an important mechanism for enforcing these relationships. Mikell argues that by the 1930s stratification in the rural areas had resulted in "two clearly defined groups":

one composed of former and present *ahenfo* [office holders] and *ikafo* [wealthy, privileged persons] ... whose cocoa wealth generated education and capital for further investment; and the other composed of ordinary folk whose small cocoa farms, impeded by inadequate capital and labor, often caused their indebtedness to the first

[20] On Akim Abuakwa, see Rathbone 1993:57–8.
[21] Crook 1986:98. The Nowell Commission report in 1939 stated that 60 percent of the farms in Ashanti Region were under one acre (Mikell 1989a:99). Presumably most households in this category farmed several small, noncontiguous farms.
[22] Mikell (1989a:132) notes that the selection of chiefs was influenced by wealth or influence: "now wealthy persons openly competed for stools."

152

group.... Debt quickly became a major problem for most farmers, and pledging valuable cocoa land became the ideal means for dealing with loans.[23]

In Ghana's cocoa belt, indebtedness took the form of land pledging – debtors "gave" their land to creditors until the loan could be repaid. Farms pledged by poor Ghanaian peasants "might be held for several decades ... therefore, for all practical purposes, such a farm was completely alienated."[24] Indebtedness thus worked to concentrate control over land and persons in the hands of the chiefly Ghanaian planter-merchant elite, adding momentum to the process of class formation. This contrasts with what happened in southern Côte d'Ivoire. There, indebtedness usually led to the mortgaging of crops (not land) to purely commercial intermediaries – especially to Lebanese merchants from the 1940s onward – who had far less political leverage over the farmers and no ready means to appropriate peasants' land or labor. In Ghana, the economic and political power snowballed in the hands of the old African political elite. The opposite was true in the cocoa-coffee zone of Côte d'Ivoire.

Having a class of capitalist farmers rise from the ranks of the chiefly elite was antithetical to the doctrines and ideology of colonial indirect rule: the contradictions of British success in Ghana bedeviled the colony's governors and administrators. The basic idea of indirect rule was to govern on the cheap by preserving the aristocratic and sacred authority of the chiefs, along with the ordinary peasant's willing acquiescence to chiefly rule. Colonial administrators had to somehow manage the political contradictions and tensions fueled by rising land values, competition for labor, and in general the growing strength of capital in southern Ghana. The chiefly establishment itself was swept up in a process of change that pulled the chiefs toward an uncertain future. On the political front, land tenure and citizenship questions fueled intense intra-stool politicking and rivalries for control over both people and land.[25] This certainly eroded the coherence

---

[23] Mikell 1989a:95. Stavenhagen (1975:148), apparently reporting findings from the 1950s, wrote that "[i]n Akokoaso, Ghana, more than 60 percent of the farmers are in debt, and of them WH Becket has said, 'their income is such that they can never aspire to escape from the vicious circle of debt.'"

[24] See Mikell 1989a:96.

[25] Under these systems of land tenure and land pioneering, expansion of the cocoa economy becomes the main force driving chieftaincy politics. Stools disputed control over certain lands, rival chiefs disputed claims to the allegiance of people in certain localities, and chiefs at various levels of the hierarchy disputed the division of surpluses appropriated in the name of the stool.

and solidarity of the neotraditional elite and often forced them to rely on the British for adjudication of their own disputes. The system was also rife with abuse and corruption. Chiefs were known to privatize stool resources, exploit tenants, abuse debtors, and forsake material and spiritual obligations to their subjects: from the 1920s onward, popular protests and anger against chiefly abuses led to an ever-rising number of "destoolments" of chiefs. More ominously, class-like tensions between commoners and chiefs simmered across the entire cocoa belt.

British administrators were forced to deal with these contradictions. They came up with all sorts of laws and reforms aimed at preventing the planter-chiefs from consolidating into a landed gentry or into a class of capitalists. Tactics ranged from trying to "retraditionalize" the chieftaincy, to squelching land markets, to auditing stool treasuries to prevent chiefs from using the levers of indirect rule to privatize revenues from stool lands.[26] Britain's attempts to put the genies of economic transformation back in the bottle did little to stabilize the political-economic order in southern Ghana. As G. B. Kay (1972) and Anne Phillips (1989) argued, the case of Ghana does indeed reveal the fundamental paradox of relying on neotraditional elites to promote the commercialization of agriculture. Jonathan Barker (1971) made the same point in a study of Senegal's groundnut basin; Karl Polanyi did so for eighteenth-century England in *The Great Transformation* (1994). We will return to this point in the conclusion.

The key fact for us here is that in southern Ghana in the 1950s, the *official prerogatives* conferred upon neotraditional elites and the *economic prerogatives* of an accumulating class were, in many ways, mutually reinforcing sources of strength in the political arena. A potent mix of political authority and economic clout produced a stratum of chiefly planters with a great deal of influence over the political behavior of peasant households, as well as a considerable capacity to mobilize community-level collective action. From the 1930s to the 1960s, this stratum proved willing and able to lock horns with the colonial and postcolonial state.

Mechanisms of Chiefly Authority. The tightly interwoven political and economic hierarchies of Ghana's indirectly ruled cocoa economy gave rich

---

[26] See Kay 1972; Phillips 1989; Crook 1986:83–4, 88; Owusu 1970:200. Indirect rule itself, formally instituted in the 1930s, was an effort toward this end. By 1940s the British were trying to prop up the viability of the Native Authorities by reforming and modernizing them – this was the point of a series of 1944 ordinances that, among other things, established stool treasuries that were subject to semiannual audits by the colonial state.

chiefs considerable leverage over their subordinates and dependents. Informal patron-client relationships were grounded firmly in the chief's control over the granting of land use rights, indebtedness, and landlord-tenant relations. The prerogative to determine who was a "stranger" and who was a "citizen" of an Akan state was exercised by local chiefs. In a system in which citizenship in the traditional polity and the status of land claims were, as Kwame Ninsin (1989) says, "inexorably intertwined," this gave the local chief (who might well be one's landlord and/or creditor) the power to define a person's economic and political rights. And as Rhoda Howard (1976:471) wrote, the "chiefs were not only chiefs; they were also large farmers in their own right, sometimes money lenders or cocoa buyers on a large scale." For peasants, these multistranded relations meant that various forms of economic insecurity, from unstable cocoa earnings to insecurity of land tenure, were personal realities very much subject to the discretion and good graces of the big men who made up the rural political-economic elite.

Economic dependency was not the only bond between chiefs and their subjects. Chiefs claimed religious and moral authority as the embodiments of royal lineages and tradition, ancient African states, and self-conscious nations. This moral legitimacy is what the British worked so hard to prop up and to harness for their own purposes. Indirect rule assumed and was predicated upon the legitimacy of the neotraditional elite, and local populations – whatever their view of the chief and even chiefly authority – were subject to neotraditional law and judicial practice (as codified by the British). Chiefs at various levels of the political hierarchy administered both civil and criminal justice, exercised coercive powers, imposed fines, and adjudicated disputes.

These ideological, legal, and economic aspects of chiefly authority were woven into a rural social order that, even with its internal strains and contradictions, served in the 1930s through 1960s as a kind of "natural" or ready-made political machinery for mobilizing the peasantry.[27] No wonder Nkrumah's Convention People's Party – like its partisan opponents, the National Liberation Movement and later the United Party – sought the support of chiefs wherever these rural heavyweights could be trusted to strengthen, rather than subvert, the party. Chiefs in the cocoa belt of southern Ghana, especially in the core Akan areas of Asante, Brong Ahafo, and Akim Abuakwa, could lead, persuade, bully, or buy the small farmers, and thereby command much of the rural vote.

[27] See Apter 1972:340–1.

Ghana's Planter-Chiefs as a "Rural Bourgeoisie." Ghana's planter-chiefs wielded considerable power over their subjects, tenants, and debtors. In this regard they were a lot like some of the other rural notables and aristocrats who appear in the cases we consider in this text – the big land-holders of the Senegal River Valley, the Islamic marabouts of Senegal's groundnut basin, and even some of the biggest Senoufo chiefs of northern Côte d'Ivoire. What makes Ghana's planter elite unique in the context of this study is the *forms of leverage they wielded over the state*. The decisive fact is that the indigenous political-economic elite in southern Ghana occupied powerful positions as cocoa producers and in the export-marketing circuit. From these positions, they could directly appropriate and valorize their share of the wealth generated by peasant producers. Most significantly, the cocoa elite could confront the state (and the European merchant houses) directly in struggles to expand the planter-chiefs' share of the wealth produced by the multitudes of small farmers growing cocoa in southern Ghana.

Ghanaian merchants in the export trade were enormously powerful compared to their Senegalese or Ivoirian counterparts. Not only did they control strategic positions in the internal commercial circuit – including distribution of credit to smallholders, transportation, and the building of storage depots – but as early as the 1910s a significant group also exported cocoa directly to Britain. The existence of independent exporters is an important indicator of the operational scale and commercial sophistication of Ghana's largest planter-merchants and of the extent to which they were able to accumulate capital. Southall (1978:195) writes that "in October 1918 one source reported that there were now a total of 292 African firms or individuals involved in the direct export of cocoa. They were independent of the services of the expatriate buyers."

Cocoa planter-brokers' growing power and ambition led them into an unbroken series of head-on confrontations with the European trading houses and the colonial state. Over the course of the 1920s, 1930s, and 1940s, brokers repeatedly attempted to force up prices by refusing to sell cocoa to European trading houses. There were major "cocoa hold-ups" in 1920–1, 1922–3, and 1930–1. In the mid-1930s the Ghanaian brokers fought to expand their share of the cocoa surplus at a time of falling world prices.[28] The European firms fought back, and in 1937 the expatriate

---

[28] Howard (1976:471) argues that a driving force behind the 1937–8 boycott was a group of wealthy farmers and coastal traders "who wanted to be able to ship cocoa direct to the European and American markets without going through European middlemen."

trading houses concluded a market-sharing or "pooling" agreement that was designed to undercut the African merchants.

It was *precisely* because the larger cocoa brokers were utilizing their dominance in the rural areas to appropriate a large proportion of the surplus of the cocoa economy at a time of declining profitability in the trade for the majority of the buying firms, that the latter came together in an arrangement whose explicit purpose was to reduce the cost of brokerage.[29]

Ghana's chiefly cocoa brokers responded to the European firms' pooling agreement by organizing and enforcing the cocoa holdup of 1937–8; it turned out to be the most successful episode of collective action waged against European trading houses in all of colonial Africa.[30] Brokers staged another commercial boycott in 1948, as the nationalists were gaining momentum. In the same year, there was also widespread and organized resistance in the cocoa belt to a government campaign to control the swollen shoot fungus by destroying cocoa farms.

This pattern of boycotts is an indicator of the commercial and financial clout of the cocoa elite as well as their capacity to undertake collective action. The cocoa big-men could wield multiple forms of power in attempts to organize, enforce, and mobilize grassroots participation in the hold-ups. Political authority wielded by the chiefs was a major asset in the cocoa brokers' confrontations with foreign buying companies and the state.

Recent work on the cocoa hold-ups reveals the extent to which the chiefs right down from Nana Ofori-Atta to the village levels in Eastern Province and Ashanti were involved in the formal organization and enforcement of the hold-ups.... By early 1948 [there was a] campaign to boycott expatriate and Syrian firms' "high priced" imports.... There is clear evidence that the chiefs throughout Ashanti and the Colony... sided with the boycott and helped to enforce it with all the resources of the NA's [Native Administrations].[31]

Rhoda Howard (1976) shows that chiefs also used their traditional powers of sanction in encouraging the hold-up of 1937–8; for example, they refused to perform funeral rites for subjects who refused to respect the selling

[29] Southall 1978:186, see also 197–202. See also Beckman 1976:46–7. On the Cocoa-Buying (Pooling) Agreement itself, see Howard, 1976:474–6.
[30] See Howard 1976:471–2, 479–80; Crook 1986; Southall 1987. On the swollen shoot campaigns, see Rathbone 1993:196; Mikell 1989a:145.
[31] Crook 1986:94, 96. On this point, see also Berry (1993:75); who argues that "[o]ne factor which may help to explain the greater frequency and effectiveness of [cocoa] holdups in Ghana [compared to Nigeria] is the different positions of Akan and Yoruba chiefs in the respective cocoa economies." See also Mikell 1989a:98; Rathbone 1993:196–7.

boycott. Wealth itself contributed to the ability of the rural elite to battle the European trading houses for control over the market. Big brokers "had the capital to buy up and hold the crops of smaller and poorer farmers,"[32] and this too was an important factor in the success of the 1937–8 hold-up.

In the wake of the 1937–8 cocoa hold-up, and also after World War II, the colonial administration encouraged and helped finance cocoa producers' cooperatives, or Farmers' Unions, in the cocoa belt.[33] It seems that this was a strategy to dilute the economic clout of the largest Ghanaian brokers. On the political front, however, the initiative had the opposite effect, for it strengthened the cocoa elite's ability to mobilize constituencies and to act in the political arena. Chiefs and big planter-traders dominated the farmers' associations and "used polygynous marriage, kinship, and patron-client networks to enhance the membership of the cooperative societies."[34] Simultaneously, cocoa big-men built up their cocoa-buying networks and the scope of their political influence. The Farmers' Unions expanded planter-traders' access to capital, for the state and the European cocoa buyers made loans and cash advances to the cooperatives. This was money that the cooperative officials could invest in their own businesses, lend to needy cooperative members and clients, or use to reward their supporters.[35] By the beginning of the 1950s, the farmers' unions were highly effective tools for rural political mobilization. They provided financial resources for the rural cocoa elite, and also political infrastructure that extended the already formidable institutional underpinnings of their power.[36]

The hierarchical structure of peasant society in southern Ghana, together with the rural elite's strategic position in the export-marketing circuit, are the key facts of this case. Ghana's rural elite, unlike its counterpart in Senegal's groundnut basin, was in a position to fight the colonial and postcolonial state for the lion's share of the rural surplus. The attributes of

---

[32] See Southall 1978:205.

[33] From 1930 onward, the colonial administration provided impetus for the formation of buyers' cooperatives, or Farmers' Unions. See Austin 1987:272–3 n. 80. However, before 1938, cooperatives bought less than 3 percent of the crop (Beckman 1976:48). In the wake of the 1937–8 holdup, officials probably came to see the development of farmers' unions as a way to curb the power of the biggest professional brokers.

[34] See Mikell 1989a:150–1.

[35] Beckman 1976, esp. 232. The new arrangements also helped big union leaders to corner markets by shutting out unlicensed buyers.

[36] This was obvious in the mobilization of the pro-CPP vote in 1951 and in the rise of anti-CPP politics after 1952. See Beckman 1976.

Ghana's rural social structure go far to explain the state-formation strategies of the Nkrumah regime.

II. Nkrumah Takes On the Planter-Chiefs: The Nationalist Era

[T]he competition which confirmed Nkrumah's leadership role between 1954–1957 [was] a struggle over cocoa and other resources which were of critical importance to the emerging state.

Mikell 1989:159

Neotraditional rulers of the leading Akan states believed that they were the rightful heirs to the British colonial state in Ghana. Before about 1945 the only challengers they had encountered were members of Ghana's professional elite of lawyers, merchants, civil servants, and teachers in the coastal cities. British administrators strove to arrange accommodations between these two groups. By the end of the 1940s they had devised a formula that seemed promising: as Dennis Austin (1964:9) describes it, Ghana was governed by a "triple ruling elite" of colonial officials, chiefs, and the African intelligentsia.

What appeared to be a rough balance of forces was upset dramatically in 1948. In Accra, the capital, and other urban centers, popular anger against colonial policy exploded in mass demonstrations and riots. Much of Ghana's coastal strip and Asante were soon engulfed in protests aimed at British rule. Within a few years, the critique would extend to the oppressive structures of chiefly authority in the countryside. Kwame Nkrumah, hitherto allied with the forces of moderate or "bourgeois" nationalism in Ghana, seized the moment to weld this unrest and discontent into what would become a populist movement organized under the banner of the CPP. The CPP claimed to represent the "common man" and demanded immediate independence for Ghana, and in doing so it foiled Britain's attempts to ensure that political modernization would proceed in a gradual and fundamentally conservative manner.

If there was a single political issue that won the CPP its first election victories in 1951, it was the struggle with Britain for control over Ghana's cocoa surplus. The CPP joined cocoa farmers across southern Ghana in attacks on the marketing-board system, promising that a CPP victory would give farmers control over the vast funds accumulated by the Cocoa Marketing Board. The party's electoral base was built largely on alliances with existing farmer-trader organizations in the cocoa areas, including the Farmers'

Unions led by planter-chiefs in Asante and beyond. Political momentum thus created was sufficient to produce a sweeping and decisive electoral victory for the CPP in 1951 (Beckman 1976:54–7).

This coalition began to crumble almost immediately; the process began as soon as the CPP grasped state power as the majority party in Ghana's new Legislative Assembly. The 1950 constitution (and its 1954 revision) gave the Legislative Assembly broad competence over domestic policy matters and also made it the key forum for negotiating the terms of Ghana's full independence from Britain.[37] Nkrumah, leader of the parliamentary majority, was elected prime minister. He formed an executive cabinet and moved to consolidate the CPP's national political hegemony, as well as its hold on the state apparatus and all the political resources that victory conferred upon the winner.

As the CPP transformed itself from nationalist party to ruling party and then to party-state, its interests and those of the Ghana's farmer-traders diverged. In 1951 the CPP had inherited control over the state's mechanisms for expropriating cocoa wealth via control of marketing circuits, and was now intent on preserving them.[38] Party leaders turned against their former allies in the Farmers' Unions and renounced their earlier condemnations of the colonial state's export monopoly. As party-in-government, the CPP showed no desire to discontinue the policy of using Cocoa Marketing Board funds for general development expenditure; it showed no desire to relinquish state control over cocoa revenues in favor of farmers and private traders. "On the contrary, the conversion of cocoa farmers' reserve funds into 'public funds' which had been opposed by the farmers proceeded at an accelerating pace" (Beckman 1976:57). The CPP succeeded in completely alienating the old farmers' organizations.

The CPP government revealed its intentions by freezing cocoa producer prices in 1951. World prices were rising, and farmers had expected a better deal from the nationalists. The government's move ignited immediate

---

[37] See Apter 1972:179–90. The Legislative Assembly was a parliament; it replaced the Legislative Council, which had an essentially advisory function vis-à-vis the colonial administration, and a jurisdiction that was limited to the coastal province (the Colony). Under the new government, most powers hitherto reserved to the British governor of the Gold Coast were delegated to cabinet ministers selected mostly by Nkrumah. (On this, see Ladouceur 1979:104–5.) The governor retained veto powers over laws passed by the Legislative Assembly. In 1954 the ministries of defense, external affairs, justice, and finance were handed over to Africans.

[38] See Allman 1993:36–40.

resistance from farmers in the cocoa heartlands and "provided the perfect catalyst for mobilizing opposition to the CPP in Asante" (Allman 1993:40). Chiefly opposition began to coalesce with the gathering of the old cooperatives into the Ghana Farmers' Congress in 1951. In the run-up to the June 1954 elections, many CPP candidates campaigned on promises to increase cocoa prices, but two months after a resounding CPP victory in that voting round, the government issued a Cocoa Ordinance that lowered producer prices by a wide margin, froze them for the next four years, and increased export duties.[39]

This precipitated a huge political crisis and was the catalyst for the formation of the National Liberation Movement (NLM) in Asante in 1954, an opposition party financed in part from the Asantehene's royal treasury. "Vote for Cocoa" was opposition leaders' slogan; the struggle was "to preclude state control over cocoa revenue."[40] Beckman (1976:67) wrote that by early 1955 the CPP's loss of control in Asante "seemed virtually complete." Ghana entered the throes of struggle over the cocoa market that pitted the farmer-traders against the state export monopoly. As many writers have commented, no one should have been surprised: it was in many ways a replay of battles that reached a climax in the cocoa hold-ups of the 1930s.[41]

Cocoa farmers' political clout and capacity for collective action had been assets to the CPP in its first campaign. All this now turned to liability as the chiefly establishment of Asante threw its full weight behind a rival political movement determined to prevent Nkrumah, viewed as the usurper of the

---

[39] The 1954 ordinance froze prices paid to farmers at seventy-two shillings per sixty-pound load for a period of four years. "The government had paid £4 a load in the fiscal year 1951/52 when the world price was £245 a ton, and many cocoa farmers felt that the government could pay £5 or £7 a load now that the world price had climbed to over £450 a ton. . . . [The government, on the other hand, was anxious to avoid inflation] and was also dependent on the surplus generated from the sale of cocoa for development funds" (Ladouceur 1979:132).

[40] Mikell 1989a:151. Ashanti region including Brong Ahafo produced half of Ghana's cocoa in the 1950s (Beckman 1976:196).

[41] See Mikell 1989a:241 and Crook 1986:94 *inter alia*. Mikell writes that the nationalist-era clash between cocoa producers and the state could have been anticipated, given the precedents of the 1920s and 1930s. In contrast to the situation that prevailed at the founding of the American Republic, for example, in the emergent Ghana property owners were being marginalized politically and excluded from direct control of the state. Just the opposite occurred in the United States: with the overthrow of colonial rule, property-holding classes consolidated their hold on state power. What would Ghana look like now if the cocoa-producing class had won the contests of the 1950s?

chiefs' rightful political mandate, as well as the illegitimate appropriator of private fortunes, from snatching power.

Fights over cocoa formed the hard core of a political agenda that was premised on the idea that the aristocrats and dignitaries of the old Akan states were the country's "natural rulers," the governors of the people under indirect rule, and the rightful successors to the British. Opposition to the CPP was voiced in the vernacular of Asante nationalism in the heart of the cocoa region, but the NLM agenda was broadened with demands for regional autonomy not only for the Ashanti Region but also for the colony's two other provinces, the coastal province known as "the Colony" and the Northern Territories. The goal was a federal (not unitary) constitution that would "break up CPP domination."[42] Leaders from Ghana's isolated and impoverished northern province were forced to take sides in this fight. They were torn between their interest in preserving northern political autonomy, including the status of royal houses in states like Dagomba and Mamprusi, and their thirst for the development revenues that only a strong central state could extract from their wealthy southern countrymen. As one northern leader put it, "We understood what federalism meant: that Ashanti wealth would largely remain in Ashanti."[43]

Political developments from 1951 onward sharpened the populism of the CPP. Upon assuming control of the government, it set out immediately to forge a highly centralized party-state apparatus that would snuff out the opposition. Starting in 1951 Nkrumah undertook to either secure the chiefs' acquiescence to party hegemony or, where chiefs resisted as they did in the core Akan states of Asante and Akim Abuakwa, to deploy all the powers of the state to undermine the political and economic authority of the rural elite, and neutralize their capacity to act collectively in the political arena. State building in the rural areas under Ghana's First Republic was aimed largely at this end. Nkrumah and his close associates surely saw this as a means to the larger ends of building a modern Ghana with a stronger and more diversified economy, and freeing ordinary cocoa farmers from the grip of a rural nobility that was enriching itself by exploiting the hard-working peasantry.

[42] See Beckman 1976:196.
[43] Ladouceur 1979:133. These are the words of Mumuni Bawumia, a northern minister in Nkrumah's first cabinet who, with some ambivalence, threw his support behind the NLM. The NLM gathered support in some parts of the North, but according to Ladouceur this was out of solidarity with anti-CPP forces rather than a deep commitment to federalism. The CPP, for its part, also mobilized and retained considerable support in the North from 1951 on. See below.

The government's strategy was three pronged. First, the regime exploited class-like tensions in the cocoa heartlands. It sought to drive a wedge between old rural patrons and their clients, and thereby free ordinary farmers from the economic and political bonds that tied them to the chiefs. Second, the CPP cultivated the support of dissident chiefs (disgruntled, subordinate, "illiterate," or peripheral chiefs) in the cocoa heartlands. Third, the party mobilized electoral support outside the core Akan states of Asante and Akim Abuakwa, including in the coastal areas of the south, where chiefly power was weaker and far less cohesive,[44] and in the Northern Territories, especially among the chiefly elite in the most powerful Native Authorities of that region. All three operations involved institution building in the rural areas, and the shape of the grassroots challenge went far in determining just what kind of institutions the regime would choose to construct.

III. Institutional Choice in the Cocoa Heartland: Rewiring the Circuits of Local Authority

In southern Ghana, the regime of Kwame Nkrumah sought to establish centralized control over a state apparatus that reached deep into localities, governing the cocoa belt intensively through a dense network of official institutions that projected state power into the micro-level dynamics of local political economies. The striking contrast with the Côte d'Ivoire is the intensely deconcentrated and interventionist character of Nkrumah's institutional strategy in the South from 1951 until his overthrow in 1966. Nkrumah's choice in this region was to centralize authority – that is, to steadily enhance central control at the expense of the authority and autonomy of the chiefs, and to do so by creating a dense network of party-state outposts that would reach deep into localities. This was administrative deconcentration, and it allowed state agents to insinuate themselves into the microcosmic world of village political and economic life. There, agents of the regime sought to usurp the political and economic authority of the planter elite.

---

[44] In the Gold Coast Colony, made up mostly of the coastal plains including the Fanti and Ga areas, "traditional institutions, particularly chieftaincy, were more firmly undermined [than in the Ashanti Confederation].... Thus indirect rule in theory became direct rule in practice" (Schiffer 1970:61). These differences had consequences for decolonization-era politics and postcolonial state building in Ghana's southern half. Owusu's (1970) account of politics in Swedru – a rural locality near Accra, a big cocoa producer, and a CPP stronghold – is a case study of what went on in the coastal zone. Only one of the southern chieftaincies – Akim Abuakwa – supported the NLM (Austin 1964:265; Rathbone 1993).

Usurpation was the name of this game: institution building in the cocoa belt represented a no-holds-barred attempt to undercut the old chiefly elite and neutralize their capacity to resist taxation and to contest the hegemony of the nationalists. To politically subordinate the cocoa belt, the CPP built state structures in the countryside that were designed to displace and suffocate the stratum within rural society that was most able to challenge the regime directly.

A. Reforms of the Party-State Apparatus

Through successive reforms of colonial institutions of rural government, the Nkrumah government shifted local balances of power, established a formidable presence at the grassroots, and took control of local administration. The turning point came in 1952, when elected Local Councils replaced the old Native Authorities as the organs of local politics and administration. This provided the opening the CPP needed to insert itself directly into rural power arenas and combat chiefly authority on its own turf. In Ghana's cocoa belt, there was a steady process of bringing local government under the direct control of the CPP, which was itself highly centralized under the increasingly authoritarian control of Nkrumah.

Administrative reform from 1944 to 1950 had aimed at bureaucratizing and modernizing the Native Authorities to provide surer footing for Britain's agents in rural Ghana, the chiefs. The Nkrumah government aborted this process. In the new Local Councils, directly elected members would outnumber members appointed by the chiefs by two to one.[45] This reform "gave the CPP tremendous advantage, both in recruitment of new members and control [of local government], while it cut down on the effectiveness of the opposition's allies, the chiefs" (Apter 1972:242). Brilliant organizing tactics and the patronage resources available to the party-in-government allowed the CPP to create local party organs across the sweep of southern Ghana and take control of elected positions in most of

---

[45] See Apter 1972:135, 195, 242–5, 251, 262. Local Councils assumed most of the functions of the local Native Authorities, including the appropriation of the revenues from "stool lands." A portion of the revenue was to be returned to the chieftaincies, but with this measure, the chieftaincy as a government institution became financially dependent upon the politicians. These were the consequences of the Local Government Ordinance of 1951, which was launched in Legislative Assembly after months of party and cabinet discussion and sustained opposition. The CPP overrode objections voiced by the chiefly establishment on almost every point.

the Local Councils. Many chiefs found themselves outnumbered by "party men" in the heart of their own constituencies. The party insinuated itself in local politics, land affairs, and chieftaincy affairs – and also undertook to countermobilize cocoa farmers into new cooperatives (more on this below) that would free them from economic dependency on their chiefly landlords, creditors, and patrons. CPP upstarts displaced the rural elites of indirect rule in many southern localities.[46]

Dennis Austin wrote that 1952 was the "beginning of the end" of the privileges of the Asante chiefs:

[T]he Asanteman Council, the Kumasi Native Authority, and the Chief's Councils within each Ashanti Division were pushed aside to make way for the new local authorities with their two-thirds elected membership.... [T]he substance of their [the chiefly establishment's] power, including the levying of the local rate, passed to new urban and local councils. The future looked still more bleak, for the views of the CPP were well known.[47]

Chiefs in southern Ghana resisted in the trenches: some even refused to turn over revenues to the new local government authorities.[48] They also took the fight to the national political arena by organizing a partisan opposition to the CPP, the NLM. It was a party of the Asante chiefs, big-men, and nationalists; they sought not only regional hegemony, but also a national electoral base that would allow them to challenge the CPP for control of the state itself.

The chiefs' perception that they were under siege was correct. From 1951 to its demise in 1966, the CPP-dominated government sustained a relentless offensive designed to cut the sinews of chiefly power in the cocoa-producing regions. Party men took more and more control of local administration in local arenas once run by the colonial Native Authorities. To this end, they used all the resources of patronage and administrative and judicial coercion afforded them by CPP control of central government.

Redrawing electoral and administrative constituencies was a key tactic in this battle, for it was possible to break up old political bastions, free subchiefs from their former superiors, and decapitate troublesome constituencies.

---

[46] On commoner vs. chief disputes in Manya Krobo (a chieftaincy near the Volta River), see Apter 1972:260–3.

[47] Austin 1964:260. Here, CPP upstarts displaced the chiefs. On the 1951 Local Government Ordinance in Swedru, a coastal district in which the chiefly establishment was weak compared to the Ashanti Region and Akim Abuakwa, see Owusu 1970:199–202.

[48] See Mikell 1989a:153–6.

Throughout the mid-1950s, many local units in the South were redrawn so that local authorities no longer conformed to the old administrative units of indirect rule; Local Councils were regrouped to remake constituencies and destabilize old chiefly strongholds.

Independence came in 1957, and in 1958 "traditionally appointed" members were abolished from the Local Councils altogether. CPP representatives were appointed as district commissioners – the party-state's administrative and law-enforcement agents at the local level – and attached to the Local Councils. A series of acts of Parliament followed from 1958 to 1961 which "seriously impaired the freedom or relative autonomy of local authorities and brought local administration firmly under central government, and therefore CPP, control."[49]

The old local government units were soon stripped of their developmentalist functions as the CPP channeled all central funds for local projects through party cells ("development committees") at the village level. Operating on "the one-party mobilization model," a corps of CPP local development officers and their assistants went out to localities to work in direct contact with rural populations. All were upwardly accountable to Department of Social Welfare agents who owed their positions to Nkrumah. As Nkrumah himself explained, "the internal life of particular villages" had until then remained "substantially unadministered." With the formation of village committees it was possible to "rest content that State Administration goes down right to the town and village levels."[50] In Swedru, a cocoa-producing locality in the coastal belt near Accra, Maxwell Owusu (1970:270–95) describes the centralization of party control over local government as happening through monopolization and "tyrannical" exercise of power by the district commissioner.

The Regional Assemblies that had institutionalized the rule of chiefs at the level of Ghana's main provinces were also attacked.[51] Given the prevailing line-up of political forces, this was inevitable: from 1954 to Ghana's

---

[49] Owusu 1970:278. On this, Schiffer (1970:72–4) writes that the CPP got rid of most Local Councils between 1950 and 1960 (the number of local councils fell from 252 to 69), only to increase the number to 155 in 1962 and 183 in 1965 to provide more patronage to satisfy alienated rank and file. The Local Councils were immobilized due to lack of funds and overcentralization of control.

[50] Nkrumah in *The Party*, April 1962, page 4, as cited by Schiffer (1970:75). By official count there were 6,058 such committees in 1963. On these local development committees, see Schiffer 1970:74–5 and Owolu 1990:83.

[51] The old system had evolved into four main regions by 1957–8, when the country was redivided into eight new regions.

political independence in 1957, the Akan chiefs had championed these regions as the building blocks of a postcolonial federalism that would guarantee them "home rule" in what were, for them, their own and rightful jurisdictions. Nkrumah's government centralized control at the expense of the regional administrations, eliminated the region as a unit of "representative government," and thus put a formal end to chieftaincy's place at the national level. "Regions" were abolished as formal political-administrative entities in 1958 when the country was redivided into eight administrative units. Once again, state builders attacked the Ashanti region, severing it in two in 1959 and creating the Brong-Ahafo region out of what had been its western flank. Chiefs of Brong-Ahafo, thus freed from Kumasi's much-resented overrule, became dependent upon the CPP.

B. Control over Land, Inputs, and Marketing Networks

CPP efforts to micromanage not only political competition but also *strategic economic exchanges* within localities were attempts to create new community-level power structures that would bypass and displace the old socioeconomic hierarchies. The CPP confronted a deeply rooted opposition movement whose leaders were bent on limiting the state's ability to appropriate cocoa surpluses from big producer-traders. Nkrumah and his strategists sought to neutralize this opposition by destroying its organizational bases, by depriving it of access to cocoa-trading profits, and by breaking up the microscopic economic hierarchies that subordinated ordinary peasants (tenants and debtors) to the chiefly planter-traders in the cocoa zone.

Shortly after its electoral victories in 1951 the CPP created a cocoa-trading affiliate, the Cocoa Purchasing Company, "which bypassed entirely the old [Farmers'] Congress leadership and existing farmer-trader organizations" (Beckman 1976:58). The party itself thus entered the cocoa trade as a licensed produce buyer – and as a direct competitor of all brokers already established in the business. Operating capital and crop-purchasing advances were made available by the government and the Cocoa Marketing Board.[52]

The CPP was now positioned to usurp the buyer-creditor role of its rural opponents. In the name of defending small farmers, the party undertook vast campaigns to distribute loans and advances to smallholders. "Nkrumah placed party officials in well-paid positions within the Cocoa Purchasing

---

[52] The government gave the CPC a £250,000 loan; additional credit was provided by the Cocoa Marketing Board (Beckman 1976:71, 60).

Company, where they could build relations with farmers by giving out loans, thereby using cocoa for political benefit" (Mikell 1989a:174). Indebted farmers were able to redeem cocoa farms that had been pledged or confiscated by cocoa brokers, middlemen, and landlords. Bonds of hierarchy and dependency were loosened; intrusion of the party-state into these intimate relationships shifted power balances in social relations of land access, production, and appropriation away from creditors (planter-chiefs) and to the state. Owusu (1970:300) writes that "[f]or electoral votes, the CPP in Swedru and in many other constituencies depended very much on the small-scale, heavily indebted peasant cocoa farmers in the surrounding country, [who were] concerned . . . with finding money to redeem a pledged couple of acres of cocoa farms." Small farmers who were freed from indebtedness to big farmers became clients of the party-state.

By the end of the 1954–5 trading season, 15,000 farmers had received loans. Very little of this money was ever repaid. The economic viability of the loan program was not an end in itself: the aim was to gain control of farmers and the market. By 1956 the Cocoa Purchasing Company controlled about one-fifth of the market.[53]

With cocoa loans and advances, the party usurped the economic and political prerogatives of the old creditors, for those who accepted CPP loans were now tied to party cadres and the party's buying centers.[54] Ruth First (1970:171–2) described the effects of the Cocoa Purchasing Company as "undermining Ghana's fledgling bourgeoisie" and "providing the party with credit and business openings with which to consolidate support. Big farmers and chiefs in the rural economy were bypassed or assailed."

As Bjorn Beckman explains it, the Cocoa Purchasing Company became a principal instrument for the promotion of a new farmers' organization, this one closely affiliated with the United Ghana Farmers' Council (UGFC).[55] The Farmers' Council was a highly centralized bureaucracy controlled by CPP in Accra. Its dense, multilayered apparatus reached downward

---

[53] Beckman 1976:61–3, 67, 76. The maximum loan was £1,500, while average yearly income of cocoa farmers was about £500.

[54] Owusu 1970:256 n. 30. In the keen competition between the CPP party-state and the NLM for clients in the run-up to the 1956 elections, loans were an equally strategic weapon for the opposition: the NLM distributed to small farmers loans advanced by British buying houses; "the CPP met this challenge by giving out cash advances to farmers who refunded [the British buyers] and were at once transferred to [CPP] buying centers" (Owusu 1970:258).

[55] Beckman 1976:58–9. The Farmers' Council was established in 1953 primarily on the basis of pro-CPP elements in the Ghana Farmers' Congress [formed in 1951 in opposition to Nkrumah] (Beckman 1976:193).

to regional-, district-, and village-level outposts, all controlled by party agents loyal to the center. Beckman called it "a centralized bureaucratic monopoly"; it took charge of cocoa buying and credit distribution, and assumed the role of monopoly provider of state-subsidized fertilizers, cutlasses, and fungicide to farmers.[56] Cocoa-trading profits and government loans fed the Council's patronage reservoirs and fueled its grassroots-level fight against the older farmers' cooperatives. "The village buying centers of the Farmers' Council became the advance posts of state and party bureaucracy in its penetration of rural society" (Beckman 1976:231).

With no organizational autonomy, and with small farmers indebted to the Council, village committees were "captives" of the party from the beginning. Farmers interviewed in Sunyani by Gwendolyn Mikell (1989b) claimed that they were held "hostage" by the UGFC and were "always outnumbered" at the village and district level by "outside elites" appointed by the CPP. The CPP organs competed directly against the old farmers' associations that were, by now, platforms and strongholds for the cocoa opposition; the party was pursuing an institution-building strategy designed to displace them completely. Unofficially, Farmers' Council leaders declared that the leaders of the old cooperatives should never be considered for leadership posts in the Council, even at the local level, "because of their suspected political unreliability" (Beckman 1976:150). In 1957 the Farmers' Council became the only officially recognized farmers' organization in Ghana.

The CPP was at the peak of its power from 1958 through 1962. During this period, the party-state reached ever deeper into the micro-level political economy of the cocoa areas. Parliament promulgated a series of laws regulating (lowering) land rents with the stated aim of protecting tenants against exploitation by landlords. Parliament also created state agencies that asserted control over the use and allocation of stool lands (i.e., lands held by paramount chiefs in the name of the Akan nations) and all revenues accruing from them. With these reforms, the state usurped chiefly power in this domain: chiefs were stripped of authority over communal lands; chiefdoms were deprived of their economic bases and left almost completely dependent upon the central government for cash infusions.[57]

In 1959 and 1960 the steady extension of state control over the cocoa trade also reached its logical conclusion: to protect farmers against "wasteful competition" in the cocoa-buying business, the regime extended the state's

---

[56] See Beckman 1976:171, 116–7, 232.
[57] See Ninsin 1989: esp. 168; Owusu 1970:273; Allman 1993:186–9; Luckham 1978:217.

cocoa monopoly to cover cocoa purchases at all levels of the buying circuit. The Farmers' Council was named the monopoly buyer, and with this degree the Council's already sprawling bureaucratic apparatus established a commanding presence in every village in the cocoa belt. Membership in the state cooperatives became compulsory and every farmer was assigned a single point of sale. CPP cadres – most of them nonfarmers – manned the buying stations. These agents of the party-state exercised a direct claim on every producers' output, prerogatives to define the terms of every farmer's sale, and authority to accept or reject each basket of produce. They also had loans, cutlasses, fungicides, and other farming inputs to distribute to promote rural development and the CPP's electoral fortunes. Cooperative officials owed their positions to the ruling party, which appointed and removed them at will in attempts to maintain centralized control over local outposts of the deconcentrated state apparatus.

Upon announcement of the state's buying monopoly in 1959, cocoa growers were informed that they would bear a new tax of 17 percent of the producer price as a "voluntary contribution" to Ghana's Second Development Plan. Assets of the older cooperatives were absorbed by the state agency. ("All our money ha[s] been taken over."[58]) Widespread rioting in the cocoa belt was met with government repression.

Monopoly control over cocoa buying and cooperative credit "permitted the national elite to extend control to the local level in ways which formerly had been impossible."[59] The state cocoa monopoly was, as Bjorn Beckman argues, essentially an exercise in political demobilization. It swept away what remained of the old farmers' unions and thus destroyed not only an important part of the entrepreneurial base of the planter-traders, but also an organizational and social base of their power. The political strategy motivating this institutional choice was clear: it was an attempt to neutralize or block the groups actually or potentially opposed to the central government's heavy appropriation of cocoa income (Beckman 1976:181). Spokesmen for the regime could not have explained it better: in an April 1961 *Dawn Broadcast*, they announced that the Council's aim was "to get farmers to support government economic policies and to help the government develop the country as a whole. Trading profits should be accumulated by the state,

---

[58] Mikell (1989a:178), who quotes from an interview with one leader of the Sunyan Cooperative Produce Buying Association. The Farmers' Council was renamed the United Ghana Farmers' Council Cooperatives (UGFCC) in 1961.

[59] See Mikell 1989a:176–7.

rather than being shared among private traders and individual farmers."[60] To make this happen, state announcers declared, farmers needed to be in organizations that were under party control.

World cocoa prices also fell between 1960 and 1965. At the end of this period, the producer price index had reached 33 percent of its 1956 level.[61] Cocoa hung on the trees because farmers could not afford to harvest and transport their crops at these prices; much of the migrant labor in the Brong Ahafo region and Ashanti region left Ghana's cocoa areas for farms in Côte d'Ivoire. In 1966 Ghanaian army officers swept the Nkrumah regime from power.

Over the next fifteen years, Ghana was ruled by a succession of six regimes. There were four military juntas and two elected governments. Of these, only those that ruled from 1966 to 1972 – the military National Liberation Council (NLC) and the civilian regime of Kofi Busia (who was himself a leading member of the NLM) – have been viewed as linked to the cocoa opposition whose presumed "right to rule" had been usurped by Nkrumah. Ideologically, rulers from 1966 to 1972 were less statist and more liberal than Nkrumah. Did they make different institutional choices in the cocoa belt?

The NLM and Busia made no definitive reversals of the usurpations of Nkrumah. Even these apparently more liberal rulers did not use state power in the service of the cocoa elite. The NLC and Busia extolled the virtues of chieftaincy, but they declined to build rural institutions that would restore the economic power of the Akan elite. Private traders were allowed back into the cocoa circuit, but without sufficient "positive backing" of the state they were unable to reestablish their positions of the pre-Nkrumah era.[62] Assets seized from the private cooperatives by the CPP (including offices, sheds, and accounts) were never returned, and private traders and private cooperatives floundered in from 1967 to 1971. A single, state-controlled cocoa-marketing system had reemerged by 1972. The NLC and Busia also declined to build institutions that would allow rural authorities in the cocoa heartlands to translate local authority into political power at the national

---

[60] Beckman 1976:101.

[61] This is an index deflated by the Accra index of retail prices. The index for 1957 and 1958 was eighty-nine; in 1959 it dropped to seventy-three and fell steadily thereafter. Beckman 1976:222.

[62] See Young, Sherman, and Rose 1981:190–9; see also Mikell 1989a:194–8; Mikell 1989b:460 *inter alia*; Nugent 1999:292 *inter alia*; Beckman 1981:151–5. On the makers of the 1966 coup, see Price 1971:370–7; First 1970:191–200; Austin and Luckham 1975.

level.[63] The cocoa elite had surely hoped for redemption under the NLC and Busia, but as Gareth Austin (1996:556) writes, "Nkrumah's victorious opponents did little to shift the balance back" in favor of the planters. Ghana's planter elite was muscled out of the way by urban professionals and by constituencies linked directly to the state itself, including the military, police, and segments of the political-bureaucratic class lodged in the Cocoa Marketing Board and the Ghana Commercial Bank. In purely local affairs, the influence of rural elites was partly restored across much of the cocoa belt, but even the Busia regime did not pursue policies or build institutions that undid the economic usurpation and political marginalization at the national level that had been engineered by Nkrumah and the CPP.[64]

When Busia was overthrown, the Akan elite lost again. Colonel Acheampong's military coup in 1972 reversed the modest liberalization of the Busia years. For the next decade, a series of governments that were associated with Nkrumah's interventionist and populist legacies reasserted control over the national state, which declined in coherence and capacity over the course of the 1970s, along with the cocoa economy itself.[65] The sharpest declines in cocoa production and in the overall health of the national economy occurred after 1975. Austin (1996:563) emphasizes the fact that "the political demoblization of the cocoa farmers was a necessary condition of the adoption and retention of the economically destructive politics of 1961–1983."

[63] See Rathbone (2000:161–3), who writes that "the NLC instituted a major commission of inquiry into electoral and local government reform which reported in 1968.... It did not recommend that chiefs once again administer and judge rural Ghanaians.... It concluded that many traditional areas/jurisdictions were unsuitable as units of newly constructed local government. They did not recommend that chiefs regain direct access to stool revenues. [Demands for a formal political role for chiefs] were quietly sidelined.... The NLC and its successors were never to restore to chiefs serious access to wealth and power." See also Berry 2001:168.

[64] The NLC and Busia regimes did offer some consolation to the chiefs, and this is a significant caveat to my argument. The 1969 constitution restored stools' authority to allocate land rights and receive land revenues, but "still place[d] strict limits on chiefs' ability to exercise fiscal or political authority independently of the state" (Berry 2001:168). The 1972 constitution "removed the right of the central government to recognize or refuse to recognize newly appointed chiefs." This right reverted to communities (Rathbone 2000:163). The 1979 constitution also recognized chiefs' land allocation prerogatives, although some argued that this was a move to facilitate land-grabbing on the part of the national elite. See Ninsin 1989:176; Wilks 1989:200–5.

[65] The Acheampong regime cultivated alliances with Northern elites at the expense of cocoa interests. See Goody 1980; Beckman 1981:156; Mikell 1989a:205, 212–3; Botchway 1998:75–9, 116.

Tension between the state and cocoa producers was a constant theme in Ghana's postindependence decades because it was largely structural, born of competition for control over the cocoa surplus. As Mikell (1989a:240–1) put it:

That cocoa producers were destined to clash with almost each successive head of state of independent Ghana should have been anticipated. The pattern was set long before independence, as cocoa farmers' organizations struggled to organize in the central and eastern areas; as cocoa middlemen operated as agents of the European cocoa monopolies in the 1920s; and as farmers engaged in the "hold-ups" and boycotts of the 1930s. The power of the producers' organizations was recognized by Nkrumah for what it was: a double-edged sword which could be as much a major political asset as it could be an economic and political liability.[66]

So it was that in some parts of Ghana, the nationalists' institution-building strategies from the 1950s onward produced dramatic breaks with colonial arrangements. It was path-switching, rather than path-dependent, behavior. Yet as we have noted, as early as the 1930s the path the British had chosen – powersharing with a neotraditional elite (classic British indirect rule) – was becoming contorted and convoluted. The powersharing strategy was becoming ever harder for the British to pursue as chiefs used their political privileges to become independent accumulators and then to challenge the economic monopolies of the British. In Nkrumah's era, Ghana reached a fork in the path. The British had found that it was not really possible to "retraditionalize" the chiefs so that they could govern over the peasantry. The choice for central rulers was now between betting on the chiefs, who as an emergent capitalist class would resist taxation (or demand many quid pro quos, limit regime autonomy, or even try to capture the national state), and betting on the peasants, who as small-scale household producers could be more easily subordinated to and taxed by the regime. Nkrumah, like Napoleon III and virtually all the African state builders from the nationalist era (including Houphouet), chose the peasants.

Since the 1960s and 1970s accounts of Ghanaian politics have often depicted the CPP as driven by an urban-based socialism, and thus as relying on the support of the petty bourgeoisie and urban workers (Fitch and Oppenheimer 1966; Apter 1972). Owusu (1970:257) corrects this view and

---

[66] Crook (1986:94 *inter alia*) makes a similar observation: The conflict between the CPP and the chiefs from 1954 onward partly represented a continuation of the struggle between the agro-commercial elite and the state, which first manifested itself directly in the cocoa hold-ups of the interwar years.

restates the essential fact of the matter: "One point needs to be stressed here, and that is the great reliance of the CPP, or the NLM for that matter, on the farmers, on the rural vote not the urban vote, to remain in power." Ninsin (1989:167–9) emphasizes the same fact, naming the cocoa- and food-producing peasantry as "pillars" of the CPP rise to power, and pointing to the party's large peasant base in 1962.

IV. Counterfactual: Powersharing outside Asante

Many have depicted Nkrumah's path switching as radicalism and have seen Nkrumahist strategies as arising from an ideological commitment to abolishing chiefly power. A look at the *regional* topography of institutional choice in Ghana during the Nkrumah era does not support that view, however.

Decolonization-era institution building in the Northern Region, home of some of the most conservative chiefs and Native Administrations in colonial Ghana, followed a strategy of political powersharing reminiscent of Senghor's choices in parts of Senegal. Dagomba, an old kingdom centered at the town of Yendi, was the bastion of a neotraditional elite whose political grip on their subjects had not been loosened much by out-migration, commercial agriculture, or modern education. Here, indirect rule was implemented in textbook fashion. Dagomba was a zone of subsistence agriculture that served as a labor reserve for export-producing zones of the South. The rural areas had almost no capacity to sustain taxation (Botchway 1998). In this part of the North, the costs of British "Native Administration" had been sustained almost entirely via direct transfers from Accra. There was little in Dagomba besides votes that was of immediate use to the nationalist regime coalescing in Accra, and these votes could be mobilized en masse by chiefs. In these circumstances, the CPP courted and eventually won over the royal house of Dagomba chiefs.[67] The nationalists manipulated and shored up the local aristocracy, preserved the boundaries of preexisting political and administrative units, allowed local aristocrats to colonize the Local Councils, and "indigenized" the CPP apparatus by co-opting the rural elite into positions of party leadership. As Martin Staniland (1975: 141) concluded in

---

[67] Staniland 1975:145 *inter alia*; Ladouceur 1979:119–78. The CPP enjoyed support in Dagomba East from the beginning. Between 1954 and 1957, the Dagomba royal house was split in a succession battle in which one lineage lined up behind the CPP, and one supported the opposition. After 1957, Dagomba along with virtually all of the North rallied behind the CPP. See Ladouceur 1979:168–75, 178.

his account of the nationalist politics in Dagomba, "the CPP took on the colour of its surroundings."

In Dagomba, transformation of Native Authority into Local Council happened without much upset or discernible change. Elections happened, but many seats were rarely contested and Dagomba's neotraditional elite saw the district's elected politicians as their agents in Accra.[68] In dealing with Dagomba, Nkrumah, like the Dagomba aristocrats themselves, behaved as a modern-day partisan of indirect rule. Staniland (1975:132) writes that the relationship between the CPP government and the Dagomba chiefs was not very different from what had obtained under colonial rule: independence narrowed the social distance between state administrators and the chiefs, but neotraditional politics continued to flourish under the patronage of the state.

The Dagomba counterexample suggests that the regime's choices vis-à-vis the chiefs and neotraditional authority in general were strategic, not dogmatic; rulers responded to threats and opportunities emanating from rural society. The fight in southern Ghana was not motivated by ideology per se, but rather by the regime's attempts to establish control over cocoa revenues that would be used to consolidate national power and build the postcolonial state.

Even within Asante and the Eastern Region – the core of chiefly opposition in the cocoa belt – the CPP behaved strategically in dealing with chiefs. It did not hesitate to ally with and enhance the power of neotraditional elites when this would strengthen the government's position in battles against its rivals.[69] In Asante and Akim Abuakwa, the CPP patronized dissident and subordinate chiefs. Many received promotions and gained more local influence. Many of the new administrative and political institutions built by the Nkrumahist state, including subunits of the party itself, were used to enhance the visibility of pro-CPP chiefs and their autonomy from the old chiefly establishment.[70] The regime's biggest move was in Brong-Ahafo, whose chiefly rulers had been subjected to what they saw as the unrightful

---

[68] See Staniland 1975:172, 132; Ladouceur 1979:101.

[69] In "Politics in Asunafo," Dunn (1975) describes what is probably the most obvious example. "The national leaders thus do not seem to have been officially opposed to the chieftaincy. They criticized the chiefs for wanting to supplant them in the future government of the country, and doing so with the aid of the British and via antidemocratic means" (Lombard 1967:226–7).

[70] Carving Brong-Ahafo out of Ashanti Region is the most dramatic example. On Swedru, see Owusu 1970:247–8, 264, 309, 327.

authority of Asante since the restoration of the Asante Confederacy in 1935. Nkrumah cultivated the support of Brong-Ahafo chiefs and fueled their aspirations of autonomy from Kumasi's overrule; carving out Brong Ahafo from the Ashanti region in 1959 was the dissident chiefs' political reward.

Across the South, the CPP government systematically manipulated stool and land disputes, supporting chiefs loyal to the party, upgrading their status, and encouraging destoolment proceedings against anti-CPP chiefs.[71] This "rewiring of the circuits of local authority," as John Dunn (1975:195) described it, was local-level state building via a strategy of penetrating localities and subjecting them to centralized CPP control. Intensive manipulation of local political economies was very much a part of this battle.

Nkrumah, like his counterparts in Senegal and Côte d'Ivoire, sought to impose political control over export-crop producing regions and to intensify the taxation of peasant farmers. To do so, the Ghanaian state established a far-flung and intrusive presence in the localities. The CPP constructed a vast patronage machine that linked rural producers to the state. Local outposts of the ruling party organized peasants at the grassroots, distributed credit and agricultural inputs, and established an official monopoly over cocoa buying. Even at the local level, control over resources and political prerogative was appropriated by state agents appointed from, and answerable to, the center.

The state apparatus was deconcentrated as the regime multiplied and expanded its outposts in the localities. In rural districts, these dense networks of local government agencies, producer cooperatives, state marketing institutions, and organs of the ruling party represented multiple and diverse points of access to state power and resources. To win support for the government, CPP agents could manipulate access to local commercial opportunities, to salaried jobs in the village cooperatives and local councils and party branches, and to agricultural inputs and credit distributed through the cooperatives.

Through these mechanisms, the CPP interposed itself between the big farmer and the small one, between creditor and debtor, and between cocoa buyer and client. In distributing credit and agricultural inputs, regulating land rents, and organizing the farmers into grassroots cooperatives linked directly to the party and the state, the CPP sought to create new patron-client structures that would displace old ones and to usurp the patronage powers of the established chiefly planter-merchant stratum.

[71] Allman (1993:186–9) provides a series of examples.

176

As time would tell, however, the Nkrumah party-state ultimately failed to uproot chiefly authority and prerogative at the micro level, where it remained embedded in relations of production and land access and in deeply personalized structures of obligation, dependency, and authority. Even when the CPP commanded all advantages of incumbency, including the full patronage powers of the state, it won only 43 percent of the vote in Asante in 1956. We also know that in those elections, almost 70 percent of the adult population in Asante did not vote at all.[72] As Allman (1993:192) writes, in spite of the CPP's deep penetration of local-level sociopolitical life and attempt to displace existing social hierarchies, and in spite of the existence of class-like tensions in the cocoa region, most ordinary peasants were, at the end of the day, neither "free laborers" nor "free voters"; they were not fully incorporated into the modern civil state.

Nkrumah's institutional reengineering did, however, achieve its immediate objective by "making it difficult for widespread opposition to arise."[73] The Nkrumah regime was not felled by mobilized rural opposition; its nemesis was a conspiracy hatched in a military barracks in Accra.

Part Two: "Local Powers Do Not Exist" – Southern Côte d'Ivoire

The postcolonial regime of Felix Houphouet-Boigny pursued a state-building strategy of administrative occupation in southern Côte d'Ivoire.[74] This meant not only extreme centralization of political authority and prerogative in the hands of the regime's direct agents, but also the building of administrative and political apparatuses that are heavily concentrated at the center. The goal of government in these regions seemed to be, to paraphrase one observer of the Ivoirian situation, to create a near absence of political life on the local level.[75] It is the exact opposite of what was observed in the central groundnut basin of Senegal, and differed starkly from Nkrumah's strategy of sending state agents to take over and micromanage villages. For rural dwellers in southern Côte d'Ivoire, administrative occupation meant that there were few points of access to state agencies, state resources, or political authorities wielding state prerogatives. The on-the-ground presence of the state was thin. Observers have been struck by the unusual degree of

[72] See Allman 1993:158–60.
[73] See Apter 1972:242.
[74] The title of Part II of this chapter comes from Nguessan-Zoukou 1990:32.
[75] See Cohen 1973:241–2.

autonomy vis-à-vis rural society and the extraordinary bureaucratic centralization that are characteristic of the postcolonial Ivoirian state. Richard Crook (1989:206), for example, has argued that what is "most distinctive" about Côte d'Ivoire in the African context "is its ability, at a very crude level of comparison, to implement its policies. The export crops have been successfully grown and marketed; the farmers get paid and receive their inputs; feeder roads get built and taxes collected."

Most analysts have explained Houphouet's institutional choices in terms of an exogenous factor – French institutional inheritance and example. France exported its administrative traditions via the colonial strategy of direct rule. The ideology-centered argument complements the institutionalist explanation: Houphouet was resolutely pro-French, supposedly pro-capitalist, and nonideological: he opted for administrative continuity and for a minimalist state. Excesses of state activism, such as using politics to stir up the rural masses or economic interventionism in peasant production, were antithetical to Houphouet's neocolonial vision of political order and development.

Cross-regional and subnational analysis, however, shows that such explanations fall short. The idea of a French model of direct rule that was applied uniformly throughout the zones of French conquest and then reproduced after independence just does not square with the facts on the ground. France and its successor states adopted the strategies of indirect rule when rulers found it expedient to do so. Modern African states were surely shaped by colonial inheritance (and rulers' ideologies), but ideas and inherited institutions were themselves shaped by what rulers confronted on the ground.

Houphouet's state-building strategies in southern Côte d'Ivoire are attributable in large part to endogenous factors – that is, to features of the Ivoirian political context that are traceable to facts of peasant life in the forest zone. Extreme centralization and concentration of the state apparatus was a reflection of the weakness of indigenous rural authorities. This in turn was a consequence of structural features of forest-zone society: relative absence of political hierarchy, broad dispersion of control over material and social resources, low levels of communal cohesiveness in villages and towns, and the extreme weakness of the precolonial political units that did survive colonial conquest. All this meant that local notables did not exercise much control over local economic resources or the political behavior of peasants. They could not, therefore, stand before the postcolonial regime as rural powerbrokers, much less rivals. Unlike the rural big-men of central

Table 4.1. *Institutional Choice in Two Cocoa Regions: Administrative Occupation versus Usurpation*

	Functional Domain		
	Provincial Administration: Party-State Apparatus	Export Marketing: Marketing Board, Co-ops	Allocating Factors of Production: Co-ops, Inputs, Land Law
Asante Region of Ghana	Spatial deconcentration Centralization of authority Usurpation	Spatial deconcentration Centralization of authority Usurpation	Spatial deconcentration Centralization of authority Usurpation
Southern Côte d'Ivoire	Spatial concentration Centralization of authority Administrative occupation	No institution building Farmers' transactions seem market-governed. Market forces	Institution building is minimal. Market forces and administrative occupation

Senegal, the Senegal River Valley, or Asante, local notables in the Ivoirian forest zone were unable to demand a share of local-level political power and inclusion in the governing institutions and processes of the state. Under these conditions, the construction of state institutions that were, to use Goran Hyden's (1983:19) phrase, "suspended balloon-like" above the rural South was a strategic move on the part of the regime: it took advantage of the particular weaknesses of peasant society as it was constituted in the Ivoirian forest zone. The same logic of institutional choice drove state building in the Casamance. Contrasts between the Asante region of Ghana and southern Côte d'Ivoire are summarized in Table 4.1.

Chapter 5 shows that there was considerable variation *within* Côte d'Ivoire. Peasant societies in the Senoufo zones of northern Côte d'Ivoire are somewhat more cohesive and hierarchical than those of the forest zone. The contrast with southern Côte d'Ivoire is less stark than the in-country contrasts examined in Senegal, but there is contrast nonetheless. The theory predicts that Ivoirian state-building strategies in the North would differ from those in the forest zone. Is this the case? If so, does the pattern of institutional outcomes in the North conform with expectations generated by the theory? It turns out that there are some real differences, and that they do run in the expected direction.

179

Map 4.2. Côte d'Ivoire

I. "Extreme Political Fragmentation" in Peasant Society

Farming societies in the Ivoirian south emerged from historical processes of precolonial settlement, colonial conquest, and peasantization, all of which worked against the concentration of power over people and land in the hands of indigenous authorities. In tracing the lineages of these societies, it is conventional and useful to divide the South into three main areas – the East, the Center, and the West. Precolonial political structures and institutions varied across these three areas, and each retains a cultural distinctiveness. However, as we shall see, by the nineteenth century the distinction between "state" and "stateless" societies that once described differences in the precolonial civilizations of the Ivoirian south had been seriously attenuated by the weakening or breakdown of African kingdoms in this region. Peasantization under colonial rule drove this process to its logical conclusion. This section makes the argument that there was a process of convergence by which rural social structures across the South came to share a common social-structural feature – the extreme localism and weakness of indigenous political hierarchy. Modern rulers' institutional choices would reflect this basic fact.

The Southeast and Center were settled over the course of the seventeenth and eighteenth centuries by Akan peoples fleeing the domination and military might of Akan states in what is now Ghana.[76] From these migratory movements arose the Baoulé and Agni ethnic groups of central and southeastern Côte d'Ivoire. Migrants brought with them the kind of pyramidal (lineage-based) political hierarchies and kingship institutions associated with Ghana's coastal Akan monarchies and the Asante empire, but Baoulé and Agni institutions never developed a high degree of centralization or wide geographic scope. As Guyer (1970:31) wrote, historians note "the absence of an Ashanti-type federal monarchy with a supreme chief anywhere in the Ivory Coast."

By the nineteenth century the Baoulé kingdom of Sakassou had dissolved into a group of small-scale and widely dispersed chiefdoms. Social organization moved toward a segmentary model characterized by "extreme political fragmentation."[77] Of the small precolonial Agni kingdoms of Sanwi,

---

[76] The first migratory movement of the Akan in present-day Côte d'Ivoire occurred in the first half of the sixteenth century. The Abron of the Koumassi region moved to what is now Bondoukou region (northeastern Côte d'Ivoire). Other groups followed in the seventeenth century in population movements associated with the rise of the Asante metropole to the East. Around 1670 to 1680, elements of the Sefwi conquered by the kingdom Denkyira fled westward and founded the Sanwi kingdom, with its capital at Krindjabo (just below Aboisso). Subgroups and split-offs from these movements formed the other Agni kingdoms, including Moronou (between present-day Bondoukou and Dimbroko) and Indénié, centered at Abengourou. The most important migratory movement came in 1720 through 1730. It arose out of power struggles in the new Asante kingdom. A vanquished faction (the Assabou group) fled to the West to form the Baoulé group. See Dian 1985:80–3.

[77] This fragmentation can be at least partially attributed to the center's inability to monopolize control over rapidly expanding North-South trade routes linking the savannah and the coast. Gold, one of this region's key trade commodities, was also widely dispersed, making it possible for small groups to split off and thereby weakening central authority. See Bredeloup 1989:27–8; Dian 1985:85; Person 1981:21. Chauveau describes precolonial Baoulé land as

Indénié, and Moronou, only the Sanwi in the extreme southeastern corner of what is now Côte d'Ivoire survived the nineteenth century essentially intact.[78] The distinguishing political features of most of Agni territory in the 1800s were localized lineage hierarchies dominated by royal aristocracies, which were centered around a number of small and weak monarchies.

The rest of southern Côte d'Ivoire was home to a great diversity of localized polities without administrative centralization above the village level. The sparsely populated West was the domain of the widely dispersed, "acephalous" societies that were, under colonialism, classified as the Dida, Bété, and Gouro ethnic groups. Chappell (1989:676) describes civilization here as a "scattering of stateless societies" that had been pushed ever westward by more aggressive intruders from the North and East. Emmanuel Terry described the Ivoirian west as "continuous milieu" without frontiers or clearly demarcated ethnic or cultural zones: to him it was "a constellation of small sovereign communities."[79]

Zolberg (1971:11) wrote that at the time of colonial contact, "there were no large-scale political entities in the Ivory Coast . . . comparable with the Ashanti in Ghana, Mossi in Upper Volta, or with the resurgent Muslim states of Mali and Senegal." This was reflected in the pattern of colonial conquest. Early on, the French were able to sign treaties with the Agni kingdom of Sanwi, with whom they had had long-established trading relations, and then with the lesser Agni kingdoms of Moronou and Indénié. In the south-central region (Baoulé country) and the Southwest (of the Dida, Bété, and Gouro), however, the French waged long and grueling wars of "pacification" against African populations who resisted village by village, hamlet by hamlet. From about 1905 to 1915 the colonizers resorted to scorched-earth tactics in Baouléland and the West. The strategy was "systematic destruction of *campements* and villages in the forest region."[80] The French carried out a widespread program of regrouping and resettlement that gathered populations into "strategic villages" set along new roads that

having "supra-village political organization as well as pronounced stratification, and the accumulation of a substantial surplus, all without a concomitant centralization of power" (Chauveau 1980:145).

[78] Stryker 1970:25. The Moronou kingdom was "reduced to an empty throne and bickering lineages in the mid-1700s by a devastating Baoulé invasion" (Chappell 1989:677). Bondoukou was subjugated and destroyed by the forces of Samory at the end of the nineteenth century.

[79] Cited by Dian 1985:84.

[80] Bonnefonds 1968:397. Bredeloup (1989:30) writes that between 1900 and 1905 the French set up thirty military posts in Baoulé territory.

182

had been cut through the forest. Communities and networks linking them together were disrupted. People lost control of their traditional lands and lineages: "they were strangers on the new land assigned to them" (Dian 1985:92).

Once control was established, an administrative strategy of direct rule developed in near-ideal form throughout the Center and West. Districts were defined arbitrarily, taking little or no account of the existence of linguistic families and following an administrative logic that would come to be defined in terms of evacuation of export crops.[81] Finding no compliant chiefs (or no chiefs at all) in many of the administrative districts they delineated, the French appointed loyal Africans – often soldiers, junior clerks, cooks, or interpreters in their employ – as their agents ("chiefs") at the grassroots. "[O]ften [they were] not even members of the ethnic group which they were appointed to control; in some cases they were not even Ivoirians, but Africans from more advanced colonies such as Senegal."[82] Official chiefs rounded up forced laborers the colonial authorities demanded for clearing land, hauling logs, building roads, and laying the railway. The administrative chiefs also acted as tax collectors. Needless to say, few enjoyed much legitimacy in the eyes of their subjects.

Most of the Ivoirian south was thus shaped by a history of precolonial political decentralization, a process of colonial conquest that was violent and extraordinarily destructive of established social orders, and direct rule through agents appointed by the colonial state. Agni areas of the Southeast had a somewhat different experience under colonial administration, for here the French found cooperative political authorities and preexisting political orders upon which to build a colonial system of rule. Throughout the Agni-dominated areas, the French drew canton limits that largely coincided with the boundaries of existing (and even some defunct) Agni microstates, and appointed members of royal families and lineage heads as cantonal and village chiefs.[83] Agni territory's colonial chiefs, like the appointed chiefs in

---

[81] Bredeloup 1989:34–6. From 1913 to 1939, *cercles* were defined and delimited as units of crop production (coffee *cercles*, cotton *cercles*, etc.). In 1947 there were sixteen such *cercles*, divided into about fifty "subdivisions." In 1939 there were 516 canton chiefs in the territory (Staniland 1970a:33, 35).

[82] See Zolberg 1964:21–2.

[83] Zolberg 1964:53. Zolberg explains for example that the *cercle* of Abengourou was divided into three cantons that corresponded to the Agni kingdoms of Indénié, Béttié, and Diabé. Chappell (1989:681) reports that the "long lost" Agni kingdom of Alangouan was reconstituted under French patronage.

other parts of the forest belt, were implicated in *corvée*. For chiefly authority, the main effect of this was to reduce legitimacy, even for indigenous elites who had enjoyed real status at the outset.[84] (The same thing happened to official chiefs in central Senegal.) Yet after about 1920, the Southeast was spared the worst of the forced-labor regime. This was partly in deference to chiefs, who were not forced to send their subjects outside of their home region, and partly because Agni and other African farmers in this region were left alone to spearhead smallholder cocoa production in the 1920s and 1930s. As we shall see, the rise of commodity production further diminished the institutional coherence and sociopolitical hierarchy that once set the precolonial Southeast apart from the rest of the Ivoirian south.

A. Rise of the Tree Crop Economy

France's *mise en valeur* of the Côte d'Ivoire centered almost exclusively on the production of tree crops – coffee and cocoa. Production of cocoa for export from this colony was initiated by Europeans, who were encouraged by the king of Sanwi to create the first plantations around Aboisso in the 1880s. Some of these declined and were abandoned by the turn of the century. African planters carried forward the momentum in this area. The geographic locus of European investment in plantations moved farther west, outside Agni territory, and into areas immediately to the north and west of Abidjan.[85] By the 1930s, about two hundred European-owned plantations, concentrated in the central-western forest zone (mostly around Gagnoa and Oumé), were a major fact of the Ivoirian economy. The European plantations were huge in size by Ivoirian standards of the time (averaging four hundred to five hundred hectares) and were worked in large part by Africans recruited as forced laborers by the colonial administration.[86] Most were run by managers hired by absentee landlords (many Abidjan-based), corporate financial groups, or trading companies (Fréchou 1955:69).

European coffee and cocoa plantations were only marginally profitable, and whatever prosperity they enjoyed turned out to be short-lived. Even

---

[84] See Firmin-Sellers 2000.

[85] French *colons* or investment groups created a few new cocoa and coffee plantations in the 1900s and 1910s. There were European plantations at M'Batto in 1895 and Tiassalé in 1905.

[86] See Frechou 1955; Bredeloup 1989:42. Hecht (1985:321–2) reports that in Divo Department in 1941, there were 22 expatriate plantation owners with average holdings of 150 hectares each. They produced 55 percent of Divo's total output.

so, the *colons'* demands for labor and other privileges from the colonial administration would have a major impact on the character of colonial rule in Côte d'Ivoire and on the politics of decolonization.

African smallholders, not the European planters, were responsible for the explosive growth of cocoa and coffee production in southern Côte d'Ivoire between 1920 and 1960. In contrast to what happened in central Senegal and Ghana's Asante region, the process of peasantization in the Ivoirian south accentuated the localized and dispersed structure of authority that already characterized indigenous societies in this region.

Rise of Commercial Agriculture in the Southeast. Agni and immigrant African planters in the Southeast led a process that would gradually push the expansion of coffee and cocoa farming across the Ivoirian south. After World War I, with logging and road building proceeding at a rapid pace in southeastern Côte d'Ivoire, the Agni turned almost en masse to cocoa farming. Land-use authorities at the community level (lineage heads) were often among the first to clear land and invest in plantations. These author- ities granted land-use rights to other lineage members and to Africans who immigrated to the Southeast to take advantage of opportunities for work or investment in commercial agriculture. By the 1950s, 28 percent of the fixed population of the Southeast was made up of foreigners.[87] In theory at least, communities represented by lineage heads retained residual claims to forest lands converted into plantations. Establishment of perennial tree crops had the effect of dramatically eroding community land rights, how- ever, for the farmer retained use rights for the life of plantations that could produce continuously for fifty years, and longer with replanting.

The rise of smallholder coffee and cocoa production thus eroded the land-use prerogatives – and with it this mechanism of control over depen- dents and other community members – of Agni royal families and lineage heads. De facto individualization of land control and the breakdown of lineage-based production units proceeded at a rapid pace in the Southeast.[88] Contributing to this process was the sheer prosperity of export-oriented agriculture in this region. Young men, commoners, and even "strangers" to Agni territory accumulated wealth, eroding dependency relations that had tied subordinate social groups to the old elite and undercutting the royal lineages' monopoly over the means of prestige.

---

[87] Chappell 1989:684. The figure was 33 percent in Agni Moronou (Boutellier 1960:139).
[88] Amon D'Aby 1958; Boutellier 1960; Chappell 1989:684.

As would be the case across virtually all of the forest zone, the limiting factor of production in the Southeast in the 1920s through 1940s was *labor*. This constraint was transcended in ways that made possible exponential increases in the amount of land under coffee and cocoa. In order to expand their holdings beyond the limit of labor power available within the household, the Agni of the Southeast who began planting cocoa in the 1920s relied on migrant laborers from poorer parts of the colony, mostly Baouléland and the northern half of Côte d'Ivoire. Some short-term laborers worked for wages, but share contracts were more common. Under share contracts, migrants farmed land that had been cleared and planted by the household head (sometimes with the help of wage labor). The owner of the trees kept the proceeds of one-half to two-thirds of the crop; what remained was the sharecropper's. The conversion of wage contracts into share contracts was not uncommon, and in the Southeast, many sharecroppers eventually received land to clear and farm on their own account.

Thus, in the oldest cocoa-producing regions of Côte d'Ivoire, land pioneering and labor influxes drove the extensive form of coffee and cocoa cultivation that became the defining characteristic of the Ivoirian *économie de plantation*. Easy access to land, migrant labor, and immigration promoted rapid increases in output by the mid- to late-1920s. By the early 1930s, the southeastern corner of the colony accounted for 90 percent of all Ivorian exports.[89]

As a result, this zone emerged as the privileged corner of what France still saw as a "backward" colony, far behind Senegal in terms of development of a colonial export economy, an urbane African elite, and a political (rather than purely military and administrative) apparatus of colonial rule. In Côte d'Ivoire of the 1920s and 1930s, the Southeast was distinguished from the rest of the colony by longer contact with the French, economic prosperity, and access to French education. Agni territory supplied France with its largest contingent of educated, acculturated, and French-speaking (*évolué*) Ivoirians.[90]

The existence of an indigenous elite of royal families and high-status lineage heads had created a foundation for rapid accumulation in the new export economy, for heads of important lineages were able to lay claim to large land tracts, allocate land to their family members, and mobilize

[89] Beugre Owo Sero and D'Alepe 1992:191.
[90] See Chauveau et Dozon 1987:267–8.

cash to hire labor. Colonial rule made lineage heads into "official chiefs" who grabbed prime land and ploughed their new salaries and cash earnings into hiring labor to clear and plant their personal cocoa plantations.[91] Heads of important Agni lineages would constitute the core of the "African bourgeoisie" of the Southeast. At the same time, as we have seen, the rise of the plantation economy redistributed property and wealth in ways that accentuated the localized and segmented nature of indigenous political organization in this area. Around 1957 Boutellier observed that in *pays Agni*,

[R]elations of hierarchy and dependency at all levels have weakened considerably or disappeared, the traditional hierarchy now exists alongside one arranged in terms of income, education, and political influence. . . . [Changes in Agni territory] have led in numerous cases to the almost complete elimination of chiefs from the framework of social life [and] . . . a diminution of the preponderance of *grandes familles*. (Boutellier 1960:205)

There has been, he wrote, a weakening of all authority, producing social disorganization and a "semi-anarchic state of affairs."

Immigration to the Southeast was a factor in this process: de facto land dispossession and settlement patterns that created extremely heterogeneous localities and towns had the effect of circumscribing and diluting indigenous authority. Agni Moronou "became a mosaic of strangers."[92] Beugre Owo Sero and D'Alepe (1992:195) called the entire Southeast "very diverse, making it a sort of melting-pot." In the most politically cohesive part of Agniland, Sanwi, indigenous Agni by 1953 constituted only about half of the local population: "out of a settled population of 32,000 in the central subdivision of Aboisso *cercle* . . . one-third were strangers. In addition, there were about 20,000 temporary immigrants working on local farms, many of whom settled in the region" (Zolberg 1964:41–2).

The political (and economic) implications of this were not lost on the Agni elite. There was a backlash in Sanwi: "[t]he land was becoming less and less Agni; land passed into foreign [non-Agni] hands, hence, the very existence of the Sanwi state was threatened."[93] In the 1950s Sanwi elites rallied around the Sanwi crown and attempted to assert their right to repossess land that had been leased to immigrants in earlier eras. By the time they acted, however, the Sanwi elite had effectively abdicated their old forms of

---

[91] See Boutellier 1960:67; Chappell 1989:683–4.
[92] Chappell 1989:682. Boutellier (1960:138) called it a "peaceful invasion" of *pays Agni*.
[93] Zolberg 1964:292. See also Boutellier 1960:136–9, 182–90; Chappell 1989.

187

political authority over land. This was truer still in the lesser precolonial Agni kingdoms.[94]

Commercial Agriculture's Frontier: The Center and West. Virtually open land access and extreme labor mobility pushed the cocoa and coffee frontier westward, creating ethnically heterogeneous villages across most of the Ivoirian south as hardwood forest fell to make way for smallholder farming. Gradually, *indigène*-stranger relations similar to those that emerged among the Agni in the 1920s and 1930s were generalized across the forest zone. Smallholder export-crop production spread to the sparsely populated West in the mid-1920s. In the wake of colonial conquest, Malinké traders from Mali and northern Côte d'Ivoire (called Dyula) had moved into the western forest zone and created commercial centers and towns across this zone. In the 1920s they obtained access to forest lands from the indigenous Dida, Bete, and Gouro and began investing in export crop production. Immigrant Baoulé farmers soon began arriving in the West. Migrants were authorized to clear forest land for their own use upon arrival, in exchange for providing labor services and/or annual payments (gifts) to those retaining "moral authority" over the land. By early 1930s indigenous households were clearing small plantations of their own. Dida of the central West began to use non-kin labor to expand their coffee and cocoa holdings in the mid-1940s. The first migrant workers were incorporated into households as "adopted relatives," but outsiders quickly established land-use rights, and less personalized relations between *indigènes* and outsiders became the norm.[95]

The 1946–1960 period was marked by huge influxes of "strangers" into the central West. Immigration in the mid-1950s was perceived in many parts as a Baoulé invasion. Within a decade after independence the Dida and Gouro were ethnic minorities in their original homelands.[96] During

---

[94] See n. 124, this chapter, on how Houphouet installed his own candidate on the Abengourou throne in 1945–7. Firmin-Sellers (1997:31 n. 7) reported that a chieftaincy dispute in Niablé in the 1950s, the geographic center of important Agni-Indiéné lineages, "failed to attract the attention of most citizens." See also Firmin-Sellers 2000.

[95] On land pioneering in the West, see Hecht 1984:270, 326; Chauveau and Dozon 1987:283; Lewis 1991.

[96] The share of immigrants among the permanent residents of Divo Department climbed sharply from 6.2 percent in 1948 to 63.3 percent in 1975 (Hecht 1984:272). Dian (1985:150) reports that in some cantons of the center-west (Gouro region), "strangers" already outnumbered *indigènes* in 1957. Zolberg (1964:40–2) wrote that "in a county in the *cercle* of

the 1950s and 1960s it became common to find household heads transacting de facto land sales to Baoulé, Malinké, and Africans from other parts of Côte d'Ivoire (and beyond). Often these sales were not acknowledged or respected by families and villages as such, creating some insecurity of tenure for immigrants and tensions in *indigène*-stranger relations that would become even more acute over time.

Colonial authorities did everything they could to accelerate the pace and sustain the momentum of land pioneering across the Ivoirian south. With the support of the administration, European loggers started in the Southeast and moved methodically westward, bringing African workers into the forest zone to cut roads and clear land. Africans and Europeans alike created new cocoa and coffee plantations in the loggers' wake. Taxation created pressure that pushed many Africans toward producing cash crops as either small farmers or migrant laborers. Even as land pioneering intensified, colonial authorities attempted to treat the local politics of land rights as a non-issue. They did not legalize the rural land claims of groups, African individuals, or indigenous authorities (including official chiefs). French administrators left their own European field agents to handle conflicts and, when the need arose, to record land claims and transfers, all in an ad hoc manner (Hecht 1985).

France's forced-labor regime was a decisive factor in the rapid rise of export-crop production. France regarded the northern half of Côte d'Ivoire (especially Senoufoland) and the entire French colony of Upper Volta as vast reserves of agricultural labor that could be channeled to the South through the use of force. In 1932 the French authorities fused the colonies of Upper Volta and the Côte d'Ivoire in order to better manage the forced-labor regime.[97] (This also helped to channel "free" Voltaic labor to the Ivoirian south and away from Ghana, where wages were higher.) Redefining the colony's boundaries had the effect of doubling the supply of labor to the *économie de plantation*. Forced labor also had an indirect effect on the pace of land pioneering in the South: until World War II colonial authorities exempted those they designated as "African planters" from this brutal and humiliating requirement. Agniland was thus spared the brunt

---

Bouaflé, originally inhabited by Gouro, two-thirds of the population is now made up of Baoulé and Malinké immigrants."

[97] This was actually a "reattachment" of Haute Volta, for the two colonies had been separated only in 1919. They were separated definitively in 1947. See Thompson and Adloff 1958:118–19. On the effect on labor supply, see Gastellu 1982:271–2.

of the forced-labor regime, and colonial authorities dangled exemption from forced labor as an incentive to encourage Baoulé and Malinké from savanna areas to create colonization villages in the Southwest.[98]

For the purposes of this analysis, the key fact is that across the entire Ivoirian forest belt, expansion of the *économie de plantation* tended to compromise the already limited powers of indigenous authorities who drew their social and institutional powers from rural communities. Land pioneering and influxes of migrant laborers created villages and localities that were not unified by common ancestry, myths of origin, or spiritual leaders. Meanwhile, the rise of smallholder commodity production and the planting of tree crops tended to break down lineages, individualize control over land, and guarantee a farmer's land-use rights for long periods of time. This eroded the prerogatives and social controls of notables who exercised moral authority over the land.[99] At the same time, because the plantation economy was based on the replication of the smallholder production unit on an ever-broader geographic scale, it did not give rise to a new strata of rural powerbrokers with control over people as well as material resources.

B. What About the Planter Bourgeoisie?

What about the much-discussed "planter bourgeoisie" of the Ivoirian forest zone? At this point in our analysis, the critical point is that the accumulation of wealth in the hands of perhaps a few hundred big planters in the Ivoirian south was *not* accompanied by the ability of the same group to accumulate political, social, and economic controls over the mass of peasant producers.[100] Big planters enjoyed respect and influence, along with the clientele that status and money can buy. However, virtually no mechanisms of social, economic, and political control over communities and localities were intrinsic to their positions and status as rich planters. This was the case around 1945, as well as in 1955, 1965, and thereafter.

In the forest, political power over communities was not inherent in the social relations of production. As we have seen, it was possible to acquire

[98] Zolberg 1964:41.

[99] See Hecht 1984; Gastellu 1982; Lewis 1991. Hecht (1985:320) wrote that the "dominant movement in the 1950s across southern Côte d'Ivoire, including Sanwi, was toward the emergence of individual land tenure and private property, including the division among individuals of unoccupied fallow land."

[100] Beugre Owo Sero and D'Alepe (1992) say that the biggest planters in the Syndicat Agricole Africain (SAA) in the 1940s were from the Southeast: they had domains of over thirty hectares and employed many wage laborers. See below.

control over land without imposing political control over people. The task of mobilizing labor was not accompanied by the establishment of durable forms of political control over local populations. Those linked to the colonial administration obtained contingents of forced laborers to work their land, but this power evaporated when forced labor was abolished in 1946. Thereafter planters hired labor, 90 percent of it supplied by migrant workers from outside Côte d'Ivoire. Across the South, workers often became sharecroppers, and sharecroppers tended to become farmers on their own account. As long as land was abundant and there were no strong political mechanisms to restrict access to it, the balance of power tended to tip in favor of the "owners" of labor power, rather than the original owners of the land. In southern Côte d'Ivoire, big farmers had to acquire labor – and were able to do so – without politically subordinating local populations.

Grassroots political culture or ideologies in the forest did little to bolster the political status or influence of successful planters. In the Center and West, very few had (or even tried to invent) spiritual or historical legitimacy as political leaders. In the Southeast, by contrast, notables of chiefly/royal status *were* among the largest export-crop producers. In the electoral struggles of the decolonization era, Agni notables did attempt to mobilize locally based electorates and campaign against the PDCI. What is important for this analysis is that this movement dissipated rapidly in the mid-1950s. All that was left of a mobilized Agni constituency by 1957 was centered in the tiny locality of Sanwi, where it was systematically repressed by Houphouet in the 1960s.[101] Thus, unlike their Asante counterparts in Ghana, members of the Agni political-economic elite were not able to mobilize deep-rooted peasant support for their political cause. Even in the Ivoirian Southeast, social relations of production, the structure of control over productive resources, and historical-ideological ties could not provide the core of the Ivoirian planter bourgeoise with powerful mechanisms of control over local populations.

The ability to build political hierarchy on the foundation of credit dependency also eluded most of the planter bourgeoisie in southern Côte d'Ivoire. Unlike the situation prevailing in Asante, where many large planter-traders were also local political big-wigs (chiefs), in the Ivoirian south most farmer-traders were regarded as strangers. Most were Dyula traders from the Ivoirian north, Mali, or Guinée who had created plantations in the forest zone after about 1920. (Prominent examples are Yacouba Sylla of Gagnoa

---

[101] See Médard 1982:73; Koffi Teya 1985:124–5.

and the Fadika family of Touba.) Dyula planter-traders used their trucks and networks of clients to mobilize votes for the nationalist cause in the late 1940s and 1950s, and in the cities of the forest zone, wealthy Dyula traders and Dyula communities dominated politics. Ultimately, however, their stranger status drastically circumscribed their political clout: although they had economic power, this could not, and did not, translate into any claims to political allegiance of the mass of the peasantry. On the contrary, their status as wealthy "foreign" merchants and plantation owners made them vulnerable targets of resentment. Person (1982:18) described pre-1945 relations between the Dyula and local populations in these terms: "[f]or forest populations, they [the Dyula] were invaders just like the French. At each revolt in the South, they were massacred in large number." Meanwhile, even as economic actors, the Dyula planter-traders were constrained: they enjoyed no monopoly of the crop-purchasing business in this zone. In the postwar years the French trading houses dominated the export trade, and the French preferred to rely on Lebanese buyers as their purchasing agents. Relations of credit dependency thus tied many small farmers to Lebanese merchants rather than to Africans who might have tried to turn financial power into community-level political clout.

On the issue of planter-traders, the Agni Southeast once again stands in partial contrast to the rest of the forest zone. As Buegre and D'Alepe (1992) explain, there was a significant stratum of Agni planter-traders in the Southeast in the late 1940s and early 1950s.[102] They competed with Dyula planter-traders who were based in the Southeast and with the Lebanese buyers who were financed by the French export houses. The political power that can come with the creditor role eluded these Agni planter-traders and, for that matter, wealthy Agni planters and all traders in the Southeast: in an amazing particularity of Agni territory, indebtedness among farmers was extraordinarily rare and limited.[103] Surely this plays a part in explaining the

---

[102] It seems that many Agni planter-traders had accumulated capital in commerce first, and then invested in export-crop production. On the history and holdings of the Assalé family of Niablé, for example, see Dian (1985:170–1) and Beugre Owo Sero and D'Alepe (1992:198).

[103] "Agni planters have traditions of saving money, one of the consequences of which seems to be the extreme rareness of indebtedness; in effect – and this is so exceptional in Africa that one must underline it – indebtedness is very limited in *pays Agni*. . . . One does not find but a few cases of indebtedness among members of the same village or lineage. . . . Savings in the form of gold is very widespread . . . [even among young farmers]. It is possible that three-quarters of all savings is in the form of gold" (Boutellier 1960:98–9). See also Gastellu 1989. Stavenhagen (1975:148, 151) contrasts the situation in Agni territory with that in southern Ghana.

anemic quality of Agni elites' efforts to mobilize electoral constituencies in the 1950s.

As for the Agni planter-trader class, it did not survive the 1950s. The commercial fortunes of many Agni traders and crop buyers were ruined by the collapse of coffee and cocoa prices in the late 1950s.[104] Most had abandoned the trucking and crop-buying business by the time of independence. In Agni territory, as across most of the Ivoirian south by the late 1950s, local-level crop buying was controlled by Lebanese buyers who worked either as agents of French buying houses or as independent merchants. Guyer (1970:74) writes that unlike what happened in next door in Ghana during the colonial period, a sizable African commercial class never emerged in the Côte d'Ivoire.

The commercial weakness of the Ivoirian planter bourgeoisie, coupled with its lack of structural economic-political ties to the mass of the peasantry, would fatally compromise its political power vis-à-vis the colonial and postcolonial state. As I will show below, the contrast with the situation prevailing in Asante in neighboring Ghana was striking. In the Ivoirian forest, the rise of a planter bourgeoisie did not reinforce or accentuate preexisting social and political hierarchies. The accumulation of wealth in the forest surely increased the status of big planters, but in general this was not accompanied by the development of concrete, micro- or local-level mechanisms of political and economic control over the behavior of peasants. Big planters could not mobilize community-level collective action.

II. Nationalist Era: Côte d'Ivoire's "Period of Politics"

In Côte d'Ivoire, the nationalist era began in 1944, when African coffee and cocoa growers organized to protest the colonial regime's blatantly discriminatory policies that favored European plantation owners. French authorities had gone to great lengths to support the *colons* during the depression years, often at the direct expense of the Africans. During World War II, Côte d'Ivoire's pro-Vichy colonial authorities outdid themselves with a series of new, racist rules and extractions. Henceforth, all the *colons*' labor needs were fulfilled by forced labor, to which African planters had no access; European

---

[104] See sources cited in the preceding footnote. On the brief trucking boom that coincided with high commodity prices in 1954, which preceded the plunge in coffee and cocoa prices from 1956 on, see also Tricart 1957:229–30; Boutellier 1960:98–9, 101.

growers received double the going rate for coffee and cocoa; and they received rationed access to imported consumer goods, agricultural implements, and inputs that none but a very few African planters (less than fifty) could obtain.[105] African planters, meanwhile, were no longer allowed to recruit migrant labor. To add further injury and insult, virtually all African planters (except those in the employ of the colonial administration) now found themselves subject to forced labor.

A. Farmers' Collective Action; Eclipse of the Planter Bourgeoisie

Most of Côte d'Ivoire's large-scale African planters were Agni lineage heads from the Southeast, and they had some experience in trying to mobilize collective action to influence state policy. In the mid-1930s Agni planters had tried to organize coffee and cocoa growers to demand better terms from the colonial administration.[106] This attempt failed. As Zolberg explains it (1964:66), the obstacles to success were the suspicions of chiefs, who worried about threats to their influence, and "ethnic antagonisms between Agni and other farmers elsewhere which hindered effective action." In 1943 the largest African coffee and cocoa growers were allowed to join the European-dominated Syndicat Agricole de la Côte d'Ivoire, a quasi-official body. One advantage of membership was access to imports that were rationed by the government during the war.

In April 1944, under the sponsorship of a progressive colonial governor just appointed by Free France (André Latrille), a group of eight African planters split from the European planters association and formed the Syndicat Agricole Africain (SAA).[107] Its core demand was restitution of a free market for agricultural labor. The SAA also demanded better prices for African growers. Membership was supposedly limited to African planters with a minimum of two hectares of cocoa or coffee, but in practice anyone willing to pay annual dues of three hundred francs was admitted. Farmers

---

[105] See Gbagbo 1982:21–3; Anyang' Nyong'o 1987:188, 209; Dian 1985:110; Zolberg 1964:67; Person 1981:22.

[106] In 1934 Agni leaders formed an Association power la Défense des Intérêts des Autochtones de la Côte d'Ivoire (ADIACI). Simultaneously they tried to organize coffee and cocoa growers in the Southeast to gain access to a government-controlled agricultural credit fund (Zolberg 1964:66).

[107] Lawler (1992:208–9) lists the founding members of the SAA as Houphouet-Boigny, Lamine Touré, Kouame Adingra, Djibrille Diake, Kouame N'Guessan, Fulgence Brou, and George Kouassi. See Syndicat Agricole Africain de la Côte d'Ivoire 1955.

had a strong incentive to pay this sum, for SAA members were exempted from France's forced labor requirement.[108]

The SAA provided an institutional framework that helped make further collective action possible. By the end of 1944 the SAA counted eighty-five hundred members, the vast majority of whom had small landholdings of two to three hectares.[109] It seems that about fifty African planters had holdings that surpassed the twenty-five-hectare threshold.[110] Of the eight founding members, four were planters from the Southeast. Beugre and D'Alepe (1992:203) suggest that the four southeasterners were the largest planters in the group, each with over thirty hectares and large numbers of salaried workers. Three of the other SAA founders were Dyulas, and one was Baoulé.

It has become conventional in Anglophone accounts of Ivoirian history to argue that the SAA, and even Houphouet's regime in general, "represented" the interests of the Ivoirian planter bourgeoisie.[111] Close inspection, however, yields an opposite conclusion. The paradox of the matter is that with the rise of the SAA, the core of the southern planter bourgeoisie – made up of wealthy Agni lineage heads of the Southeast – was eclipsed as a leading force in national politics. Big Agni planters who helped found the SAA did not try, or were not successful, at using it as a vehicle for consolidating political bases of their own. They did not use the SAA to organize small planters in their home areas.

As things turned out, the SAA rank and file was made up of small farmers "concentrated in the two Baoulé-dominant *cercles* of Bouaké and Dimbokro. Most of the other members were scattered throughout the forest zone, with the exception of the Southeast. This area, which produced 53 percent of the coffee and cocoa grown in the Côte d'Ivoire, accounted for only 10 percent of the membership."[112] The political effects

---

[108] See Zolberg 1964:67; Campbell 1973:207–9; Gbagbo 1982:26–32.

[109] Dian (1985:111) writes that the "quasi-totality of African planters in 1945–6 had less than twenty-five hectares."

[110] From Anyang'Nyong'o (1987:188), we can infer that in Côte d'Ivoire during World War II, there were about fifty African planters with twenty-five or more hectares of coffee and/or cocoa under cultivation, for fifty was the number that qualified by this standard to obtain imports under wartime rationing.

[111] Amin (1967) was actually the first to make this argument. Subsequent francophone authors have generally discounted it. See Gastellu 1989; Fauré and Médard 1982.

[112] Zolberg 1964:67; cited by Anyang'Nyong'o 1987:207. Half of the SAA's total membership in 1944 came from the circles of Bouaké and Dimbokro.

of enfranchising farmers with smaller, newer landholdings in the central-South were immediate. The only Baoulé in the SAA founding group, Houphouet-Boigny – canton chief of Yamoussoukro, a medical doctor, and one of the colony's wealthiest African planters – was elected president by the SAA members in September 1944. Once elections determined the locus of power within the SAA, numbers of voters and votes, not wealth or class standing, defined the political outcome. There also would be consequences for postcolonial economic strategy: rulers would support the small peasantry, rather than capitalist farmers.

In 1945, the SAA allied with small, Abidjan-based ethnic and voluntary associations to form the Bloc Africain and elect Houphouet as the Côte d'Ivoire's representative to the French Constituent Assembly.[113] In March 1946 Houphouet consolidated his organizational base in a new political party named the Parti Democratique de la Côte d'Ivoire (PDCI). In the French National Assembly, Houphouet forged an alliance with the French Communist Party, which pledged to support his campaign to end forced labor in France's African colonies. In a stunning, personal victory for the parliamentary deputy from the Côte d'Ivoire, France abolished forced labor by a March 1946 law that bore Houphouet's name. Flush with success and riding a tidal wave of popular support across the French colonies of Afrique Occidentale Française (AOF), the Houphouet-led PDCI was the principal catalyst for the formation of an AOF-wide mass nationalist party, the Rassemblement Démocratique Africain (RDA), in Bamako in October 1946.[114]

Abolition of forced labor produced major shifts in the structure of the plantation economy and in regional geopolitics in Côte d'Ivoire. It sounded the death knell for the European-owned coffee and cocoa sector, for the plantations could not operate profitably when their owners were forced to pay competitive wages to African workers.[115] Most Europeans abandoned or sold their coffee and cocoa domains. A reciprocal effect of the Loi Houphouet-Boigny was that "those abruptly freed from forced labor could start plantations of their own" (Dian 1985:110). So it was that 1946–56 became a decade of anarchic land rush on the Ivoirian frontier. Many have

---

[113] Loucou 1976:11–12. "Houphouet would spend the next thirteen years in the shifting coalition cabinets of the Fourth French Republic, usually in the Health Ministry" (Chappell 1989:686).

[114] See Person 1981:24–5.

[115] As Bredeloup (1989:42) writes, "their technical/agronomic knowledge and their financial means were insufficient to sustain the large plantations."

described this as a Baoulé colonization of the Ivoirian West.[116] As a result of this process, the small, new plantations of the Center and West displaced the vast, old plantations of the East as the main source of dynamism in the Ivoirian plantation economy. For the old Ivoirian planter bourgeoisie of the Southeast, the rise of Houphouet in the late 1940s thus marked not only political defeat, but loss of economic hegemony as well.[117] The SAA bureau constituted in November 1947 did not include any Agni members.[118]

Labor to fuel this postwar boom in land pioneering was supplied by migrant wage laborers. They came by the tens of thousands to the forest belt from the savannah regions of northern Côte d'Ivoire, mostly Senoufoland, and from Mossi territory of Haute Volta.[119] Capturing this labor flow – that is, directing it away from Ghana (where wages were higher) and to the Ivoirian South – was another feat for which Houphouet could claim some political credit. Acting both as a party-builder and head of the SAA, Houphouet sought alliances with the *grands chefs* of the savannah zone – the paramount chief of the Senoufo, Gbon Coulibaly, and the far more influential Moro Naba, chief of the Mossi aristocracy of Ouagadougou.[120] Both agreed to direct their subjects to the coffee and cocoa plantations in southern Côte d'Ivoire, where African farmers now promised migrant laborers better terms than their European rivals.[121] Below we show that Houphouet's strategies for building alliances with rural leaders in the more hierarchical and cohesive societies of the savannah zone were the opposite of those pursued in southern Cote d'Ivoire.

[116] See for example Chappell 1989:684. On the westward shift in the center of gravity of the plantation economy, see Nguessan-Zoukou 1990:91–2.

[117] Chauveau and Dozon (1987:267–8) see the election of Houphouet to the French Assembly in 1945 as marking the political defeat of the Southeast. On the erosion of the economic hegemony of the Southeast, see also Anyang'Nyong'o 1987:213. As of the early 1970s, the southeastern departments of Abengougrou, Aboisso, and Adzopé were still areas with high concentrations of large coffee and cocoa domains (Dian 1985:174, 176). In the rest of the South, large plantations do not appear to be concentrated in particular localities – rather, they are scattered across a wide geographic area.

[118] There were two members from Bassam: Lamine Touré of Odienné, who was the vice-president, and Djibril Diaby, the *secretaire archiviste* (Syndicat Agricole Africain de la Côte d'Ivoire, 1947).

[119] By legislation of September 1947, made effective in February 1948, France reconstituted the colony of Haute Volta. See below.

[120] See Gunderson 1975:84–5; Anyang'Nyong'o 1987:212.

[121] Under the forced labor regime, the Moro Naba and Gbon Coulibaly had supplied 30,000 and 6,500 forced laborers, respectively, to the European plantations in southern Côte d'Ivoire. This "human traffic" continued after the abolition of forced labor, with the support of the northern chiefs (Anyang'Nyong'o 1987:211–2).

B. Building the PDCI

The PDCI began organizing electoral constituencies in the Ivoirian south. For this, it turned away from the SAA practice of relying on prominent planters and Baoulé cantonal chiefs as its local agents. Houphouet's initial party-building strategy was to rely "almost exclusively" on Africans who staffed the ranks of the colonial bureaucracy.[122] Civil servants stationed in up-country towns were appointed by the party's central committee to found PDCI branches and represent the party in the localities (Zolberg 1964:119).

Dyula traders (and planter-traders) soon became prominent as PDCI agents in the forest zone (Person 1982:18–24). Most were strangers who hailed from northwest Côte d'Ivoire and Mali. As political operatives, their great asset was that they were plugged into the Dyula social and economic networks that crisscrossed the Côte d'Ivoire and linked it to RDA heartlands in the savannah. Most of the towns of the Ivoirian forest belt were majority Dyula, and Dyula PCDI organizers soon dominated politics in these urban centers.[123] They used their cash and transport vehicles to promote the PDCI cause. Even in remote rural localities, a Dyula trader was often the PDCI man.

Outsiders thus played the role of local political organizers. Analysts often deal with this anomaly by pointing out that Muslim traders were usually the most literate individuals around. Yet this explanation seems excessively apolitical. The PDCI also relied on Dyula immigrants as its agents in cities and localities in the Southeast, which were home to Côte d'Ivoire's best-educated and wealthiest rural populations. Relying on outsiders as party agents can also be understood as a political choice: it bolstered the autonomy and hegemony of the center. This strategic logic was surely at work in Agni territory, where rural society was perhaps best equipped to contest the PDCI's new monopoly. Person (1982:25–6) wrote that as the political alienation of the old Aboisso and Abengourou planter bourgeoisie mounted from 1945 on, the RDA/PCDI "relied on the muslim minority against the rich Agni planters who had at first supported the SAA."

From the very beginning, in the rural South the PDCI relied on agents with no political standing or base of their own. Houphouet's strategy reflected the reality he encountered in the localities: across the forest zone,

---

[122] See Zolberg 1964:101, 119.

[123] Using data from Abidjan, Dimbokro, Abengourou, Man, and Agboville, Barbara Lewis (1971:285–7) writes that "northerners . . . equal and usually exceed the number of urban inhabitants from the region in which the center is located." See also Person 1982.

the indigenous political elite was too weak to demand political inclusion. Even the wealthy, neotraditional political elite of the Southeast proved unable to mobilize a popular base of decisive political weight.[124] Houphouet's party-building strategy took advantage of the political weakness of rural communities in the forest zone.

C. Counterfactual: Powersharing with the Moro Naba

There are counterfactuals that provide support for this argument. One is the case of the Senoufo region of the northern Côte d'Ivoire, which is a focus of Chapter 5. Another is the case of PDCI electoral strategies in Mossi territory of Haute Volta, which was an integral part of Côte d'Ivoire from 1932 to 1947, and thus a part of Côte d'Ivoire at the moment of Houphouet's rise to power.

In the 1940s, the Moro Naba Saga II, chief of the Mossi aristocracy at Ouagadougou, brokered flows of forced and migrant labor to the South. After 1945 he also brokered Mossi votes. When Africans were granted representation in the French parliament, the Moro Naba demanded that the Mossi be represented by "sons of the soil," not by strangers, like Houphouet, from southern Côte d'Ivoire. The Mossi aristocracy also asserted their longstanding demand that Haute Volta be detached from Côte d'Ivoire and reconstituted as an autonomous colony.

In his first bid for a seat in the French parliament in 1945, Houphouet was very nearly defeated by the Moro Naba's candidate.[125] "Houphouet

---

[124] Agni elites' attempts to mobilize southeastern planters had fizzled out in the 1930s. In 1944 they were unable to grab control of the SAA. In 1945–7 the political center of Indiéné (Abengourou) was so weak that Houphouet, with the support of Governor Latrille, succeeded in overriding the hostility of the Indiéné aristocracy and having his brother-in-law, a son of the ruling family, imposed as Chef Supérieur. The dethroned king was Essey Bonzou, identified by Thompson and Adloff (1958:122) as "king of the Agnis." This particular episode of conflict persisted until 1956. One effect was to further weaken the chieftaincy in this region. The Agni chief installed with Houphouet's backing, Amoakon Dikhe, was born of a Senegalese father and Agni mother; he was the only Muslim in the royal family and was closely linked to the pro-PDCI/RDA immigrant Dyula community in the Abengourou area (Person 1982:23–5). See Lombard 1967:238. The PDCI also meddled in other chieftaincy disputes in Agni territory in the 1950s (Staniland 1970b:385).

[125] This was the 1945 elections to France's first Constituent Assembly. The tally was 12,650 for Houphouet and 11,620 for the Baloum Naba Tenga Ouedraogo, the Mossi candidate (Skinner 1989:181; Thompson and Adloff 1958:123–4). Kouame Binzème, an Agni lawyer who was supported by an organization called CAPACI (Comité d'Action Patriotique de la Côte d'Ivoire, which evolved into the PPCI in 1946), received a few hundred votes (Gbagbo 1982:34; Thompson and Adloff 1958:123–4).

then recognized the importance of the Mossi aristocracy."[126] According to Semi-Bi Zan, for the June 1946 elections, Houphouet promised to support demands for the reconstitution of the colony of Haute Volta in exchange for the Moro Naba's withdrawal of his candidate.[127] Six months later, in the November 1946 elections to the French National Assembly, Houphouet agreed to press demands for the reconstitution of Haute Volta in exchange for the Moro Naba's endorsement of a National Assembly list made up of three candidates: Houphouet, Ouezzin Coulibaly, a major RDA leader from western (non-Mossi) Haute Volta, and Kaboré Zenda, a candidate named by the Moro Naba himself to "represent the Mossi." "The list was a brilliant success" (Zan 1996:86–7). After that, the colonial administration grew hostile to the PDCI and the RDA, and Houphouet found it impossible to maintain an alliance with the pro-French Mossi elite.[128]

Houphouet's attempt to cut a deal with the Mossi elite is instructive. It suggests that the party-building strategies he pursued were the product of shrewd survey of local political topography and its regional contours, rather than some idiosyncratic preferences of his own or, as some have suggested, the importation of the French Communist Party's highly centralized organizational model. In 1946 Houphouet tried to deal with the Mossi aristocrats just as Senghor dealt with the Mouride elite: Houphouet treated the Moro Naba as a *grand electeur* and offered him considerable political autonomy within his circumscribed domain in exchange for the votes of Mossi subjects. This was the polar opposite of PDCI strategy in the Ivoirian south. Would the regional difference in institutional choice have persisted if Haute Volta had remained part of Côte d'Ivoire? By this book's hypothesis, it would have. It seems, however, that Houphouet himself was not eager to find out. He consistently endorsed the proposal to detach Haute Volta from Côte d'Ivoire.

The issue was soon resolved. In May 1947 the PDCI/RDA and its parliamentary ally, the French Communist Party, passed into the opposition in French politics. Power struggles in France and the gathering winds of the Cold War changed the political climate in French West Africa. Colonial authorities launched an all-out administrative repression of the RDA, now branded as a communist movement. Subtraction of Haute Volta from the

[126] Zan 1996:87.
[127] Zan 1996:87. See also Zolberg 1964:76 and Lawler 1992:216.
[128] See Skinner 1989:181–3.

colony of Côte d'Ivoire in September 1947, thereby removing it from RDA and PDCI influence, was the first move in this process.[129]

D. Crushing and Rebuilding the PDCI

In late 1948 the governor of Côte d'Ivoire, Laurent Péchoux, launched an all-out campaign to crush the PDCI.[130] Extreme political pressure for the next two years produced acute social tensions in localities, a series of bloody incidents, and wide-scale disruption of the organizational apparatus and political network that had been constructed by the PDCI. As Zolberg (1964:101) writes, "Because civil servants constituted the backbone of the PDCI organization, the party was extremely vulnerable to this administrative pressure." Many of the original founders and general secretaries of local PDCI branches were harassed, fined, or jailed by the administration. Some were beaten. A great many withdrew from the party.

As a result, party leaders came to rely even more heavily on Dyula traders as their intermediaries with the rural population. Strangers in the forest zone continued to act as the party's local agents.[131] As a political strategy, this is extraordinary: as Barbara Lewis (1971:292) writes, the entire period of postwar political mobilization in Côte d'Ivoire was a time of frequent localized expression of resentment against the Dyula as produce buyers (given the frequency of disputes over credit and crop payment) and as land seekers (given the frequency of disputes over land rights). In the late 1950s Zolberg observed some of the net effects of this party-building strategy:

At the local level, the general secretaries, often immigrants from other parts of the country, do not derive their authority from local support but rather from their office in the party hierarchy. They are dependent for appointment and for their continued existence on the territorial executive and particularly upon Houphouet-Boigny personally. Although these persons are often unpopular and resented because of their economic role [as traders], Abidjan has always insisted that all communications be channeled through them.[132]

---

[129] Zan 1996:88–9. The non-Mossi western region of Haute Volta was strongly pro-RDA and pro-PDCI.

[130] Morganthau 1964:190–3. On the series of bloody incidents, see Gbagbo 1982:95–7; Lawler 1992:219–24.

[131] See Person (1982:21–5), who reports that after 1948 Muslim traders were PDCI general secretaries for about half the local party sections in the Ivoirian south.

[132] Zolberg 1964:196, see also 186–7.

There were attempts to capitalize on the political liabilities of the PDCI, but they were not very successful. French *colons* and, from 1948, the colonial authorities themselves encouraged the emergence of regionally based (ethnic) rival parties in the Southeast and Southwest.[133] It is not surprising that the most significant of these was centered in the Southeast, home of an established planter bourgeoisie and an indigenous political notability that was linked to the colonial administration. Southeasterners themselves had not delayed in trying to organize a political response to Houphouet. In 1945, the French-trained (Agni) lawyer from Aboisso/Sanwi, Kouamé Binzème, ran unsuccessfully against Houphouet on the ballot for France's Constituent Assembly. Binzème and some associates also tried to build up a farmers' association to displace the SAA in the Southeast (and North).[134] In 1946 these efforts crystallized into the Parti Progressiste (PP), which was led by Agni intellectuals including Binzème.[135] Like earlier southeastern/Agni political associations, the PP traded on its association with the precolonial monarchies, the Agni chiefs, and the prestigious professional credentials of its French-educated spokesmen.

The PP operated under the sponsorship of the colonial administration during the period of administrative repression of the PDCI, and seems to have received financial support from French *colons*. Meanwhile, in the Gagnoa area, Bété resentment of immigrant (and strongly pro-Houphouet) Baoulé and Dyula populations crystallized in a Bété-backed political party that also received encouragement from the colonial authorities.[136] Another rival party emerged in the Northwest.

For this analysis it is most significant that leaders of these rival parties proved unable to mobilize and then broker significant blocs of rural votes during the "period of politics" in Côte d'Ivoire. As Person put it, these small, weak parties were "total failures" that collapsed when administrative

[133] Person 1982:22–3; see also Zolberg 1964:129, 140, 144, 199–201.
[134] Tidjane Dem (a Muslim businessman from Korhogo) was Binzème's northern partner (Staniland 1970b:384). See also Zolberg 1964:75.
[135] PP leaders were Kwame Binzème, the Ponty-trained teacher Kacou Aoulou, also from the Southeast, and Tidjane Dem. Gbagbo (1982:34) writes that in 1945, Binzème was an intellectual with "no real hold on the population." On PPCI in Bongouanou (Agni Moronou) in the 1950s, see Staniland (1970b:387–8), who writes that the PP "rested on its connections with and support of the [Agni] chiefs and the French administration."
[136] This was the Parti Socialiste (SFIO) of the Côte d'Ivoire, led by Dignan Bailly. See Morganthau 1964:174, 181; Lewis 1971; Person 1982:26; Gbagbo 1982:95–7; Chauveau and Dozon 1987:272–3, 275–6.

support for them was withdrawn after 1951.[137] Although this is a bit of an overstatement in the case of the PP, the larger point is well made. Throughout southern Côte d'Ivoire, including in Agni territory, rural society lacked the hierarchical cohesion that would have enabled indigenous authorities to mobilize large rural constituencies and thereby to press their claims to political authority and resources on the new elite at the center.

The PDCI broke with the French Communist Party in September 1950 and the period of administrative repression began to draw to a close.[138] By 1952, Houphouet had reconciled with the colonial administration and embraced France's vision of "new partnership" between the metropole and the colonies. His political ascent was now virtually unobstructed, for in rural Côte d'Ivoire there was no organized political movement that could block him, and even very few local leaders and personalities who were strong enough to demand a price for incorporation of their followings into the PDCI.

Two years of systematic attacks by the French authorities had seriously weakened the organizational infrastructure of the PDCI. The institution-building strategy that Houphouet chose at this moment was shaped decisively by the political realities he confronted in the Ivoirian forest zone: he proceeded to consolidate power without rebuilding the party's mass base. Power was concentrated in Houphouet's hands. Grassroots organs were not reactivated. As Ruth Morganthau (1964:211) said, "the PDCI remained disorganized. [Houphouet] appealed over the heads of his associates to the masses. The status of every other Ivory Coast leader became dependent upon his personal relationship with Houphouet." Under Houphouet's autocratic hand, the PDCI established a "practical monopoly over access to political life."[139] Henceforth the party would serve as a political vehicle for integrating various elements of the would-be Ivoirian political elite – civil servants, students returning from France, trade union leaders, big planters and planter-traders, leaders of the now-marginalized rival parties – into a political class dominated by a supreme leader.

[137] Person 1982:22. However, as many have noted, one residue of these parties was the further politicization of the *indigène*-stranger cleavage in the South. Baoulé and Dyula "strangers" in the forest zone were associated with PDCI, while people indigenous to the South (e.g., Agni, Bété) were smeared as "traitors" to the PDCI cause (Morganthau 1964:208–9).

[138] Person 1981:26. PDCI disaffiliation with the PCF was a compromise brokered by François Mitterrand. Repression of the PDCI continued through 1951. Person (1982:22–3) calls the June 1951 elections "the low water mark for PDCI."

[139] See Zolberg 1964:188–90.

The PDCI dominated the political stage completely until April 1957, when it formed the first autonomous Côte d'Ivoire government. The Ivoirian political elite that crystallized at that moment was the product of what already was a politically centralized and spatially concentrated structure of power. Those elected as deputies to represent southern constituencies in the precursor to the first National Assembly were party men chosen at the center with no local power bases of their own, and no control over local instances of the party. "At the highest level, most of the members of the [PDCI] Comité Directeur had spent their adult life away from their native region – in some cases outside the Côte d'Ivoire – and did not have an independent base of political support; hence, they derived their authority from their office in the party."[140] Thompson and Adloff (1958:131–2) reported "widespread absententionism" in the elections for the 1957 Territorial Assembly, Côte d'Ivoire's first African government.

The political weakness of rural societies in the forest zone is a striking fact of nationalist-era politics in Côte d'Ivoire that has been obscured by the myth of the political clout of the Ivoirian "planter bourgeoisie." There were indeed several dozen large-scale Ivoirian commercial farmers in Côte d'Ivoire in 1944, but the core of this social group was made up of southeasterners whose political influence and clout were eclipsed decisively by the rise of the SAA and then the PDCI. A new class of big African planters emerged in the Center and West in the 1950s, but as a process of class formation, this was at least as much an *effect* of the PDCI's rise (when well-connected party men gained access to new sources of cash and loans, some of which surely went to buy out European planters) as its cause.[141]

Social structure in southern Côte d'Ivoire goes far in explaining the political weakness of rural interests in this zone. The rural South was marked by the absence of social hierarchy, low levels of cohesion and solidarity in village communities, and the limited powers and legitimacy of indigenous rural authorities. Agniland is a partial exception that helps to prove the rule,

---

[140] See Zolberg 1964:197.

[141] There was massive land pioneering in the West in the 1950s, and we can assume that many large plantations were created in this process. With the retreat of the colony's approximately two hundred European plantation owners after 1946, we can presume that many of their large domains were sold to Africans. Such transfers may be the origins of a new Ivoirian political-cum-planter bourgeoisie that arose in the 1950s and 1960s, after the PDCI had control of the state. In one case, a 450-acre coffee and cocoa plantation owned by a French settler was purchased by Houphouet in 1963 and given to the Veterans Association of Man (Lawler 1992:239). Many more large plantations were created for members of the political class in the 1970s.

for even here, an indigenous elite that was rich in social capital – material wealth, aristocratic title, Western education, good connections to colonial authorities – was unable to mobilize a mass base to support its claims to a share of the postcolonial state. Within Agni territory, the tiny Agni kingdom of Sanwi stands out as a micro-exception that again helps to prove the rule. Sanwi, the most politically coherent and institutionalized of the Agni states in the twentieth century, remained a site of organized political initiatives to press demands on the regime now coalescing in Abidjan. Houphouet crushed Sanwi political mobilizations in 1959–60, 1961, and 1969 with localized repressions that resulted in many arrests each time. This case is discussed below under the heading of Sanwi exceptionalism.

The most serious opposition facing Houphouet in the late 1950s came from "free-floating" elements of the urban elite, not from the rural areas. Challenges to the extreme narrowing of the political arena in Côte d'Ivoire came from students returning from France, many of whom objected to the form of neocolonialism that was under rapid construction in Côte d'Ivoire; from civil servants bitter over the betrayal of the French Communist Party and the rest of the Left; and from trade union leaders loyal to the RDA, the AOF-wide nationalist movement now disavowed by Houphouet. Co-optation was the regime's strategy for dealing with these disaffected elements: individuals were offered jobs in the party and civil service. The institutional apparatus of the party grew only where it was needed to absorb and contain resistance to the regime: a PDCI "youth wing" and labor organization were created in Abidjan. Opposition among intellectuals and returning students persisted, however, and the pace of Africanization of the civil service slowed down: "For a while between 1957 and 1959 it [the PDCI] felt it could count more on loyalty from the Europeans than from the African intellectuals" (Morganthau 1964:214).

As Côte d'Ivoire moved toward internal political autonomy, the French colonial authorities played yet another political card. France initiated a process of spatial deconcentration of the state apparatus and of devolution of central authority.[142] Between 1952 and 1955, three coastal cities (including Abidjan, the capital) and one interior city (Bouaké) became fully autonomous municipalities with elected mayors and councils, and independent budgets. In 1955 another five cities became partially autonomous municipalities with appointed mayors and councils. The constitutional

[142] On this, see Staniland 1970a:39. The four full communes were Abidjan, Bingerville, Grand-Bassam, and Bouaké.

205

and legal framework for the new *communes* was copied directly from the French model. Staniland notes the irony of the colonizers' last-minute embrace of populism and sees the decentralization initiatives as an unambiguous attempt on the part of the French authorities to dilute the influence of the Ivoirian political elite that now gathered at the center. Upon coming to power, Houphouet reversed this move toward "democratic decentralization."

III. Institutional Choice in Southern Côte d'Ivoire: Administrative Occupation

The fragmented and atomized social structures characteristic of the peasantries of the Ivoirian south meant that capacities for sustained collective action were low. The brilliance of Houphouet's strategies for governing and taxing the south is that they reinforced this very feature of rural society. Because local authorities were weak, the regime of Houphouet ignored them. It did not build networks of rural political institutions to link local power centers to the state; it did not channel resources into the hands of provincial powerbrokers in order to enhance their political authority and fuse it with that of the regime; it did not try to promote the rise of a new strata of rural leaders.

Under the postcolonial regime, the Ivoirian south was striking in its *absence* of ruling-party politicking, organization building, and official consciousness raising. The state provided little incentive or impetus for political organization or collective action of any kind. Observers spoke of the stifling and stagnation of political life at the local level.[143] Michael Cohen argued in 1973 (pp. 241–2) that the government avoided spending money in the localities because state money generates political activity. Barbara Lewis wrote in 1971 (p. 293) that the PDCI sought to minimize political group formation at the local level.

This governing strategy had institutional correlates: there were few official sites, positions, or organizations on the local level that offered direct access to state wealth or power. Local interests had few sites to colonize or capture, provincial political entrepreneurs had little cause to mobilize rural populations to further their ambitions, and political machines were not built to link local networks to national hierarchies. There was no elaborate network of state institutions in the forest belt. This made for a state

---

[143] See Cohen 1973; Médard 1982:70; Stryker 1971a.

apparatus that was spatially concentrated and therefore distant from the localities. The state's rural outposts were projections of highly centralized forms of political authority and prerogative: virtually all state resources and prerogative were tightly controlled from the center. In the southern half of the country, direct agents of the center governed peasantries. Even the officials stationed in the regions and localities enjoyed little autonomy from Abidjan.

In the rural South, Goran Hyden's (1983:19) description of the African state as suspended in mid-air is apt. The appearance of "ungroundedness" was produced by the extreme centralization of authority in, and spatial concentration of, the state institutions that structured Ivoirian political space. Ungroundedness was a two-dimensional effect: it reflected not only the concentration of state administrative capacity and prerogative at the higher levels of the bureaucratic hierarchy, but also the thinness of state presence in the localities. These features of state design were manifest in the three institutional and functional domains we track here: provincial administration and the political *encadrement* (organization) of the peasantry, official strategies to promote coffee and cocoa production, and state regulation of the export-crop marketing circuit. What some have perceived as the unusually high degree of administrative capacity in the Ivoirian provinces was no doubt related to the remarkably centralized and concentrated structure of control.

Although indigenous political authorities were weak, the regime was not complacent about its ability to dominate and control the forest zone. On the contrary, Houphouet seemed to fear above all else the possibility that political entrepreneurs would try to ignite the explosive mixtures of ethnic *indigène*-stranger and class-like tensions that were inherent in the Ivoirian *économie de plantation*.[144] Such tensions led to violent uprisings in Gagnoa in 1970 that were suppressed with much bloodshed by the regime. Stryker, a close observer of Ivoirian politics in the 1960s, pointed out that this kind of conflict is more easily isolated and suppressed when it does *not* occur in an arena that provides access to modern organizational resources.[145] Houphouet's regime seems to have understood its challenge in precisely these terms. The challenge was to reproduce the dispersion, fragmentation, and extreme localism of rural social networks, communities, and identities. Avoiding the politicization of local social divisions, communal solidarities,

---

[144] See Chauveau and Dozon 1987:276–80.
[145] See Stryker 1971b:134.

and class-like consciousness was crucial not only to maintaining the political hegemony of the regime, but also to sustaining the expansionist momentum of the plantation economy.

A. *Territorial Administration and Party Structure*

This book argues that where postcolonial regimes strive to co-opt or displace powerful indigenous authorities in the rural areas, they build party-state apparatuses that burrow deeply into the foundations of local political authority. In the coffee and cocoa zones of Côte d'Ivoire, by contrast, the regime of Houphouet made the opposite institutional choice, and this in response to weakness of indigenous political authorities and peasant societies' low levels of political structuration. The institution-building strategy was one of administrative occupation: Houphouet built a ruthlessly centralized and highly concentrated party-state that gave rural interests few sites of access to the state and state power, and few sites that would-be political entrepreneurs at the local level could use as scaffolding to advance their own political ambitions and/or the interests of rural Ivoirians.

In the 1960s and 1970s Houphouet presided over a progressive *deinstitutionalization* of the territorially structured political apparatus, that is, of the ruling party and of the (meager) structures of local government inherited from colonialism. The state's presence in localities in the South was limited almost completely to a military-style territorial administration in which rural populations were subjected to an ever-tightening grid of prefectorial control. Christian Potholm (1970:270) observed that of four African countries he studied in the 1960s, the only one to display less interest in "political development" than Côte d'Ivoire was the Republic of South Africa.

Ruling Party. The on-the-ground presence of the PDCI weakened considerably between 1950 and 1960. The party's decline as an organizational reality continued unmitigated over the course of the 1960s, so much so that Stryker (1971b:136) and others described it in the early 1970s as "dilapidated and atrophied." In the countryside in the South, the machine politics and co-optive functions of the PDCI withered away.

Under Houphouet, the geographical scope of electoral districts expanded in the 1950s. This process reached its logical extreme at the time of independence when the entire country was brought together in one electoral unit. "The electoral system was reduced from nineteen constituencies in 1957 to four in 1959, and then to a single nationwide constituency in the year of independence, with all National Assembly candidates running at large, without opposition, after personal selection by the president and party secretary general."[146] From 1960 until the political opening of 1980, Ivoirians cast a single vote for or against the list of PDCI candidates for the National Assembly.

This meant that deputies in the Ivoirian National Assembly had no electoral constituencies to represent, answer to, or promote. Tessy Bakary writes that most *deputés* had no geographical base of political support, and in fact no popular base at all.[147] Like the parliamentary deputies from the Lower Casamance that were discussed in the last chapter, oftentimes the Ivoirian deputies were not even indigenous to the regions they were supposed to represent. Bakary described the Ivoirian National Assembly as little more than a club of "the President's Men." It is not surprising that rates of participation in the PDCI five-year election rituals were low, for as Bakary argued, deputies in the parliament failed to create, maintain, or perpetuate mechanisms or incentives for electoral participation.

At local levels, the PDCI apparatus consisted of little more than secretary generals who were appointed by Abidjan to represent the party at the lowest level of the administrative hierarchy, the *sous-préfecture*. No elections were held and no PDCI political organization existed at the *sous-préfecture* level. The main function of the secretary generals was to organize the local sale of PDCI party cards and collect annual fees for national identity cards. Many peasants perceived these obligations as the modern-day equivalent of paying the colonial head tax. There is a clear contrast with the system that developed in central Senegal, where party notables bought batches of party cards to distribute to their actively patronized electoral clienteles. In Côte d'Ivoire, the PDCI's local agents in the forest zone lacked their own electoral clientele and political bases, as had been the case in the 1950s. Local instances of the party were not renewed or rejuvenated in 1960, and often secretaries-general were the very individuals who had assumed these posts a decade before.[148] Many were perceived as strangers in the localities they worked. Nguessan-Zoukou (1990:39) describes the rapport between PDCI secretary generals and local populations as "very distant."

---

[146] Zartman and Delgado 1984:5.
[147] See Bakary 1986. See also Bakary (1991:76), who writes that "[l]iterally, elected officials represent no one but themselves." Stryker (1971a:96) and Widner (1994:131–3) echo this point.
[148] Zolberg 1964:196.

209

So ungrounded was the PDCI as an institution – so concentrated and centralized in structure and process – that the roles and prerogatives of the secretary generals were minimal and contact between them and authorities in Abidjan was "intermittent, at best."[149] Local agents of the party were kept out of any real brokerage, activist, or decision-making role in the party or administration. They seemed to play virtually no role as propagandizers, coalition builders, constituency organizers, local patrons, or intermediaries. In some cases, party organization at the local level was so dilapidated that the *sous-préfet* was charged with responsibility for collecting party dues from local residents.[150] On paper, the PDCI claimed to have village cells (*comités*), but in many localities these did not exist. Where cells existed, their main purpose seemed to be the collection of annual fees for identity cards.

It is very clear that the PDCI did not serve as a network for channeling state resources from the political "core" to the periphery in exchange for votes and political support. By the early 1950s it had ceased to serve as a conveyor belt for elevating local-level political entrepreneurs into the national political scene. There were political personalities in Houphouet's regime who were supposed to represent one or another ethnic group or up-country town. Yet the typical pattern of elite creation in southern Côte d'Ivoire was the exact reverse of patterns observed in many other places – in central Senegal, for example, or in northern Cote d'Ivoire (as we shall see in the next chapter) – where rural big-men use local power bases to propel their own ascent up the national political ladder.

In the Ivoirian south, things did not work this way: big-men lacked autonomous power bases. Houphouet would often recruit into politics what Tessy Bakary (1991) called a "newly educated nobody." *After* incorporation into the national-level political class, some would work to become personalities in their home localities. After the mid-1970s Houphouet expressly required high-ranking state officials to do so: he required them to establish coffee and cocoa plantations in their native villages and exhorted them to invest in village improvement projects to show their concern for the folks back home.[151] In this way, prominent politicians of the regime's

---

[149] Stryker 1971b:136. See also Nguessan-Zoukou 1990:39.

[150] See Widner 1994:131–2.

[151] Woods (1994:471–2) writes that "almost without exception, hometown development associations are set up by prominent individuals residing in Abidjan.... [T]he vast majority of [association leaders] were either members of the PDCI, high-level bureaucrats and/or deputies in the National Assembly." See also Dubresson and Vidal 1991. Contrast also with Kenyan politics as described by Bates (1989:87).

own creation were imposed on the localities. Highly personalized linkages between center and periphery were sometimes established. Yet the big-men were dependent upon power and status bequeathed from above, and thus remained within the orbit of the president's control.[152] Contrast this with the situation in the Wolof groundnut basin, where those aspiring to national office required the blessing and patronage of rural powerbrokers, especially the Sufi marabouts.

Municipal Government. As the party atrophied, so too did other spatially deconcentrated political structures inherited from the 1950s. In the mid-1950s, a reform-minded colonial administration had created the legal framework for autonomous and semi-autonomous municipal government in Côte d'Ivoire. Five urban centers were granted some financial autonomy and the right to elect municipal councils and mayors. At around the same time, the French authorities created department-level "general councils," which were supposed to be political bodies that would represent populations living outside the urban centers. General councils were supposed to accommodate respected rural leaders and local-level influentials.[153] We can safely presume that this group included cantonal chiefs (or their associates) who had been loyal to the French during the period of repression of the PDCI.

The Ivoirian leaders who took the reins of internal self-government in 1957 chose to undo these institutional innovations, thereby reversing the process of deconcentration and political devolution (decentralization) set in motion by the French.[154] Staniland (1970a:38) declared that in Côte d'Ivoire, "[l]ocal democracy was choked off." No municipal elections were held anywhere in Côte d'Ivoire between 1956 and the early 1980s; cities and towns had no taxation powers or managerial autonomy, and even the ruling party "was largely an irrelevant organization in the urban areas."[155] In six of the eight Ivoirian municipalities in 1970, the office of mayor was occupied by the administrative prefect.[156]

---

[152] With the opening of electoral competition in the 1980s, this began to change. Support in the regions and localities became political capital that could be used to advance one's position in the national arena. See Dubresson and Vidal 1991.

[153] See Staniland 1970a:38–9.

[154] On this reversal, see Stryker 1970:210; Staniland 1970a:38–9.

[155] Cohen 1974:230. On the cities, see also Cohen 1973:227–40; Stryker 1971a. On mayors, see also Bakary 1986:218.

[156] See Stryker 1970:208.

By the 1970s, many Abidjan-based members of Parliament had added the post of mayor to their resumés. These, however, were positions void of political resource or prerogative; they were little more than honorific appointments.[157] Médard wrote in 1982 that the municipal councils had disappeared.[158] As for the provincial general councils, after independence they ceased to exist. Nguessan-Zoukou (1990:28–9) argues that the municipal governments and departmental councils were aborted "because they threatened to become a counterweight to the omnipotence of the prefect. . . . To prevent the emergence of local political personalities, the regime chose to ignore the laws creating local bodies."

The Ivoirian pattern is the opposite from what was observed in Senegal, where most towns serving as departmental seats became full *communes* in the 1960s, each with an elected mayor and council. In central Senegal, these new municipal governments became regional leaders' stepping stone to the National Assembly. Ziguinchor, the capital of Lower Casamance, was the exception. Ziguinchor remained under the control of a state agent linked directly to the center (the regional governor): it conforms closely to the pattern we see in Côte d'Ivoire. These two cases thus provide support for the hypothesis that where rural society was not hierarchically structured, regimes did not build institutional sites that would have allowed new political entrepreneurs to consolidate power. Nguessan-Zoukou (1990:28–9) made this argument in the late 1980s: the Ivoirian regime, he said, did not create local government bodies because it feared that "personalities who might emerge from such institutions might be strong enough to give the impression of contesting the power of the center."

There seems to be something to Michael Cohen's (1973:241–2) observation about Ivoirian rulers avoiding the expenditure of money in localities because government spending creates political activity. Nguessan-Zoukou describes "ridiculously low" levels of state investment in social services in localities in the forest zone, except in the personal political constituencies of Houphouet himself in the Baoulé districts around his own hometown,

---

[157] In Côte d'Ivoire all skilled municipal employees were recruited and paid by the central government (Garnier et al. 1992:14).

[158] Médard 1982:70. See also Stryker 1971a:97. Côte d'Ivoire embarked upon a policy of administrative decentralization and "democratization" in the early 1980s that created new communes (the first since 1956) with elected municipal councils and reinvigorated electoral competition for these seats. See Bakary 1986. Dimbokro, one of the new communes created in 1980, remained under the control of the prefect at the end of the decade (Bredeloup 1989:83).

Yamoussoukro.[159] Others have noted low levels of investment in social services (education and health) in the Côte d'Ivoire compared to other lower-middle-income countries, or to Ghana.[160] As wealthy as Côte d'Ivoire was in the 1960s, when the country was in full economic boom, services deteriorated in secondary urban centers of the South such as Agboville and Dimbokro.[161]

Territorial Administration. The system of territorial administration that was imposed on the forest zone was a near-perfect model of direct rule. Virtually the only linkages between core and periphery were bureaucratic, and these were remarkably insulated from local political pressures and influences. One observer described the postcolonial process of state building in the rural areas as the "bureaucratization of local political life."[162]

Territorial administration was structured into a tight hierarchy. This was one part of the colonial legacy that the new rulers in Abidjan chose not to discard. Abidjan also accepted France's demarcation of administrative units, which had been drawn in the 1920s and 1930s with virtually no reference to precolonial political or social groupings (save in the East and, as we shall see, the North). Abidjan did, however, make some innovations as rulers built a postcolonial institutional apparatus to control the hinterlands.

Its choices were almost the opposite of those made in Dakar. Whereas Dakar's initial choice was to deconcentrate territorial administration by making the old *cercle* subdivisions the basic units of territorial administration in 1960, Abidjan chose to create a new rung of administration *above* the *cercles*. Between 1956 and 1961 the government placed the colony's nineteen *cercles* under the territorial authority of four regional governors, who were called *préfets*.[163] These prefects were the regime's top law-and-order agents

---

[159] Ngessan-Zoukou 1990:31, 125. See also Garnier et al. 1992.

[160] Schultz 1975:81. This shows up in aggregate statistics: Côte d'Ivoire's quality of life indicators that are lower than average for lower-middle-income countries (Garnier et al. 1992). On the low level of state-financed social services, see also Stryker 1970: 241.

[161] See Cohen 1973:232; Bredeloup 1989.

[162] See Staniland 1970a:126.

[163] In Senegal, the *cercles* disappeared and the *cercle* subdivision became the basic unit of territorial administration (renamed "department" or prefecture). In Côte d'Ivoire, the new supra-*cercle* jurisdictions were first named "regions," then renamed "departments" or prefectures. In Côte d'Ivoire *sous-préfets* were stationed at the level of the old colonial subdivisions.

outside the capital city. All were appointed by the Ministry of the Interior. "There was a clear concern with tightening central control."[164]

Again in contrast to central Senegal, the departments in the Ivoirian south were not electoral constituencies or political units in any other sense.[165] Prefects and *sous-préfets* were serving officers in the Ivoirian army, and were referred to by their local subjects as *mon commandant*. Colonial cantonal chiefs lost all coercive powers and administrative prerogative: they faded away, yielding their place as local representatives of the state to the *sous-préfets*. In a very short time, the kind of bureaucratized apparatus of political control observed in Casamance was imposed across virtually all of southern Côte d'Ivoire.

Starting in the mid-1960s, when consolidation of the party-state was complete, there was a steady *de*concentration of the state's military-style presence in the rural areas. From four prefectures ("departments") in 1956, the number went to six (1966), nine (1969), then twenty-four (1974), thirty-two (1978), and forty-nine (1985).[166] The number of *sous-préfectures* also increased steadily from the late 1960s. Prefectorial administration is the only part of state apparatus in southern Côte d'Ivoire that underwent systematic deconcentration in the first two decades of independence.

In military fashion the prefects and *sous-préfets* were rotated from post to post, and from region to region, as their careers developed and as the regime pushed forward with repeated restructurings of the Ivoirian political space. Even the *sous-préfets* were not indigenous to the localities they administered. Stryker wrote that "the sub-prefect is always a stranger in his assigned district (by official policy to discourage nepotism), and he is usually as dependent upon interpreters as was the [colonial] commandant."[167] Even within the spatially deconcentrated prefectorial apparatus, manned by direct agents of the state from top to bottom, little administrative prerogative or autonomy gravitated down to the man-on-the-spot. *Sous-préfets* had no budgetary or disciplinary powers, they often lacked staff or technical support, and they usually had few or no local connections to help them accomplish the task at hand. When local troubles broke out,

---

[164] Staniland 1970a:113–18. In the last decades of colonial rule, Côte d'Ivoire was divided into nineteen *cercles*, fifty subdivisions, and about five hundred cantons. The new "regions" or prefectures were created in 1959, but prefects were not appointed until 1961.

[165] The exception to this was the year 1959, when the four "regions" were electoral constituencies for the Legislative Assembly election.

[166] See Stryker 1971a:92–4; Médard 1982a:65.

[167] Stryker 1971a:95. *Sous-préfets* were usually rotated every two years.

it seems that Abidjan-based authorities were often called in to handle the problem.[168]

To keep administrative authority tightly centralized, Abidjan did not rely solely on the military-style chain of command.[169] In this area as in many others, Houphouet often trusted Frenchmen more than his own country-men to remain insulated from political influences that might erode the hegemony of the center. Four years after the 1957 administrative reform, only one of the nineteen *sous-préfets* was an Ivoirian; their immediate supe-riors were Ivoirians in only about half of the cases (Staniland 1970a:115). Throughout the prefectorial administration the pace of Africanization was surprisingly slow. In 1964 there were more Ivoirian *sous-préfets*, but they were monitored by inspectors attached to the Ministry of Interior; eight of the nine inspectors were French. As late as 1968 the prefects were shadowed by deputies, virtually all of them Frenchmen, who were empowered to take over in the prefect's absence.[170] Insulating the state apparatus from local po-litical pressures by relying on Frenchmen and other foreigners as the state's agents was a pattern of governance observed at virtually every level of the governmental hierarchy in postcolonial Côte d'Ivoire, from Houphouet's inner circle on down. In 1979 there were at least 10,000 French advisors and technical agents working in the Ivoirian government.[171]

Ascendance of the state in Côte d'Ivoire was thus accompanied by atro-phy of political parties and electoralism. A skeletal but reliable apparatus of territorial administration was imposed on rural localities. The regime's state-building strategy produced institutional structures and processes that were strikingly evocative of a military occupation of the South: overall, the apparatus was spatially concentrated; power was centralized, often in the hands of military officers; the chain of command was hierarchical and tight; and the state was aloof and distant from localities. In contrast to the

---

[168] On reliable but limited administrative penetration of localities and the weakness of the *sous-préfets*, see Stryker 1970:241. On the need to call in a high-level delegation to handle a local disputes, see Staniland 1970c:628; Bonnal 1986:26–8.

[169] On the contrary, "the prefectoral corps was liable to intrigue because of its strategic place in the political system. The prefect of the Southeast department and two sub-prefects in mid-western districts were imprisoned in 1963 for alleged involvement in the [alleged] plots against Houphouet-Boigny" (Staniland 1970a:122).

[170] Staniland 1968:315. Of the prefectorial deputies in 1968, only one was an Ivoirian. Some of the French prefectorial deputies were former colonial subdivision commanders. On the French inspectors, see Staniland 1970a:122.

[171] *Africa Confidential*, 20, no. 21 (17 October 1979):7. Chappell (1989:692) reports that Ivoirianization of the government reached the 70 percent level in 1984.

institutional choices made in Senegal's groundnut basin (or in northern Côte d'Ivoire, discussed in the next chapter), in southern Côte d'Ivoire there was no party apparatus to co-opt provincial leaders or upstarts in order to defuse their oppositional potential, mediate and contain factional or communal competition in the towns and countryside, or share power at the local level with rural notables in exchange for their political support. This helps explain rulers' autonomy vis-à-vis local political actors and groups in southern Côte d'Ivoire. Autonomy, however, was bought at the price of institutional mechanisms and political relationships that would have embedded central authority in local sociopolitical life.

Stryker (1971a) and others (e.g., Zolberg 1971) have spoken of "the missing middle" or "institutionally constricted middle" in postcolonial Côte d'Ivoire. They are referring to the absence of political institutions and networks at the regional, departmental, or *sous-préfecture* level to link center and locality. This is what we have referred to as spatial concentration of state institutions, and it made for a governing apparatus that offered few footholds and points of access to would-be political entrepreneurs in the southern provinces. Staniland (1970c:629, 632) and Nguessan-Zoukou (1990) noted that Ivoirian rulers' institutional choices served this preemptive function: absence of middle-level institutions meant that rural political entrepreneurs lacked bases from which local support could be leveraged into the arena of national politics. Very similar causes produced the same effects in Lower Casamance, as we saw in Chapter 3.

B. Control over Factors of Production: Land, Purchased Inputs, Credit

In promoting smallholder coffee and cocoa production, the regime of Houphouet-Boigny avoided the aggressively interventionist development strategies pursued by many of its neighbors. In comparison with what had been going on in central Senegal or the Ghanaian forest zone, Ivoirian policies governing access to factors of production (land, credit, purchased inputs) appeared laissez-faire. It is true that producer prices were set by the state, input prices were subsidized, and extension agents passed out cuttings to start new coffee and cocoa trees. Yet Ivoirian rulers did not build a heavy institutional apparatus or resort to intensive bureaucratic regulation to structure the labor process, investment, land access, or the dissemination of new technologies.

What explains this institutional strategy? The answer does not lie in the regime's ideology (although ideology surely helped justify and reinforce rulers' choices) or, as some have suggested, in the interests of a capitalist planter bourgeoisie. Rather, rulers' institutional choices in the rural development domain were perfectly consistent with a larger strategy of avoiding all moves that would stir up local politics in the forest zone or contribute to the institutional structuration of rural political space. The Houphouet regime built institutional infrastructure that was spatially concentrated at the center, and that promoted the ruthless centralization of political and administrative authority. Rulers simply declined to adopt rural development strategies that would inject political resources into the rural areas or that would build platforms that could be used for local political organization. They avoided political entanglement at the grassroots.

Even without much of an institutional apparatus to promote rural development, Côte d'Ivoire was able to double its coffee output and triple its cocoa output between 1955 and 1970, thanks to the grassroots dynamics of tree-crop production in the Ivoirian forest belt and the availability of a land frontier.[172] Increases were almost entirely due to the replication of the smallholder production unit on an ever-wider geographic scale. The downside was the replication of weaknesses in the Ivoirian plantation economy that had become obvious in the 1950s: low and stagnant yields, soil depletion and erosion, and low-quality output.[173] The Ivoirian government was well aware of these problems in the 1960s and 1970s, but chose not to tackle them in any concerted manner. After the mid-1980s the old problems became serious obstacles to sustaining output levels. They also compromised the price competitiveness of Ivoirian crops on international markets, raising basic questions about the future and sustainability of the Ivoirian *économie de plantation*.[174] Houphouet may have been politically

---

[172] Dian 1985:98–9. These crops accounted for about 75 percent of all Côte d'Ivoire exports in 1960.

[173] The quality of Ivoirian coffee fell steadily between 1948 and 1954, from 72 percent classified in the highest grade in 1948 to 6 percent so classified in 1954. *Marchés Tropicaux* (no. 495, 7 mai 1955:1245) described this as Côte d'Ivoire's "Number One problem." Meanwhile cocoa quality declined from 71 percent superior grade in 1948 to 12 percent superior grade in 1952 (Frechou 1955:81; see also 59–61). By this time (mid-1950s) plantations in the Southeast were showing signs of aging and falling productivity. In the 1990s problems in the cocoa sector centered on the aging of plantations and low and falling yields usually attributed to "anarchic" production methods. See also Boutellier 1960:202; Anyang'Nyong'o 1987:198–9; *Marchés Tropicaux*, no. 2380 (21 juin 1991): 1553.

[174] Ivoirian yields have remained low and stable over time. Yields are about three hundred to five hundred kilograms per hectare (kg/ha). With intensified techniques they can reach 1500 kg/ha (Atta 1992:9). Malaysia and Indonesia became major producers in the

shrewd in avoiding state activism and entanglement in the coffee and cocoa economy, and thus requiring nothing more than compact and tightly controlled (spatially concentrated and centralized) rural development institutions, but the opportunity costs in terms of investment and innovation were high.

Land. At the time of independence, the postcolonial regime inherited the commanding heights of an economy in full expansionary drive, propelled from below by the spread of smallholder coffee and cocoa production. It also inherited 16 million hectares of virgin forest. The regime's institutional choices in this domain sanctioned the land pioneering that had driven the expansion of coffee and cocoa farming since the 1920s. As Chaveau and Dozon (1987:257) argued, Houphouet knew from early on "how to play upon Ivoirian realities ... [as he did in the economy,] where his liberalism was and remains in accord with the extensive and expansionist tendencies of the local plantation economy."

Postcolonial rulers' choice in the land domain was *not* to build authoritative institutions to govern and regulate land access. By the Code Domanial of 1963, all land not "in use" or held under private title was to be registered in the name of the state. The code was never implemented, however. Instead, Houphouet simply declared that "the land belongs to the one who cultivates it."[175] By these rules, Ivoirian law recognized neither customary land rights or communal land jurisdictions (in the South), nor private property in land.

Most social scientists have emphasized the fact that neither de jure nor de facto Ivoirian law recognized customary, communal, or hereditary land rights. Person observed that communities' rights were systematically ignored in all affairs, including land, calling official land policy "a Promethean drive to make all of Côte d'Ivoire tabula rasa."[176] The state's goal seemed to be "to dissolve the basic communal units of rural society" (ibid.) and to concentrate in the state itself the only legally recognized power to dispose of land in a definitive manner. This can be seen as part and parcel of an institution-building strategy that produced a spatially concentrated state apparatus and that centralized authority in the hands of state agents:

1980s. Yields there are often three times African levels. See also *Le Monde Diplomatique*, "Chute des cours du cacao: Qui croit encore aux 'miracle' Ivoirien?" no. 417 (Dec. 1988):14.

[175] See *Marchés Tropicaux*, no. 907 (30 mars 1963): 789; Ley 1982; Gastellu 1982:275.

[176] Person 1982:29. See also Person 1981:29.

the community was not recognized as a political unit, and no resource-management or asset-allocation powers were conferred upon it.[177]

At the same time, the Ivoirian state declined to recognize private property in land. The state refused to grant individuals the right to permanently alienate land, and rulers did not commit themselves to enforcing land sales or protecting private property in land. Few social scientists have emphasized this aspect of land policy, which surely must be taken as evidence of the *weakness* of capitalist interests in the agrarian sector. Boutellier (1960:195) is an exception: he noted that for immigrants in the southeastern forest zone, insecurity of land tenure had negative consequences for investment. The point is generalizable. Although land sales (or sales of land-use rights) to immigrants were very common throughout the forest zone from the early 1950s onward, these transactions were not always recognized as final by the seller, or as legitimate by the seller's heirs and family members (Chauveau 2002).

What happened in practice? Throughout much of the forest zone, the state's direct agents – prefects, *sous-préfets*, forestry officers – allocated land to immigrants and issued *authorizations d'occupation*.[178] They accommodated local land practices by recording the sale of land-*use* rights (not outright sales) for lump-sum payments, just as colonial administrators had since the late 1940s.[179] Prefects and *sous-préfets* also settled land disputes informally, on an ad hoc basis, for the state had declined to provide clear legal guidelines for arbitration of conflicts between individuals and families. It was as Boutellier (1960:204) had observed in Agni territory in the late 1950s: land tenure relations were conducted in an institutional void ("juridical void"). In effect, Ivoirian rulers chose neither to deny nor to guarantee the land rights of two groups – original inhabitants and immigrants – who held conflicting claims to the same land.[180]

Ivoirian rulers chose not to build institutional structures (codified rights, law, institutionalized procedures or sites for land arbitration) to govern

---

[177] This contrasts with the situation that prevailed in central and northern Senegal, where the state gave communities legal standing as political entities with jurisdiction over land use, and thus effectively institutionalized the land powers of established indigenous authorities. The pattern in southern Côte d'Ivoire is, however, *similar* to that observed in Lower Casamance, where the state's direct agents (*sous-préfets*) emerged as land arbiters.

[178] See Dian 1985:93–5, 146; Hecht 1985:333; Lewis 1991. *Authorisations d'occupation* do not bear ownership and cannot be transmitted to an heir.

[179] On sales in the West, see Hecht 1985:323–8 and Köbben 1963; on the Southeast, Dian 1985:95. See also Tricart 1957:217.

[180] See Lewis 1991; Gastellu 1982:274–5.

access to this factor of production, and the choice was deliberate. Rulers profited from land pioneering: it sustained the expansionist dynamic of the Ivoirian economy. Yet this involved the de facto alienation of land to strangers (immigrants), which meant the de facto dispossession of indigenous communities. This is why land rights were (are) such a politically explosive issue in the forest zone. In many *sous-préfectures* of the Southwest, immigrants made up more than two-thirds of the total population in the 1960s and 1970s. In Divo area, for example, Barbara Lewis found that original Dida inhabitants had ceded use rights to most of their land.[181] Throughout the West, which was the dynamic frontier of the plantation economy in the 1960s and 1970s, indigenous inhabitants boiled with resentment toward the immigrant Baoulé and Dyula who owned most of the coffee and cocoa farms. (Even in the Southeast, land dispossession was a major political issue in the late 1950s and early 1960s, and it reemerged with a vengeance in the late 1990s.)[182] For indigenous Bété populations of the Southwest, Houphouet's dictum "The land belongs to he who farms it" was something close to a degree giving Baoulé farmers carte blanche access to Bété lands and freeing immigrant land seekers from any obligations to indigenous host communities. In 1970 land conflicts between indigenous Bété farmers and Baoulé "foreigners" produced a Bété uprising in Gagnoa. The national security forces intervened. Estimates of the number killed run from several hundred to 4,000.[183] One 1998 report quoted Ivoirian politician Kouame Affouet, who spoke on behalf of aggrieved Bété: "[As far as many Bété are concerned,] Houphouet knew exactly why he made that [1963 land] declaration. He knew his people [the Baoulé] had exhausted all their forest lands and the only way to ensure that they got more land was to encourage them to go West. . . . You see, in those days, everyone was afraid of Houphouet" (Dzisah 1998).

The Houphouet regime found it expeditious to try to atomize and privatize local conflicts, rather than to collectivize and politicize them by bringing the issue into the public sphere. In effect, rulers' institutional strategy in this domain denied *all parties* claim to state resources in the fighting out of local conflicts.

---

[181] See Zolberg 1964:41–2; Hecht 1984; Lewis 1991:10.

[182] See Boutellier 1960:138, 189, 194–204.

[183] The spark was an attempt to block a 1967 Baoulé land invasion (Koffi Teya 1985:124). See Lewis 1991; Baulin 1989:62 n. 5. Chauveau and Dozon (1987:279–80) link the 1970 events to party struggles of the 1950s, which themselves were rooted in long-standing issues of land control.

One net result is that decades-long land tensions continue to simmer, periodically breaking out into violence and fueling ethnic conflict in the Ivoirian south. This has been a major fact of Ivoirian politics in the last decade.

Meanwhile, at the summit of the political hierarchy, members of the Ivoirian political class interpreted Houphouet's 1963 land degree as an open invitation to use state power to appropriate land for themselves. From 1970 Houphouet encouraged this explicitly, fueling what Dian (1985:155) called an anarchic land race among party cadres and civil servants.[184] High functionaries and PDCI personalities received land attributions from Houphouet or his ministers of state; in many cases, land that had been classified as forest reserve by the colonial administration was declassified for this purpose. Land so granted was often cleared at state expense for the creation of functionaries' coffee and cocoa plantations. Bassett (1993:149) writes that, thanks to post-independence political privilege and connections to the state, "[i]t is common knowledge that members of the Ivoirian political elite are among the largest landholders in the country."

Labor. As Bernard Founou-Tchuigoua (1979) has insisted, an open immigration policy was the necessary complement to the regime's land strategy. It was perhaps the regime's most decisive contribution to sustaining spectacular increases in coffee and cocoa output in the 1960s and 1970s. In the South, virtually all nonfamily labor was foreign.[185] Almost 80 percent of the migrant workers came from Mali and Haute Volta/Burkina Faso. Together with the migrant labors from other West African countries, these immigrants constituted somewhere between 20 and 30 percent of the rural population of the Ivoirian south in the first two decades of independence. The existence of what one analyst called "an exploited sub-peasant class at the bottom of the scale" (Schultz 1975:85) helps explain why farmers in the forest zone opted for extensive rather than intensive strategies of agricultural production. With abundant labor, there were fewer incentives to increase labor productivity or improve crop quality. It is also extraordinary that immigrant workers, whose fate and fortunes could be decided on a whim of the state, were allowed to vote in the periodic rounds of elections that took place after independence. This continued into the 1990s and is

---

[184] See also Gastellu 1982:275.
[185] See Lucier 1988:259.

another measure of Houphouet's distrust of and lack of a secure hold over indigenous populations in the Ivoirian south.

Purchased Inputs. The institutional choices that conformed most strikingly to the administrative occupation model were the choices made in the classic domain of "rural development" – that is, in state efforts to promote improved production techniques and the use of purchased agricultural inputs. Houphouet's regime did not try to use rural development programs as a way to mobilize rural political support or organize political clienteles in the southern provinces. Instead, in matters having to do with production techniques and inputs, the Ivoirian regime chose to intervene hardly at all. In the coffee and cocoa sector, input-distribution programs were extremely limited in ambition and scope and handled through skeletal institutions with virtually no grounding in rural communities.

Intensification of cocoa and coffee production hinged on promoting the use of fertilizer, pesticides, fungicides, and high-yielding varieties. This in turn required distribution of credit (to enable farmers to purchase inputs) and dissemination of new growing techniques so that farmers could make good use of the improved inputs. The parastatal agency SATMACI (Société d'Assistance Technique pour la Modernisation Agricole de la Côte d'Ivoire), created in 1958, assumed responsibility for these tasks from the 1960s to the 1980s.

In the Ivoirian south, rulers never embraced the kind of "integrated rural development" that became conventional practice in the development industry in the early 1970s. Rather, SATMACI's domain of competence was defined in terms of product, not territory, and its mandate was defined narrowly, as a coffee and cocoa extension service.[186] SATMACI dealt with individual household heads on a one-on-one, voluntary basis. It focused on cash-crop farming issues at the household level only (not questions of infrastructure, social services, marketing, food crop production, etc.). With a mandate defined so narrowly, rulers ensured that SATMACI could not cultivate territorially defined constituencies, become entangled in community-level politics, or be used by political entrepreneurs for such purposes. The agency was also politically insulated in classic Ivoirian fashion:

---

[186] By 1970 SATMACI shared the field with parastatals that focused on palm oil and coconut production in the South. The palm-oil parastatals created outgrower schemes; most of the outgrowers were foreigners from Upper Volta/Burkina Faso (see Anyang'Nyong'o 1987:226).

foreigners assumed prominent managerial and technical roles. Hinderink and Tempelman (1978:98) describe SATMACI in the years from 1960 through 1970 as devoted to a "thoroughly technocratic approach" and "still organized and mainly staffed by French expatriates."

SATMACI's major campaigns in the 1960s and 1970s aimed at regenerating coffee and cocoa plantations by replacing old trees with improved varieties, and encouraging the use of pesticides and fungicides. Following the example set by the French colonial administration, SATMACI's principal activity was distributing improved-variety seeds and plantings free of charge to farmers.[187] By 1986 the cumulative result was that improved (hybrid) plantings accounted for 18.2 percent of the total (Crook 1990:658). SATMACI also subsidized the costs of inputs like fertilizers, but did not oblige or pressure tree crop farmers to use them. Most never did.[188] According to Widner (1993:31), fairly reliable studies undertaken in the mid-1980s suggested that fertilizer use "was minimal. Only 7.6 percent of cocoa farmers and 15 percent of coffee farmers used chemical fertilizers; 22 percent of the cocoa farmers and 15 percent of the coffee farmers used insecticides." SATMACI did sponsor a few more ambitious programs, but these were of marginal significance to the forest zone at large. Small numbers of farmers volunteered to participate in the development of SATMACI-supervised "block farms" (demonstration farms), for example, and some formed "voluntary groups" to receive special SATMACI training and special rates for inputs.[189]

A similar story can be told about credit. The Ivoirian south had a Caisse Nationale de Crédit Agricole (CNCA), but it lent almost nothing to "village planters" after about 1962. Around 1968 a Banque Nationale de Développement Agricole (BNDA) was created, partly to increase the flow of credit. In the fiscal year 1968/69, however, the BNDA lent only CFA

---

[187] *Marchés Tropicaux*, no. 495 (7 mai 1955):1191–2, 1243–5; Dian 1985:112. In 1955, 26 million plants were so distributed.

[188] In 1969, 93 percent of all fertilizer imported to Côte d'Ivoire was used on crops other than coffee and cocoa (Stier 1972:74). In 1991, 80 percent of the fertilizer consumed in the Côte d'Ivoire was used for cotton and rice (*Marchés Tropicaux*, no. 2380 (21 juin 1991): 1559).

[189] Anyang'Nyong'o 1987:200. "Voluntary groups" consisted of about thirty farmers: each purchased inputs at a reduced rate. Those who met SATMACI standards for pruning and the like received a bonus (rebate). In some areas, SATMACI also offered rebates for new plantations created according to SATMACI norms. In 1985 Dian (1985:117–21) reported that a total of about U.S. $10 million (3.3 billion CFA francs) had been distributed in rebates.

6 million to coffee and cocoa growers, out of a total of CFA 1 billion in agricultural loans. Figures for the fiscal year 1969/70 are much the same: CFA 45 million went to coffee and cocoa growers, out of a total that exceeded CFA 2 billion in loans.[190] Government-financed credit programs did become more widespread for a brief interlude in the 1970s, but this was not connected to any effort to build up rural cooperatives or otherwise broaden SATMACI's mandate.[191]

What is most important for this analysis is that only 10 to 15 percent of farmers in the South ever became engaged in government-run agricultural improvement programs (Crook 1990:658). The regime did not build credit schemes to finance investment or create dense institutional networks in the rural areas to guide, administer, and monitor a state-led agricultural modernization process. True, SATMACI existed, but it was politically insulated, run under the centralized control of direct state agents, and did not operate through local outposts in the villages. By the end of the 1980s most observers judged its overall impact on Ivoirian coffee and cocoa production to have been minimal.

With cheap labor and plenty of unmortgaged land, the vast majority of planters could get by without intensifying production through the application of capital in the form of fertilizers and other purchased inputs. The technical requirements of producing (low-quality) coffee and cocoa are low. Farmers had little incentive to invest in quality-enhancing techniques since the state, which set official prices of the purchase of coffee and cocoa, did not pay a premium for better produce. Most coffee and cocoa exported from Côte d'Ivoire continued to be produced on small farms, 85 percent of them less than 5 hectares in size (with most holdings around 2.5 hectares), using what agronomists called "traditional" production techniques. *Marchés Tropicaux*, on the basis of the official Côte d'Ivoire agricultural census of 1974–5, passed this judgment on the coffee sector: 99.65 percent of all

---

[190] See Stier 1972; Anyang'Nyong'o 1987:221–3.

[191] In the 1970s the Banque Nationale de Développement Agricole (BNDA), working through SATMACI, increased the scope of its credit programs in the rural South. Kouassi (1993:74) implied that in the mid-1970s about half of all agricultural credit went to coffee and cocoa producers. This seems to have come almost exclusively in the form of seven- to eight-month "consumption" loans to members of rural cooperatives receiving SATMATCI's technical assistance (Dian 1985:359). Large numbers of rural households (about 24 percent) seem to have received these loans in the mid-1970s, even though the cooperative movement was small and weak. Anyang'Nyong'o (1987:244) noted that a particularly large percentage of all households in Aboisso (75 percent) received BNDA consumption loans in 1975.

Ivoirian coffee is produced in the "traditional coffee sector, that is to say peasant holdings. . . . Yields are weak and the care given to the trees is quite minimal [*assez sommaire*]."[192] In spite of nearly stagnant productivity, for twenty years, from 1960 to about 1980, the Ivoirian government got what it wanted – increases in exportable output.

C. Commercialization of Coffee and Cocoa

What was the regime's strategy for extracting rural surpluses? The central feature of this strategy was the decision to leave the direct purchase of coffee and cocoa in the hands of private traders. Farmers were paid on time, in cash. The government regulated (stabilized) buying prices and financed the export circuit, but farmers were never forced to sell export crops directly to state officials.

This meant that in contrast to the export-crop producing regions of much of West Africa, in southern Côte d'Ivoire there was no compulsory network of village-level marketing institutions (cooperatives). Without compulsory cooperatives, forest zone communities lacked what are, in other contexts, important points of access to state resources and key sites for accumulating power at the community level. In the coffee- and cocoa-producing zone, the regime of Houphouet extracted rural surpluses through the atomized and seemingly apolitical processes of a regulated market.

Commercialization of coffee and cocoa was structured by the state (officially fixed producer prices and licensed buyers), but buying and selling transactions were privately managed and they remained marginally competitive. Around 1970 about a dozen large, private export houses sat atop the commercial hierarchy.[193] Under terms set by the state (the Caisse de Stabilisation) and using finance capital mobilized by the government on their behalf,[194] the export houses advanced cash to a limited number of private buyers, or *traitants*, who organized and financed crop buying on the ground.

By the end of the 1950s most *traitants* financed directly by the export houses were Lebanese businessmen who operated within family-based

---

[192] *Marchés Tropicaux*, no. 1693 (21 avril 1978):1068.

[193] SEPRIC/SEDES 1970:77–9. Through a process of concentration, the number was reduced to six or seven by the early 1980s. See Mahieu 1984:9–10.

[194] The central bank (BCEAO) made crop-financing loans to Ivoirian-based private banks. This cash was reloaned to the export houses.

business groups.[195] It seems that there were about 190 of these big coffee and cocoa buyers in the fiscal year 1968/69, and about 60 or 70 in the early 1980s. The large-scale buyers, in turn, advanced funds to their own purchasing agents, or *acheteurs*. These subcontractors were usually Africans. Most of them drove light trucks owned by their employers.[196] They scoured the countryside, buying crops at the farm gate from small producers. Mountains of produce were delivered to rural collection centers, where the commodities were inspected and turned over to licensed private transporters – most of them independent African merchants/truckers – who carried coffee and cocoa to storage depots in Abidjan or (after the early 1970s) to southern coffee-processing plants. When the harvest was sold on the international market, private agents at all levels of the commercial circuit collected a state-mandated profit margin. The government of Côte d'Ivoire kept the rest, which added up to a very hefty margin of about 60 percent of the world market price in normal years between 1960 and 1974.[197]

At the lowest levels of the crop-buying circuit, competition among the *traitants*, and the buyers' drive to expand their profit margins, encouraged

---

[195] *Marchés Tropicaux*, no. 495 (7 mai 1955):1244–5; Tricart 1957; see also Beugre Owo Sero and D'Alepe 1992. Of the traitants surveyed by SEPRIC/SEDES in 1970, 55 percent were Lebanese and 23 percent were "other foreigners" to the Côte d'Ivoire. Ivoirian traitants made up the remaining 22 to 23 percent. The research agency deemed its sample to be representative. Lebanese and other foreigners were overwhelmingly dominant in coffee buying. On an individual level, the Lebanese and foreigners generally operated on a much larger scale than their Ivoirian counterparts (SEPRIC/SEDES 1970). In Divo in 1980 there was one Lebanese buyer "who handled more than half of the [Divo] region's cocoa" (Hecht 1983:340). See Boone 1993.

[196] In 1970, 91 percent of the 451 acheteurs surveyed by SEPRIC/SEDES were Africans (86 percent of these were Ivoirian). Of the total, 70 percent drove vehicles owned by the traitants (SEPRIC/SEDES 1970:83–8).

[197] Most sources divide the f.o.b. price of Ivoirian coffee and cocoa between producers (50 to 60 percent of f.o.b.), the export tax (22 to 23 percent), and commercial intermediaries (the remainder). That underestimates the state's share, for the difference between the f.o.b. and the world market price was also pocketed by the state (in the form of Caisse de Stabilisation profits). Thus, in normal years (i.e., from 1960 to 1974 and 1982 to 1987) the peasant received about 25 percent of the world market price of Ivoirian coffee and cocoa, about 10 to 12 percent went to commercial intermediaries, and all the rest went to the state. See Terpend 1982; Lee 1980:636. In all years between 1966 and 1988, farmers' returns in current CFA francs remained stable or increased, maintaining the illusion of rising prices. Yet *real prices* between 1960 and 1975 averaged about half of the 1950 level. Real producer prices between 1976–7 and 1984 were lower than the 1960 price in all years except 1977–8, when they finally crept back up to the 1950 level (Ridler 1988:1522; *Marchés Tropicaux*, no. 1693 (21 avril 1978):1074).

226

crop purchasers to extend credit to farmers. By making a preharvest loan and using the next crop as collateral, peasants were effectively "tied" to one buyer. De facto interest payments were deducted from the farmer's returns at harvest time. These arrangements reproduced the colonial buying relations known as *la traite* in their classic West African form.[198] As Bonnefonds (1968:413) wrote, the Ivoirian "peasants buy . . . on credit, and are at the mercy of those who purchase their crops." Most African nationalist leaders and African governments in the 1950s and 1960s deemed these debt ties to be exceedingly exploitative of farmers, and the call to free peasants from usurious rural traders was one justification for the rise of state purchasing monopolies (and compulsory selling "cooperatives") in rural West Africa.[199] The Ivoirian government also blamed the ills of the rural marketing system on unscrupulous private traders. Unlike its neighbors, however, the Ivoirian regime was content to fix (stabilize) the coffee and cocoa purchase price and then leave almost all crop buying and rural lending in private hands. Government credit schemes administered through SATMACI did become more important in the mid-1970s, but in the early 1980s farmers once again became heavily dependent upon private buyers for credit.[200]

Houphouet's regime did provide a legal framework that allowed farmers in the coffee and cocoa zone to form selling cooperatives (GVCs, or Groupements de Vocation Coopérative).[201] Cooperatives were officially recognized as buying agents, and thus were allowed to retain the state-mandated commercial margin normally collected by the private buyer. The government also allowed (pressured) cooperatives to retain this "rebate," or *ristourne* (rather than distributing it among the members), to invest it in community-improvement projects, such as the construction of health

---

[198] See Kipré 1983:232; Bonnefonds 1968; SEPRIC/SEDES 1970:86. In 1971 *Le Monde* described merchants' interest rates as "usurious," saying that as a result of these high charges, peasants often received only 10 to 15 percent of the fixed price at harvest time (*Le Monde*, "Les paysans de la Côte d'Ivoire envient la richesse de leur Caisse de soutien des produits agricoles" (1 juin 1971):10, cited by Campbell 1973:273).

[199] In fact, in 1944 the SAA called for cooperative selling arrangements that would eliminate private middlemen from the coffee and cocoa trade (Zolberg 1964:67).

[200] Terpend 1982. A 1990 government report explained that "the trader makes up for the quasi-absence of credit in the rural areas" (République de Côte d'Ivoire, Direction Centrale des Grands Travaux 1990).

[201] On colonial-era provident societies (SIPs) and their successor institutions, which played a marginal role in the Ivoirian forest zone, see Hirschfeld 1975; Manso 1981; Stryker 1970:237–40; Anyang'Nyong'o 1987:195.

clinics.[202] Where GVCs existed, local notables often did monopolize management, profit personally from their positions, and use the rebates to promote their own ends.

The facts that are critical here, however, are: (1) farmers were not obliged to participate in GVCs, and few did; (2) the state did not finance the cooperatives; and (3) each village was allowed to create *only one* cooperative. Where a cooperative existed, however inactive or "fictive" or dysfunctional it might be, the playing field was closed to new organizational entrepreneurs. Meanwhile, for farmers who did not stand to benefit from the existing cooperative arrangements, "exit" prevailed over "voice," defusing much of the cooperatives' potential as a source of conflict (and dissipating organizational impulses that existed in some localities). In fact, most producers did decline to participate in the collective marketing arrangements: 90 percent of all coffee and cocoa was handled by private buyers in the 1960s; 80 percent was handled privately in the 1980s.[203] Some rural development experts deplored the "passive attitude" of Ivoirian coffee and cocoa planters (SEPRIC/SEDES 1970:87). Other observers concluded that the state was "discouraging local initiative" and "deliberately keeping [the cooperatives] on a short rein."[204] Stryker (1970:215–16) argued that "the Ivoirian regime [was] opposed to the project of rural collectivities from the beginning."

Many analysts have attributed the regime's choice of institutional arrangements in coffee and cocoa marketing to ideology: because of its liberalism and pro-capitalist bent, Houphouet opted for relatively hands-off methods for the internal commercialization of coffee and cocoa. This book suggests that that the explanation lies in political factors linked to rural social organization in the Ivoirian south. For the internal marketing of coffee and cocoa, the regime opted for a *concentrated institutional structure* – that is, one that did not involve the creation a far-flung network of state

[202] "Manipulations and pressures are exerted on the members of the cooperative as to the affectation of the [*ristourne* or rebate] . . . in accordance with the wishes of administrative and political authorities" (*Forum Economique*, 10 juin 1991:3).
[203] Hirschfeld (1975:60) reported that GVCs handled 10 percent of all coffee and cocoa during the 1962–3 harvest. This figure fell to less than 1 percent of all coffee and 2.2 percent of all cocoa in 1969–70. GVC's share of coffee and cocoa production climbed thereafter, reaching about 16 percent of each crop by 1973–4, where the GVC share more or less stabilized. In 1985 coffee/cocoa GVCs handled 19.6 percent of national production. On the 1980s see *Marchés Tropicaux*, no. 2380 (21 juin 1991):1552. Crook (1990:660) reported that in 1987, 93 percent of GVC operations were financed by private buyers.
[204] Stryker 1970:215–6; Schultz 1975:84.

outputs in the localities. Meanwhile, control over Abidjan-based marketing institutions was *centralized* in the hands of a narrow, Abidjan-based political elite. In designing this system, the regime made choices that were consistent with its other institutional strategies in the forest zone.

The market-based commercialization system offered no political resources or institutional footholds for would-be political entrepreneurs in rural localities. Rural export circuits bypassed chiefs, big planters, respected local personalities, and the PDCI general secretaries. Ironically, this market-based buying system allowed central rulers to exercise more control over the coffee and cocoa surplus than a heavily bureaucratic marketing system would have, for the center did not have to share with rural notables.[205]

At the same time, the regime's institutional choices in the marketing sphere helped it to cope with the explosive problems the regime confronted in the domain of land tenure. Ethnic tensions ran high in communities across the entire forest zone. To make matters worse, the *indigène*-stranger cleavage sometimes ran along class-like divisions. This was the case in much of the Southwest, where the largest farmers and landholders tended to be strangers. It was also true in parts of the East, where large Agni planters were landlords and where immigrants could find themselves exploited, politically marginalized at the village level, or both.[206] Politicization of the resulting tensions (in the form of nativist ideologies; xenophobia; challenges to the state's authority to sanction land pioneering; ethnic-based claims for a redistribution of surpluses between wage laborers, sharecroppers, and landholders, etc.) has been an ever-present possibility:

---

[205] The Ivoirian government liberalized the GVC regime at the village level at the end of the 1980s, but it did not throw political caution to the wind. According to United Nations Development Project/International Labor Organization (UNDP/ILO) analysts, the Ivoirian technostructure and "modern political and administrative authorities" did not want to see the creation of regional-level cooperative unions. The political authorities feared that the "creation of more hierarchy" in the cooperative structure would produce "new sites for skimming resources" [*prélevement*] and sites for fights over resources. According to UNDP/ILO, the regime also feared that opposition parties would grab control of the regional-level cooperative unions. See Programme des Nations Unies pour le Développement, Bureau International du Travail, Government of Ivory Coast (PNUD/BIT/IVC) 1991:18, 24, 28.

[206] Since colonial times, the failure or paralysis of cooperatives in the Ivoirian south has often been attributed to precisely these kinds of tensions. See Boutellier 1960:196, 205; Manso 1981; Anyang'Nyong'o 1987:201–2, 239 n. 66; PNUD/BIT/IVC 1990:16–17; Atta 1992; Widner 1993a:314–15. On "exit" and "voice" in the GVCs, see Lewis 1992.

many analysts of postcolonial Côte d'Ivoire defined it as the Houphouet regime's central fear, and the regime's greatest challenge in governing the South.[207]

By leaving export-crop marketing in the South in private hands rather than instituting compulsory producers' cooperatives, the regime eliminated one obvious catalyst and focal point for political competition and conflict within localities. Within villages, tensions that existed between original inhabitants and strangers over collective buying and selling transactions, control of marketing institutions, and the use of GVCs rebates were surely dampened by the fact that membership in cooperatives was not compulsory. Also, GVCs were not very important to the village economy – this also had a depoliticizing effect. In this way, the private marketing system played a role in the regime's efforts to keep potentially destabilizing *indigène*-stranger tensions under control and to depoliticize village life.

Farm-gate purchases obliged individual farmers to strike ad hoc deals with private traders. Traders competed among themselves to obtain farmers' produce. Poorer farmers bargained over credit terms from a position of weakness. Richer farmers bargained from a position of strength, and often were able to win back a share of the buyer's profit margin. Private deals meant that in practice the real per-kilo purchase price varied by farm, despite the fact that the state mandated uniform rates. The private, ad hoc, and even quasi-competitive nature of buying, selling, and lending transactions reinforced the often-noted atomistic tendencies inherent in smallholder commodity production. In this sense, the marketing process reinforced barriers to collective action and consciousness among farmers.

Meanwhile, the politically strategic functions of export-crop marketing and rural credit distribution remained in the hands of an outsider group with no political ambitions of its own (other than staying on the good side of power wielders in Abidjan). Lebanese traders dominated export-crop marketing and rural credit – controlling an estimated 80 percent of the business in the 1970s and 1980s. As politically vulnerable outsiders, the Lebanese community had virtually no capacity to fight the state for a larger share of the rural surplus. The regime's power vis-à-vis the merchants

---

[207] Médard (1982:83) and Chauveau and Dozon (1987:272–3 *inter alia*) called the *indigène*-stranger opposition in the forest zone "the principal cleavage within Ivoirian society." See Boutellier (1960) on Agni Moronou in the 1950s. Events since the mid-1990s in Côte d'Ivoire seem to confirm Chauveau and Dozon's analysis.

was reflected in the low prices the regime paid for the services of this group and the resulting "efficiency" of the Ivoirian export-crop marketing circuit.[208]

Under these arrangements, cocoa and coffee farmers tended to identify the Lebanese merchants, rather than the state, as the source of exploitation in the commercial circuit. The regime itself played this card overtly, targeting rural merchants as the source of the peasantry's exploitation, deflecting attention from its own appropriations of the rural surplus, and positioning itself as the defender of peasants' interests. To the extent that the system worked like this, the regime's political and economic interests were well served.

The political weakness of the Ivoirian merchant interests in the 1950s – that is, of Dyula and Agni traders – helps explain why the Houphouet government was able to get away with leaving the crop-buying circuit in non-African hands. The most important indigenous merchant interests in Côte d'Ivoire, the Dyula planter-traders in the South, had limited bargaining power. They were themselves foreigners in the forest zone, squeezed between European and Lebanese trading houses, and dependent upon the regime's protection in the South. As most Dyula traders were crowded out of the crop-buying business by Lebanese merchants in the late 1950s and 1960s, they concentrated on the transport business, where access was regulated by the postcolonial state (via licensing). The coffee and cocoa transport business developed as a "reserved sector" for the Dyula trading community, whose members were regrouped into a corporatist Transporters Association that was patronized and controlled by the PDCI and Houphouet.[209]

Large Agni traders did have more social capital to trade on in the Southeast, but this was not converted into clout in dealing with the state. Agni

---

[208] From the 1960s to the 1980s about 12.5 percent of the f.o.b. value of Ivoirian coffee and cocoa was going to the crop buyers, most of them Lebanese. See Terpend 1982; Fieldhouse 1986:192. As for trucking, the business appeared in the 1960s and 1970s to be virtually "nonprofitable" due to the small scale of most operators, competition among them, and the "disorganization" of the transport circuit (République de Côte d'Ivoire, Ministère de l'Economie et des Finances 1973; SEPRIC/SEDES 1970:83–4). See also IDET-CEGOS 1963:77–8; Amin 1967:136.

[209] For a detailed analysis, see Lewis 1980:84–5. As Bredeloup (1989:89) later wrote, "The state fears that the Dyula entrepreneurs will constitute a counter-power, an independent class. They are therefore carefully solicited by the state.... The state maintains a sort of 'personal clientelism' and watches to see that their economic ambitions do not translate into demands for political voice or more autonomy."

society was so socially fragmented and economically atomized by the 1950s that Agni political entrepreneurs were only marginally successful in using their wealth and political birthright to mobilize Agni constituencies. Agni elites were thoroughly marginalized in the national political arena by the time of internal self-rule in 1957: Beugue and d'Alepe suggest that Agni merchants might have been able to rebound from their commercial failures of the late 1950s if the political defeat of the Agni elite had not been so complete.

IV. A Counterfactual: Sanwi Exceptionalism

A set of highly localized events in Sanwi, southeastern Côte d'Ivoire, is significant because Sanwi is an exception that helps to prove the rule. There was indeed some variation in rural social organization in the forest zone of Côte d'Ivoire. In Sanwi, there was a measure of political cohesion and hierarchy that was otherwise lacking in a forest zone characterized by leveling and lack of political hierarchy. Social-structural differences produced small but distinct variations in the political capacity of indigenous society in the forest zone.

In the election year 1956–7 an important PP leader, Kacou Aoulou, ran as a PDCI candidate. Some Agni of Sanwi refused this move toward co-optation and chose instead to fight to retain political distinctiveness and cohesion, and thus some possibility for autonomous action, for their small region. They organized support for the Liste pour la Défense des Intérêts du Pays Sanwi (Candidates for the Defense of Sanwi Interests) in the 1956–7 elections. Sanwi was at this point coterminous with the central subdivision of the Aboisso *cercle*, with a settled population of about 40,000 people distributed among 119 villages and settlements.

On the eve of independence, Sanwi elites tried something more drastic. They organized a last-ditch effort to renounce the authority of the regime that had installed itself in Abidjan. An Agni delegation traveled to Paris in early 1959 to demand autonomy for the Sanwi state – they found legal grounds for this in the protectorate treaty signed by Sanwi and France in 1843. Finding no support for their initiative in France, a Sanwi government-in-exile was established in Ghana. This episode culminated in several hundred arrests in Côte d'Ivoire. The accused were tried in Abidjan, found guilty in spring 1960, and subsequently released. In 1961 a second "affaire Sanwi" ended as the first – in several hundred arrests. A new intrigue in

1969 also ended in several hundred arrests.[210] Sanwi alone among the Agni microstates of the Southeast exhibited some sustained political cohesion and capacity for political self-organization.

After the decade of repression, the Houphouet regime did in fact create institutional mechanisms for dealing with Sanwi that differed from those built elsewhere in the forest zone. In 1970 the regime recognized a Mutuelle pour le Développement Economique et Social de la Préfecture d'Aboisso (MUDESPA), a local development association that, as Dwayne Woods described it, would serve "as a means of bringing the Sanwi community back into the political system." The thirty-six Abidjan-based members of the "interest group" representing Aboisso/Sanwi won concessions from the regime in 1970, including recognition of the king of Sanwi and restoration of land taken over by the French and by the government of Côte d'Ivoire. Dwayne Woods also credits MUDESPA with "the development of villages" and blocking the creation of a set of new agro-industrial estates that had been planned by the parastatal SODEPALM (Woods 1994:476).

With the complete political submission of Aboisso, the regime reincorporated the elite of this zone. A new, deconcentrated site of political organization (MUDESPA) was allowed to exist, and concessions on land and kingship allowed for what was, at least, a symbolic devolution of political legitimacy to nonstate actors. These initiatives were small indeed, but that was in keeping with the limited scale of the political challenge that Aboisso/Sanwi posed to the regime in Abidjan.[211] The concessions can perhaps be seen as commensurate with the political gain the regime saw in cutting a deal with the Sanwi elite after twenty years of antagonistic relations.

Rulers' institutional choices in southern Côte d'Ivoire departed from those of Nkrumah in the Ghanaian cocoa belt in three ways. First, the Ivoirian state maintained an administrative presence that was "suspended from

---

[210] See Zolberg 1964:199–200, 277, 289–93; Chappell 1989:681; Contamin and Fauré 1990:191; Chauveau and Dozon 1987:277, 279.

[211] PNUD/BIT/IVC 1990:30 *inter alia*. Sanwi exceptionalism was again evident in the late 1980s, when the regime lifted the rule restricting each village to only one agricultural cooperative (GVC). In the Aboisso region, GVC proliferated as "traditional families" organized their long-standing clienteles of small planters into cocoa-selling associations. Many of the new GVCs failed, but where GVC leaders had social capital and could provide real services to small farmers, these unions were a success.

Abidjan," rather than trying to insert its administrative authority into the intimate, village- and even household-level workings of the export economy. Second, Ivoirian rulers adopted laissez-faire policies toward access to, and use of, basic factors of production (land, capital, inputs). And third, in the export sector, the Ivoirian regime relied upon privately handled buying and selling transactions. Social-structural differences go far in explaining why state building proceeded along such different trajectories in these two regions.

A key structural attribute of peasant society in the Ivoirian forest zone was its political and economic fragmentation – the absence of institutionalized political hierarchies, the dispersion of political and economic power, and the cultural heterogeneity of localities. These features of peasant society made it possible for the Houphouet regime to rely upon relatively "hands-off" economic strategies in exploiting coffee and cocoa producers. They also made it possible, and expeditious, to govern the rural South through an administrative apparatus that offered local political entrepreneurs or notables no access to state power. Analyses that attribute the exceptional aspects of state policy to the clout of a rural bourgeoisie are off the mark: Houphouet's strategies reflected and reinforced the political weaknesses of peasantries in the South, rather than the power of capitalist planters.

Some of the net political effects became clear with time. In the 1980s and early 1990s world coffee and cocoa prices plummeted. In the fiscal year 1989/90 the Ivoirian government halved producer prices. Although many farmers felt betrayed by the regime,[212] they were not able to mount forms of collective action that posed a serious threat to the government's policy-making autonomy, much less to state authority. Contrast this to what happened in Senegal when real groundnut prices fell in the late 1970s: there, powerful rural leaders (the Islamic marabouts) won groundnut price concessions from the government by threatening that their followers would neglect export-crop cultivation and concentrate on food crops.[213] Note also the contrast with southern Ghana in the 1930s, where cocoa farmers and traders organized the spectacular 1937–8 "cocoa hold-up" aimed at forcing foreign buying houses to disband a pooling agreement that depressed cocoa purchase prices. Big Asante producers' political and economic authority over small farmers was key in explaining the success of the Ghanaian "hold-up." So why were Ivoirian farmers unable to press the government for a

[212] See Widner 1993a.
[213] See Cruise O'Brien 1984.

234

better deal in the cocoa crisis of 1989–90? Part of the explanation must lie in the weakness of grassroots authority and communal institutions in the Ivoirian coffee and cocoa belt. Taken together, these cases suggest that rural modes of social and political organization can be an important determinant of farmers' capacity to act collectively in their confrontations with the state.

From the 1960s to the end of the 1980s the Ivoirian regime was well served by administrative and political structures that tended to produce political stagnation in the forest belt. Rulers' institutional choices helped prevent organized challenge from below and deprived would-be rivals of opportunities to establish constituencies and clienteles of their own. This institution-building strategy, however, left central rulers without the local footholds and provincial alliances they would need to manage and contain local social conflict when the need arose.

Conclusion

Cocoa and coffee were known as "rich crops" in the first decades of African independence. Labor demands are low (compared to cotton farming, for example), and profits are high: international buyers pay more for luxury beverage crops than for commodities like groundnuts or cotton, which were destined to become part of the basket of wage goods for the European working class. So it was that coffee and cocoa created and sustained West African peasantries that were wealthier in the 1960s than those anywhere else on the continent. Large commercial farmers in southern Ghana and southern Cote d'Ivoire have often been described as West Africa's rural bourgeoisies.

Working deductively from Marxist or pluralist theory, it was easy to argue (as many analysts did from the 1960s to the 1980s) that these strata would be favored by postcolonial rulers. Indeed, the argument that because they were large-scale commercial producers (who, following the logic of Mancur Olson, were presumed to have a high capacity for collective action), they were favored, was made explicitly in the case of Côte d'Ivoire.[214] By this logic, Nkrumah (at least in the 1950s, before he embraced socialism) should have been equally solicitous of large-scale cocoa farmers and traders.

In fact, both regimes sought to undercut the political influence of the largest and best-established commercial farmers early on, from the early

---

[214] See for example Amin 1967; Bates 1981; Rapley 1993.

1950s. Rulers in both countries worked hard to prevent nascent rural bourgeoisies from using the state to advance their class interests. In Côte d'Ivoire, the wealthy producers from the Southeast were pushed out of the political arena as Houphouet consolidated his political hegemony after 1954. Under Houphouet's rule, agricultural policy was always aimed at stabilizing a peasant-centered cocoa and coffee sector, not favoring capitalist farming in this sector. Producer prices, transportation rates, processing policy, and the buying circuit were all structured to encourage the extension of land under cultivation and to maximize the tonnage of low-grade output. Ivoirian cocoa and coffee policy did not advantage producers with locational or technological advantages, or those with the capacity to invest in crop buying, processing, or productivity- and/or quality-enhancing inputs.[215]

Meanwhile, there seems to be no evidence in the Ivoirian case that the largest or most advanced producers ever united to protest against what we might call the "anticapitalist" biases in coffee and cocoa policy, or to press for policy that would have been better tailored to their needs, interests, or comparative advantage.[216] It seems that Houphouet routed those most likely to represent large-scale commercial cocoa interests in the first rounds of political competition in the late 1940s. Once Houphouet secured control of the state, government policy created economic disincentives to further capitalization in the cocoa and coffee sector. The regime also bought off some of the key actors in the large-scale cocoa and coffee sector by co-opting them into far more lucrative positions in the Abidjan party-state: members of an incipient capitalist farming class left the rural areas and took up membership in the bureaucratic bourgeoisie. The ranks of the Ivoirian political class are filled with the sons of leading cocoa and coffee farmers from the 1950s.

In Ghana, there was a head-on battle between the nationalists and the big cocoa elite. It began in the early 1950s and went on for another decade; in fact, it has never been resolved decisively. The Ghanaian agrarian bourgeoisie was far more powerful economically (as producers and as traders), and far more confident politically, than its counterpart of wealthy cocoa growers in southeastern Côte d'Ivoire. Class tensions were far more acute in the Ghana cocoa belt in the 1950s than anywhere in Côte d'Ivoire. This is more evidence of the social structural differences across the two cases.

---

[215] See Gastellu 1989.

[216] See Fauré and Médard 1982; Gbetibouo and Delgado 1984:125; Rimmer 1984:170; Crook 1988:129–30; Gastellu 1989.

It turns out that central rulers' overriding goal was similar in both countries. State builders did not seek "rural transformation" or modernization per se. If they had, they would have banked on the largest and most economically advanced producers. The goal was to achieve forms of rural political demobilization that would make it possible to tax peasants indirectly, via state control of exports. For all the ideological difference between Houphouet and Nkrumah, both regimes employed fundamentally populist ideologies in pursuit of this end.[217] Rulers positioned themselves as defenders of what Houphouet called "the brave peasants." Houphouet and Nkrumah both identified private rural merchants (and in the Ghanaian case, landlords) as the enemy of common folk.

From the mid-1950s on, achieving success at rural political demobilization required very different institutional strategies in the two cases. Although farmers produced the same crop – cocoa – on both sides of the Ghanaian-Ivoirian border, rulers employed very different strategies in attempting to influence social relations of production, structure access to productive resources, and control marketing circuits. The Ghanaian regime's strategy involved intense interventionism at the local level, a rush to build new institutions in the localities to displace old ones, and state agents' deep implication in local-level politics and disputes of all kinds. This contrasts sharply with the Ivoirian government's aloof presence and "the absence of local political life" in the forests of southern Côte d'Ivoire. The endogenous theory of institutional choice proposed here locates the origins of these differences in rural social organization: the two regimes confronted rural societies that differed in their capacity to challenge nationalists' control over both agricultural surpluses and the political behavior of ordinary peasants.

In devising means to govern and tax cocoa producers, Nkrumah confronted direct resistance mounted by large-scale cocoa farmers and traders (and supported by much of the peasantry in Asante), who contested not only the new state's claim to cocoa wealth, but also Nkrumah's and the CPP's claims to state power. So explosive was this confrontation that, in little more than a decade, it destroyed the Nkrumah regime and crippled one of sub-Saharan Africa's most prosperous farming economies.

Ghana's cocoa producers were remarkable in the context of decolonizing Africa, not only for their prosperity, but also for their capacity to mount organized challenges to the colonial and postcolonial states. As we have

---

[217] On populism, see Chege 1988.

seen, their *interest* in challenging the postcolonial state was traceable in part to the wealth of big producers, and their positions as landlords, creditors, and cocoa traders. They did not believe that they needed the state to underwrite their local influence and privilege. Even more to the point, the Asante elite were determined not to allow Accra to drain cocoa wealth from their region and then, to add to the injury, use it to accumulate power at their expense.

The Akan chiefs' *ability* to mount direct resistance to the central state – their capacity for collective action – was related to structural and political facts of rural society. The ability to mount direct resistance to the state's claims on the rural surplus was rooted in the hierarchically structured political economies of the Akan states under colonial rule. The rural elite, which was organized by and around the chiefly planter-merchant stratum, wielded multiple sources of leverage and influence over the behavior of smaller-scale and poorer producers. Under colonial rule, many of the planter-chiefs had established controlling positions in both the "sphere of production" and the "sphere of circulation" in Ghana's protocapitalist cocoa economy. Institutions of British *raj* in Ghana – most notably the Native Authorities and the farmers' unions that were created after 1938 – had also been used as instruments of power accumulation by the same chiefly class. Many planter-chiefs had cinched control of rural political constituencies in Ghana's cocoa heartland. CPP efforts to micromanage not only political competition but also *strategic economic exchanges* within localities were attempts to create new community-level power structures that would bypass and displace the old socioeconomic hierarchies. It was a strategy of usurpation.

In Côte d'Ivoire, where rural societies were atomized or weakly structured at best, cocoa producers had no social-political infrastructure for collective action, and thus very little by way of political organization, leadership, or resources that could be mobilized as a counterweight to new rulers at the center. Here we encounter the proverbial "sack of potatoes." Even where aristocratic and wealthy cocoa producers in southern Côte d'Ivoire viewed Houphouet and the Baoulés as usurping their rightful places in the successor state (Sanwi in the early 1950s is the obvious case), the geographical reach of even the most prominent Ivoirian chiefs was small, they had no hold on marketing circuits, and they did not exercise much economic leverage over the farmers they claimed as constituents. Because socioeconomic hierarchies were so weak, there was no ready-made rural infrastructure for contesting the hegemony of the regime in Abidjan.

Houphouet was not pressed to rewire the circuits of local authority; the status quo of a demobilized and atomized peasantry suited the state's purposes perfectly. The challenge for Houphouet in the Ivoirian south was to *prevent* rural political entrepreneurs from getting a hold of resources and institutions that could be used to organize followings and accumulate influence. For this, administrative occupation was the institution-building strategy of choice: it provided rural actors with no footholds in the state and no points of access to state resources. This kind of "liberal" approach would have been political suicide for Nkrumah in Ghana, for the cocoa-producing elite would have enjoyed full freedom to mobilize against the center.

5

The Geopolitics of Late Development

Expanding the scope of commercial agriculture was integral to state formation in the postcolonial period, for "development" could extend the reach
of the state and strengthen a regime's grip on new regions (and new producers). In the best of circumstances it also helped fill state coffers with export
and tax revenues. Viewing postcolonial development through statist lenses,
it is easy to miss how political – and how constrained – African rulers'
choices really were about where, when, and how to promote structural
transformation in rural social relations and modes of production. Rulers
were constrained by their rural allies' demands and refusals, by fears of the
political consequences of rural socioeconomic change, and by possibilities
and limits to change inherent in indigenous modes of agricultural production. The endogenous theory of institutional choice focuses attention on
these geopolitical factors. In so doing it helps measure the considerable
extent to which institutional and market structures of African economies
have been shaped by the rural societies that central rulers have sought to
tax and govern. Leaders who now seek to defy or willfully transform these
constaints continue to do so at considerable political risk and cost.

   This chapter focuses on two regions that were economically peripheral at
the time of independence: the Senegal River Valley, which divides Senegal
and Mauritania (and thus constitutes Senegal's northern border region),
and the Korhogo region, which is the center of gravity of Côte d'Ivoire's
northern half. The chapter seeks to explain when, why, and how postcolonial
regimes chose to promote market expansion in these particular zones (as
opposed to others). In other words, we push the endogenous theory of
institutional choice to explain the place and timing, as well as the mode, of
state-led rural development. This analysis works in four ways to test, refine,
and extend the theory developed in preceding chapters.

First, the cases offer additional empirical support for the causal theory advanced in Chapter 2. Deepening incorporation of these two regions into national markets in the 1970s was part and parcel of state-building strategies aimed at consolidating powersharing alliances with rural elites in hierarchical agrarian societies. In both cases, the politically successful solution (equilibrium solution) to the institution-building problem was powersharing. This means that even when postcolonial rulers were at the peak of their power – when partisan opponents had been eliminated, one-party states were entrenched, and international financial backers were generous and forthcoming – governments in Senegal and Côte d'Ivoire chose to bargain with, make concessions to, and share power with provincial chiefs and aristocrats. Indirect rule was thus confirmed as a viable institutional option in both of these former French colonies. This constitutes additional challenge to rival theories that attribute rulers' institutional choices to inherited colonial doctrines (in this case, to the doctrine of French direct rule).

Second, the cases document in-country contrasts. They highlight the unevenness of institutional topography in West Africa, even within any one state. In-country contrasts reinforce the argument against theories that focus on national-level (statist) determinants of institutional choice. Postcolonial rulers in Côte d'Ivoire – generally viewed as the most statist, ideologically coherent, and bureaucratic of all France's successors in Africa – chose a strategy of administrative occupation in the South, as we saw in the last chapter. In the Korhogo region, by contrast, rural threats and opportunities pressured the regime to embrace powersharing. Determinants of this difference must be endogenous to the rural areas; they cannot be found in national-level factors such as regime ideology or French neocolonial influence. As William Munroe (1995) suggested in a recent study of Zimbabwe, state building remained an essentially local project.

Similarly, in the Senegal River Valley, national rulers chose institutional strategies that were the exact opposite of those pursued in another peripheral zone of Senegal, Lower Casamance. Explanations that focus on Senegalese rulers' obsession with "national institutional uniformity" cannot account for this difference. Looking at the Senegal River Valley is doubly useful from an in-country perspective, for it also helps generalize findings from the Wolof groundnut basin. Many analysts have seen powersharing in the groundnut basin as the product of factors that are sui generis to that region (i.e., the profoundly cultural, mystical, and curiously modern phenomenon of Mouride marabouts' influence over the peasants). In

241

the Senegal River Valley, Dakar built powersharing arrangements with an indigenous rural elite whose power appears to be less mystical and more tightly rooted in the kind of everyday, material factors (especially land-holding patterns) that we have emphasized in this text, and that also go far in explaining outcomes in the Wolof groundnut basin.

These cases serve present purposes in a third way. In both settings, rulers' institutional choices *change over time*. Both can be read as cases of "path switching." Can this be squared with a theory that explains institutional choice in terms of rural social structure? I argue that it can. Logically, there are at least three possible solutions to the conundrum: rural social structure can change, rulers can make or correct mistakes, and goals of central rulers can change. In the Korhogo region, Ivoirian rulers switched paths to address the adverse political consequences of past "mistakes." In the Senegal River Valley, we can say that changes in social structure altered the needs and interests (preferences) of rural elites and their allies at the center: new insti-tutional strategies were developed in response to these shifts. Explanations deduced from the theory itself capture basic determinants of institutional shifts in the regions examined here.

Finally, these chapters uncover empirical material that does not fit neatly into the typologies presented in Chapter 2. Two partial anomalies invite extensions of the theory. We encounter the first in a subregion of the Senegal River Valley. State-engineered settlement schemes in the Sene-gal River delta created a pattern of rural social organization not anticipated by the theory. It gave rise to political dynamics also not included in the original possibility set. There is a second anomaly in the Senegal River Valley. In the Middle and Upper Valley in the 1960s, rulers pursued what can be described as a "mixed" institutional strategy. It was a combination of economic non-incorporation and political powersharing. In the 1970s, this strategy gave way to a form of powersharing that is closer to the ideal type.

Taken together, the two main cases presented in this chapter show that regimes chose to "develop" peripheral territories when and where they cal-culated that institution building would shore up the state's hold in those particular regions. This is the logical corollary of the argument advanced for Lower Casamance. There, Dakar forewent rural development for the first two decades of independence because state investment and institu-tion building threatened to empower rural actors who seemed destined to challenge the regime's hegemony.

In Korhogo and the Senegal River Valley, where powersharing served the center's interests, the regimes' rural allies seemed to have followed their part in state-building dramas as they are hypothesized here: they were willing collaborators in "rural development" if and when they calculated that state building would reinforce their own standing and influence in their home areas. Powersharing alliance gave the more powerful of the two sets of rural elites considered here – those in the Senegal River Valley – a measure of veto power over institution-building (economic development) initiatives that might jeopardize their control over their dependents, tenants, and subjects. We observed the same dynamic in the Wolof groundnut basin, where political stability was bought at the cost of policy innovations such as land reform, universal primary education, and increases in real producer prices that could have contributed to more technical innovation in agriculture.

Part One: Path Switching in Northern Côte d'Ivoire

> From a study of different regions of the Ivory Coast, it is quite clear to me . . . that each sub-elite has evolved a distinct structure in its relations with the national level.
>
> Staniland 1970c:624

The Korhogo region of northern Côte d'Ivoire was the geographic target of a concerted push to produce state-led economic development. Institutional vehicles of this development were marketing and input-distribution agencies and rules designed to promote cotton production. The timing and character of the Houphouet regime's institutional choices came largely in response to demands from provincial elites for political incorporation and powersharing.

In analyzing institutional choice in northern Cote d'Ivoire, this chapter traces variation in strategy across both space and time. It highlights variation across regions within Côte d'Ivoire, and also documents change over time in rulers' state-building choices within this one region. The focus is on the densely settled and populous Senoufo region of northern Côte d'Ivoire, which constitutes the demographic core of the country's northern half. The capital city of this region is Korhogo.[1] Peasant society here is more cohesive and hierarchical than in most of the Ivoirian forest zone. An endogenous theory of institutional choice predicts that state-building

---

[1] Korhogo is one of five main population centers in Côte d'Ivoire. The others are Abidjan, Bouaké, Man, and Daloa-Gagnoa.

strategies in the Korhogo region would differ from those pursued in the South, and this in fact is what we find.[2]

Zigzags in the historical trajectory of institutional development in this region help put this book's argument to the test. In dealing with the indigenous elites of the Senoufo region, Ivoirian state builders switched strategy twice. French colonial rulers collaborated with the Senoufo nobles, as did nationalist politicians in their first attempts to mobilize support in this region. In the mid-1950s, however, Houphouet-Boigny organized against the provincial elite. The regime's institutional choices were aimed at usurpation; the strategy resembled what we observed in the Asante region of Ghana. Then, in the 1970s, Houphouet reverted to powersharing. What explains the strategies themselves, and the zigzags, if the pattern of rural social organization did not transform radically – in two opposite directions – over the course of this short period?

The anomaly here is the usurpationist strategy of the late 1950s and 1960s. It is a deviation from the expected course of powersharing; it can be viewed as an "off-the-path" choice on the part of central rulers. In the Korhogo region, there was a measure of hierarchical cohesion in Senoufo society that gave northern elites some bargaining power in dealing with the regime in Abidjan. The limited (and indeed declining) capacity of these elites to generate or extract rural wealth on their own, however, placed them in a position of dependency vis-à-vis the postcolonial state: they needed new ways to maintain their socioeconomic privileges in Senoufo society, and for this they looked to Abidjan. In these circumstances, the regime is expected to build economic and political institutions to share power, more or less along the lines of what happened in the Wolof groundnut basin. What happened?

Political factors that are not fully theorized in this analysis seem to explain the regime's usurpationist drive in the late 1950s and 1960s. In the 1950s, when the PDCI sought to consolidate rural support in the Senoufo zone, French administrators pressured their allies, the Senoufo cantonal chiefs, to participate in repression of the PDCI-RDA. This was also France's policy in the rest of Côte d'Ivoire. The nationalists countered by playing the populist card in Korhogo, as they did in the South. That is how the PDCI became an anti-chief party in Senoufoland. The party built a political machine in

---

[2] On the Malinké region centered on Odienné, and the precolonial kingdom of Kabadugu, see Toungara 1996. Postcolonial politics and state building in Odienné also conform to the powersharing pattern.

Table 5.1. *Path Switching in Northern Côte d'Ivoire (Korhogo)*

	Functional Domain		
	Provincial Administration: Party-State Apparatus	Export Marketing: Marketing Board, Co-ops	Allocating Factors of Production: Inputs, Land
Korhogo 1960s	Spatial deconcentration Centralization of authority	No institution building	Institution building is minimal.
	Usurpation	Market forces	Market forces
Korhogo 1970s–1980s	Spatial concentration Devolution of authority	Spatial deconcentration Parastatal agency works with local elites.	Purchased inputs: parastatal agency and local elites Land: local elites
	Powersharing	Some powersharing	Some powersharing

the Korhogo region, and in the 1960s regional party leaders used it to try to usurp the positions and authority of Senoufo elites. Sure enough, however, over the first decade of independence it became increasingly clear to rulers in Abidjan that this institution-building strategy was dysfunctional. It was not serving their interests. Failure to co-opt the indigenous political elite had raised the specter of regionally based mobilization against the center. It also retarded the regime's effort to promote peasant production of a taxable commercial crop in this region. The regime was being "punished," as it were, for straying from the politically optimal strategy of powersharing. This story has a trial-and-error dimension that closer inspection would reveal in most of the cases considered here.

What Ivoirian rulers needed at the end of the 1960s were new institutional arrangements that would allow them to govern and tax Senoufoland in an effective manner. This is exactly what they chose. In 1970 the regime broke with the usurpationist politics of the nationalist period and embraced institution-building strategies aimed at powersharing with the indigenous provincial elite. This contrast is sketched out in Table 5.1. Senoufo elites and the Houphouet regime found common cause in an institution-building strategy centered on erecting a deconcentrated network of PDCI, rural development, and marketing institutions in the Korhogo region. Some devolution of authority to local elites occurred as leading clans took control of the regional party. Land-tenure prerogatives that had been challenged by the party-state in the 1960s were restored to Senoufo leading families in the 1970s, and central rulers channeled improved agricultural inputs and farming incomes to the lineage-segment heads who presided over the large, extended households of this region.

I. Hierarchical Cohesion in Senoufo Society

Frustrated by the difficulty of "pacifying" African societies in the southern forest zone, French troops cut a straight line northward, up the Comoé River, to reach the more open woodlands and grasslands of the savannah. In 1903 they conquered and occupied Korhogo, the political center of the Senoufo region. From the military and administrative base it established in Korhogo, France opened a new front in its war against the Baoulé and other forest-zone populations. After more than a decade, they brought

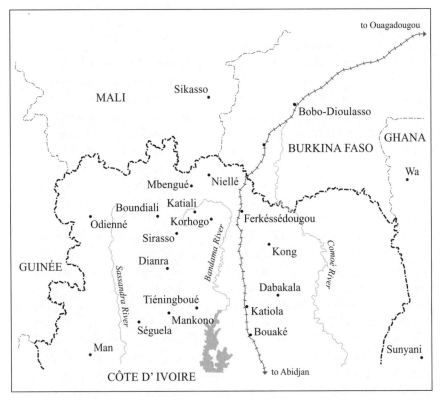

Map 5.1.   Northern Côte d'Ivoire

246

"the interminable resistance of anarchic forest peoples" to an end and placed all of modern-day Côte d'Ivoire under French rule. In retrospect it is clear that a precedent had been established, for Senoufoland would remain a re-. gion of geostrategic importance to colonial and postcolonial architects of Côte d'Ivoire.

In 1903 Senoufo society was more centralized and politically cohesive than the African societies of most of the forest zone. This cohesion was partly a result of the very recent past. In the 1890s (1892–8) Samory Touré, the last of West Africa's great empire builders, descended from the Guinée highlands to conquer and occupy much of what is now northern Côte d'Ivoire.[3] Conquest caused massive upheaval in the Senoufo zone. War, pillage, and upset forced many Senoufo to leave their dispersed and largely autonomous village settlements to seek the protection of the largest of the Senoufo chiefdoms, Tiembara, which had acquiesced to Samory's overrule. Most settled in new villages located in what became known as the *zone dense* (zone of dense settlement) in a fifty- to seventy-kilometer radius extending mostly southward and westward from the town of Korhogo, seat of Tiembara.[4]

In the safe zone around Korhogo, Samory ruled through the Tiembara chief and the existing structures of the chieftaincy.[5] This means that at the end of the nineteenth century, Gbon Coulibaly, the Tiembara chief, governed the Senoufo under a precolonial version of indirect rule. These arrangements helped extend and consolidate Gbon's authority over other Senoufo chiefdoms of the region. Samory himself was an ambitious

---

[3] The kingdoms of Kong, Bondoukou, and Bouna were subjugated and destroyed. See Stryker 1970:25.

[4] Coulibaly 1978:46, 58. According to Coulibaly, the Tiembara (Kiembara) chiefdom was founded in the fourteenth century (and by some accounts, earlier). Senoufo populations now inhabit the region stretching from Boundiali to Kong (about 200 kilometers along an east-west axis) and from Katiola to the Mali border (about 230 kilometers along the north-south axis), a region that includes the towns of Boundiali, Korhogo, Diawala, Niellé, Mbengué. (The "voltaïque cousins" of the Senoufo, also called "Senoufo" by Coulibaly, inhabit most of what is now western Burkina Faso.) In Côte d'Ivoire, the Senoufo population is spread very unevenly across this region, with almost 40 percent of the total – 103,000 of 277,000 in the 1970s – concentrated in the Department of Korhogo, which is one of three main administrative jurisdictions covering the Senoufo region. Population density in the Korhogo Department (the so-called *zone dense*) is sixty to eighty inhabitants per square kilometer; in the northern and southern reaches of the Senoufo zone, population density is only five to twenty inhabitants per square kilometer. See also Hinderink and Tempelman 1978:95; Person 1981; Bassett 1984:25, 2001.

[5] See Gunderson 1975:87, 180; Coulibaly 1978:48–50, 110.

centralizer and state builder. During his short rulership he superimposed on Senoufo institutions an administrative system that amounted to "the most ambitious indigenous centralizing effort in the history of this area."[6] Stryker (1970:60) writes that Samory's empire in what is now Côte d'Ivoire "achieved a degree of administrative linkage on a larger scale than any other precolonial polity in the history of Ivory Coast." European imperialists would inherit this legacy. When France defeated Samory in 1898, it asserted control over a Senoufo population that was less dispersed and more politically centralized in the Korhogo zone than it had been a generation before.[7]

About half of the population of present-day Côte d'Ivoire lived in the northern savannah region at the time of French conquest. Senoufo were the large majority: in 1960 they constituted a large majority of the rural population of northern Côte d'Ivoire and about 80 percent of the population of the Korhogo region.[8] Senoufo lived as sedentary agriculturalists and acted as hosts to small populations of pastoral Peul who lived on the margins of Senoufo society. Dyula traders were also present as strangers in Senoufoland: their presence increased during the Samory wars and again with the expansion of colonial commerce under French rule. Coulibaly (1978:51, 53) describes Dyula settlements as "islands of minor importance submerged in a Senoufo universe."

Senoufo villages were physically compact and highly cohesive: they were organized around deeply rooted village institutions (sacred forests where meetings were held and collective decisions were made, initiation societies), strong gerontocracy, caste structures, hierarchies of "founding" and "settler" lineages, and the hierarchical landlord-stranger rules that structured farmer-herder relations.[9] Villages themselves were interconnected via hierarchies that formed chieftaincies that were controlled by the foundling lineages of a certain area. In the Senoufo heartland at the turn of the century,

---

[6] Stryker 1970:25, 60. Martin (1971:164) describes Samory's empire as a system of 10 military provinces with 162 subdivisions. France was eager to destroy him: they did not want "any independent states in or adjoining their new colonies in Guinea and Ivory Coast" (ibid.).

[7] The exact opposite was true in the case of the Baoulé: there, monarchical organization regressed markedly in the nineteenth century (Person 1981:21).

[8] On 1900, see Stryker 1971b:128. In the 1960s Senoufo made up 10 percent of the national population (Hinderink and Tempelman 1978:93). Bassett (1984:245) reports that in 1980 Senoufo still made up 80 percent of the rural population of the Korhogo region.

[9] On physical layout of Senoufo villages and on caste, see Coulibaly 1978:80–3.

chieftaincies were nested in a hierarchy of chieftaincies: when France occupied Korhogo in 1903, twenty-six of the twenty-eight Senoufo chiefs of the *zone dense* recognized the primacy of Tiembara and its chief, Gbon Coulibaly.[10] France had come upon an indigenous political infrastructure that was broader in scope, and somewhat more hierarchical and centralized, than what it confronted elsewhere in Côte d'Ivoire.

Sinali Coulibaly (1978:107) wrote that "land is the source of political authority" in Senoufo society, and this was reflected clearly in Senoufo political institutions: control over land was the basis of hierarchy within chieftaincies, villages, lineages, and lineage segments. Chieftaincies were controlled by the senior males of Senoufo founding lineages. They served as political authorities, arbiters, and allocators of land.[11] Land chiefs (*tarfolo* chiefs) made land grants for the creation of new villages within the lineage's territory. New villages recognized the political primacy of the dominant lineage, paying tribute in kind and labor. Some writers have used the term "semi-feudal" to describe the relationship that tied settler villages to the founding lineages of the Senoufo chiefdom of Katiali.[12] When the leader of a settler village died, his successor had to regain permission from the *tarfolo* of the central village to continue using the land, and the *tarfolo* could refuse this request.[13] These rules helped reproduce the authority of the chieftaincies – that is, of central villages – over settler villages.

Coulibaly (1978) and others explain that such relations were particularly important in the Korhogo region. This is because many new villages were established in the last decades of the nineteenth century, around the

---

[10] Stryker 1970:81. This area included three small cantons in what is now Sirasso *sous-préfecture*, southwest of Korhogo. See also Launay 1982:16, 23.

[11] Coulibaly (1978:109) nuances this generalization: with the population influxes to the *zone dense* after the 1880s, some villages ended up with more newcomers than original inhabitants. In some cases, village chiefs were chosen from the numerically dominant group, while the land chiefs represented the founders. This arrangement was not the general rule.

[12] Bassett 1984:21–4. See also Bassett 2001. Katiali and its six satellite villages covered an area of 569 square kilometers. Coulibaly points out that in contrast to European feudalism, in the Senoufo system land belongs to families (lineages), not individuals. Also in contrast to European feudalism, among the Senoufo political authority and authority over land are/were, in theory, separable: the former is invested in chiefs; the latter is invested in lineages (Coulibaly 1978:111–12).

[13] See Coulibaly 1978:119–20; Bassett 1984:20–1.

time of the Samory wars. Hierarchy was reinforced by the fact that the most powerful Senoufo chieftaincies used the political instability of that era to force their weaker neighbors into political submission by revoking their land rights – that is, forcing them into the position of de facto settler villages.[14]

Important Senoufo chieftaincies comprised many, sometimes several dozen, villages. The highest-ranking land authorities (the *tarfolo* chiefs) were represented at the village level by subchiefs or village headmen, who were themselves the oldest members of the settler village's founding family. If the village was large, it would be divided along lineage lines into "quarters," each with its own subchief. This made for political cohesion within chiefdoms and a chain of command in which the most important land issues and local disputes were passed upward to chieftaincy-level authorities for adjudication.

Within Senoufo lineages and villages, authority and hierarchy were rooted in control over agricultural production and labor. Until the 1930s, village or quarter lands were communal lands: they were held in common and tilled on a communal basis under the supervision of chiefs or subchiefs.[15] The product of this collective effort was stored in cylindrical communal silos that graced the skyline of Senoufo villages. Subchiefs controlled this food stock and were responsible for providing for subsistence from this store. As a mark and reinforcer of privilege in village society, some individuals had the right to devote several days of the work week to cultivating an *individual* plot. The right to produce, consume, and accumulate "privately," as it were, was reserved for male elders (including chiefs, headmen, and lineage-heads) and married women with children.

Labor power was the scarce resource in this system. The labor power of young people, especially young men, was the key asset, and it was allocated in ways that worked to affirm social cohesion and hierarchy. A "young man" in Senoufo society is an unmarried man, and in this society men married around the age of thirty-five. Because youths were not allowed to have individual plots, their labor power was a floating resource whose allocation was determined by other political and social rules. The main claim on their labor was held by the community as a whole: youths worked mostly on

---

[14] Coulibaly 1978:48–9, 109–10, 112. He describes these processes of political centralization (from 1860 to 1900) as the "feudalization" of Senoufo political institutions.

[15] See for example Bassett 1984:29, 20, 173.

communal fields. Privileged individuals – male elders – also held more particularistic claims on the labor power of youth. This was institutionalized in the most important of the Senoufo village institutions – the *poro* initiation societies.[16]

Youth were organized into *poro* societies, which along with the closely related institution of village-level sacred forests were a powerful source of communal coherence and continuity. *Poro* played a key role in controlling and deploying the labor power of youth, for young men in the last (seven-year) phase of the twenty-one-year initiation process were given the job of tilling the individual plots of the elders.

During the last *poro* ceremony period, the young Senoufo has to work hard without compensation on the lands of village elders, he has no rights whatsoever ... the elders control the land, the women, and the labor supply of the village.... In fact, Senoufo society still [1978] can be considered very rigid because of its strong gerontocracy. At the same time, it is rather egalitarian, since every male who completes poro will eventually [become] a village elder. (Hinderink and Tempelman 1978:95)

Elders' control over the circulation of women (marriage contracts) reinforced the hierarchy in production relations. By laboring in the fields of chiefs and elders, male youth also earned the right to marry, and did so in unions arranged by the notables.

As Bassett writes (1984:53–5), slave labor was also a prominent part of the indigenous class structure and the Senoufo mode of production. Household production depended in part on the work of so-called hut captives, the descendants of war captives or slaves who, by the second or third generation, "often enjoyed benefits typically associated with a master's free sons and daughters" (ibid.:53). Larger and wealthier households included more descendants of captives. So-called hut captives and young men did much of the work on the larger Senoufo production units, especially collective fields and lineage-based fields controlled by chiefs and lineage elders.

Some observers have noted that there was a certain democracy and egalitarianism in the Senoufo system, for all married males could reach elder status. It is important not to forget, however, that most people could not aspire to this status (women, non-Senoufo, descendants of captives), and

[16] See Coulibaly 1978:98–105.

that not all elders were of equal rank. There were hierarchies of founding and subordinate lineages, and these remained nested in the hierarchical structure of chiefdoms. Wealth and household size were additional sources of social stratification. Wealth enabled men to marry more wives, have larger households, cultivate more land, and thus produce more.

II. French Indirect Rule

France's strategy of rule in the Senoufo heartlands of northern Côte d'Ivoire was the exact opposite of the strategy it adopted in the southwestern part of the colony. In this part of the North, the colonial authorities sought to govern by "co-opting the Senoufo traditional structure of governance" (Stryker 1970:81). France's choices are explained largely by the opportunity structure it encountered: in Senoufoland, France found powerful and willing indigenous collaborators. Gbon Coulibaly, leader of the Tiembara chiefdom, "welcomed the French as liberators" and sought to collaborate with France to solidify and extend his rule.[17] France embraced the opportunity to govern through its new ally: colonial authorities named Gbon Coulibaly paramount chief and undertook to harness Senoufo chiefly hierarchies to the colonial cause.

A colonial system of indirect rule was up and running in the Korhogo region a decade before France had crushed the resistance of the Baoulé and other forest peoples to the South. Around Korhogo, France created a colonial administrative division (*cercle*) that coincided with the established boundaries of the Tiembara chiefdom.[18] France also respected the geographic authority of the local chiefs, and cantons were delimited along the lines of preexisting political boundaries. Nephews of Paramount Chief Gbon Coulibaly were appointed as cantonal chiefs throughout the Korhogo region.[19] Beyond Korhogo, France restored some of the Senoufo chieftaincies that had been conquered by Samory at the end of the nineteenth

[17] Lawler 1992:207; see also Bassett 1984:47–8.
[18] What is now considered the "Sénoufo region" was made up of the colonial *cercles* of Korhogo, Boundiali, Ferkéssédougou, and Tagbana (which included Dabakala and Katiola). Most of the area outside Korhogo *cercle* was not under Korhogo (Tiembara) authority. Katiola, for example, was the capital of "*pays Tagouana*" and not under Korhogo's authority. See Nguessan-Zoukou 1990:130. On colonial administrative boundaries, Coulibaly (1978:57) argues that the cantons were basically traditional units, delimited according to "historical circumstance."
[19] See Gunderson 1975:169, 180; Zolberg 1964:53.

century, thereby winning the support of those who were reinstated. In contrast to their strategy in most of southern Côte d'Ivoire, French administrators made "a concerted effort to respect customary successions to chieftaincy and only rarely replace local rulers by outsiders. . . . Indigenous chiefs were thus granted a certain degree of independence in that they 'ruled' over their former provinces."[20]

French rulers depended upon a politics of collaboration with Senoufo elites at the provincial, cantonal, and village level. Their strategy was to buttress local chieftaincy and gerontocracy, to work through those social hierarchies to enforce order and acquiescence to French overrule, and to extract agricultural commodities and labor. In the early years of French rule, Senoufo peasants toiled in the communal village and lineage fields to produce foodstuffs requisitioned by French armies to fuel the colonial war in Baouléland. Chiefs invoked traditional claims on their subjects' labor power to organize villagers for this task and were paid by France for their services. Chiefs and lineage-heads also deployed their "traditional prerogatives" in recruiting young men and the descendants of captives to serve as porters and construction workers for French merchant houses and the colonial administration. "As influential collaborators for a relatively weak state and fledging mercantile houses, canton chiefs enjoyed a considerable amount of political and economic power" (Bassett 1984:57).

This collaboration with Senoufo elites meant that there was a huge gap between colonial practices in this region and France's formal doctrine of direct rule. There was also a blatant contradiction between French strategy in the Senoufo region and one of colonialism's core legitimating doctrines: the abolition of slavery. Bassett writes that the colonial administration "supported the 'class interests' of chiefs and relatively wealthy peasants possessing many slaves," and that one way of doing so was to buttress precapitalist production relations between slaves (descendants of captives) and masters. "The colonial administration found it useful not to intervene in these relations, for liberation of the slaves would be detrimental to European commercial and industrial interests. The state also did not want to run the risk of alienating slave owners" (Bassett 1984:54). When it came to the daily work of imperialism, political expediency trumped doctrines and ideologies that had wide currency in Paris.

---

[20] Bassett 1984:50, 52. Bassett notes that Gbon Coulibaly sought to extend his authority over areas that were previously independent of Korhogo, and that the canton chiefs of Niellé and Mbengué refused to accept this.

A. Extracting Cotton and Labor

France's appetite for the produce and labor power of the Senoufo grew in the 1910s and 1920s. Cotton was long established as a staple crop in the Senoufo region, and in the 1910s the French decided that this was the agricultural commodity they wanted from northern Côte d'Ivoire. Established Senoufo elites remained the linchpins of the colonial system of extraction. Senoufo chiefs were made responsible for filling village quotas.[21] This rule reinforced France's stake in confirming chiefly control over communal labor, village fields, and the product thereof.

From the 1910s to about 1930 cotton destined for the colonial state was produced in a perversion of the traditional way. It was cultivated communally on village fields under the supervision and control of chiefs and headmen. In contrast to the old system, however, the product of this collective effort was not a public good: chiefs and lineage-heads sold the cotton to the French, used the proceeds to pay head taxes, and kept the rest for themselves. Additional cash incentives (credit, bonuses, commissions) were offered to canton chiefs and village chiefs who exceeded village production quotas. Colonial authorities undertook to intensify production in the late 1910s and 1920s, and chiefs enforced the rules of the ever-more demanding production regime. Now peasants were forced to monocrop, obey strict weeding schedules, and follow new rules in applying purchased inputs. "Those who failed to follow directives were beaten."[22] Bassett writes that "although circle 'guards' [locally perceived as 'soldiers'] visited each canton to oversee the selection, clearing, and planting of cotton fields, the administration ultimately needed influential chiefs to see that its orders were carried out."[23]

Sales of cotton to the colonial authorities increased in the 1910s and 1920s, but raw labor power soon rivaled cotton as Senoufoland's leading export. A brutal forced-labor regime was one centerpiece of France's civilizing enterprise in Africa. In Côte d'Ivoire, the Senoufo region bore a disproportionate share of the pain. France viewed the Senoufo region as a reservoir of manpower that could be coercively mobilized by France's local

---

[21] "In a display of his cooperation with the colonial administration, Gbon Coulibaly, canton chief of the Kiembara, planted 2 ha. of cotton in 1911 to serve as a model for surrounding villages.... In 1916, each taxpayer was forced to cultivate 8 ares of cotton (100 ares = 1 hectare)" (Bassett 1984:67).

[22] From Bassett 1984:115.

[23] See Bassett 1984:49. See also ibid.:67, 116; Campbell 1973:295.

agents – the chiefs – and sent to work in the rapidly growing economy of the forest zone. Demand for forced laborers from the Senoufo region increased steadily from the early 1900s onward. In 1918 as many as 1,200 men were removed from the fields and homes of Senoufoland and sent to work as forced laborers in the South. Many were whipped, beaten, crushed, or killed by disease as they cleared roads, laid railway, hauled logs, tapped rubber, and created plantations for the colonial state and private French business. Noble Senoufo families were spared the worst of these abuses, for they could send the descendants of captives to fulfill forced labor requirements while their junior kinsmen remained in the village.

France intensified the pressure over the course of the 1920s and 1930s. In 1928, the year the railway reached Ferkéssédougou, France conscripted 8,000 Senoufo into forced labor. In Kong Cercle, about 15 percent of the active male population was removed from the villages and agricultural work force.[24]

The heavy weight of France's extractions strained the capacity of Senoufo villages and households to provide for subsistence needs. Forced cultivation of cotton and food crops, the head-tax regime, and the colonial *corvée* all deprived Senoufo households of land and labor previously dedicated to food production. "The very fragile situation of many households collapsed in 1929 after adverse ecological conditions (locust invasions and drought) reduced crop yields" (Bassett 1984:74). Famine struck northern Côte d'Ivoire.

B. France Shores Up the Lineage Heads

The appalling misery of Senoufoland in 1929 contributed to a process of deeper change in local authority relations and in the organization of production. The system of multi-lineage collective fields began to break up: food and labor shortages meant that this institution was no longer able to guarantee a subsistence minimum for its members (Bassett 1984:134–9). The old collective fields gave way to a more segmented system of collective production – a system based on lineages. This change eroded the power of village-level and canton chiefs in two ways. First, many were implicated directly in the failure of the old system: they had abused their power and authority. Corrosion of what had once been legitimate authority, and the collapse of their ability to provide a safety net for their subjects, weakened the chiefs. French commanders in the Korhogo region began to complain

[24] Kong's estimate is for 1930 (see Bassett 1984:75, 124). See also Lawler 1992.

and worry about the declining authority of chiefs around this time. Second, breakdown of the largest communal fields deprived the village and canton chiefs of their most important mechanisms for appropriating agricultural surpluses from their subjects. Bassett (ibid.) writes that by 1930 the canton and village chiefs' control over commodity production – institutionalized in collective production on the village fields and in the colonial practice of paying chiefs for the product of this collective labor – was being widely contested by village elders and lineage notables. Lineage heads had shared in the right to appropriate the product of the collective fields in the earlier period. In the 1920s they began to demand the reinstatement of this prerogative, and to thus rein in the authority of the official chiefs.

Due to famine, there was no official "cotton campaign" in northern Côte d'Ivoire in 1931 or 1932. As Senoufoland recovered from this food crisis in the 1930s, it became clear that a change in social structure had occurred. Lineage-based production units – the farming unit based on a lineage segment composed of a household head's younger brothers and maternal nephews, their wives and children, and possibly descendants of captives – were now established as the main units of agricultural production.[25] Village fields and village granaries – which had been under the direct control of the village chiefs – were mostly gone. Henceforth, as we shall see, the cantonal and village chiefs would be more dependent upon agricultural surpluses that they could produce themselves, and more dependent upon the state.

Bassett (1984:134–5) explains that in 1932 French authorities attempted to address the agricultural crisis and "crisis in native command" in the Korhogo region by making two changes in administrative structure and practice. First, they reorganized the "native command." France reduced the number of canton chiefs (thereby enlarging the geographic area under the control of the remaining chiefs), and "further recompensed canton chiefs for their services to the state by granting them monthly salaries." This was supposed to discourage the canton chiefs from monopolizing the profits generated by peasant producers. "At the same time, 'councils of notables' comprised of village chiefs and lineage heads were formed within cantons as a means of strengthening the indigenous chief system and to check the excesses of the canton chiefs" (ibid.).

The second change cut in the same direction. Like the change in administrative structure, it represented an attempt on the part of French

---

[25] Bassett 1984:139, 173; see also Hinderink and Tempelman 1978:97.

commanders to solidify a political and economic partnership with Senoufo village chiefs and lineage heads (elders), partly at the expense of the canton chiefs. Henceforth, France would target its commodity-production policies at the lineage heads, who would now be paid directly for output produced on the lineage-based collective fields (Bassett 1984:139). Cotton production remained compulsory for the peasants of Korhogo, but France hoped that the new system of remuneration would create incentives for farmers to increase the quantity and quality of output. A related innovation was the creation of colonial provident societies (SIPs), which were supposed to promote cash-crop production by distributing seeds.[26] The cotton output of Korhogo *cercle* grew over the course of the decade from 500 tons in 1933 to 800 tons in 1939 (Bassett 1984:79). By the mid-1940s cotton was the main commercial crop of the North. Income from cotton would further segment the village community and tend to reinforce wealth and status hierarchies based on controls over the labor of youth, women, and the descendants of captives.[27] A secular process that would persist for the rest of the century had been set in motion: the quest for political stability and the commercialization of agriculture was pushing central rulers away from the official canton chiefs and toward firmer alliance with the village chiefs and elders who controlled production within the large, extended households of this region.

Moves toward "peasantization" of the Senoufo population weakened the official cantonal chiefs. At the same time, this process affirmed – and even reinforced – the land and labor prerogatives of lineage-heads and village elders, and their authority over villages and members of their extended households. Shoring up the system of communal production within extended families helped lineage notables recapture control over the labor power of youth, and thus to shore up gerontocracy in the Senoufo social order.[28] With the creation of "councils of elders," these developments

---

[26] It seems that in the colonial period, these never provided credit. On the SIPs in northern Côte d'Ivoire, see Bassett 1984:75.

[27] The Compagnie Française de Développement de Fibres Textiles (CFDT) entered the scene in 1951. It worked through a system of producer incentives targeted at large households. See Campbell 1973; Boone 1992:112, 175.

[28] Hinderink and Tempelman 1978:97–8; Bassett 1984:162–4, 175. The *poro* system continued to exist, and the young men still had to work for village elders, who kept control over land, women, and the labor force. Extended-family farms were still controlled by elders, which helps explain, according to Hinderink and Tempelman (1978:98), the continued high rates of outmigration of youth from this region. A similar dynamic also helps explain out-migration from the Senegal River Valley.

were institutionalized in the administrative machinery of the colonial state.

III. The Nationalist Era: Houphouet Zigzags to Gain Advantage

In 1944, on the eve of the nationalist era in Côte d'Ivoire, the colonial administrator Gaston Joseph described the Senoufo as "cultivators, extremely attached to the land, hardworking,... and obedient to powerful chiefs."[29] France, however, had gone too far in exploiting these attributes of Senoufoland. Under the wartime regimes of Vichy and Free France, military and forced-labor quotas doubled. So too did production quotas for rice. "Hunger became common."[30] The labor drain and crop requisitioning again pushed many households below the subsistence level, and Senoufoland experienced localized famines in 1942 and 1943.

The "massive suffering" that France inflicted on Korhogo from 1939 to 1944 is what it took to rupture the forty-year collaboration between the French authorities and Korhogo paramount chief Gbon Coulibaly. As Lawler (1992:207) writes, Gbon Coulibaly had welcomed the French to Korhogo in the 1890s. "He had supported them throughout World War I, collaborated during the interwar years, providing forced labor and assisting in the collection of taxes and tribute; had supported the recruiting drive for soldiers to defend France in 1939; and when France fell in 1940, he was able to live comfortably with colonial authorities who'd switched allegiance to Vichy." Gbon's goodwill toward France finally expired in 1945, when he openly joined Houphouet-Boigny's fight to end forced labor in the African colonies.

Gbon Coulibaly would remain faithful to Houphouet until Gbon's death in 1962. This was an enormously important alliance for Houphouet: a leader with widespread political influence in a densely populated part of the savannah zone was a key resource for the PDCI-RDA in 1945 and 1946. Gbon "commanded almost mystical respect" among the Senoufo;[31] he was "venerated by all the peasants and influential among Muslims of the North."[32] Gbon's open calls for the end of the forced-labor regime (better late than

[29] Cited by Lawler 1992:13.
[30] Lawler 1992:208. Bassett (1984:148) reported that in the month of April 1936 – that is, before wartime increases were imposed – France drafted 850 men from Korhogo *cercle* to work as forced laborers.
[31] See Lawler 1992:210.
[32] See Person 1982:27.

never) surely bolstered esteem for the octogenarian chief in the eyes of almost everyone in the region.

Gbon responded to the Syndicat Agricole Africain's (SAA's) call in 1945 for "free wage laborers" from the North by "having his chiefs provide Houphouet with 1,500 men" (Lawler 1992:210). In 1945 and 1946 this powerful and influential chief led the Senoufo population en masse into the PDCI-RDA. Senoufo votes – along with those of their Voltaïque "cousins" in what was then called Upper Côte d'Ivoire (now Burkina Faso) – clenched Houphouet's victories in key electoral battles of the early post–World War II years.[33] Gbon and the cantonal chiefs strongly backed Houphouet's successful bid for election to the French parliament in 1945 and 1946. With the suppression of forced labor in May 1946, Houphouet became a national hero. Nowhere was enthusiasm higher than in the Senoufo zones of the North.

Dramane Coulibaly, a railwayman and son of the paramount chief, became the chief *interlocateur* between Houphouet and the venerated Gbon. Dramane emerged as the regional leader of the PDCI-RDA. He campaigned aggressively for Houphouet in Senoufo-Voltaïque regions of Côte d'Ivoire and Upper Côte d'Ivoire, which included the RDA strongholds in the Bobo-Dioulasso area. In Korhogo, Dramane spoke with Gbon seated at his side. Alliance with prominent Senoufo notables was pivotal in Houphouet's national-level political strategy: by some reports, Houphouet had promised to make Dramane his prime minister.[34] Houphouet appeared to be on course for the kind of powersharing deal that France had pursued in this region since the beginning of the colonial occupation.

This trajectory was disrupted in 1949 when French authorities lashed out against the PDCI-RDA. As the campaign of political repression against the PDCI-RDA moved into high gear, colonial authorities exerted intense pressure on the canton chiefs in Senoufoland to play the part of France's loyal agents. The cantonal chiefs were so economically and politically

---

[33] See Zan 1996:89. Recall that what is now Burkina Faso was called "Upper Côte d'Ivoire" from 1932 to 1947, when it was actually part of the French colony of Côte d'Ivoire. This region voted along with the rest of Côte d'Ivoire in the first electoral campaigns of the nationalist era. Support for the RDA in the western, Voltaïque/Senoufo regions of Upper Côte d'Ivoire was very strong; the definitive separation of the two territories in 1947 was an attempt on the part of France to weaken the PDCI-RDA.

[34] On these alliances, see Lawler 1992:225–6. She notes that Gbon Colibaly mobilized the *anciens combattants* and thus "provided the PDCI-RDA with the nucleus of a political machine in the North" (1982:210).

dependent upon France that most did not resist. By this time, most had no independent economic base – their control over communal labor and output had collapsed in the 1930s. Many were so resented by local populations that their personal authority derived almost completely from links to the colonial state. Colonial officers appear to have had no trouble in turning the cantonal chiefs against the PDCI-RDA (Gunderson 1975:83–5).

One notable exception was Paramount Chief Gbon Coulibaly. For his loyalty to Houphouet, Gbon was evicted from the paramount chieftaincy and replaced by his son Bema, who positioned himself as "leader of the pro-France faction of Senoufo cantonal chiefs." Dramane Coulibaly remained the chief PDCI-RDA militant and loyalist in the Korhogo region. For this he was sent to prison in 1950.[35] Antagonism between the Senoufo establishment (centered on the leading notables and canton chiefs) and the PDCI would structure Korhogo politics throughout the 1960s.[36]

In the face of hostility from France and the Senoufo canton chiefs, the PDCI-RDA resorted to the institution-building tactic it employed in the South. Party strategists recruited their agents among those whose jobs and livelihoods depended on neither the colonial state nor the cantonal chiefs. In the Senoufo region, the PDCI-RDA relied on Dyula merchants, as it did in the South. Like the Dyula traders who had taken up residence in the South, those living in Senoufoland were mobile, had access to cash, and were connected to commercial and social networks that spanned the RDA's entire territorial reach. Person reports that from 1946, "in the North, the quasi-totality of RDA *responsables locaux* [secretaries of subsections of the party, which were organized within the colonial administrative subdivisions] were local traders, Muslims without exception."[37]

The power the Senoufo cantonal chiefs still wielded over their subjects was registered in a pronounced erosion of the PDCI vote in Senoufoland after 1950.[38] Although the Senoufo were "among the most ardent supporters" of the party, Houphouet's party won only 20 to 30 percent of the vote in this region in the National Assembly elections of 1951 (Zolberg

---

[35] Person 1992:27. Governor Pechoux's treats and reprisals eventually lead Gbon to distance himself from Houphouet in 1950.

[36] See Lawler 1992:225–6.

[37] Person 1982:25, see also 21–4. Senoufo religion was animist. Person reports that by 1940 "most of the Senoufo ruling class had rallied to Islam," but most still practiced the indigenous religion as well. He refers to the Senoufo as "more-or-less Islamized peasants of the North."

[38] Lawler 1992:213; Person 1982:23.

1964:139–40). French authorities apparently concluded that keeping voters away from the polls was the best they could do in the Senoufo region. In spite of Korhogo's demographic weight, the French did not even try to create a rival political party in this region.[39]

Rapprochement between the French and Houphouet came in 1953, clearing the way for territory-wide ascendancy of the PDCI. In Korhogo, this turned the political tables on the pro-France cantonal chiefs. Now they were not only on the political defensive, but also abandoned by their French patrons and thus virtually disarmed in their confrontations with the nationalists. Houphouet's first response was to reactivate the political machine headed by Dramane Coulibaly and staffed in the villages by Dyula PDCI party militants. This machine was geared to counter and subvert the authority of the chiefs in this region.

Off-the-Path Choices

Dramane would remain the political boss and patron of Korhogo until 1970. As party chief in this region, he waged political war on the cantonal chiefs and used the levers of bureaucratic power and access to the party-state to shower party patronage on his allies and constituents.

When the venerated paramount chief Gbon Coulibaly died late in 1962, Dramane Coulibaly consolidated his hold on the PDCI political machine in Korhogo. Dramane used this instrument to marginalize the former cantonal chiefs and alienate much of the rest of the Senoufo chiefly hierarchy, including the notables and elders at the village level. Dramane ruled as a regional strongman. His closest collaborator was the regime's highest-ranking administrative officer in Korhogo (the prefect), an officer named Huberson who was a prominent PDCI stalwart and an outsider to the northern region.

As Gunderson (1975:124–5) explains it, the regional PDCI under Dramane and Huberson relied on coercion, corruption, and patronage politics to enforce its dominion. Dramane and Huberson marginalized Senoufo notables at virtually all levels of the chiefly hierarchy and recruited their

---

[39] The French did create a rival political party centered on Séguéla and the Malinké zone of the Northwest. Instead of trying to create a rival party in the Korhogo region, France recruited Tidjane Dem, a Muslim businessman from Korhogo and the son of one of Samory's lieutenants, to run on the PP ticket. This allowed the PP to present itself as an alliance of eastern and Muslim/northern interests. (Tidjane Dem had run against Houphouet on the nominating ballot for the October 1945 first constitutional assembly elections.) See Zolberg 1964:70, 138–9.

agents and allies among political outside groups: the Dyula merchant community, Senoufo commoners and other underdogs in the old Senoufo political hierarchies, and "upstart chiefs" who sought to escape the overrule of the old founding families. Dramane pursued a power-consolidation strategy of usurpation; he went so far as to bully peasants into providing local PDCI officials with the forced labor and agricultural commodities that had once been the reward of chiefs.

As the 1960s wore on, this usurpationist strategy proved to be economically and politically counterproductive in the Senoufo region. The problem that the regime in Abidjan would face was that it lacked effective political agents in a peasant society that retained a strong communal identity and viable, indigenous communal institutions.[40] Dyula PDCI militants exercised no political or economic authority over ordinary Senoufo farmers. They did not control access to land, agricultural labor, or the means of social reproduction and status promotion. Outsider traders and social underdogs were not in a position to manipulate hierarchical relations of political and economic dependency to get ordinary Senoufo farmers to remain loyal to the postcolonial party-state, to convince local leaders to submit to the political status quo in Abidjan, or to organize production to generate the export crops Abidjan wanted.

Political Penalties. The political costs of attempts to displace and usurp the positions of the Senoufo elite in Korhogo became clear in the 1960s. Houphouet had actually tried to ward off problems by creating space in the *national-level* party-state for those at the pinnacle of the Senoufo chiefly hierarchy. Members of the Korhogo ruling family were quite systematically co-opted into elective and appointed offices in Abidjan, where they would be removed from day-to-day politics at home. Most prominent was Gon Coulibaly, grandson of the old paramount chief, who was a member of the National Assembly from 1959 onward. In the 1960s Gon was known as leader of the "anti-Dramane faction" of the Korhogo political elite. He made it his mission to work against the Korhogo PDCI and "to lobby party and administrative officials to work in harmony with Senoufo chiefs" (Gunderson 1975:131). Other prominent members of the Coulibaly clan held high-ranking administrative and technical posts in Abidjan. Bema Coulibaly, another enemy of the Korhogo PDCI, retained the title of

---

[40] Gunderson 1975:189. As Gunderson points out, neither group had "the ability to manipulate significant economic resources."

canton chief of Korhogo and continued to act as head of the Senoufo chiefly establishment in that area (although he lived in "exile" in Kiemou, a town about thirty kilometers south of Korhogo, for most of the 1960s).

Co-optation of a few prominent members of the Korhogo ruling clan via the granting of Abidjan-based offices did not prove sufficient to neutralize the Senoufo region as a zone of possible opposition to the central rulers. In the 1960s Houphouet paid a political price for failing to co-opt the Senoufo notability effectively, and for condoning the usurpationist strategy pursued by those in control of the Korhogo PDCI.

In the early 1960s, suspicions, discontent, and rumors of conspiracy were rife in Senoufoland. Tensions throughout the country reached a crescendo in 1963, when Houphouet announced the discovery of a far-reaching conspiracy against his regime. Houphouet used what have become known as the *faux complôts* (pseudo-plots) of 1963 and 1964 as an occasion for general intimidation of the Ivoirian political elite. Member of Parliament Gon Coulibaly was among those who found themselves on the receiving end of this treatment. Gon was accused of using Senoufo cultural associations as a front for subversive activity against the regime. He was stripped of his parliamentary immunity and threatened with arrest.[41] Korhogo canton chief Bema Coulibaly was also implicated and harassed. In acting to intimidate members of the Korhogo chiefly establishment, Houphouet betrayed a fear that indigenous political structures and social solidarities in the Senoufo region could be used against the center.

Northerners were highly visible in the next round of political disturbances in Côte d'Ivoire, which came in the late 1960s. Student-led protests in 1969 sparked widespread political discontent and criticisms of the PDCI. Northerners were prominent in these protests, and in the "national dialogues" Houphouet organized to allow representatives of various corporate groupings to vent their grievances against the regime.[42] The complaint of the northerners was that their region was impoverished and relegated to backwater status in the national political economy. In voicing this protest, spokesmen for northern interests could credibly claim to speak on behalf of mobilizable rural constituencies.

---

[41] See Gunderson 1975:113; see also Launay 1982:121. Gon Coulibaly was released after a short time. Canton chief Bema Coulibaly was subject to political harassment from the Korhogo PDCI. On the pseudo-plots of 1963–4, see Médard 1982:72; Amondji 1986:67; Diarra 1997.

[42] On the dialogues, see Médard 1982:77–81; Amondji 1986:109–14; Widner 1993b:50, 54–5.

Frustration with the halting pace of rural development in the North in the 1960s (a point we discuss next) thus found overt political expression at the national level. Rulers in Abidjan had mounting political incentives (as well as economic incentives) to "bring development" to the North, and thus secure the integration of the North into a national political economy centered on Abidjan. The costs of politically alienating Senoufo notables rose over the course of the 1960s.

Economic Costs. There was a major push to introduce high-yielding cotton varieties (Allen variety) in the Senoufo *zone dense* from the beginning of the 1960s. (It was accompanied by efforts to intensify rice production.) Initial attempts to bolster cotton output relied on colonial-style coercion. Villages were forced to fulfill cotton quotas by working on plantations prepared by the Compagnie Française de Développement de Fibres Textiles (CFDT), a French corporation devoted to increasing French West Africa's cotton exports.[43] It had operated in Senoufoland since 1951. In the 1960s Senoufo villages that failed to meet their quotas were reported to the Ivoirian state agents responsible for law enforcement, the *sous-préfets*. *Sous-préfets* were known to employ the rural *gendarmerie* to enforce cotton-production quotas in recalcitrant villages and on reluctant chiefs.[44]

Peasant resistance to the "cotton program" of 1960 and 1961 was widespread and worrisome to the regime. State agents backed off from the coercive tactics by about 1962; this was accompanied by a fall in marketed cotton output. Many households withdrew from cash-crop production to concentrate their energies on food crops.[45] Faced with labor scarcity and low cotton prices, most households chose not to engage in commercial cotton production.

In 1964 the state and the CFDT developed a cotton strategy that relied on producer incentives and the "traditional" household production unit. Producer prices were henceforth subsidized by the state.[46] These subsidies,

---

[43] See Campbell 1973:249–53, 259–60. The CFDT's initial strategy was to work through a system of premiums targeted at large households. This was consistent with the approach the colonial regime had adopted in the 1940s. Costs of the cotton program in Côte d'Ivoire were covered by France's Fonds d'Aide et Coopération (FAC) until 1966.

[44] Campbell 1973:295; Gunderson 1975:124. Bassett (1984:201) writes that in 1960 and 1961 "coercion was used to force recalcitrant chiefs and households to cultivate cotton."

[45] See Bassett 1984:203, 206; Campbell 1973:284–5, 295, 298–9.

[46] The Caisse de Stabilisation reimbursed the CFDT for the difference between the state-mandated producer price and the price the CFDT said it was willing to pay. See Campbell 1973.

264

and the inputs that would now be distributed by the CFDT and the government's agricultural agents, were targeted at large peasant households in Senoufoland – that is, households that were relatively rich in both land and labor. New cotton programs would thus benefit households headed by Senoufo village chiefs, lineage heads, and prominent elders. Extension agents charged with increasing rice output gravitated toward the same strategy. Irrigation was required for rice, and access to land near streams in Senoufo villages was under the control of elders. In contrast to what was happening in the domain of party building and rural administration, in the domain of rural development post-1964, "[t]he elders were the intermediaries through which the outsiders worked."[47]

To recruit the support of Senoufo dignitaries, the outsiders played on their interests and fears. The CFDT and the extension agents worked to convince the elders that expanded cash-crop production would stem the out-migration of Senoufo youth. This would bolster the elders' ability to sustain large households, help support the elders' status and prestige, and help sustain the vitality of community institutions (Gunderson 1975: 156–73).

When it came to stemming out-migration of Senoufo youth, there was clear convergence between CFDT/state interests and those of Senoufo notables. Those interested in rural development in the Senoufo region became convinced in the 1960s that cotton's success would depend upon the survival and viability of the "traditional" extended-family production unit. The key was that the extended household guaranteed the peasant farmer access to a robust supply of household labor (non-wage labor). As a 1965 study financed by France's Ministry of Cooperation had argued, the success of the cotton-promotion programs in the North "would depend upon the social relations determining the supply of labor. . . . The traditional socioeconomic unit of extended household had to remain intact."[48] Most important was the survival of the largest households, defined by the experts as the top 20 percent in terms of landholdings, for they could produce on a scale that would optimize the use of productivity-enhancing inputs

---

[47] Gunderson 1975:155. "Among those who showed an interest in rice cultivation, members of founding compounds, particularly those who had been recognized as chiefs, were in a better position [than most people] to take advantage of the new opportunities for improved rice production" (ibid., 152). SATMACI was in charge of rice promotion until this job was taken over by the Société pour le Développement de la Riziculture (SODERIZ).

[48] Campbell 1973:292. The report is SEDES, *Région de Korhogo: Etude de Développement Socio-Economique*, 8 volumes (Paris, 1965).

(oxen and fertilizers).[49] High rates of out-migration from Senoufoland – estimated at about 25 percent of the active male workforce in the 1960s and 1970s, and almost half of the men in the 20–29 age group – depleted the all-important non-wage labor force, the productive potential of Senoufoland's extended households, and hopes for developing cotton as an export crop.[50]

Outsiders did not have to work hard to convince local dignitaries that out-migration was a social and political problem. As Gunderson (1975:156, 173) put it, "the presence of youth was essential to the continued dominance of the elders." Out-migration, he wrote, was "a main cause of the erosion of their power." In trying to respond to this problem, Senoufo elders had few options other than the one proposed by the state. Agricultural extension agents in Senoufoland argued that cash-cropping within the household production unit would allow the elders to keep youth productively employed at home, in Senoufoland. Cotton cultivation would "keep youth close to the villages, where they could participate in village ceremonies and ensure that village institutions would not disappear" (ibid.:156). In the absence of well-developed private markets for agricultural produce, farming inputs, and long-term finance, Senoufo notables had few economic alternatives for enhancing the viability of local agriculture.

The post-1964 cotton and rice programs were more successful than postcolonial rulers' intial attempts to use direct coercion to extract marketable commodities from Senoufo households. In the mid- to late- 1960s Senoufo notables – heads of "founding families," especially those recognized as chiefs – emerged as the biggest beneficiaries of state- and CFDT-sponsored agricultural intensification schemes. Sons and nephews of Korhogo's ruling family were among the most prominent beneficiaries. By 1970 Chief Bema of Korhogo was cultivating about four hundred hectares of rice on tracts of land flooded by the Bandama River (Gunderson 1975:170).

In their attempts to increase marketed agricultural output (and exports) from the Senoufo region, extension agents and the CFDT found themselves at cross purposes with local PDCI leaders and militants who were trying to *undercut* the old Senoufo leading families. The Korhogo PDCI was antagonizing and fomenting discontent among the old Senoufo elite just when the

---

[49] Bassett (1984) defined "large households" in Katiali as those with more than seven hectares of land.

[50] Bassett 1984:225. Estimates for the twenty to twenty-nine age group are for 1975 to 1980 (ibid.).

agricultural services were attempting to work through the old social institutions to expand commodity production in this region. Houphouet himself
apparently felt that he had lost control of the Korhogo PDCI and political
battling internal to this region.[51] The political status quo was increasingly
dysfunctional given Abidjan's goals, which included power consolidation at
the national level and promoting taxable agriculture in the best-endowed
and most populous region of the North.[52]

IV. Institutional Choice: Abidjan Reverts to Indirect Rule

As early as 1965 Abidjan began to act: central rulers began to try to limit
the excesses of PDCI militants in the Korhogo region and to sideline some
of the Dyula party officials who were viewed as opportunistic outsiders by
much of the local population.[53] In 1965 Houphouet responded to political
restiveness in Korhogo by promising "a massive infusion of state resources"
to develop the North.

In the effort to govern and tax Senoufoland, the Houphouet regime
eventually found it expeditious to seek partnership with the indigenous notables who exercised leadership and economic authority in this region –
the Senoufo elders and the heads of large extended households, and heads
of "founding lineages" who were key in determining the allocation of land
between and within villages. In Senoufoland, rural social organization (especially village hierarchies, communal cohesion, land tenure rules, and modes
of labor control) gave these indigenous authorities a small but significant
measure of bargaining power vis-à-vis the Houphouet regime. This small
measure was enough to distinguish them from their counterparts in the
South – local big-men in the Agni, Bété, and Baoulé zones – who never
secured any powersharing deal with the center.

Dramane's strategy had been one of usurpation of the authority, privileges, and positions of the Senoufo chiefly elite. That Dramane and Prefect

---

[51] In the national daily *Abidjan Matin*, the president himself made a special plea to the respective factions in the Korhogo region "to put aside their squabbles in the interest of regional
progress and harmony" (*Abidjan Matin* [29 March 1963]:3, paraphrased by Gunderson
1975:114).

[52] Gunderson (1975:114–28) writes that Houphouet realized that he did not have control
over the factional squabbling in the Korhogo region and perceived it as dysfunctional. The
Dramane faction was distributing the patronage resources of the state as they saw fit in
order to build up their own political bases, mostly among the nonfarming Dyula.

[53] See Gunderson 1975:119.

Huberson had pursued this option with vigor in the face of its mounting political and economic costs reveals a degree of autonomy on the part of the regional PDCI that was unusual in the Côte d'Ivoire context, and that was perhaps itself a product of the strong political localisms and factionalisms indigenous to this region.

A. Party-State Apparatus

In the embittered atmosphere of 1969 and 1970 Houphouet undertook an extensive reengineering of the local state in the Korhogo region. There was a clear about-face in the power-consolidation strategy: the central state reverted to a mode of rural governance that resembled the indirect rule strategies employed by France from 1890 to 1950 in Korhogo, and that also resembled the powersharing strategies governments have pursued in central and northern Senegal. Abidjan's goal was to incorporate the Senoufo elite and larger numbers of rural inhabitants in Korhogo into party affairs and agricultural development programs.

In the 1970s and 1980s Houphouet adopted a state-building strategy aimed at taking advantage of social-structural realities of peasant society in the North. By the logic proposed here, two facts are key in accounting for this outcome.

First, village-level elites still exercised authority and influence over the members of their communities. Notables controlled land, marriageable women, the labor power of unmarried men, and labor and food within large extended households. Continuing influence of the elders was surely also related to the existence of customs and beliefs that legitimated gerontocracy, especially in settings where village cohesion remained high. Institutions such as sacred forests, *poro* initiation societies, and communal livestock corrals remained salient features of local political and economic life, producing a measure of coherence at the village level that distinguished this region from most of the rest of Côte d'Ivoire.[54] Hierachical relations among villages remained an important axis of local authority in the Senoufo region,

---

[54] See also Gunderson (1975:124), who writes that "Senoufo questioned the legitimacy of individual chiefs who had been guilty of misdeeds in the past but were not willing to contravene all local norms and jettison the indigenous political-social order." Analysts of local government and politics in the Korhogo region in the 1990s note that village-level institutions still produced a measure of cohesion at the village level that distinguished this region from most of the rest of Côte d'Ivoire. See Garnier et al. 1992:80, 82.

and this also stood in contrast to the far more atomized patterns prevailing in the South.

The second fact is that Senoufo notables posed no direct economic challenge or competition to the regime. On the contrary, notables' capacity to generate and appropriate rural surpluses had come to depend upon their ability to engage in commercial cotton and rice production. Success in these endeavors, in turn, had come to depend on access to loans, inputs, and markets controlled by the state. All the ingredients of a successful powersharing solution were present in this situation. And as the politics of the 1960s had shown, there were costs to the regime of *not* finding some way to politically incorporate Senoufo notables and to harness their authority to the state's.

In 1970 the Korhogo PDCI led by Dramane Coulibaly – which had been based on "Dyula, commoners, and others without legitimacy in the local context"[55] – was dismantled. The PDCI political machine was rebuilt around the neotraditional chiefly hierarchy in Senoufoland. Occasion for overhaul of the regional PDCI was provided by the "renewal elections" of 1970.[56] Dramane was sidelined and his allies and agents were purged from their positions in provincial administration and the party. Gunderson reports that in the 1970 PDCI elections the Senoufo heartland, virtually all Dramane's lieutenants at the three levels of the regional party apparatus – the prefecture, *sous-préfecture*, and village levels – lost their positions. In regional administration, Prefect Huberson and all sub-prefects aligned with Huberson and Dramane met the same fate. Of all Côte d'Ivoire's twenty-four prefectures in 1970, only one non-Senoufo circumscription (Dimbokro) experienced political and administrative turnover of the same scope (Gunderson 1975:131–3).

Purges in the Korhogo region created space for incorporation of the neotraditional Senoufo elite into an already deconcentrated party-state apparatus. Abidjan orchestrated PDCI campaigns in Korhogo that gave symbolic support to local Senoufo leaders, institutions, and ideologies. Gon Coulibaly, leader of the "pro-chief" PDCI faction in Korhogo, replaced Dramane as the regime's intermediary in Senoufoland: Gon was introduced in the government-controlled media as "the new political leader of the

---

[55] See Gunderson 1975:124–5; Garnier et al. 1992.

[56] In Katiola, a Senoufo town not under the direct authority of Korhogo, the government began replacing PDCI militants who were seen as being at loggerheads with the administration and not aiding development efforts as early as 1962 and 1965 (Gunderson 1975:120).

Korhogo region" (ibid.:133). To reinforce the point, Houphouet named Gon Coulibaly one of three vice-presidents of the National Assembly around 1971. The political star of Korhogo chief Bema Coulibaly rose along with Gon's.

Throughout the region, the PDCI apparatus was colonized by leading Senoufo clans. The process was often quite straightforward, given that in this region of Côte d'Ivoire (in contrast with most of the South) boundaries of political-administrative units corresponded to colonial cantons which themselves had often been etched along the lines of precolonial political jurisdictions.[57] In PDCI elections of the 1970s, clans of canton chiefs captured local party machinery not only in Korhogo but also in the important Senoufo towns of Sirasso and Dikodougou. Sons of old canton chiefs were elected as deputies to the National Assembly.[58] Throughout the region, individuals with close ties to village chiefs replaced Dramane's men at PDCI offices at the prefecture and sub-prefecture levels. In the villages, sons and nephews of Senoufo chiefs were recruited to be PDCI party secretaries. New party directives came along with these changes in personnel: "[p]arty leaders at all levels were encouraged to pay appropriate deference to chiefs."[59] Across the board, many of the usurpations – some petty, many significant – of the Dramane era were undone. Gunderson (1975:155) observed that overhaul of the PDCI apparatus "permitted those villages with closer ties to the Senoufo chiefly hierarchy to emerge victorious and strengthened vis-à-vis the newer villages which had been identified with Dramane's leadership."

Incorporation of the established Senoufo notability into the party-state apparatus represented a devolution of political prerogative in this region. Individuals with their own local-level connections, clout, status, interests, and constituencies displaced the state's direct agents and appointees in the region: now locally rooted actors were in position to dispense party patronage on behalf of the Ivoirian regime and to broker access to the higher instances of the state apparatus. In the 1970s and 1980s, "traditional leaders were absorbed into modern posts," and deconcentrated instances of

---

[57] In 1962 Korhogo Department was still divided into thirteen cantons. Some chiefs had authority over several dozen villages. In 1975 the Department of Korhogo was cut into eight *sous-préfectures* which corresponded more or less to old cantons (five were swallowed up). See Coulibaly 1978:57–8.

[58] In Sirasso the son of the canton chief was elected PDCI secretary-general in 1980; his uncle was elected to the same post in 1990 (Garnier et al. 1992).

[59] See Gunderson 1975:134–5.

the state apparatus such as the PCDI committees became indistinguishable from local gatherings of Senoufo notables.[60] National-level politicians now sought support in Korhogo by courting the Senoufo chiefs.

It is a measure of devolution that the ability of the state's direct agents (the prefects and *sous-préfets*) to manipulate electoral competition in the Korhogo area diminished. Their room for maneuver was constrained by communities' preferences for electing notables with connections to Senoufo chieftaincy posts (as in Sirasso in 1990). Observers regarded local party structures in the Korhogo region as more accountable to local constituencies than local party units elsewhere in Côte d'Ivoire, and this too can be taken as a measure of both devolution and the political distinctiveness of this region.[61] One particularity in the rules of local party competition also underscores the specificity of this region: in Korhogo PDCI secretaries-general at the *sous-préfecture* level were elected (via queueing) rather than appointed to office.[62] This represented a measure of devolution of prerogative that was specific to this region: it seems that the regime counted on hierarchical cohesion at the local level to produce acceptable electoral results.

Unlike their counterparts in much of southern Côte d'Ivoire, prefectural administrators in Senoufoland since 1970 have worked through the hierarchy of Senoufo villages and village institutions in regulating local conflicts and problems of landlord-stranger relations. When clashes between Senoufo farmers and Peul pastoralists intensified in the 1980s and 1990s, for example, state agents looked to Senoufo institutions to perform policing and dispute-adjudication functions that might otherwise have been provided by the state itself, or not at all.[63] Much of what we can see in the structure and processes of the post-1970 party-state in the Korhogo region

---

[60] Garnier et al. 1992:85. See also Crook and Manor 1998:154, 159; Bassett 1993:147–9.

[61] Garnier et al. 1992:85–7

[62] This rule was put in place in 1980 (Garnier et al. 1992:85).

[63] Diallo (1995:40–1) wrote that in local disputes, "the lack of material and financial means of the *sous-préfets* – and doubts about their competence and honesty – lead peasants to seek other solutions. Disputes between farmers and herders are increasingly regulated at the local level with the aid of Senoufo hunters (*donxobele*)." The rise of banditism in the North also led the prefects to solicit the collaboration of these hunters. "Armed with traditional hunting rifles, they do police patrols at night in the villages which are, as it were, submitted to curfew. . . . Punishments inflicted on herders [for crop damage] are often excessive and reveal an abuse of power on the part of the hunters who have a tendency to substitute themselves for the administration. Nonetheless, the administration is still an indispensable intermediary." Diallo (ibid.) also notes that Senoufo chiefs formed committees to govern access to dams (watering points) and keep Peul away. See also Gunderson 1975; Bassett 1993, 2001; O'Bannon 2000.

seemed designed to harness the communal coherence of this region to the state's cause and to capitalize on the authority of village and regional-level notables.

B. Rural Development

The post-1970 reorganization of the PDCI in Korhogo, and of local administrative processes in this region, elevated the official political standing of the old Senoufo notability. Henceforth, the deconcentrated party-administrative apparatus that had been built in the 1950s and 1960s would be used to co-opt leading clans of the Senoufo region into alliance with the Houphouet regime. The year 1970 also marked the government's inauguration of major economic initiatives in this zone that would confirm the land-use powers of Senoufo founding lineages and draw local leaders – elders and lineage-segment heads – into a deconcentrated network of parastatal institutions that would help shore up their local prerogatives and also link them to the state. As A. Bonnal writes (1986:22), the government wanted to give the region more economic dynamism without disturbing the existing equilibria between social and ethnic groups.

What emerged after 1970 was a form of powersharing that made for center-periphery institutional linkages that were distinctive in the Ivoirian context. Powersharing required an institutional apparatus that was more deconcentrated, and that devolved more state prerogative to locally rooted actors, than the governing machinery that had been imposed on the South.

Resources for institution building came in the form of major regional development initiatives aimed at *Le Grand Nord*, and targeted for the most part at the Senoufo region. The regional development agenda was worked out in direct consultation with regional elites. According to the World Bank (1978:148) the planning process constituted "a major exception" to the norm in Côte d'Ivoire in that it "took place outside of the regular planning process and involved political bodies in the provinces to a meaningful extent. Local officials were able to stress regional goals and to exercise greater control [than elsewhere in Côte d'Ivoire] over the allocation of funds." Most observers describe the resulting spending initiatives as primarily politically motivated. As Dwayne Woods (1989) put it, redistributive policies and cash transfers aimed at "reintegrating northern notables and elites into the national economic system" and diffusing northern resentment over the vast regional growth disparities that had emerged in Côte d'Ivoire. Official publications presented the development agenda for the

Greater North as an effort to "reinforce national unity" and make possible harmonious relations between North and South.[64] Institutional linkages and resource transfers born of this initiative shored up the new (renewed, really) alliance between the national center and rural elites in this part of the Ivoirian periphery.

The Ivoirian government incorporated the Korhogo region ever more tightly into the national space over the course of the 1970s. In the process, it chose strategies of rural development aimed at slowing the drain of rural labor, maintaining the land-redistribution prerogatives of the leading Senoufo clans ("founding families"), and shoring up the prerogatives family heads and elders exercised over youth, land, and production. What evolved was a rural development program based upon a deconcentrated set of input-distribution and cotton-marketing institutions. These institutions permitted limited but significant devolutions of authority over resources and local decision making to indigenous rural elites.

The new approach to regional governance and taxation was very successful at increasing yields and total output. Some accounts reported a tenfold increase in yield per hectare for Ivoirian cotton between the early 1960s and 1980. Côte d'Ivoire's total output of commercial cotton rose from about 29,000 tons in 1970 to 143,000 tons in 1979. The Senoufo region produced 55 percent of this total. By about 1982 almost half of all cultivated area in the Korhogo region was under cotton.[65]

The CFDT evolved into an Ivoirian parastatal, becoming the CIDT (Compagnie Ivoirienne de Développement des Fibres Textiles) in 1973.[66]

---

[64] Woods 1989:480; Nguessan-Zoukou 1990:132–5. As part of the "New Deal" for the North, the regime selected six sites for sugar production/refining complexes that would "bring jobs to the region" and thereby help keep Senoufo men close to home. This initiative fell far short of expectations, but it consumed half of the national budget for agricultural development in 1977 and 1978. See Woods 1989. The complexes were sited around Ferkéssédougou, outside of Korhogo's jurisdiction; Nguessan-Zoukou describes them as "foreign bodies in Senoufoland" and writes that most of the plantation and factory workers were from southern and western Côte d'Ivoire (ibid.). See also Watts and Bassett 1985; Fauré 1982:52–3; Lele, van de Walle, and Gbetibouo 1989.

[65] Bassett 1984:134, 195, 204. The Malinké region to the far southwest of Odienné (Monkono, Dianra, Tiéningboué) produced 33 percent of the national total (Nguessan-Zoukou, 1990:139, 145). In the Senoufo region in the early 1980s, 45 percent of cultivated land was under cotton; swamp rice accounted for 10 percent of the cultivated area.

[66] The state took 55 percent ownership and the CFDT retained 45 percent. See Campbell 1984. Tidjane Dem, leader of the partisan opposition to the PDCI in Korhogo in the early 1950s, was named CIDT director in 1973. This appointment was another marker of the political reversal that had taken place in the region.

As a practical matter of corporate management, however, little if any prerogative was transferred from the French to Ivoirian civil servants, northern politicians, or regional-level Senoufo leaders in the 1970s and 1980s. French managers and technicians retained control over decision making, as was generally the case in the parastatal agencies devoted to promoting coffee and cocoa production in southern Côte d'Ivoire. Rulers in Abidjan opted for highly centralized control over the cotton parastatal; in the Korhogo region there was nothing akin to the kind of parastatal "agency capture" that helped underpin a powersharing arrangement between the state and rural elites in central Senegal. Yet in institutional structure and practice the CIDT *was* different from rural development agencies in *southern* Côte d'Ivoire. This was true in three main respects.

First, the CIDT was mandated to carry out "integrated rural development" within a territorially defined zone of Côte d'Ivoire. For rural development agencies of the South, by contrast, mandates were defined in functionally specific terms only. Clients of the coffee and cocoa parastatals were approached as individual producers, not as members of rural communities or territorially defined political constituencies.

Second, the CIDT distributed inputs to farmers on a yearly basis – credit, oxen for animal traction, seeds, fertilizers, and pesticides. As we have seen, for peasant growers of cocoa and coffee in the Ivoirian south there was no comparable institutionalization of long-term relationships between a state agency and farming households, and no comparable input-distribution programs or apparatus.

Third, in the northern region the state built a deconcentrated institutional apparatus to handle cotton marketing. This was very different from the market-based approach employed in the cocoa and coffee zone. In the cotton zone, the CIDT operated through an extensive network of rural cooperatives that purchased the yearly cotton crop and deducted input costs from farmers' earnings. In the 1980s northern cooperatives handled 80 to 90 percent of the cotton crop, in contrast to the 10 to 20 percent of the export crop that was marketed by cooperatives in the South.

Why did the Ivoirian government build rural development and marketing institutions in Senoufo region that were so different from those that existed in the South? Let us deal first with the agronomic argument, which is that the technical requirements of cotton production and processing determined the form of interventionism the state had to pursue. It is true that cotton is more input intensive (and thus capital intensive) and labor intensive than coffee or cocoa, and this is especially true when "green revolution" technologies are applied. Cotton also requires more supervision and monitoring of farm labor. Planting and weeding requirements are stringent, and even more so under the input-intensive strategies in use in northern Côte d'Ivoire after 1970. Does cotton itself, rather than rural social organization, explain why the Ivoirian government chose a more deconcentrated and devolved institution-building strategy in the North?

The answer is that the sociopolitical facts remain primordial, in the sense that making cotton the crop of choice was itself a strategy adapted to the facts on the ground. It may be that getting African peasants to produce cotton that can be profitably exported by the state requires intensive government (or corporate) intervention in the production process, and thus deconcentrated rural development institutions. Even so, such undertakings require local social and political "inputs" that are not present in all rural settings.

In their initial attempts to gain access to a local supply of cotton in the Côte d'Ivoire in the 1940s, French interests had looked to the area around Bouaké. This is mostly Baoulé country. Around the time of World War II, cotton was the most important commercial crop marketed in the Bouaké area.[67] Cotton production eventually proved unviable in the Baoulé region for two reasons. First was the explosive take-off of the coffee and cocoa economy in the South, which offered farmers higher returns for less labor and encouraged the migration of Baoulé farmers to core coffee- and cocoa-producing areas.[68] Second was the exporters' perennial interest in keeping producer prices low and, as the 1950s progressed, their growing interest in upgrading the quality of Ivoirian cotton. Requisite degrees of control, coordination, and supervision of the labor process were difficult and costly to achieve.

These are the considerations that led the CFDT and French planners in the 1960s to identify *household* labor of the kind available in the

---

[67] The Institut de Recherches du Coton et des Fibres Exotiques (IRCT) set up a cotton research station, one of three in French West Africa, in Bouaké in 1946. Gunderson (1975:145) reported that circa 1958 Korhogo was producing 2.5 times as much cotton as villagers around Bouaké.

[68] Mafeje (1991:139) compared cotton to coffee in these terms: Cotton production is small scale, labor intensive, and often most successful when undertaken with family labor. Coffee is less labor intensive, suitable for larger-scale production, doable with hired labor, and in short, "a lazy man's crop."

Senoufo region, and the existence of "hardworking farmers" and cohesive, family-based production units, as critical to successful cotton production.[69] Nguessan-Zoukou (1990:131) offers a strong version of this point by saying that "it seems that in Côte d'Ivoire, only Senoufo peasants are capable of the discipline required [for growing cotton at the price and quality required by exporters]. Cotton cultivation has not had the same success in Baoulé country (Bouaké, Dimbroko, etc.), where soil and climatic conditions are essentially the same, if not better."[70]

Rulers interested in taxing and governing northern Côte d'Ivoire were responding to local socioeconomic and political realities when they chose to promote cotton in the Senoufo region in the 1970s, and to embrace the socially conservative "improvement approach" as a way of doing so. Rural social organization thus shaped strategies of state building in this region. These factors must be invoked to explain why the state chose interventionist developmentalism and powersharing in the North when it had eschewed such strategies in the South.

When the regime defined "integrated rural development" as the CIDT's mission in the North, state agents were drawn immediately into community-level issues involving land and labor use, food crop production, and landlord-stranger relations. Why did rulers in Abidjan choose to implicate the state in these matters when they had consciously avoided such entanglements in the South? One reason was that state capacity was enhanced in the Senoufo region by the existence of indigenous political infrastructure that could be harnessed to the regime's projects. Another is that by the end of the 1960s the regime did not fear "capture" of its grassroots apparatus by hostile political forces. On the contrary, Abidjan had discovered an interest in co-opting and even shoring up the indigenous political infrastructure that existed in the Senoufo region. Rulers in Abidjan obviously calculated that the state's cause could be furthered by embedding institutions of the modern state in village-level and even inter- and supra-village Senoufo political institutions. Under these conditions, integrated rural development became politically tolerable (not too risky, that is) and even desirable for those interested in state building in this region.

---

[69] It was also essential that land not be a purchased input that would add to the farmers' production costs.

[70] See also Campbell (1973:287), who writes of Agni farmers' rejection of cotton as a cash crop.

CIDT cotton strategies in the Korhogo region centered on providing improved inputs to peasant farmers working within the "traditional Senoufo production unit." This was the household concession organized around a lineage segment and headed by an elder.[71] Households were composed of the household head's married uterine brothers and their wives and children, unmarried brothers and nephews and nieces, and other family dependents. All the household's active male and female workers worked at least three or four of the six-day Senoufo week on a communal field presided over by the household head.

The linchpin of the CIDT strategy in the 1970s was providing oxen for animal traction to large households – those that were relatively rich in both land and labor.[72] Implementation of this plan increased inequalities that were already pronounced in the Senoufo region. In a region where almost half of all households cultivated less than half a hectare of cotton in the 1970s, one study reported that "the average large household" cultivated over seven hectares. Bassett reported that households employing CIDT-supplied oxen in the 1970s cultivated on average three times more land than, and earned three times the income of, households relying on manual cultivation.[73] For the very largest households, the state went even further: tractors were provided (on credit) by the CIDT. Around 1980 the average number of working adults in tractor-owning households in the town of Niellé was ten. In the town of Gbon, it was 26.4. Bassett mentions one household in Katiali, to the north of Korhogo, that claimed forty-one working adults.

Fertilizers and pesticides were also supplied on credit by the CIDT. Although payment for inputs was deducted from farmers' earnings when the

[71] The physical layout of the concession may suggest something about its internal dynamics: concessions are compact, all buildings are contained within a circular outer wall, and there is one central courtyard and one single exit to the exterior (Coulibaly 1978:84–6).

[72] Nearly two hundred inhabitants of the region received oxen (on credit) for animal traction between 1967 and 1970 (Gunderson 1975:146–7). This experiment was then replicated on a wide scale between 1970 and 1980, when the area under cotton benefiting from ox-drawn cultivation in northern Côte d'Ivoire rose from about 1 percent to 33 percent of the total (Bassett 1984:208). Around 1993, animal traction was used on 57 percent of the area cultivated in Boundiali department (Diallo 1995:38).

[73] Bassett 1984:237–8 (for the Korhogo region). Nguessan-Zoukou (1990:131), citing results for the Korhogo region in 1972–3, reports that 99 percent of all households cultivated less than 3 hectares, and that 45 percent cultivated less than half a hectare. In Bassett's sample of the town of Katiali, the average "large household" counted 6.3 able-bodied adults and cultivated 7.3 hectares. "Small households" in his sample averaged 3.7 adults and 2.68 hectares (ibid.).

cotton was sold to the state (the CIDT), there was nonetheless a significant transfer of resources to the larger households of the region: the state subsidized cotton production at an average rate of about 43,000 CFA francs per hectare (about $140 per hectare) in the late 1970s.[74]

There does not seem to be a record of explicit political manipulation of these input-distribution programs, or of any de facto devolution of control over CIDT operations to rural elites who used CIDT inputs as patronage resources to build up electoral clienteles. On the contrary, it seems that once the overall thrust of the cotton-promoting strategy was set, the CIDT's day-to-day rural operations were governed by more or less apolitical criteria.[75]

However, it is also clear that the CIDT "improvement approach" – working within the existing land tenure regime and relations of production and targeting large households – had built-in biases that bolstered and reinforced Abidjan's political strategy. Targeting large households meant that CIDT interventions would benefit the prominent regional leaders and community members who had been recognized as local dignitaries and given places in the party-state apparatus by the political reforms of 1970. At the microscopic level of the household, CIDT input-distribution programs reinforced the capacity of lineage-segment heads to maintain large households, along with the elders' authority over the subordinate farmers in the household (unmarried men and women) who had no direct access to the agricultural inputs such as oxen that were provided by the CIDT.

When it came to management of another basic input, land, there was a clear decision on the part of central rulers to reinforce the authority of the elders, notables, and founding families of the Korhogo region. This represents a de facto devolution of authority in this domain; the term seems especially appropriate in this case, given Senoufo complaints that the Ivoirian state and the Korhogo PDCI had violated (usurped) local land prerogatives with impunity in the 1960s. After the political turnabout of 1970, much of the old order was restored, and lands that had been handed over to "upstart" chiefs and villages by Dramane Coulibaly were returned to old founding lineages. Rural development in the 1970s was to proceed on the basis of respect for "traditional land tenure."

[74] Bassett 1984:247. On cotton subsidies, see also Campbell 1973:268–70.

[75] Bassett reported (1984:223) that "the CFDT and the state extended services and production inputs to young and old alike" – the problem was that village youth had a very hard time gaining access to land, which was monopolized by the elders, and presumably thus credit and a cotton crop of their own that could be used as collateral for getting fertilizers and pesticides from the parastatal. See Lele, van de Walle, and Gbetibouo 1989.

In the mid-1990s Diallo wrote that "[i]n the Senoufo region, land is still regulated in the customary fashion. Here land cannot be sold or exchanged, in contrast to what happens elsewhere in Côte d'Ivoire. The land tenure regime is communal. Lineage heads accord land-use rights to members of the community. Outsiders are granted revocable use rights only."[76] Within family concessions, elders continued to monopolize control over most land: even in the 1980s, unmarried Senoufo men – normally those in the fifteen to thirty-five age bracket – still had virtually no direct access to land.[77] Bassett reported that in a sample of thirty-eight households in the village of Katiali (population 1,600) in the early 1980s, only one unmarried man cultivated his own, personal field. Elders were reluctant to give subordinate men land access because "they were primarily interested in exploiting the labor of young men in their own fields."[78] Elders' control over food, women, marriage contracts, and *poro* institutions reinforced this hierarchy.

For land allocations between lineages and lineage segments, CIDT interventions also respected leading families' land prerogatives. For the most part, indigenous authorities were also left to negotiate landlord-stranger relations. The state did encroach on these landlord prerogatives in the late 1970s and 1980s by encouraging the sedentarization of Peul (Fulani) herders in Korhogo region. Livestock initiatives undertaken by the state agency SODEPRA encouraged new Peul migration to the area.[79] This contributed to mounting conflict between Senoufo farmers and Peul herders from the mid-1980s onward. As tensions flared, SODEPRA and the prefectorial administration reiterated a commitment to respecting Senoufo landholders' claims, respected indigenous landholders' rights over so-called vacant lands, and "vowed greater respect for local customs."[80] This

---

[76] Diallo 1995:41–2. "No land is privately owned or has ever been sold in the Katiali region. For the time being, customary land-use rights prevail" (Bassett 1984:276).

[77] Bassett (1984:238–9) reported that for the 38 households of Katiali, "male household heads controlled approximately 90 percent of all fields cultivated in the village. Women's personal fields only amounted to approximately 10 percent of the area cultivated. Other kin (nephews, sons, younger brothers, parents) exerted least control over household production, with their individual fields amounting to less than 1 percent of the total area cultivated in the village."

[78] See Bassett (1984:225).

[79] SODEPRA is the Société pour le Développement des Productions Animales.

[80] Bassett 1993:144, 147. See also Diallo 1995:39. Bassett (ibid., 144) notes that respecting indigenous land rights was often easier said than done, for "sometimes there were so many conflicts at the local level between Jula [Dyula], Senoufo, and various segments of Senoufo villages and lineages that it is hard to endorse one set of claims as 'fundamental' or 'legitimate.'"

reaction was the precise opposite of state agents' response when analogous confrontations erupted in southwestern Côte d'Ivoire in the late 1980s.[81] In all these areas, there were clear contrasts with the land-access rules and norms prevailing in southern Côte d'Ivoire.

C. Export-Crop Marketing

Here too, Ivoirian rulers made institutional choices that took advantage of communal coherence and village-level political hierarchy in Senoufoland. At the time of reconfiguration of the regional party-state apparatus in 1970, the export-crop marketing apparatus was redesigned. Private buying agents were eliminated from the cotton-buying business in the Korhogo region in the early 1970s and replaced by producer cooperatives, or Groupements de Vocation Coopérative (GVCs). These grower cooperatives collect, weigh, and arrange for the transport of raw cotton to the CIDT's cotton gins, where grades and weights were checked by CIDT evaluators.[82] A deconcentrated network of about 500 GVCs – over half of them in the Senoufo region – handled 90 percent of the cotton purchases in Côte d'Ivoire in 1989.[83]

The United Nations Development Project compared GVC dynamics in northern and southern Côte d'Ivoire in 1990. It found that compared to GVCs in other parts of Côte d'Ivoire, in the Senoufo region village chiefs played a larger role in GVCs, villagers had slightly more confidence in these institutions, and GVCs were organized in a more hierarchical manner (that is, information was more centralized in the hands of GVC leaders).[84] Access to these institutions was also the province of elders: Bassett (1984:238) reports that cotton selling was organized such that the heads of extended households "monopolized cotton income."

In Senoufo country, the regime eventually came around to what we hypothesized at the outset to be the politically expedient solution to taxing and governing this region. Important Senoufo clans and notables secured institutionalized positions within the postcolonial state, occupied positions in

[81] There, the regime vowed commitment to the principle of "the land belongs to the user."
[82] Campbell 1973:273; Garnier et al. 1992:84. See also Watts and Bassett 1985:16.
[83] *Marchés Tropicaux et Méditerranéens*, no. 2380 (21 juin 1991):1552. There were 332 cotton GVCs in 1985; they commercialized 82 percent of the cotton crop (ibid.; *Fraternité Matin* [Abidjan, 17 mars 1988]:23, 25).
[84] Programme des Nations Unies pour le Développement, Bureau International du Travail, Government of Ivory Coast (PNUD/BIT/IVC) 1991.

distributive institutions that allowed them to tap inflows of state resources to the region, and were assertive in political gatekeeping and recruitment in ways that sometimes compromised the prerogatives of state administrators stationed in Senoufoland. In Korhogo, de facto power devolutions to indigenous political elites were more extensive than in the South. This made for a measure of powersharing in this region that contrasts with the strategy of administrative occupation by which Houphouet governed the South.

What emerged in Korhogo was a *watered-down* version of the kind of powersharing strategy modeled in Chapter 2. Measured in terms of what the theory leads us to expect, this outcome is close to the mark. The elites of the Korhogo region were relatively weak compared to the rural aristocracies in, for example, central Senegal, and what emerged in Korhogo was a powersharing arrangement more limited in scope than what rulers constructed in the Wolof groundnut basin. Where there is attenuated rural hierarchy, we see limited powersharing. This finding should increase our confidence in the theory, for it should be able to accommodate variations in degree as well as differences in kind.

Powersharing in northern Côte d'Ivoire was a response to the existence of a rural elite with bargaining power vis-à-vis the center, and also a state-building strategy that shored up regional powerbrokers and the kind of "decentralized despotism" that Mamdani (1996) has described. By 1970 the Houphouet regime had come around to this politically expeditious state-building strategy, but it had the paradoxical effect of helping construct *Le Grand Nord* as a geopolitical actor on the national stage. Rural development was the means by which the powersharing alliance was consolidated and anchored in the structures and processes of agrarian society: this was also the case in the Wolof groundnut basin of Senegal, and as we shall see, the same pattern unfolded in the Senegal River Valley. Korhogo and the neighboring Odienné region in the Northwest remained economically disadvantaged parts of Côte d'Ivoire, but they both possessed the political asset of local institutions that empowered and helped to organize local notables.

In 1993, after a quarter century of powersharing, the Senoufo chiefly family of Gbon Coulibaly could be described by one observer as "perhaps the one family in Côte d'Ivoire which can rival the Houphouet-Boignys in the extent of their political-economic power base" (Rapley 1993:114). Côte d'Ivoire's northern elite was in a position to assert itself in the 1990s, when death of "the father of the nation" and deep economic crisis disrupted established patterns of core-periphery alliance and caused the ruling coalition constructed by Houphouet to unravel. The so-called *Grand Nord* emerged as a political force, led by ex-PDCI politicians and regional notables who could mobilize electoral constituencies far more reliably than their rivals, the Abidjan-based politicians of the South.

Part Two: Path Switching in the Senegal River Valley

The dominant feudal class has not found a way to make its lands prosper.

Dumont 1972:189

The Senegal River arches 1,000 miles across the Western Sahel, forming the border between Senegal and Mauritania. During the rainy season, water from the Fouta Djallon highlands in modern Guinée flows down the mountains and toward the sea, flooding the lowlands along the last 360 miles (600 kilometers) of the river's course. These yearly floods irrigated the alluvial soils that sustained the ancient states and civilizations of the Senegal River Valley. Before the twentieth century, grain surpluses produced in the river valley made it the breadbasket of this part of the Sahel. Massive southward emigrations from the river valley in the late 1700s and early 1800s peopled entire zones of what is now Senegal. Islam was diffused southward from this region. The river served as the avenue of France's fateful commercial and military penetration of the Western Sahel. Only in the last century did the Senegal River Valley – "the fertile land between two deserts"[85] – become peripheral to the political economy of this part of Africa.

Dreams of commercial agriculture in this region have exerted an inexorable pull on Senegal's governments. Visions of reclaiming the Delta from the sea-water tides that rise into the mouth of the river during the dry season, and of irrigation in the Delta and the fertile Middle Valley, date to the earliest periods of French occupation. In the early 1800s French military governors saw agricultural development in the river valley as a way to "put to work locally a population of slaves that can no longer be transferred overseas."[86] In the 1910s there were attempts to hold back the sea's "salty tongue" to permit European settlers to farm in the Delta. A major anti-salinization dam was built at Richard Toll, near the Delta's upper limit, in 1947. Large-scale pump irrigation soon followed, bringing industrial-scale rice and sugar production to the Delta in the 1950s.[87] In the late 1970s

---

[85] See Boutillier et al. 1962:1.
[86] See Mathieu, Niasse, and Vincke 1986:220.
[87] See Mathieu, Niasse, and Vincke 1986:220, 228.

and 1980s the state finally intervened in production in the Middle and Upper Valley to create and finance small-scale rice irrigation projects. By the 1990s river floods throughout the entire basin were governed by the massive Manatali hydroelectric dam, situated in the Kayes region of Mali and run by the Organisation de la Mise en Valeur de la Vallée du Fleuve Sénégal (OMVS) in the name of the governments of Mali, Senegal, and Mauritania.

Until the construction of the Manatali dam, the socioeconomic topography of the river valley was the force that determined the pace, geographic locus, and character of state efforts to expand commercial production. Even with the dam, considerations of local politics still go far in determining the shape and thrust of Senegalese government interventions.

In Senegal, the river valley is divided into three distinct subregions: the Delta (Saint-Louis to Dagana), the Middle Valley (Dagana to the Matam area), and the Upper Valley (the zone around Bakel). (See Map 5.2.) Each has presented different opportunities and challenges for central rulers. In terms of natural endowment, the Middle Valley has always been deemed the most promising for commercial agriculture. Here, the river flows through an alluvial valley as much as twelve miles (twenty kilometers) wide. In normal flood seasons, the water rose twelve feet to irrigate the entire valley, nourishing both soils and crops. Geopolitical factors long militated against developmentalist options, however. Until the early 1970s Dakar state builders declined to construct new institutions to spur transformations of what was, by about the 1930s, basically a subsistence economy subsidized by labor exports to central Senegal and Dakar.

In the Middle and Upper Valley, there was very little commercial agricultural production from about the 1940s to the 1960s. Under these conditions, the theory presented in Chapter 2 predicts that rulers will choose a strategy of "non-incorporation" because of the region's economic marginality. In the Middle and Upper Valley, we see an outcome that has some but not all features of the ideal type. Dakar rulers' actual strategy in the Middle and Upper Valley in the period from 1940 to 1970 can be characterized as *partial* non-incorporation. While Dakar undertook no institution building in the spheres of rural production and marketing (as the theory predicts), there *was* vigorous institution building – and powersharing – in the narrowly political domains of provincial administration and party-centered machine politics. What we encounter here can be described as a "mixed" strategy: it involved economic non-incorporation and political powersharing.

283

The anomaly may be rooted in the paradoxical combination of a near-subsistence economy and steep social hierarchy. In the abstract, we would not expect stark social differentiation when the level of social surpluses is so low, for there is very little for the dominant stratum to appropriate. It must be axiomatic that unless a provincial elite in these economic circumstances receives infusions of outside resources, such a configuration is not sustainable over time. These factors – precariousness of social hierarchy and resource transfers from outside – do seem important in explaining the drama of change in this region in recent decades.

In the Middle and Upper River Valley, there have been deeply rooted social and political constraints to the commercialization of agriculture. The most important of these are the extraordinary rigidity of social hierarchies and land tenure regimes in these zones, and powerful opposition on the part of indigenous rural elites ("feudal oligarchies") to innovations that would erode their control over the river's fertile floodplain. These same rigid hierarchies provided Senegal's colonial and postcolonial regimes with a reliable infrastructure for political control of the river valley. To govern the river valley, Senegal's governments latched onto this conservative elite. Indigenous forms of authority and political control were embedded in the institutions of the modern state.

Colonial and postcolonial rulers pursued a political strategy of indirect rule in the Middle and Upper Valley. Dakar allowed the oligarchic families to capture and control deconcentrated networks of party-state institutions in these zones. Alliances between the central authorities and the land-holding elite crystallized at every level of the party-state apparatus, from village chieftaincies and local cells of the ruling party to the highest reaches of government in Dakar. During this period, the traditional economic bases of the old nobility narrowed. Colonial conquest destroyed the old river trade, and the agricultural economies of the Middle and Upper Valley turned inward to the production of millet and sorghum and to herding – all destined primarily for local use. Access to the state replaced sharecropping and old modes of taxation as the river valley elites' main source of wealth. Out-migration helped sustain households. External resources were surely important in sustaining social hierarchy in the face of economic stagnation (and decline) in this zone.

What is most interesting for our purposes is the "path switching" by which the institutional choices from about 1940 to 1970 gave way, in the 1970s and 1980s, to strategies designed to promote "rural development" and a more complex form of powersharing. This shift is largely explicable

Table 5.2. *Path Switching in the Senegal River Valley*

	Functional Domain		
	Provincial Administration: Party-State Apparatus	Export Marketing: Marketing Board, Co-ops	Allocating Factors of Production: Cooperative, Land
Middle and Upper Valley 1960s	Spatial deconcentration Devolution Powersharing	No institution building Non-incorporation	No institution building Non-incorporation
Middle and Upper Valley 1970s and 1980s	Spatial concentration Devolution of authority Powersharing	Spatial deconcentration Devolution of authority within the PIVs Powersharing	Spatial deconcentration Devolution of authority within PIVs and CR Powersharing

in terms of changes in rural social structure: the indigenous social order that had provided such a convenient foundation for modern state building was eroding. Long-term secular changes were surely at work, but the crisis of Sahelian drought in the early 1970s brought things to a head. For both rural elites and central rulers, the mixed institutional strategy of 1940 to 1970 no longer sufficed to contain political risks and produce the desired political benefits.

Central rulers shifted to an all-out powersharing strategy in the Upper and Middle Valley in the 1970s and 1980s. This shift is summarized in Table 5.2. State-led rural development became the order of the day. Deconcentration of the state apparatus received a mighty impetus, and was accompanied by de facto devolutions of state authority and prerogative to the regime's political allies, the Senegal River Valley aristocracies.

This mode of extending state authority into rural hinterlands of the Middle and Upper Valley conforms with hypotheses presented at the outset of this study. And as Balans, Colon, and Gastellu (1975), Linda Beck (1996a), and others have argued, it is a pattern of political consolidation that closely parallels the one seen in the central groundnut basin. The economics of state building in these two regions has been quite different, however. In the groundnut basin, the regime allied with a rural elite who reproduced their political and social power by sponsoring land pioneering and patronizing the peasant producers of Senegal's main export crop. In the Middle and Upper River Valley, by contrast, the regime allied with rural elites whose social and political power remained rooted in limiting and controlling access to fertile lands devoted to food-crop production, and in sharecropping.

The Delta is a distinct subregion: it is the last 120 kilometers of the Senegal River, starting at Dagana, and is the broadest section of the flood-plain. Here, state building proceeded along a different trajectory. This sub-region appears in the following pages in three ways: as a counterfactual, as part of the larger geopolitical story of state building in the Senegal River Valley, and as a theoretical anomaly. The Delta provides counterfactual sup-port for our main argument about the Middle and Upper Valley, for lack of indigenous social hierarchy in the rural areas to the west of Dagana ruled out powersharing as a strategy of national integration, and also created con-ditions propitious for building state institutions that would promote more radical economic change (because there was no indigenous oligarchy for the regime to protect). This is key to the geopolitics of development in the River Valley: it explains why state-led economic development for the first half of the twentieth century focused on the Delta, even though the eco-logical constraints to commercial agriculture were more formidable there than in the Middle River Valley.

The Delta also turns out to be a theoretical anomaly, given our starting point: a pattern of social organization not anticipated by the theory evokes an institutional response also not included in the original possibility set. This "case within a case" has properties that are unusual for West Africa but prevalent in East Africa. It adds another cause-effect scenario to the original repertoire.

I. Rural Society in the Senegal River Valley

A. Middle and Upper Valley

The Middle Valley stretches along four hundred kilometers of the river basin. It is called the Fouta Toro after the Foutanke kingdom established in the Middle Valley around 1515. Society here is Halpulaaren – made up of Toucouleur and Peul speakers of the Pulaar language – but given the numerical and social predominance of the former, it is often referred to as "Toucouleur society." Its political center is the city of Matam. The Upper Valley is a Soninké zone. It covers an eighty-kilometer stretch that is centered on the city of Bakel.

At the end of the colonial period, these were economically isolated parts of Senegal that lived off of subsistence production of millet and sorghum,

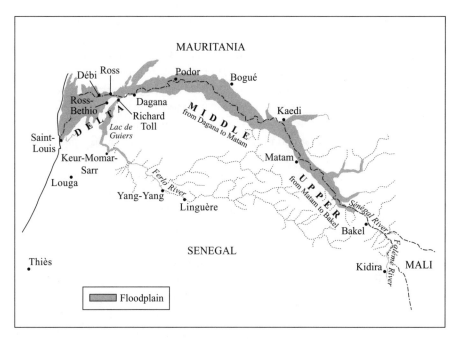

Map 5.2. Senegal River Valley, Including the Delta

and the seasonal out-migration of workers destined for the cash-crop-producing regions and urban areas of Senegal. Politics and society in the Middle and Upper Valley were structured in rigid hierarchies that were themselves factors in explaining the region's economic stagnation.

Toucouleur society was dominated by a group of powerful ruling lineages that controlled the narrow and fertile floodplain, which rarely extended more than ten miles from the river.[88] Alliances and struggles for hegemony among these dynastic lineages played (and continue to play) a major role in the evolution of the Fouta. From 1778 to 1865, following the theocratic revolution against the Foutanke monarchs, the Fouta was loosely united under a weak Islamic state headed by a ruler (Almamy) elected by representatives of several dozen dominant families that were of varying size and importance. The strongest of these sought supporters among the

---

[88] Klein 1972:421; Boutillier et al. 1962:57. The size of the floodplain is highly variable. As Seck (1991:308) writes, in the first decades of independence the size of the floodplain (counting both sides of the river – Senegalese and Mauritanian) was estimated at 400,000 hectares in an "average year," of which 100,000 was cultivated. See also Bethemont 1986:5, 66.

others and used diverse means to win them, including the distribution of land and attributions of positions of territorial command. French penetration and military conquest of the Senegal River Valley destroyed the formally centralized theocratic state. Pacification was declared complete in 1891 and the region was annexed to the colony of Senegal. France made alliances with leaders of the Fouta's dominant lineages, who continued under colonial rule to struggle among themselves for hegemony.[89]

During the precolonial regime of the Almamyat, "the feudal structure of Toucouleur society endured and probably rigidified."[90] A powerful conservative aristocracy maintained strict control over the fertile floodplain in a zone of high population density and pressure on the land. Rights to land use and water use (for farming in the floodplain, gardening, rain-fed agriculture, grazing, and fishing) were orchestrated to vary across time, space, and citizenship categories to take advantage of the physical topography of the river basin and the yearly rhythms of rising and falling waters. Rigidity and complexity in the land tenure regime limited possibilities for the extension and intensification of agriculture, and thus contributed to emigration from the Fouta to the south, including Wolof regions. This turns out to be a constant in the modern history of this region.

The land tenure regime in the Fouta Toro underpinned a complex social hierarchy structured along the lines of class-like status groups and castes, lineages, age groups, and gender.[91] The status-group and caste system defined the basic hierarchy of land rights. As Niang (1975) and others have argued, it accentuated rigidities and inequalities in land access and use.

At the top, the freemen, RimBé, occupy the leading social rank and possess the largest and more fertile lands of the river valley. The superior caste of this group, the ToroBé, a religious aristocracy composed of the most influential families of the land, possess vast land domains. Below [the "freemen"], are artisanal castes

---

[89] On the Almamyat, see Boutillier et al. 1962:17–8, 56; Griffeth 1968:185, 189; Klein 1972:424–9.

[90] See Boutillier et al. 1962:17. The pulaar word for aristocrats or dignified persons is *TooroBé* (*toorobé* [pl.] or *toorodo* [sing.]).

[91] Park (1993:12, 293–302) stresses the economic functionality of these arrangements in an agrarian society based on flood-recession agriculture, where floods and rains are highly erratic across both time and space. "In the long term, the most viable form of tenure is some form of corporate (institutional) holding of a portfolio of lands in many different soil types and located at different altitudes. . . . This is completed by traditional seasonal reallocation of plots . . . by political authorities. Social and political hierarchy establishes priority among claimants, avoiding a free-for-all." Park's perspective highlights risk management as an overriding socioeconomic logic in this kind of ecological setting.

(ironworkers, leather workers, weavers, fishermen, woodworkers, griots, etc.). At the bottom are slaves, transmitted by inheritance, who have no property rights. (Dumont 1972:184).

Real power was centered upon the elite, who controlled large domains composed of noncontiguous land tracts. This oligarchy usually cultivated some land, but also lived off rents and tithes they received in return for access to land.[92] Even as the prosperity of agriculture declined in the twentieth century, the land tenure regime remained the linchpin of political and social hierarchy in the Middle Valley. Niang said in 1975 that land rents continued to play "a very important role in reinforcing political authority and the prestige of the elite."[93]

Surveys in the 1950s showed that a high proportion of the cultivated fields in the Middle and Upper River Valley were rented:

Overall, 37 percent of the fields are rented by farmers who have no rights at all to these lands and who pay rent in money, kind, or days of work. . . . [T]he cost of rent is never less than 10 percent of the harvest and frequently runs up to 50 percent. . . . An additional 30 percent of the fields are farmed by people holding [secure] cultivation rights who must pay dues and tribute to the *maîtres de la terre*.[94]

Boutellier et al. (1962:57) wrote that in the *cercles* of Matam, society displays "truly feudal aspects, with large land domains cultivated by [descendants of] captives." These so-called captives (also referred to as slaves, vassals, or serfs) comprised one-fifth of the population of the Fouta Toro in the late 1950s.[95]

Throughout, production was organized at or near the household level. The extensive land domains of the oligarchy and sharecropping thus co-existed with a form of peasant production, or what Boutillier et al. (1962: 116–7) described as a system of small familial proprietorship.

The Fouta Toro was divided into discrete territorial units or provinces, each known as *leydi*, which were laid out as long strips bisected by the river and which comprised land on the river's high wet banks, in the floodable basin, and on the sandier and higher lands that lay beyond the flood basin

---

[92] Boutillier et al. (1962:116–17) wrote that some of the large landholdings predated the sixteenth century, but that most seemed to date to the period from 1515 to 1778, which came to an end with the establishment of the Almamyat.

[93] See Niang 1975:150.

[94] Boutillier et al. 1962:116–17. Their surveys were done in 1958.

[95] Control over them "was transmitted by inheritance, absolutely like durable goods, livestock, and land" (Boutillier et al. 1962:53–4). See Park 1993:24.

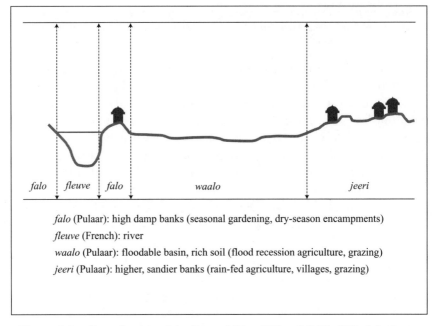

falo (Pulaar): high damp banks (seasonal gardening, dry-season encampments)
fleuve (French): river
waalo (Pulaar): floodable basin, rich soil (flood recession agriculture, grazing)
jeeri (Pulaar): higher, sandier banks (rain-fed agriculture, villages, grazing)

Figure 5.1. Cross Section of the Senegal River Valley (Middle Valley) (redrawn with permission from Barreteau 1998:14)

(see Figure 5.1). The *leydi* are often described as "microstates," for under the last period of unified authority, the Almamyat, each *leydi* functioned as a largely autonomous unit of political, economic, and social management. Access to and use of the river valley's resources were regulated within these units. After colonial conquest, each *leydi* was halved into northern (Mauritanian) and southern (Senegalese) administrative sections.[96] This did not undermine social hierarchy in the Fouta Toro.[97] On the contrary, France did not challenge the existing land-tenure system, or the hierarchical political structure of the microstates of the Middle Valley.

[96] Splitting the leydi in two "aggravated the decline of the traditional resource management system," which was centered on what Elkins (1995:10) calls a "time sharing system" whereby groups of farmers, herders, and fishermen had use rights to land in the floodplain during different times of year.

[97] Boutillier et al. (1962:117–29) argued that "from the end of the eighteenth century of the beginning of the nineteenth, the era of upheaval, including the French occupation and the political changes that accompanied it, profoundly modified the land tenure situation. Over the 1880 to 1910 period, the situation stabilized." Other writers stress continuities in the feudal-like social structure of the Fouta Toro.

Within the *leydi* microstates, only certain lineages of the noble *toorobé* strata occupied positions of political power. These ruling dynasties supplied the provincial leaders who held positions of *chef de territoire*, village chief, and imam.[98] The weight of this stark hierarchy was attenuated by the fact that politics was also structured by the parcellization of authority into ever-smaller territorial and social units (e.g., groups of villages, villages, residential quarters). Even units at the bottom of the pyramid guarded significant autonomy. Residential quarters within villages, for example, "constitute independent political entities and are jealous of their autonomy at the level of organization of production."[99] Parcellization or fracturing of power created the basis for serious factional politics within villages and microstates.[100]

In the Upper Valley, twentieth-century political and social structure is similar in its main outlines to that of the Fouta Toro. Society was organized along the lines of three endogamous strata (freemen and nobles, casted groups, and descendants of slaves) and dominated by a land-controlling nobility. The floodplain is narrower in this eighty-kilometer stretch of river, and perhaps because of this, social hierarchy is even steeper here than it is in the Fouta Toro.[101] Dominant families control large contiguous land domains and others "acquire access to cultivable land via one or several of an array of payments, depending on the quality of the land and the customary relationship between the landowner and the farmer" (Bloch 1991:240–1). Temporary out-migration to other parts of the Sahelian zone, especially central Senegal, and more recently to France, has been an economic mainstay of the Soninké zone for much of this century.[102] Inflexibility in the land tenure regime helps explain the prominence of temporary migration as a strategy for accumulation and/or risk management.

B. The Delta

For the last 120 kilometers before it reaches the Atlantic, from just west of Dagana to Saint-Louis, the Senegal River spreads out into branches and tributaries to create a wide delta covering an area of about 5,000 square

---

[98] Beck 1996a:178; A. B. Diop 1965:23.

[99] Dia and Fall 1991:152, 141. The authors provide the example of the residential quarters of Kaskas, the largest village in the *arrondissement* (population 4460 in 1986) of which it is the *chef-lieu* (Department of Podor).

[100] Dia and Fall 1991:150. See also Schmitz 1991:7.

[101] See Bloch 1991:252.

[102] On Soninké migration, see Adams 1977b; Adams and So 1996; Manchuelle 1997.

kilometers. Senegal's largest freshwater lake, the Lac de Guiers, "an extraordinary reserve of freshwater in the Sahelian 'desert' of the Ferlo," extends southward from the river.[103] In stark contrast to the upriver Toucouleur and Soninké societies, the Delta was (and remained for the first half of the twentieth century) distinguished by very low population densities and the absence of political structuration, well-defined land rights, and a political aristocracy. The major factor limiting the agricultural potential of the entire zone was the incursion of seawater into the river delta during the dry season. In the twentieth century it became a frontier zone receiving immigrants from various parts of Senegal and Mauritania.

II. Colonial Strategies

After frustrated attempts to open the Delta to European settlers in the 1910s, the French gave up on this region and focused instead on encouraging peasant-based groundnut production in central Senegal. Immediately after World War II, Senegal's colonial administration once again took up the challenge of developing the commercial agricultural potential of the Delta. Dams were built at the two ends of the Lac de Guiers in 1947 and 1956. The first was the anti-salinization dam at Richard Toll; it opened the door to large-scale pump irrigation and commercial development in the surrounding zone. A state agency, the Mission d'Aménagement du Sénégal (MAS), developed six thousand hectares of rice fields in this area in 1953. The experiment was a disappointment and the land was eventually taken over and converted into sugar estates by a private French firm, the Compagnie Sucrière Sénégalaise. Investment was accompanied by the in-migration of an ethnically heterogeneous population (about 60 percent Wolof, 19 percent Peul) of fisherman, farmers, and laborers.[104] Development of the Delta would continue in earnest in the 1960s.

Senegal's governments have viewed the Delta as almost a tabula rasa, where dreams of commercial agriculture and social engineering are unconstrained by any preexisting order. The opposite has been true in the Middle and Upper Valley.

As Linda Beck (1996a:182) writes,

[u]nder French colonial policy in the Fuuta [Fouta], remarkably similar in practice to British indirect rule, the colonial state sought the assistance of the provincial

---

[103] See Mathieu et al. 1986:220.
[104] See Le Gal and Dia 1991:162–4; Seck 1991:319.

dynasties in administering the region.... Certain toorobé families who were co-operative allies maintained or even enhanced their power and status in Tukulor [Toucouleur] society, while those associated with resistance to colonial rule found themselves excluded from access to colonial economic and political resources.

France established cantonal chieftaincies within the existing territorial jurisdictions and named members of Toucouleur and Soninké *grandes familles* to these posts. When Sociétés Indigènes de Prévoyance (SIPs) were created to collect and manage seed stocks in the Toucouleur and Soninké zones, these too fell into the hands of leaders of the dominant aristocratic families. As was the case in the groundnut basin, the SIP were used by local elites to reinforce their own wealth, control over local agricultural surpluses, and political hold on local populations.[105]

In the early 1970s Balans, Coulon, and Gastellu (1975:43–5) argued that the authority and hegemony of the land-controlling oligarchy had not been fundamentally degraded by colonial (and early-postcolonial) rule. This is partly because of limited economic development in this zone, "but partly because of the policy of the central [colonial] authorities themselves, who refused to overturn the established order and preferred instead to accommodate themselves to the existing social and political structures." The choice was not made simply for convenience or by default, but rather reflected French authorities' fears of destabilizing social forces and "an authority crisis" in the Fouta Toro. One fear was of Islamic prophetic or renewal movements which, "if allowed the liberty to spread, would gravely damage the authority of the *toorodo* aristocracy" (ibid.:47–8) and, presumably, might eventually challenge Mouride hegemony in the central groundnut basin. Balans et al. wrote that the French colonial authorities hampered and repressed Islamic prophetic movements in the river valley, usually to the advantage of the region's longstanding elite. Limited economic

---

[105] In 1972 P. Laville reported on the case of an SIP of Bakel where, as was the norm in the river valley and groundnut basin, the SIP was controlled by the colonial *commandant de cercle* ("president" of the SIP) in collaboration with a few notables. The vice-president (VP) of the SIP of Bakel, a local notable, "made his children, relatives, and vassals the managers of seed stocks [requisitioned by the SIP].... Each head of household had to deposit the requisite quantity of the harvest at the closest storage point, and then ... an identical amount with the VP who turned a share over to the *commandant de cercle*, after having distributed handouts to his courtiers and servants. The VP constituted a large clientele by distributing, willy-nilly, tickets for the purchase of imported consumer goods (e.g., beans, rice, cloth). Lastly, at meetings of the *conseil d'administration* [of the SIP], the VP was careful to make sure that proposals of the president were adopted, without discussion, by all members present" (P. Laville as cited by Gentil 1986:35).

development in the Upper and Middle River Valley – not only under colonial rule but in the 1960s as well – was partly a reflection of this conciliatory attitude toward the oligarchy (ibid.:45).

Under colonial rule, the Fouta Toro became a quasi-monocultural region devoted to the production of millet. In spite of a natural endowment favorable to agriculture, economic output stagnated and even declined. Grain exports to Mauritania and other parts of Senegal, which had totaled about fifteen to twenty thousand tons per year in the years preceding World War II, fell to about five thousand tons a year in the 1950s.[106] Household production was oriented essentially to family use. Surpluses circulated on the margins of monetary circuits and were traded mostly on the basis of barter. Virtually none of the output of the large domains was sold outside of the river valley. Cotton production regressed dramatically under colonial rule.

Integration of river populations into the national and international economy during this period had occurred largely via labor migration. This process "left unchanged the essential features of local food crop production and social structures (i.e., relations of production and power, and notably relations of land access and appropriation).... [T]echniques and modes of production were unchanged" (Mathieu 1991:200). Everywhere, hand-held hoes and family labor predominated. As Boutillier et al. put it, there was "no terraced agriculture, no fertilizer, ... no sign of progress."[107]

Temporary emigration to Senegal's groundnut-producing regions and urban centers, and to France, was in part a consequence of economic stagnation in the Middle and Upper River Valley.[108] Control of the land by the conservative oligarchies of the Upper and Middle River Valley limited the total amount of land under cultivation. Large landholders tended to cultivate or rent only a portion of the land under their control, leaving arable land idle while "others are obliged to rent land to secure subsistence, and may opt to procure land by other means, including migration."[109] Boutillier and his collaborators (1962:131) reported that in the late 1950s,

---

[106] Boutillier et al. 1962:256; see also van chi Bonnardel 1978:442.

[107] Boutillier et al. 1962:106; see also Bloch 1991:252.

[108] Manchuelle (1997) stressed the extent to which temporary migration among the Soninké is a long-established strategy for accumulating wealth that can be invested in building up social status at home. Even in the twentieth century, he argues, it was not the poorest, or those with the fewest opportunities at home, who emigrated. Manchuelle's argument helps explain how such steep social hierarchy could develop and persist in a zone where agricultural surpluses are limited.

[109] Boutillier et al. 1962:131–2.

68.5 percent of farmers in the upper parts of the river valley complained of land shortage. Downriver, in much of the Fouta Toro, it was 42 percent.

Toward the end of the colonial period, rates of temporary out-migration from this region became so high that they *caused* regression of agricultural output, especially the Fouta Toro.[110] Migration from the Middle Valley to Senegal's urban centers was estimated at a rate of 25 percent of the active male population (fifteen to fifty years old) between 1945 and 1960. Soninké rates of emigration were at least as high. Emigration produced a stream of remittances to the river valley that helped sustain households, and even improve the situation of some, in spite of overall stagnation or regression in output.[111] Population in the Middle River Valley grew by an annual rate of 2 percent in the 1950s.

III. Decolonization Politics

In the immediate post–World War II years, the Toucouleur chiefs of the Fouta Toro were lined up squarely behind Senegal's leading politician and deputy to the French National Assembly, Lamine Guèye. These political brokers were among the first courted by the upstart politician Léopold Senghor in the fiscal year 1948/49, as he set out to fracture Lamine Guèye's rural political coalition. Senghor's strategy was to form a rival political party that would unite Senegal's rural peripheries against the urban core. Control of the Senegal River Valley was a major prize in this electoral contest, for the population of the valley (excluding the regional capital, Saint-Louis) was about 300,000, equivalent to about 60 percent of the Mouride population in the groundnut basin.[112] Almost half of the river valley's population was in the Fouta Toro alone. In the late 1940s Senghor scored a key victory in winning the support of a major Toucouleur political leader, Saidou Nourou Tall.

Saidou Nourou Tall was head of an important group of noble families in the Fouta Toro. He was also a major Tidjane marabout with a powerful

---

[110] Boutillier et al. 1962:106, 256; Boutellier 1963:117; A. B. Diop 1965:36, 53, 71–5; Péllisier 1966:30. The Fouta Toro served as a labor reservoir for the Dakar service sector after World War II. The Toucouleur population in Dakar in 1957–8 numbered between about 20,000 and 30,000.

[111] In 1958, 40 percent of the monetary revenue of Toucouleur households came from migration (Boutiller 1963:117).

[112] Seck 1991:303. The population of the Fouta Toro around 1980 was 300,000. Of this, 10,000 were in Matam, the capital city of this zone.

institutional base within the Tidjane order.[113] Having rendered great service to French colonial administrations over the course of several decades (including service as chaplain of the French African troops under Vichy during World War II), Sedihou became deeply involved in decolonization politics in the late 1940s and 1950s. In 1947 he established an urban political base for himself by creating an ethnic association of Toucouleur emigrants in Dakar, the Union Générale des Originaires de la Vallée du Fleuve (UGOVF). The Union spread quickly to the Fouta, and the UGOVF became an important political force.[114] Senghor "wooed the UGOVF by stressing his desire for a Tukulor [Toucouleur] assistant in the BDS and later by appointing Mamadou Dia, a Tukulor whose family came from the River Region," as his right-hand man (Behrman 1970:89). Dia also had great appeal in Mouride zones, where he was born and spent his boyhood. Lamine Guèye denigrated Senghor's tactics as "regional bribery" (ibid.:88).

Senghor's alliance with Saidou Nourou Tall was cemented well before Senghor's decisive win in the 1952 Territorial Assembly elections. The major families of the Fouta Toro then lined up behind Senghor. By the mid-1950s small splinter groups of the Toucouleur elite that had remained loyal to Lamine Guèye were incorporated into Senghor's party. Factionalism within the towns, provinces, and villages of the Middle and Upper River Valley persisted within the ruling party. It was managed on an ongoing basis through "long and difficult negotiations between central and local party elites"[115] and, as Beck (1996a:217) reports, was "generously accommodated" within the UPS.

The nobility of the Fouta Toro perceived a very high stake in nationalist-era politics in Senegal. Although well-informed analysts have viewed socioeconomic order in the Upper and Middle Valley as remarkably stable from the 1910s to the mid-1970s, it seems that in the 1950s the provincial elite of the Fouta Toro perceived ground shifts that could erode their power. Boutillier et al. believed that there were factors at work in the late colonial

---

[113] According to Behrman (1970:184–5, 51), Saidou "directs Abdul Aziz [Sy], current head of the Tijani branch, in political matters. . . . Saidou is current head of the most important Tukulor Tijani [Tidjane] branch but technically subordinate to Abdul Aziz Sy." His extensive relations with the colonial administration date to the 1910s; by 1957 he had received twenty-four medals for service to France. See also Morganthau 1964:147.

[114] Beck 1996a:183. "In 1953 the UGOVF split into warring factions and lost its political control of the Tukulor" (Behrman 1970:89).

[115] Schumacher (1975:39) so describes the handling of dissident UPS factions in Saint-Louis, Podor, and Matam in 1956 and 1959. See also Schmitz 1991.

period – emigration, regression in agricultural output, and possibly other factors as well – that contributed to a weakening of the rights of large landholders. Large landholders "collected their dues and payments more irregularly, and at a diminishing rate," and there were signs of reinforcement of cultivators' use rights. "This evolution, slow as it is, is distinct enough that the inhabitants of the valley are beginning to be conscious of it. . . . We are in effect witnessing today a crystallization of opinion hostile [to these trends], naturally coming from the large landed families of the Fouta."[116] Their political power, Boutillier et al. argued, was in "rapid decline." Fouta nobles used the national political arena to stake out their position:

To slow or reverse the erosion of their privileges in the land tenure system, the large landholders have come together in an association, the active members of which naturally include all the "big names" of the Fouta. [O]ne can read in Dakar's daily newspaper (*Paris-Dakar*, 2 July 1958) a declaration made by this association, issued from Matam, which shows clearly its objectives:
  It warns *arrivistes* ["newcomers," upstarts] who attempt to appropriate land to which they hold only "use rights," and warns certain low-ranking bureaucrats who, by their ignorance or in search of profit, take the side of these *arrivistes* under the fallacious pretext that "the land belongs to everyone," that the Association de Propriétaires Coutumiers et Cultivateurs de la Vallée du Fleuve [Association of Traditional Landholders and Farmers of the River Valley] is ready to intervene whenever any of its dues-paying members is in difficulty. . . . They note that the French respected their land rights. (Boutillier et al. 1962:130)

Boutillier and his coauthors suggested that for the Toucouleur oligarchy, protecting the old land-tenure regime was not an end in itself. The premise of the 1958 Matam declaration, they argued, was that the Senegal River Valley held economic potential for Senegal and Mauritania, and that the state-led *mise en valeur* of the river valley was imminent. "The large land-holders want to be prepared to profit from the hydro-agricultural improvements that are being planned so that they can eventually consolidate their position and benefit from the general revalorization of the land that will surely follow the realization of these projects" (ibid.).

Meanwhile, the most politically visible of the Fouta oligarchy, Saidou Nourou Tall, was himself a principal actor in the critical party and electoral events of 1957 and 1958. Saidhou played the leading role in organizing the Tidjane and Mouride *grands marabouts* into a Conseil Supérieur des Chefs Réligieux opposed to what the rural religious elite perceived as excessive

---

[116] Boutillier et al. 1962:129–30, see also 117.

nationalism and social reformism among some of Senegal's urban politicians. This pressure guaranteed the 1958 split in the UPS, when the recently incorporated left wing of the party (the "Young Turks") walked out to form the PRA-Senegal. Expulsion of the reformers left the original UPS elite and the Islamic marabouts to lead the country to a decisive and conservative vote in the 1958 referendum on Senegal's independence. Saidou's prominent role in these events has been understood in the context of his position in the Tidjane brotherhood ("he directs Abdul Aziz Sy [Grand Khalif of the Tidjane brotherhood] in political matters").[117] Yet as the head of a group of important Toucouleur families in the Fouta Toro and a major UPS heavyweight in that region, it is sure that his influence was also felt there.

UPS political control of the Senegal River Valley in the 1950s was rooted in the alliances Senghor negotiated with the ruling elite of the Fouta Toro in the late 1940s and 1950s. The Fouta oligarchs made shrewd assessments of their interests in the national political and economic developments of this era. They displayed something closely resembling class consciousness and were capable of acting on their own account on the national stage. In the 1960s the state-building strategies of the Senghor regime institutionalized this alliance and worked to shore up the power and privileges of the landed elite in the Fouta Toro.

IV. Institution Building in the River Valley

Harnessing the agricultural potential of the Senegal River Valley was a major preoccupation of the newly independent government of Senegal. All efforts in the 1960s were focused on the delta region, a zone that was technically more difficult (but politically easier) to exploit than the Middle Valley. This choice reflected social and political obstacles to the commercialization of agriculture in the Middle Valley.

A. Institutional Choice in the Delta

Although colonial-era experiments had been mostly disappointing, the nationalist government in Dakar was not willing to give up on the dream of irrigated rice production in the Delta. In the early 1960s the state itself led the charge. In 1965 a new parastatal regional development agency, the

---

[117] Behrman 1970:184–5.

Société d'Aménagement Economique du Delta du Fleuve Sénégal (SAED), was charged with this mission.[118] SAED was given a sweeping mandate to create thirty thousand hectares of farmland in the Delta and to produce sixty thousand tons of rice in ten years. Land appropriated directly by the state under Senegal's 1964 National Domain Law was placed at its disposition.[119] Over the next seven years, SAED spent FCFA 5.5 billion (about $18 million at the time) to develop rice production on an industrial scale in the Delta.[120]

SAED ran settlement schemes that created what would be officially defined as a rice-producing peasantry in this zone. The parastatal brought thousands of immigrants to the Delta. It trained the immigrants and organized them into producer groups that were assigned terrains defined by axes of the hydraulic grid. Producer groups were brought together as "village sections" of "cooperatives" created by SAED, and these became part of Senegal's national cooperative system. SAED used the cooperatives to furnish inputs to farmers (on credit backed by the national development bank, the BNDS). All output was purchased directly by the state agency. By the 1970s about ten "totally mechanized" rice estates of over one thousand hectares each had been built. In less than a decade, the process had created what looked to many (including some of the farmers) like a nearly proletarianized workforce cultivating SAED land (Adams 1977a).

SAED established technical outposts and deconcentrated administrative stations throughout the zone. Land access and use, irrigation equipment, inputs, and the production process itself were all managed directly by state agents, who were often perceived by farmers as taskmasters.[121] The government maintained the partial fiction that laborers on the SAED rice estates were independent household producers. In fact, however, the organizational system "left little autonomy to the farmers, and this created many operational problems, including farmers' refusal to reimburse debts, delays in delivery of inputs and equipment, poor maintenance of infrastructure, and

---

[118] SAED replaced the Organization Autonome de la Vallée (OAV), created in 1960 as the successor to the MAS, the colonial agency that developed the rice estates at Richard Toll that were eventually taken over and converted to sugar cane by the private firm CSS (Seck 1991:22–5).

[119] Under the 1964 law, most of the Delta was designated as *zone pioneer* and thus as land that would be managed directly by the state.

[120] Of this, 66 percent was externally financed (Seck 1991:22).

[121] Adams 1977a:41 *inter alia*; Adams and So 1996:107. Farmers had to comply with SAED regulations in order to receive credit and other support. Sanctions could be taken against farmer groups not in full compliance with regulations. See Gellar 1990:139.

high production costs" (Le Gal and Dia 1991:163–4). These and other technical and operational problems plagued the large-scale SAED rice estates in the 1960s and early 1970s. By 1975 SAED had developed 10,500 hectares, but this was only 35 percent of its original objective, and overall results were "weak and unstable" (Seck 1991a:22). SAED reported that the Delta produced over 18,000 tons of rice in 1983, but costs were high.

In the Delta, political and institutional outcomes have been influenced as much by human geography as they have been upriver, but outcomes have been very different. State building in the Delta in the 1960s produced a network of institutions managing industrial-style rice estates. Authority was centralized in the hands of state agents. At the same time, there was spatial deconcentration of the official institutions that served as sites for the micromanagement of the irrigation system and of the producers themselves (control of the irrigation grid, SAED technical services, producer groups, cooperatives). Even villages and so-called village cooperatives on the large estates of the Delta were unilateral acts of the state: they were socially heterogeneous and, according to observers, "lacking in coherence."

The logic laid out in Chapter 2 does not anticipate this form of state conquest of a zone hitherto marginal to the national economy, or this mixture of centralization of authority and spatial deconcentration of the state apparatus in a politically egalitarian rural society, where no rural elite challenged the regime. In settings like this, we expect centralization of authority in the hands of state agents, but not the kind of spatial deconcentration of governmental institutions that is observed in the Delta. Yet in looking at the Delta in the 1970s and thereafter, we also find a "peasantry" that does not conform to any ideal types specified at the outset: this one was created by the state, through a settlement scheme. The entire phenomenon is unusual for most of West Africa, where the development of commercial agriculture took place largely within in the context of preexisting social and political orders and/or was fueled by population movements that were not engineered directly by the state. State-made settlement schemes are associated with large-scale irrigation projects, such as Office du Niger in Mali or Gezira in Sudan, and are also found in East Africa and southern Africa where governments resettled Africans whose land had been forcibly appropriated by Europeans.[122]

To create a peasantry in the Senegal River Delta, Dakar rulers selected spatially decentralized institutions that operated under tight central control.

---

[122] The Ujamaa villagization program in Tanzania is another example.

In terms of the typology proposed in Table 2.2, the institutions of the Delta were isomorphic to those that placed peasant farmers under direct state control in Asante, and that thereby usurped the indigenous cocoa-producing elite in that region of Ghana.

The difference between the two cases is that in the Senegal River Delta there was no preexisting elite to usurp. In the Delta, top-down control and spatial deconcentration of the state apparatus were the sine qua non of a social-engineering project in which the state provided the rules, political and social infrastructure, and all the material resources necessary for commercial agriculture. We are looking at an institutional strategy that may be specific to modern settlement schemes in which peasantries are created *de nouveau* by the state.[123]

We return to the Delta in the chapter's conclusion, after considering two distinct phases in Dakar's attempt to maintain its political footing in the Middle and Upper River Valley.

B. *Institution Building in the Middle and Upper Valley, 1960–1972*

State building in the Middle Valley in the 1960s seemed aimed at little more than institutionalizing linkages between the Toucouleur dynasties and central rulers. Dakar's goals appeared to be entirely political: in the 1960s there was no effort to increase, capture, or transform agricultural surpluses in this region. The economy of the Fouta stagnated and even declined over the course of the decade, and high rates of temporary out-migration continued to be a major source of monetary revenue for families in this region. As these economic changes chipped away at the old sources of the Toucouleur elite's authority and wealth, the *toorobé* dynasties' standing in the region became ever more dependent upon access to the center.[124] The status and clout of the landholding oligarchy became more contingent upon controlling patronage resources and wielding political prerogatives that were, in effect, devolved to them from the center.

---

[123] Under these conditions, farmers may be more accurately described as proletarians, or as semiproletarianized, as we have noted above. Outgrower schemes may also be organized within this institutional model.

[124] Beck 1996a. This explains, she argues, the rock-solid support for the ruling party in the Fouta Toro. Beck contrasts the Fouta elite's persistent dependence on Dakar to the growing economic and political autonomy of the Mouride elite of the groundnut basin, which has been fueled by their investments in commerce in the 1980s and 1990s. See Boone 1992, 1994b.

From 1960 to 1972 postcolonial state building in the Middle and Upper River Valley proceeded through limited but politically significant spatial deconcentration of institutions and de facto devolutions of state authority to the established rural notability. This allowed the regime to distribute access to state resources and prerogative more broadly amongst the indigenous elite of this region. Many observers noted that in the Middle River Valley, "the *toorobé* dynasties represented the [party]-state" and virtually monopolized all local- and regional-level positions in the administrative and party apparatus.[125] The Fouta elite was also well represented in the National Assembly, at the ministerial level of government, and at top levels of the Dakar-based bureaucracy.[126]

In the Fouta Toro there was no dramatic reworking of administrative jurisdictions and existing political units. The old elite of the cantonal chieftaincy "assumed new roles in the party-state, such as mayor, deputy, minister, or high-ranking bureaucrat" (Beck 1996a:209). Leading families held positions at all levels of the hierarchy and across a range of functional domains. They became regional and local UPS leaders and retained control over the cooperatives. Even local cells of the rural reform movement, Animation Rurale, fell under the sway of the local oligarchy (as they did in the groundnut basin). In the villages, chiefs, cooperative representatives, and party cell leaders were political allies or clients of the *toorobé* elite. Some described the process as the "traditionalization" of modern political power in the Middle and Upper River Valley.[127]

The ruling party electoral machine, already thoroughly implanted in the river valley at the time of independence,[128] took root in densely structured networks and hierarchies of rural society. Party dynamics and intraparty political competition in the Fouta were animated by grassroots factionalisms based on residence (including villages and village quarters), family, and caste. Factionalism was accommodated via progressive

---

[125] Beck 1996a:163. See also Behrman 1970:32; Balans, Coulon, and Gastellu 1975:64–8 *inter alia*; Schmitz 1991.

[126] From positions in the central state, members of some of the most politically powerful families of the Fouta Toro influence matters of direct concern to them. For example, Beck (1996a:204) notes that Senegalese author Cheikh Hamidou Kane, who is a member of one of the most politically powerful *toorobé* families, was in the 1990s Senegal's minister of water resources.

[127] Beck 1996a:210; Balans, Coulon, and Gastellu 1975; Bloch 1991.

[128] The regional capital city of Saint-Louis was an exception. It was ex-SFIO and then a PAI bastion (Schumacher 1975:30).

deconcentrations of the party-state apparatus. Parcellizations of authority, as in the creation of new subunits of the party apparatus, gave all parties access to "positions and spoils" (Schmitz 1991:7–8). Atop the party hierarchies were the heads of landholding families, the *toorobé* elite, considered to be the "great electors" of the Fouta Toro. They "monopolized nominations to the PS party list," delivered the region's votes to the ruling party, and "appointed" delegates from the river valley to Senegal's National Assembly.[129]

As for state agents posted in the region, Boutillier et al. wrote in the early 1960s that they, along with most Toucouleur intellectuals, deferred to the policy preferences and political prerogatives of the oligarchy. Even those who favored a more egalitarian social order in the Fouta Toro "could scarcely endorse this overtly, [for] they could put themselves in difficulty in their own personal situation" (1962:129).

Dakar had cemented its political alliances with an indigenous elite in the Upper and Middle Valley that was systematically opposed to irrigation projects that could threaten their land rights and social clout. Although development planners nurtured dreams for irrigated rice production in the Middle Valley in the 1960s,[130] prevailing political arrangements seemed to preclude state-led attempts to develop irrigated agriculture in this zone. Landholding families' social and political power rested in part on their ability to limit access to the fertile floodplain. In a zone of land shortage, a good part of the floodplain (which lay under their control) was uncultivated. Sharecropping, which was integral to reproducing the sociopolitical order, seriously restricted possibilities for innovation or intensification of production on much of the best land. Virtually all analysts believed that the small production units and rudimentary farming practices of this zone could not generate the large surpluses needed to cover the costs of irrigation. Dakar, however, had chosen to build on the status quo in this zone, not to try to reorder it. Senegal's 1964 National Domain Law, which among other things officially abolished the rights of "traditional landholders" to collect land rents or dues, "passed unnoticed" in the Middle

---

[129] Beck 1996a:174, 188. In the 1960s two members of the National Assembly were considered "appointees" of Saidhou Nourou Tall (Behrman 1970:116).

[130] SAED's plans for irrigation in the Middle Valley date to 1968. The Organisation de la Mise en Valeur de la Vallée du Fleuve Sénégal (OMVS) was created in 1972. It is an international organization that brought together the governments of Mali, Senegal, and Mauritania to coordinate efforts to control river floods to produce hydroelectric power and develop irrigated agriculture in the valley.

and Upper River Valley. Civil administrators in the region were party to the "conspiracy of silence" that helped perpetuate the old relations of land access and political subservience.[131]

In the Upper and Middle River Valley in the 1960, the regime did little to stimulate economic activity of *any* kind.[132] In 1960 the colonial trading companies closed their outlets along the river. Organized ferry service declined, but the ferry was still used by travelers and by peddlers who conducted small-scale merchandise trade along the river. In 1969 the government of Senegal withdrew the ferry service completely in response to Mauritania's decision to prohibit transport of its national commerce via Senegal. The road from Saint-Louis to Matam, the "capital" of the Fouta Toro, was not finished until 1971.

As of 1965 there were only seven agricultural cooperatives in the Senegal River Valley, the Delta included.[133] Virtually none of the agricultural output of the Upper and Middle Valley was commercialized through these agencies. Production in this zone centered on millet, which was consumed by the producers, traded or bartered locally, or sold on parallel markets in the region.[134] The principal political and economic function of the cooperatives in this zone was to distribute loans to what must have been a narrow clientele, presumably comprised at least in part of cooperative officials and their allies and dependants.

Etienne Le Roy (1991:175) described Dakar's overall strategy in the Fouta in the 1960s this way: "Confident of the political support of the populations of this economically marginal zone, the political men of Dakar tended to forget about them and their problems."

C. Path Switching: State Building during the Irrigation Years, 1975–1990

It took a crisis of biblical proportions to soften the rural elite's opposition to the state-led development of irrigation projects that could upset the social balance in the river valley. This cleared the way for an across-the-board intensification of the Senghor regime's interventions in this zone.

Between 1972 and 1983, Sahelian drought was so severe that the survival of rural society in the Middle River Valley was threatened. For almost

[131] Niang 1983; Crousse, Mathieu, and Seck 1991; Beck 1996a:186–7.
[132] On the ferry and roads, see van chi Bonnardel 1978:371–4.
[133] van chi Bonnardel, 1978:627 n. 116.
[134] van chi Bonnardel, 1978:628 n. 131. As van chi Bonnardel (1978:571) put it, "in these conditions, the cooperatives serve no commercial functions."

a decade the river's floodplain was reduced to about 25 percent of its normal size, and rain-fed agriculture became impossible in much of the Fouta Toro.[135] Peasants devised new coping strategies. In the Upper Valley, around Bakel, peasant groups began to invest earnings repatriated from France in small motorpumps that could be used to draw water to fields created on river banks that lay above the normal floodplain, and on land that was not controlled directly by the old oligarchy.[136] Soninké farmers planted sorghum, maize, and rice, a crop hitherto confined to the Delta. So successful were the early attempts that this model of collective "self-help" – the creation of what would later be called "irrigated village perimeters" (*périmètres d'irrigation villageois*, or PIV) – diffused spontaneously throughout parts of the Soninké zone and the Fouta Toro. According to Béthemont (1986:67), about ninety hectares of land were so irrigated in the Upper and Middle Valley in 1974. The technology diffused rapidly. About four hundred hectares were irrigated by farmer- and village-owned motorpumps in 1975.[137]

In 1976 the Government of Senegal intervened massively to centralize control over the existing irrigation projects and to develop rice-producing PIV all along the Middle and Upper River.[138] SAED was the chosen instrument. All observers argue that state intervention on this scale would not have been possible without the consent of the rural elite of the river valley, who until then had been uninterested in any such form of "rural development."[139] One PIV president explained it in these terms: "When

[135] The total floodplain of 400,000 hectares was reduced to less than 100,000. Rainfall from Matam to Saint-Louis, which had averaged about 290 mm a year, the minimum amount necessary to raise rain-fed crops, fell at Podor to 73 mm in 1983. The zone from Matam to Saint-Louis was hardest hit. Around Bakel, the rain was more abundant and regular, and rain-fed agriculture was sustained (Béthemont 1986:65–6).

[136] The use of motorpumps was pioneered in the Bakel region by migrants, returned from France, who sought to invest their savings in productive activity. See Aprin 1980; Adams 1985; Bloch 1991. Jaabe So, who spearheaded part of this process, explains the story himself in *A Claim to Land by the River* (Adams and So 1996).

[137] Seck 1991:23. Béthemont (1986:67) says that there were 12 PIVs in 1974, worked by 880 households. Mathieu (1991:203) says that PIV covered 20 hectares in 1974 and 200 in 1975. Official numbers were not produced until the coming of SAED in 1975–6.

[138] "Well, the Minister of Rural Development came and had a look [in 1973]. The vegetable garden was beautiful then: tomatoes, onions, cabbage. When they came back to the village, I was standing next to the Minister; he didn't know me; he only knew Robert [Robert Aprin, the French technican hired by Jaabe So]. He said: I must say, these people are hard-working. I only wish it was for our benefit" (Jaabe So in Adams and So 1996:121–2). Jaabe So is founding president of the Fédération des Paysans Organizés en Zone Soninké de Bakel. His organization did not want SAED involved in their business.

[139] See for example the contributors to Crousse et al. 1991.

someone is drowning and you hold out some object to him, even if it's a knife, he'll grab onto it in order to save his own life; it is in this spirit that SAED was accepted."[140] With the intervention of the state, the number of hectares officially developed as PIV along the Senegalese side of the river would reach about eighteen thousand by 1988 (Seck 1991:23).

So it was that a kind of exogenous shock – the drought – produced an economic crisis that threatened the reproduction of the old social order in the river valley, and that also gave rise to social innovation in the form of new village-level development associations, farmer-led investment, and new agricultural and land-use practices. A net effect was shifts in prevailing balances of socioeconomic power away from the old elite. For Dakar and the oligarchy, these changes raised the costs and diminished the benefits of the state-building strategy pursued in Upper and Middle Valley the 1960s, which we have described as a mix of political powersharing and economic non-incorporation. Rural elites made recalculations about what was necessary to ensure their survival as a dominant stratum.

If state-led irrigation itself posed risks to the Fouta and Soninké elite, it is clear that these risks were attenuated greatly by up-front concessions made by the regime in Dakar. Control over land tenure issues was conceded to the established oligarchy. "Deliberate non-intervention in the land tenure domain"[141] was a sine qua non of SAED action. Paul Mathieu (1991:210) wrote that "[t]his was a realistic position and no doubt a major factor in the rapid spread of irrigated agriculture throughout the valley. Development rested essentially on the consensus of holders of traditional rights over use of the lands in question."

Massive drought in the Upper and Middle Valley thus spurred an intensification of Dakar's efforts to support its allies in this region and also opened the door to intensive state efforts to harness the regional economy to the national project. Dakar's best scenarios promised to save the valley from economic backwardness, diversify commercial agriculture in Senegal, and rescue the country from its dangerous dependence upon imported rice, its main food staple. The political strategy for making this happen centered on powersharing with the old oligarchies that represented the Senegalese state in these hinterlands. Dakar seized upon an irrigation strategy that could be pursued within existing social relations of land access and labor use. From 1976 to the mid-1980s the regime built new social and economic institutions

[140] Quoted by Bloch 1991:243.
[141] Mathieu 1991:198.

306

for promoting the partial commercialization of agriculture in this region – the state-made PIV, PIV producer groups and cooperatives, and later, rural councils. Fouta and Soninké elites pursued a strategy that complemented Dakar's: theirs was "a strategy of mastery of institutions [which] succeeded almost everywhere in the valley" (Bloch 1991:245). The new, deconcentrated outposts of the state that were created during the irrigation years fell under their political sway or control.

From 1976 on, SAED and the Senegalese Ministry of Public Works created PIV in the Fouta Toro and the Soninké zone of the river. Bulldozers prepared sites of twenty to thirty hectares. These were supplied with motorpumps and irrigation networks. By 1982 about ten thousand hectares had been constituted as PIVs; by 1988 when this reached eighteen thousand hectares, irrigated perimeters existed at several hundred sites along the Upper and Middle River.[142] Following the original model, most were created on dry lands near the river that had been devoted to rain-fed agriculture in the past, and where flood recession agriculture was not possible even in normal years. Many large landholders continued to resist the introduction of pump irrigation on their most fertile lands in the river's floodable basin.[143]

Households in existing villages and groups of villages cultivated small parcels – rarely more than one-quarter hectare in size – within the PIV. Farmers gained access to particular irrigated parcels through "producer groups," or cooperatives, which were made up of representatives of the 80 to 120 households working each PIV. Under terms established by SAED, these new entities were supposed to elect presidents and vice-presidents who would be responsible for land matters within the PIV and for dealing with the parastatal agency. SAED's job was to "centralize control;" to provide

---

[142] Seck 1991:28–9; Béthemont 1986:67. Numbers vary somewhat by source. SAED reported that there were 26,000 farmers working PIV in Senegal in 1983 (Mathieu 1991:203). PIV were developed at more than 1,000 sites throughout the entire river basin, including the Delta and land in Mali and Mauritania. Frankenberger and Lynham (1993:81), apparently referring to 1987, say that despite the growth of state and private irrigation projects, "it is estimated that only 13.8 percent of the 240,000 hectares of suitable land on the Senegalese side has been brought under irrigation."

[143] For example, "in the Department of Bakel, the great landholding family of Diawara, the Saaxo family, claimed to have purchased their lands from Bacili kings before the colonial period. They accepted the first PIVs of Diawara and of Moudery on their dry land near the river, but when it was a question in 1985–6 of creating new irrigated perimeters in the floodable basin, the Saaxo family resisted and the development took place on the riverbanks.... This family is refusing to surrender customary rights over a land tract destined for development into a perimeter" (Bloch 1991:244).

motorpumps, fuel oil, and technical assistance; and to work through the producer groups to supply farmers with fertilizer and credit for rice production. In the course of things SAED swallowed up the autonomous PIV created in the pre-1975 period.[144]

The PIV model was supposed to incarnate a "semi-communitarian" or "semi-traditional" model of peasant production, just like the groundnut cooperatives in central Senegal.[145] The practical meaning of this in the Senegal River Valley was that the PIV were dominated by representatives of the local oligarchies. Those allocating land and negotiating with SAED were members, political allies, or clients of the *toorobé* dynasties.[146] Creation of these new bodies thus caused no abrupt rupture in already established patterns of party politics in the Senegal River Valley, or indeed in older political arrangements in this region. In 1991 Bloch wrote that "[s]ince the creation of the first PIV [in the community of Moudery, Bakel Department] fifteen years ago, there has never been an open election for the leaders of the *groupement de producteurs* attached to the PIV" (1991:26). Catherine Elkins described one of her cases in much the same terms: "The rice project started by SAED had been turned over the village's traditional leaders" (1995:21).

PIV land was distributed on a basis that turned out to be highly consistent with traditional modes. It seems that in the early years of SAED intervention, when conditions in the Fouta Toro were most desperate, the widespread introduction of PIV had a certain equalizing effect, giving most villagers the chance of access to land closer to the river. Long-standing holders of land rights in the Fouta Toro did not try to monopolize large surfaces or the best of the newly irrigated land.[147] Land allocation took place within traditional norms, but once allocated, farmers' use rights seemed secure and free of overhanging social obligations and dues. Yet land tenure practice in effect evolved within a couple of years "toward forms of land-use and land-tenure relations very close to the old land practices" (Mathieu 1991:210).

---

[144] Bloch 1991, 1993. See also Aprin 1980; Adams and So 1996.

[145] Mathieu 1991:198.

[146] Beck 1996a:209–10; Schmidt (1991:7) wrote that "we found that in the majority of cases, it is the small local oligarchy...that has placed its members at the head of the offices that direct the local cooperatives." As Niasse put it, "the traditional *toorodo* elite is clearly predominant" (cited by O'Bannon 1995:16).

[147] See Mathieu 1991. It seems that this was not always the case around Bakel, where the old elite immediately took over the first PIV for their own benefit (Niasse 1991:110–11).

The PIV and the producer groups were both distributive and political institutions. In this regard they functioned much like the groundnut co-operatives in central Senegal. They were points of access to state-provided resources, and they were dominated by the established, indigenous elite. Soninké and Toucouleur leading families benefited directly from government credit channeled through the PIV, as well as from other side-payments.[148] Meanwhile, credit, subsidized agricultural inputs, and even access to cultivable land – all channeled through the PIV and producer groups – provided sustenance for their allies, dependents, subjects, and clientele.

As a structure for the commercialization of rural surpluses, the system set up by SAED never worked as its architects had envisioned. SAED was supposed to buy the rice harvest and deduct from farmers' earnings the costs of inputs and services provided by the state. This did not work out in practice, for SAED did not commercialize more than about 35 percent of the rice produced in the Upper and Middle Valley.[149] Most rice produced on the PIV was consumed by the producers themselves or sold on local informal markets. Because SAED did not appropriate a surplus from the producers, it could not extract payment for credit, fertilizer, pumps, and gas oil – much less for the development of the land itself. Gradually it became clear that state-sponsored rice irrigation projects were above all subsidizing subsistence production in this region.[150] Costs of production on the small plots in the PIV proved to be too high to make this kind of farming commercially viable.[151] Analysts argued that generating larger, commercializable

---

[148] In one of Elkins's study sites, a "*toorobé* central leadership lineage" created a PIV to get access to credit for rice cultivation from the government, and then invested the money in commerce (1995:35). Beck (1996a:197) makes note of "side payments" to nobles in the Fouta Toro whose land privileges were compromised during the 1975 to 1984 period.

[149] The average rate of SAED commercialization of PIV rice in 1983 was 37 percent. Meanwhile, PIV rice accounted for only about 2.4 percent of all rice commercialized by SAED in 1983 (that is, 440 tons of a total of 19,000 tons commercialized by SAED) (Mathieu 1991:203).

[150] Fertilizer was subsidized at a rate of more than 50 percent up to 1986. Motorpumps for PIV startup were distributed free by the state and less than 25 percent of the value of those put in place thereafter was amortized. Credit was extended without interest, and SAED was supposed to be repaid when farmers sold their rice harvest to the state (Mathieu 1991:200–7). See also Béthemont 1986:68–9.

[151] Commercial viability of the irrigation projects in the Middle and Upper Valley was, from the beginning, obviously just one of several state objectives. The same could be said of development strategies in Senegal's groundnut basin in the 1960s, although this may not have been so obvious at that time.

surpluses would have required the introduction of tractors or animal traction; development of more land, more difficult land, and larger tracts; and intensification and closer supervision of the labor process.[152] Irrigation was possible within the context of old land-tenure relations and patterns of labor use, but only economically viable if heavily subsidized by the state.

Given state subsidies covering a very large share of the monetary costs of irrigated rice production, the PIV were relatively successful and increased rapidly in number from 1976 to the mid-1980s. Links between the Fouta and Soninké elite and rulers in Dakar were further institutionalized over the course of this period. In 1980 and 1982 Communautés Rurales and Rural Councils – institutions provided for in 1972 reforms aiming at administrative decentralization throughout Senegal – were set up in the river valley.[153] Land parcels within irrigated perimeters developed by SAED would henceforth be allocated by elected Rural Councils. These same bodies would also take charge of land matters within the much wider territorial jurisdictions of the new Communautés Rurales.

Given the history of state institution building in this region it is not surprising that the Rural Councils became instruments of the already dominant nobility. As Cheikh Tidjane Sy put it, the powers of the Rural Councils were "confiscated by the traditional feudal elite."[154] In Schmitz's view, land management prerogatives held by the state under Senegal's 1964 land law and the 1972 reforms were straightforwardly conferred upon the river valley's leading landholding families:

The CR [Conseil Rural] has great power over the land allocation. If one knows that the rural councilors usually come from the families that supply the "political personnel" at the head of the "microstates" [of the Fouta Toro], then this means that the land is managed through the "patrimonial-clientelist" sphere, and not by the

---

[152] See for example Boutillier et al. 1962:132; Seck 1991:30–1; Barreteau 1998:24.

[153] The Department of Bakel is part of the region of Sénégal Oriental (now Tambacounda). Elections for Rural Councils were not held here until 1982 and the councils were not actually constituted until 1984.

[154] Sy 1988:16. Bloch (1991) provides many examples. One case appeared at first to SAED agents to be anomalous: "The president of the CR de Kidira [Bakel zone] is a *maccudo* (descendant of halpulaar captives or "slaves"); SAED agents were very impressed by this until they realized that they were dealing with an individual who was dependent upon the Sy family, the dominant family of Bundu. In a meeting we had in 1987 . . . in the presence of the president of the CR and several representatives of the Sy family, the president did not dare speak" (Bloch 1991:244 n. 2).

administration, even if the *préfet* and *sous-préfet* are supposed to have a supervisory role [*rôle de tutelle*] vis-à-vis the president of the CR. . . . The local elite was thus able to lock up control over usable land. (Schmitz 1991:13)

As the state continued to create PIV, Rural Councils attributed tracts of irrigated land to their own members. "Thus the CR attributes a large property, developed by the state, to the president of the Rural Council himself, who happens to be a noble. It is generally true that the CRs attribute land to members of the CR and other influential persons" (Bloch 1991:250).

There was an intimate connection between land politics as institutionalized in the new Rural Councils and the reproduction of the ruling party's political hold on the river valley. Rural Councils were elected from party lists in a majority-take-all system. In the Fouta Toro, a de facto one-party state within a state, this made the Rural Councils "tools of the [ruling party]," as Lam said, as well as tools of the rural oligarchy.[155] State building in the Senegal River Valley during the drought years made central rulers' ability to govern the populations of this region ever more dependent upon their alliance with long-standing rural powerbrokers.

A decade of state investment in small-scale irrigated agriculture in the river valley, from 1975 to 1985, did not profoundly challenge the old socioeconomic order in this region. And as had been foreseen in the early 1960s, irrigated rice farming within existing socioeconomic structures did not, in general, prove to be commercially viable. When the rains returned to the Fouta Toro in the mid-1980s, large numbers of producers abandoned both irrigation and rice production and returned to old methods of producing traditional food crops. Writing in the 1990s, Elkins (1995:20–3) stressed the inability of most households in the Middle Valley to ever fully recover from the drought, and their growing dependence on rotational migration to Dakar, commercial activities, and wage employment in the Delta.[156]

Progressive scaling back of SAED and withdrawal of producer subsidies between 1985 and 1990 all but ensured that this trend would hold.[157] Many

---

[155] Lam 1992:121–2. See also Beck 1996a:187–8.
[156] See also Frankenberger and Lynham 1993:84–5.
[157] Senegal's Nouvelle Politique Agricole (1984) called for "disengagement" of the state and moves toward "true pricing." In 1987 the new Caisse Nationale de Crédit Agricole du Sénégal (CNCAS) took over SAED's credit-allocation functions throughout the entire valley. New interest rates were set at 13.5 to 15 percent. In 1989 in the Department of Matam, one-third of the PIV surfaces were not cultivated (Mathieu 1991:211; Seck 1991:12, 30).

PIV were abandoned. Irrigated agriculture in the Upper and Middle River Valley became the affair of those who could afford it, or those who could exploit it "according to tenure systems very close to the traditional system, sharecropping, which is generally not compatible with [*nuisible à*] irrigation."[158] SAED created PIV that were, in effect, owned by powerful individuals. Bloch (1991:246–7) provides a few examples from Bakel: Since 1986, Moudery III, a PIV in the CR of Moudery, Department of Bakel, was "reserved for the deputy to the National Assembly and his family (thirty hectares). . . . Moudery V [was] reserved for the president of the Rural Council [a noble] and his allies. . . . He thus has what he calls his 'own perimeter.'" Meanwhile Rural Councils were known to attribute or even sell some land to outsiders, raising the specter of land dispossession for the region's most vulnerable farmers.[159]

In Senegalese national elections in the 1990s, the ruling party scored its highest rates of electoral support in the Fouta Toro.[160]

Dakar's institutional choices in the River Valley until the 1990s reflected the regime's high adversity to political risk. Perhaps they also show a respect on Dakar's part for the profound precariousness of the subsistence economies in this region. Yet populations of the river valley and of Senegal as a whole have also paid the economic and political opportunity costs of strategies that built modern state authority on the foundations of old oligarchies. One cost is that innovations in land use, irrigation, and investment have been tightly constrained, leaving ordinary farmers perhaps more vulnerable than they might otherwise have been to the effects of damming the Senegal River in the 1990s.

Completion of the Manatali dam in 1987 gave a supranational authority, the OMVS, near total control of the river valley's most crucial asset, the floodwaters. OMVS management disrupted flood recession agriculture along the entire length of the river in Senegal.[161] This creates a situation of new indeterminacy (Barreteau 1998). The river valley in the late 1990s

---

[158] Engelhard 1991:51; Bloch 1991:250, 250 n. 3.

[159] See Niasse 1991:110; Mathieu 1991:198, 211.

[160] That is, in the Departments of Podor and Matam (Beck 1996a:160–1, 344).

[161] See for example Elkins 1995:14, 17: "Erratic artificial floods released since 1989 by managers of the Manatali Dam on the upper Senegal River in Mali have been costly and destructive. . . . Their principal effect has been to disrupt the natural floods and flood-recession agriculture."

was buffeted by an untenable combination of conservative machine politics aimed at maintaining the ruling party's electoral control (although the resources at Dakar's disposal had diminished greatly) and what is a potentially radical process of economic interventionism and change.

Changes were also under way in the Delta subregion during the 1980s and 1990s. Inequalities within the farming population emerged over time, with government prerogative and resources necessarily playing a large role in this process. In the Delta, Mathieu, Naisse, and Vincke (1986:232) spoke of a peasant aristocracy made up of village chiefs and cooperative officials. They were first in line to benefit from the progressive devolution of political and economic prerogative that would come with "decentralization" and downsizing of the state. Meanwhile, a very different dynamic took shape: collective consciousness among small farmers and farm workers developed in some areas, sometimes *in opposition to* the state. For example, a peasant association called the Foyer de Ronkh, founded in 1963, became locked in combat with SAED over crop payments, credit, and farming practices. In the mid-1970s it was affiliated with a large number of youth associations and economic self-help groups in the Delta zone.[162] Groups like these found considerable support from foreign nongovernmental organizations (NGOs) in the 1980s and 1990s.

Between 1980 and 1987 the Senegalese government gradually pulled back from managing large-scale rice estates in the Delta (Seck 1991:25–6). In 1980 some land in the Delta zone was turned over to newly constituted Conseils Rurales. There was a speculative "land rush" as Rural Councils gave land away to Dakar functionaries, Mouride marabouts, merchants, SAED and CSS technicians, and others "eager to turn a rapid profit before salinization sinks the yields from irrigation."[163] Between 1981 and 1983 the quasi-totality of the irrigable land bordering the Lac de Guiers was subject to demands for land *affectations* (land grants). "Forty percent of these requests were made by persons not residing in the two CR's concerned. Demands from local farmers were made by 'the peasant aristocracy': village chiefs, presidents of cooperatives, etc." (Mathieu, Naisse, and Vincke 1986:232).

---

[162] The example of Ronkh "has inspired several youth movements...spreading like an oil spill [*tâche d'huile*] in all the region around Saint-Louis" (Niang 1991:6). See also Gentil 1986:214–15; Diop and Diouf 1992a; Barreteau 1998.

[163] See Schoonmaker-Freudenberger 1991:6.

Over the course of the 1980s, as more SAED land in the Delta was turned over to the Rural Councils,[164] peasant associations that were organized as producer cooperatives also presented land claims to the Rural Councils. At the same time, they sought to take advantage of credit and agricultural extension facilities provided by SAED, other state agencies, and NGOs.[165] Some observers lamented the peasant associations' lack of political clout ("they are ignored in the big discussions about the future of the region, construction of dams, etc.").[166] Others worried that the peasant associations did not have the technical or financial means to develop irrigated agriculture.[167] Even with these limitations, it is noteworthy that these associations have coalesced and have been able to advance collective demands on state agencies at the local level.

Rural society as it now exists in the Delta was born of state intervention, including the building of deconcentrated institutional structures for top-down control of immigrants on settlement schemes. In the parts of the Delta targeted for settlement schemes, no preexisting rural society was there to refuse or thwart this process. Yet the process itself produced a rural social order marked by economic and political hierarchy, and tensions amongst newly coalesced social groups. Local hierarchy, competition over local resources, and competititon over state and other external resources became starker as central rulers scaled back their ambitions for taxing this zone, and as Dakar devolved land allocation and other prerogatives to local actors. The Delta case thus adds a scenario to the original repertoire of institution-building strategies and their social determinants, but its implications for rural development and democracy are indeterminate on the basis of this brief discussion. Do settlement schemes create new rural aristocracies? Or do they spawn egalitarian and representative leadership? What determines the outcomes? We leave this puzzle to future researchers.

---

[164] By a 1987 presidential decree, all land in the Delta formerly designated as *zone pioneer* and managed directly by SAED was declared *zone territoire* and turned over to Rural Councils (Niang 1991; Le Gal and Dia 1991:169).

[165] Seck (1986:16 *inter alia*) shows that the rise of these peasant associations in the Delta after 1980 was linked to a shift in SAED strategy: SAED now prioritized the development of "intermediate-sized" estates that would be worked by more ethnically homogenous and cohesive peasant groups. The producer groups would have more autonomy, but still receive SAED training and inputs. In the 1990s agricultural credit was provided by the Caisse Nationale de Credit Agricole (CNCAS), financed by the Caisse Centrale de Coopération Economique (CCCE) and the World Bank.

[166] Gentil 1986:216.

[167] Mathieu, Niasse, and Vincke 1986:232, 236.

314

Conclusion: Why Institutional Strategies Change

If you take the first decades of independence as your time frame, northern Côte d'Ivoire and the Senegal River Valley appear as cases of relatively late development. The drive to build new institutions to govern and tax these regions peaked in the 1970s and early 1980s, at a time when rulers already had firm control over the core export-producing regions of Côte d'Ivoire and Senegal. Imposing state-led developmentalism in the Korhogo region and the Senegal River Valley entailed changes in the institutional strategies central rulers had originally "chosen" in these parts of rural West Africa. We thus have institution-building trajectories that can be taken as cases of path switching.

This book explores the proposition that rulers' institutional choices in taxing and governing the countryside (state forms in the countryside) are largely determined by political dynamics in rural society itself. This may sound overly deterministic. If it is correct, then how can we explain more or less abrupt changes in rulers' choices – that is, in their institution build-ing strategies – such as the changes we observe in these two cases? Path switching often occurs abruptly, over the short time period of only a few years, whereas rural social structure and political capacity surely evolve more incrementally. When (why) do rulers' institutional choices change?

Three possible answers can be deduced from the proposed theory. They can be considered in light of the cases of strategy shifting examined so far.

Social-Structural Change

Strategies can change, or shift, when rural social structure changes. Rulers alter their institutional strategies when there is a change in the interests and/or bargaining power of rural elites. This can happen gradually or abruptly. Something like this happened in the upper and middle reaches of the Senegal River Valley, where economic decay and grassroots responses to Sahelian drought worked to erode the dominance of the rural elite. Like elites everywhere, rural notables in the river valley embraced the develop-mentalist initiatives proposed by the center because the notables came to see innovation as necessary to shoring up and perpetuating their own power. Central rulers undertook institutional innovations as a way of helping to save faltering allies.

A similar logic can be applied in southern Ghana. In Asante, Nkrumah abandoned the powersharing strategy of the British and pursued an

315

usurpationist strategy instead. This, too, could be counted as a case of path switching that is traceable to social-structural change. Over the course of the 1930s to 1960s, provincial notables who had acquiesced to overrule by the modern state began to challenge the economic hegemony of the center. The strengthening of their positions as economic operators surely explains Asante elites' growing willingness and ability to challenge the center. This presented dilemmas for the British colonial administration that were never clearly resolved. Britain tried without success to stem social-structural changes by holding back the commercialization of land, and also tried to use colonial institutions to "retraditionalize" the chiefs. In other words, the British tried to change rural society (to modify the interests of Asante elites and the nature of their political power) so that rural society would better match the colonial government's institutional choice. This did not work.

As many have observed, colonialism ultimately failed to come up with political formulas that could provide a framework for economic growth for much of Africa, and this was dramatically evident in the case of southern Ghana. Peaceful transfers of power of the 1950s and 1960s to nationalist governments in Ghana and elsewhere were admissions of this failure; decolonization was itself strategy switching on the part of the Europeans. Changes in rural society, and the growth of urban populations, created tremendous pressures for modifications in the form of the state.

Risks and Mistakes

Rulers' tolerance for political risk can change (that is, they can decide to take risks they avoided in an earlier period), they can make mistakes, and they can correct mistakes. Rulers can be induced by new, exogenous pressures to adopt politically risky institutional strategies (i.e., stategies that are not expected, given our theoretical starting point, to enhance their ability to govern and tax the rural areas). Presumably such gambles can pay off, but they can also end up looking like "political mistakes." So it was in Lower Casamance. By about 1980, economic decline in central Senegal pressured Dakar to adopt a new, politically risky institutional strategy in what rulers had long perceived as a politically dangerous region. Dakar gambled and lost, for the resulting ungovernability of Lower Casamance has prevented the center from reaping gains from its attempt at institutional change.

Alternatively, rulers can switch paths to address the adverse political consequences of "past mistakes." This is what happened in the Korhogo region, where the 1960s experiment in administrative occupation produced a backlash that forced rulers back onto the powersharing path.

"National integration" obviously also involves interregional strategies, risks, and trade-offs, and a fuller account would have to take this into account. As we saw in Chapter 3, by 1980 central rulers in Senegal undertook a politically risky land strategy in Lower Casamance, but the explanation for this lies partly in Dakar's attempts to open a land frontier for its land-hungry Mouride allies, whose social power lay in the groundnut basin. In making institutional choices in the countryside, the stakes have been high and central rulers have been forced to game risk and trade-offs as well as reward.

Rulers' Goals Can Change

A change in rulers' goals can also cause path switching. For example, rulers can decide to stop taxing and governing parts of the countryside. They can abdicate some of the prerogatives of rule. In the 1990s the downsizing of the African state led rulers to virtually abandon regions they had previously tried to govern much more intensively. This is close to what happened in parts of the Middle and Upper Senegal River Valley in the 1990s. Residents of the river valley were informed that rulers had switched to an institutional strategy called "democratic decentralization." Central rulers devolved authority and prerogative to localities, but local actors often found that what they had been handed was "an empty envelope."[168] Devolution of power was not accompanied by the resources, enforcement powers, and protection of the central state.

When governments choose to dismantle or scale back state presence in the countryside, they incur new political risks, most notably when this allows rural social groups to organize autonomously in opposition to the center or with the goal of supporting a takeover of the center. These are precisely the sorts of pressures that drove state building in the 1950s through 1980s. Similar kinds of pressure on the center have been much in evidence in West and Central Africa in the last decade.

---

[168] This is how one Rural Council president put it in a discussion with Brett O'Bannon (2000).

6

![horizontal bar]

Conclusion

It is ironic that in African countries centered on the production of export crops, central rulers in the 1960s through 1980s relied most heavily for political support on the constituencies they hoped to tax the hardest – the peasants. For all the talk of "urban bias" in postcolonial Africa, the fact remained that rural constituencies and electorates provided these regimes with the ballast they needed to sustain attacks from the unions, intellectuals, students, lumpenproletarians, and even civil servants in the cities. This dynamic was in clear evidence after 1990, when internal and external pressures to move toward multipartism, and to reform the local state via administrative and political decentralization, gave rulers new occasion and new impetus to return to the rural areas to mobilize rural electorates. Regimes founded by Senghor, Houphouet, and Nkrumah sought to renew the electoral mandates they had received at the outset, in the 1950s, and to counterbalance the urban-based opposition that organized under the banners of pro-democracy movements. In striking and decisive ways, politics in the current era revisits the founding crises of the postcolonial African state.

John Lonsdale wrote in 1980 that there were three sources of variation in postcolonial Africa's political experience: the nature of the colonial regime, the political character of the nationalist movement, and the organization and dynamics of indigenous rural societies (Lonsdale 1981). This text has maintained a single-minded focus on the third factor, and argued that it has been even more determinant of broad political trajectories, state forms, and perhaps even the viability of the center than Lonsdale's formulation implied. The point is perhaps more salient now than ever, for the terms of center-periphery alliance, and the structure of the local state, are up for renegotiation in Africa, as in most of the developing world.

318

Conclusion

Across Africa, the political conditions that promoted national integration and underpinned smallholder agriculture between the late 1940s and the 1980s are being transformed, either by default or by design. Changes in international politics and the global political economy have weakened central states. These changes have been accompanied by the rise of a "new international development agenda" that is supposed to empower almost all that is local at the expense of the center. Multipartism, decentralization, privatization, and the end of state-led rural development – these are official leitmotifs of the remaking of African states today. Reforms under way since the 1980s are supposed to shift the burden of political and economic initiative (and bargaining) downward, to citizens and farmers and communities in the regions and small towns of Africa. This vision guides ambitions to remake state-society relations in Asia and Latin America as well.

Federalization, consociational strategies that establish semi-autonomous regions, and decentralization are variations on a theme: proponents of all such devolutions argue that they will enhance participation and representation in government and unleash economic innovation. Hechter (2000) argues that devolutions that produce modern forms of indirect rule can have the advantage of defusing subnationalist opposition movements that can sap the authority and finances of the center. In studies of the United States, E. E. Schattschneider offered a less sanguine view of devolution, which he viewed as the localization and privatization of social conflict.[1] Under any scenario, regional or provincial politics only becomes more obvious and decisive in shaping possibilities for political stability, material progress, and the preservation of states in Africa and throughout the developing world.

So far in African studies, analysts have devoted little attention to variation in rural political settings and in center-periphery power balances. The problem of national integration (or territorial integration) has not received sustained attention from academic analysts since the 1960s. The theoretical field has been dominated by conceptualizations of rural society and "the African peasantry" that stress cross-case structural similarities and that make general arguments about the political weakness, marginality, and irrelevance of the rural masses.[2] The politics of core-periphery linkage has

---

[1] Schattschneider (1960:12), as cited by Rimmer and Wobbles 2000:30.

[2] Some dissenters argued that as "freeholding peasantries," at least some agrarian societies were strong enough to either escape the grasp of the state by "exiting" from the formal economy (Hyden 1980) or, if they were led by large-scale or prosperous farmers, to lobby for good agricultural policy (Bunker 1987; Bates 1981).

been understood largely in terms of patron-client relations and the manipulation of tribalist ideologies, and thus as essentially ad-hoc or ideological, rather than as institutionalized in state structure. The superficiality of core-periphery linkages has often been presumed. (Paradoxically, the territorial integrity of the state has also been taken mostly for granted.) At the same time, local arenas are often conceptualized as prepolitical (as in the "natural" village community) or apolitical (as in the model of atomized smallholders as a sack of potatoes). Studies of the African state since the 1970s have not paid much attention to what Mamdani (1996) calls the local state, its structural connections to the center, or the mechanisms that produce the territorial grounding of state power.

The main point of this book is that rural political topography in sub-Saharan Africa is highly uneven, and that because of this rural localities and provinces have been incorporated into the modern state in highly variable ways and to varying extents. To delineate this political topography is to lay the basis for explaining a wide variety of social phenomena and political processes, as G. William Skinner's work suggested for China (Little 1989:79). Even patron-client relations in Africa vary in their legitimacy, staying power, dependence on state resources, and implications for collective action. As African states relinquished control of markets in the late 1980s and 1990s, and as the winds of multipartism swept across political landscapes, observers have been confronted with new evidence of the enduring political salience of region and regionalism in African politics, spatial unevenness in the depth and robustness of state-society linkage, and variation in the capacities of subnational groups to mobilize politically, self-govern, and innovate.

In every decade since the 1950s there has been case-specific empirical work on politics in rural Africa, core-periphery linkage, state building in the provinces, and local state reform. In some of this work, cross-case differences have been detailed and analyzed. Close observers have noted that specificities of local context go far in determining the actual effects of top-down attempts to establish or redefine political and institutional process or linkage.[3] Even so, there have been few attempts to model patterns of local or regional variation or to theorize their political effects (especially for the postcolonial period).[4] This may be because local political dynamics seem

---

[3] Recent examples are Harbeson 1990; Beck 1996; Forrest 1998.
[4] An exception is a superb literature on East Africa that explains different modes of rural social protest in settler colonies (Kenya and Zimbabwe) in terms of the level of commercialization

fundamentally contingent, deeply historical, and almost infinitely variable. Jeffrey Rubin (1996) makes this case explicitly in his studies of regional variation in core-periphery linkages in Mexico. He documents local specificity in the ways in which the postrevolutionary party-state of the PRI (the Partido Revolucionario Institucional) was implanted in different peasant societies in Mexico, and argues that the variations are so complex that they simply defy the kind of theorization that is valued in political science. Rubin is surely correct at some level. The problem is that without theory, it is difficult to accumulate and amplify insights from research, to think about causality (to hypothesize or "predict"), and to make nonarbitrary assessments about how structure and agency interact in any given context. Perry Anderson (1974:7–8) framed the generality-versus-specificity dilemma in the historical sociology of Europe in these terms:

> Often, either "abstract" models were constructed or presupposed – not only of the absolutist state, but equally of the bourgeois revolution or the capitalist state – without concern for their effective variations, or "concrete" local cases were explored without reference to their reciprocal implications and interconnections.... The practical consequences of this division are often to render general concepts – such as [mode of production] – so remote from historical reality that they cease to have any explicative power at all; while particular studies – confined to delimited areas or period – fail vice-versa to develop or refine any general theory.

Anderson's claim resonates in African studies, where models of the African state, or African peasantry, have tended to be too general to register the effects of rural political forces that can vary – in politically decisive ways – across space. Absence or failures of theory in African studies can carry additional costs. Conceptions about African idiosyncrasy and the ultimate unknowability of political cause and effect ("the irrationality of events") are more likely to prevail, and to rationalize failures of will and politics that would not stand in other contexts.

This study has proposed a model of rural social variation and its institutional and political effects. Although some will surely find the claims too broad, they will perhaps agree that most of the existing work on rural political trajectories is too ideographic. And insofar as the model here was deduced from general principles about collective action, state building, and

---

of rural labor. See for example Arrighi 1970; Saul 1973; Berman and Lonsdale 1992; Furedi 1989. Freeholding peasantries are distinguished from sharecroppers and proletarians. Another literature contrasts patterns of rural government and politics in Kenya and Tanzania (Barkan 1984). Insights thereof have not, however, been widely generalized outside these particular contexts.

political choice, it can travel beyond West African cases to agrarian society and core-periphery linkage in other regionally divided countries – including South Africa, Mexico, Brazil, India, Iraq, China, and the former Soviet Union – where rulers undertake reforms of center-local relations in provincial and regional settings that differ widely in their political organization, dynamics, and established connections to the center.

In this conclusion, I offer an assessment of the model that is based not so much on how well it fits with the empirical materials presented here (that is done in earlier chapters) as on its ability to speak to a few pressing practical and theoretical concerns. The discussion is organized under five headings: variation in rural political capacity, form and reforms of the local state, the fate of the center, rural Africa and the failure of developmentalism, and structure and choice.

I. Variation in Rural Political Capacity

Much of the general work on African politics portrayed peasantries not only as homogenous across space and politically unstructured, but also as uniformly excluded and oppressed by the state. As African states were weakened by economic crisis and then neoliberal reforms in the 1980s and 1990s, liberal notions of civil society were grafted onto this basic state-versus-society model.[5] Rural society, defined in opposition to the state, came to be seen as made up of local communities or associational networks that were more or less egalitarian and composed of either "free" political agents or natural communal groupings that were linked by shared interests. Rural communities were therefore presumed to possess inherent (democratic) self-governing capacity. Some pointed to the continuing vitality of local political institutions like chieftaincy, and argued that these enhanced rural Africa's potential for democratic self-governance. Skeptics like Mahmood Mamdani stressed the authoritarian and even reactionary nature of institutions that structured political life in many provincial settings; these concerns have been echoed in much recent research on decentralization, multipartism, and community resource management in Africa.[6] Recent discussions of the essential political character of rural Africa have thus produced three competing models – provincial Africa as politically inert, as

---

[5] See examples and critiques of this conceptualization in the various contributions to Harbeson, Rothchild, and Chazan 1994.

[6] See for example Beck 1998; Blundo 1998b; Ribot 1999; Munro 2001.

progressive, and as authoritarian – yet little by way of theory or research to get a handle on the debate.

The preceding chapters suggest that what we have here is, in part, an empirical question, in the sense that the political character of agrarian society in Africa differs across space. What appear to be competing characterizations can actually be capturing different realities in different rural settings.

We have proposed a map of regional political organization that emphasizes variation, and that thus advances the discussion. Localities are modeled as structured political arenas that vary in their degree of hierarchy, social cohesion, intensity and nature of internal divisions, modes of labor control and land allocation, capacity for collective action, and autonomy. Society at the microscopic level can be structured by gender, lineage, caste, ethnic, landlord-stranger, creditor-debtor, and class-like relationships. These can constitute powerful mechanisms of sociopolitical cohesion and control. Meanwhile, there are various forms of connection to the center, and these have often been constituted via "fusions" of state and local power. Resulting syncretisms are captured better in Marxian and Gramscian conceptions of societal power as shored up by the state, or Foucault's visions of state power insinuated in microscopic social processes, than in liberal models that imagine society in opposition to the state.[7]

This study identified a set of "ideal type" variations in rural social organization and advanced hypotheses about their political effects.

For peasantries engaged in production of agricultural commodities for the market, the differences emphasized here are the degree of hierarchical cohesion (which affects bargaining power of rural actors) and the manner in which rural elites appropriate a share of rural wealth (which shapes their interest in collaborating with the regime). In the typology of rural sociopolitical organization that was proposed in Chapter 2, zones of commercial, peasant agriculture fall into three broad types: hierarchical (vertically cohesive) societies in which elites appropriate agricultural surpluses directly (as in capitalist production), hierarchical societies in which elites are economically dependent upon the state, and nonhierarchical societies. There is a fourth category in the typology of social-structural variation: it is really a catch-all for rural societies that are not engaged in commercial agriculture. Labor-exporting zones, nomadic societies, and zones of pure self-provisioning fit into this category. They are regions that are weakly

[7] See for example Gramsci 1988 and Foucault 1980.

incorporated into the modern state: builders of the French colonial empire referred to them dismissively as *l'Afrique inutile*.

This schema directs attention to the highly uneven sociopolitical topography of most African countries and to the implications of this for state building, economic development, regime maintenance, democracy, and state preservation. Regional variations that matter have to do with settlement patterns, property-rights regimes, the scope and salience of non-state political institutions, modes of market access, and cultural homogeneity (shared language and belief in a shared future, shared social institutions). These factors make a difference for how, how thoroughly, how durably, and how democratically regional and subnational populations are (or are likely to be) incorporated into the "national" state. A thicker description could theorize these aspects of rural life in processural terms or as sites of ongoing struggle and renegotiation, rather than as structural features of rural settings. I agree that that would capture more of the complexity of local reality, and I hope that this study contributes to such refinements.

The six regions that served as the principal case studies were observed in two main time periods: the colonial era with an emphasis on the 1940s and the nationalist struggles of the 1950s, and the independence years when African countries reached the high-water mark of postcolonial state building, the era from about 1960 through the 1980s. Each case study tracked state building across three functional domains of state action: territorial administration, rural development, and crop marketing. In the course of the analysis, subregional variations were encountered. These called for brief consideration of several subcases that expanded the empirical scope of the study.[8] The typology draws attention to basic contrasts in the political character and dynamics of regions and rural communities. A few contrasts in the make-up of the local political arena seem particularly stark, suggestive of new avenues of research, or relevant to current discussions of states and state reform in Africa.

The reality and continuing political salience of rural social hierarchy – rooted largely in land-tenure regimes – is impossible to miss. Fauré (1993:325–6) captured this in his flat assertion that "local networks of political domination in Africa are frequently strongly hierarchical and

---

[8] There were side glances at seven additional cases. They are, in Senegal, the Senegal River Delta, the Sine part of the groundnut basin, and Upper and Middle Casamance; in Côte d'Ivoire, the distinction between the Southeast and Southwest, and the case of Sanwi; and in Ghana, Dagomba and the coastal strip of Ghana.

personalized, often forming a monopoly at the level of the local community." This basic fact of life in much of provincial Africa belies images of inherent egalitarianism or natural democracy. Where dominant lineages or members of old aristocracies control land or market access, possibilities for autonomous political action (including associational autonomy) on the part of individuals are extremely restricted. As Allman (1993) noted in her studies of Asante in Ghana, when these conditions hold, possibilities for engaging ordinary farmers as full or "free" participants (citizens) in the formal political sphere are limited.

Mamdani trained the spotlight on rural despots – the state's agents in the localities – but in doing so seemed to suggest that all were sheer creations of the center, and thus susceptible to changes in political priorities and direction at the top, and also likely to be overthrown in the event of any genuine empowerment of rural citizens. There is however a politically important difference between rural despots who were imposed on localities under the governing strategies we have called administrative occupation and usurpation, on the one hand, and home-grown notabilities on the other. The former conform more closely to Mamdani's model: they have shorter time horizons, and have less incentive and power to cultivate and patronize local dependents and followers, and are more dependent upon the center than the latter. Home-grown notabilities' power and influence is older, multi-stranded, and more deeply rooted. They have long-term stakes in reproducing the specifically *rural* sources (both ideological and material) of their privilege and influence. Pure agents of the center who have been parachuted into the rural areas – such as the *sous-préfets* and politicians who govern rural populations in southern Cote d'Ivoire or Lower Casamance – occupy positions far more tenuous and insecure than the old locally dominant lineages and aristocracies whose staying power has been remarkable in places like central and northern Senegal, and the Asante region of Ghana.

In rural societies that are not steeply hierarchical, political arenas are more open. Here we find the greatest potential for progressive reform, and also perhaps the greatest potential for political volatility and instability. In cases where there is social egalitarianism, what seems decisive is the presence or absence of mechanisms of horizontal cohesion and coordination. This was one lesson of the comparison and contrast between southern (especially southwestern) Cote d'Ivoire and the Lower Casamance, and we return below to the implications of this for our original model of rural social variation. What the empirical material showed was that horizontally cohesive Diola society in Lower Casamance has exhibited considerable capacity for collective action and for enforcing downward accountability on community-level political leaders. It seems that the kinds of microscopic political institutions that can work, as Elinor Ostrom (1990) has shown, in the effective management of common-property resources (enforceable rules, norms of reciprocity, and criteria to determine community membership and divisions of labor) can have analogous or spill-over effects in the political sphere. The Diola case also suggests that horizontal cohesion can work as an impediment to top-down attempts to manipulate local political processes.

In southwestern Côte d'Ivoire, there is an absence not only of indigenous rural hierarchy, but also of integrating social institutions in general. Central rulers selected a governing strategy of administrative occupation, as in Lower Casamance, but in southwestern Côte d'Ivoire this helped perpetuate a provincial institutional void. A net effect is up-country political life that is prone to explosions of conflict within communities that neither Abidjan rulers nor prominent local personalities and officials can control. In southern Côte d'Ivoire conflicts are taking the form of communal conflict over land tenure rules. There are virtually no local political arenas or institutions that exist to serve as sites or conduits for collective dispute resolution, goal setting, local conflict management, or state intervention. Capacity for sustained rural collective action (as opposed to sporadic destructive outbursts) seems particularly low in cases like this, as Elinor Ostrom's work would suggest. Possibilities for local institution building may be the most open-ended in these settings, in the sense that there are few preexisting structures to bias the outcomes, and that one can envision a wide variety of potentially workable forms. Possibilities for success are also perhaps the most remote in these settings.

A well-studied case that is not analyzed here sheds additional light on this issue. The part of southeastern Nigeria sometimes referred to as Iboland is similar to Lower Casamance in its absence of steep social hierarchy and the presence of strong mechanisms of horizontal social cohesion. This part of Nigeria was the site of what some have called anglophone Africa's most successful experiments in local government in the 1950s and 1960s. Horizontal associations taxed themselves to mobilize capital for local investment projects, democratic politics was open and competitive, and constituents exercised voice in trying to keep their representatives accountable. The local government institutions were crushed by Nigeria's federal government in 1966. It is difficult to resist comparison with the case of Lower Casamance, where similar logics of horizontal cohesion and political decentralization organize rural society. It was geographer Paul Pélissier who identified the Diola in 1960 as more ready for democracy than people anywhere else in rural Senegal. There may be particular structural configurations of rural society – lack of steep hierarchy, presence of horizontal cohesion – that are particularly propitious for the development of democratic local government.

Openness of local political arenas in relatively nonhierarchical societies seems to have another important effect. The phenomenon of community leadership by successful "native sons" or intellectuals – including teachers and those who have left the rural areas to make their fame and fortunes in the capital cities – seems more prominent in these settings. Urbanites organize "hometown associations" in places like southeastern Côte d'Ivoire (and, incidentally, in the coastal areas of central Senegal, where hierarchy is also weak) to provide capital and leadership for local investment projects. Elementary and high school teachers are prominent in community politics in these settings. Once you notice this difference, it does seem logical that outsiders or intellectuals are more likely to be local innovators in rural societies without aristocracy or rigid gerontocracy. In much of the Senegal River Valley, by contrast, stark social hierarchy appears to have been an impediment to economic and social innovation on the part of successful emigrants. Until the drought of the 1980s, at least, emigrants' remittances that were invested in public goods tended to go into mosques and other symbols of order and continuity.

Two cases underscored limitations of the original typology of rural social organization, and thus called for a more inductive process of theory refinement or reformulation. The first was Lower Casamance, where the presence of integrative mechanisms not provided for in the original typology – that is, mechanisms of horizontal cohesion – proves to have great political salience, as we have just noted. The fact that this configuration is by no means unique to Lower Casamance means that it needs more systematic and explicit consideration. A second anomaly was encountered in a subregion of the Senegal River Valley, the Delta zone. The peasantry here was, in effect, *created by* the state through a settlement scheme. Rural society in this subregion did not fit neatly into the original four-part typology, and was animated by social dynamics that seem to be particular to the circumstances of its origins. Given the prominence of settlement schemes in East African landscapes, especially in Kenya, Tanzania, and Zimbabwe, this is another social configuration that would have to be incorporated into a more complete theory.

II. Forms and Reforms of the Local State

This text places the spotlight on the political calculations that shape rulers' choices about what kinds of local states to build to integrate regions into the national political space, govern rural populations, and structure the distribution of power and prerogative between central rulers and local notabilities. By placing the argument in a time frame of several decades, the analysis underscores the basic fact, all too often overlooked in the recent literature on reform of the local state in Africa, that current rounds of institutional restructuring are played out in settings that are minutely structured by preexisting core-periphery linkages and by long histories of center-local conflict and bargaining. The analysis here assumes that regimes design core-periphery linkages to better tax and control regional populations, and in so doing it highlights the fact that achieving these objectives has constituted a central and decisive challenge of state formation in modern Africa. Rulers can be expected to try to institutionalize (lock in) and maximize the political advantages vis-à vis the regions that they secure by winning control of the central state. The terrain charted in this book shows that rulers' institution-building strategies produce forms of local state that can differ across space, even within a single country. This is because rulers' institutional choices are forged in response to different kinds of regional political opportunity and challenge.

Institutional structure itself can thus be modeled as the result of bargaining and competition between central and local actors. This analytic formula can be contrasted to two alternatives. The first alternative is the set of models of institutional change in the African countryside that see "reform" in terms of the unilateral (autonomous) choices of central governments. Such models are often found in public administration literature. Yet even politically explicit models of the African state can contain what is essentially the same mistake. As Burman (1984), Mamdani (1996), Scott (1998), and others have pointed out, the entire problem of rural or territorial governance has often been defined as inherently administrative – that is, as technocratic, developmentalist, necessarily top-down, and ultimately requiring little more than effective assertion of state authority – rather than as political in the sense of involving struggles over the purposes and meaning of the national state, of authority and power in the regions, and of the local community itself. Colonial rulers in sub-Saharan Africa rarely admitted that governing rural Africa was a political process; they insisted instead on defining the exertion of state power in the countryside as simply "native administration." Models emphasizing the autonomy (and even the neutrality) of central rulers often carried over to postcolonial studies of territorial administration and rural development. Central rulers have been viewed as relatively unconstrained by provincial social forces, because of either the overwhelming power of the center, the weakness of rural society, or the self-evidently beneficial character of the institutional and economic changes ("reforms") the center seeks to impose. State reform in sub-Saharan Africa in the 1990s, especially political decentralization and economic liberalization in the rural areas, has often been understood in these terms.

A second alternative to a bargaining model of institutional choice is the set of models that define rulers' choices as a more or less straightforward response ("supply response") to societal demands. This work builds on the basic intuition of pluralist explanations of governmental policy outcomes. These theories are found in the public choice literature on federalism and the rise of other forms of limited government (Buchanan and Tullock 1962; Weingast 1995). This approach has not had great resonance in African studies because most analysts would insist on conceptualizing African ruling elites as actors or interest groups (or social classes) in and for themselves, rather than as neutral processors or mediators of societal demands. African cases thus help to reveal what is unacknowledged and assumed in the public choice model: the logically prior existence of a constitutional order (which would itself register a balance of power between rulers and ruled) that defines the national unit and makes rulers responsive to powersharing demands.

The approach advanced here goes beyond both state-autonomy and public-choice (or pluralist) approaches by locating and charting the effects of center-periphery bargaining. It focuses attention on the *existence* of subnational variations in "the local state" and in institutional frameworks of center-regional relations, and *explains* this variation in African contexts, where national integration itself is an ongoing and contested political process. This approach complements and extends a new and growing literature in political science on territorial politics and national integration.

Two general assumptions of core-periphery bargaining models are, first, that the interests of central rulers (the central state) are distinct from and, when it comes to issues of taxation and local autonomy, potentially at odds with those of regional actors, and second, that there is variation in the strength of regional actors. Analysts differ in theorizing the sources and effects of these variations in bargaining strength. Some recent work undertaken outside the African context has attributed differences in regional political clout to locational or ideological factors, institutional factors such as political party structure, resource endowments, and/or group size. Examples of this can be found in bargaining models that have been employed recently in studies of federalism and decentralization politics in post-Soviet Russia.[9] Katherine Stoner-Weiss (2001), for instance, offers an explanation for variation in the autonomy vis-à-vis the center of constituent units of the Russian Federation. Drawing on a repertoire of classic political economy concepts, she defines the political strength and interests of regional elites in terms of their cohesiveness as a group (which is determined in her model by group size), concentration and specificity of assets in the regional economy, and regional elites' economic autonomy vis-à-vis the center. The last variable is a function of the presence or absence of exportable assets (oil, minerals, foodstuffs) and the extent to which regional economies are subsidized by the federal budget. Stoner-Weiss's approach, like the argument developed in this book, is consistent with long traditions of theorizing in both historical and "modern" political economy that see macropolitical outcomes as determined from the bottom up; that is, by variation in the power and interests of societal actors in their confrontations with central states.[10]

By incorporating Africa into this stream of research we have moved the discussion in two new directions. The analysis here emphasizes social-structural determinants of variation in regional capacities for collective action and in the bargaining power of regional actors. It thus reconnects the study of territorial politics to work on modes of production, property and property-rights regimes, class and communal structure, and social-structural transformation. This study also innovates by insisting that the

---

[9] See Treisman 2001, who sees an ideational variable ("regional oppositional sentiment") as one key factor in explaining regional political strategies in the former Soviet Union, and Solnick 1998 on the Soviet Union itself. On Latin America, see for example Willis, Garman, and Haggard 1999, who emphasize party structure as a determinant of local actors' interests and bargaining strength, and Snyder 2001a, who also stresses institutional factors. Hechter 2000 and Yang 1996 identify distance from the center as a key variable. On the United States, Alston and Ferrie 1999 provide a social-structural account (focusing on changes in rural modes of production) to explain how regional elites' interests vis-à-vis the center can change over time.

[10] Levi 1988, Rogowski 1989, and Frieden 1991 produced influential variants of this approach in the 1990s. The basic logic is stark in Marxist historical sociology, as well as in the work of Barrington Moore and some of his academic contemporaries and descendants, such as Tilly 1966 and Skocpol 1979.

330

institutional frameworks that set the terms and rules of core-periphery interaction in any given setting *are themselves* products of earlier rounds
of center-regional bargaining, and thus cannot be taken automatically as
"independent variables" in analysis. This argument really cannot be avoided
in any setting where institutions are contested, unstable, or undergoing reform. A complete causal explanation would surely have to account for variation in purely state-centric factors. The heuristic advantage of the more
parsimonious model, such as the one we have opted for here, is that it
makes it possible – in theory, of course – to isolate and study some of the
macropolitical and institutional effects of societal variation.

The present study required an analytic device for describing variation in
the design of institutions linking center and rural periphery in West Africa –
that is, in the design of the local state.[11] I postulated that, in effect, institutional structure and process vary along two distinct dimensions, one
having to do with spatial concentration or deconcentration of the state apparatus, and the other having to do with the extent to which governing authority and prerogative is devolved to local actors. This model produced four
different "ideal type" institutional configurations. These were named powersharing, usurpation, administrative occupation, and non-incorporation.
Case studies showed that the ideal types did capture significant cross-case
differences in the design and functioning of state institutions in the six main
regions studied here.[12] Institution-building trajectories charted in the chapters also showed that rulers' institutional choices can change over time, and
vary across space within the boundaries of one country. Most importantly,
the cases tested the argument about the conditions under which central
rulers would choose each particular strategy. The basic argument was that
rulers choose on the basis of calculations about whether rural elites will
be useful allies, threatening rivals, weak *interlocateurs* who might however
engage in local-level entrepreneurialism to enhance their bargaining power
vis-à-vis the center, or simply politically nonexistent or irrelevant. Where
there are useful allies, we expect a local state that institutionalized powersharing between central and local elites. Threatening rivals are targets

---

[11] To do this, we reconfigured existing understandings of substantive (that is, real rather than
de jure) variation in patterns of state intervention/incorporation of rural African societies.
Existing literature has, in effect, focused on either differences in degrees of interventionism
(mostly in economic realm) or radicalism, referring mostly to the extent to which populism
was used as a tool against the neotraditional elite.

[12] In the Senegal River Valley we encountered a mixed or hybrid institutional strategy that
was not anticipated in the original typology.

of state building aimed at usurpation. Where local political arenas are open to political entrepreneurs, administrative occupation (which preempts the development of autonomous local institutions) is expected to be the institutional strategy of choice. Non-incorporation is a strategy that is likely in zones that are not politically threatening or economically interesting (i.e., not taxable) as far as central rulers are concerned.

What are the implications of past institutional choices, and of the different institutional scenarios, for new rounds of local state building? What are implications for the likely course of the de facto devolutions now under way, and for the kind of "genuine democratic decentralization" that is an official objective of the de jure reforms that many African countries have undertaken since about 1990? What do the different institutional scenarios imply about the likelihood of breakdown of institutional links between center and rural periphery, and what might happen in such an event? Let us consider these matters in general at first, and then see what happened in the 1990s rounds of local state reform in three of the cases considered in preceding chapters.

Where indigenous elites wield nonstate forms of power over their subjects and dependents, and yet have become economically dependent upon the center, we find institutionalized powersharing arrangements (spatial deconcentration, devolution of authority) that allow regimes to rule the countryside indirectly, through these chiefs and notabilities. Such configurations of power and interest produced a kind of "decentralized despotism" (Mamdani 1996) that was one of the most enduring forms of local state in twentieth-century Africa. It was resilient because it was rooted locally, most notably in land-tenure rules. In future rounds of local state building, central rulers can be expected to work to shore up the influence of rural elites *as long as* these regional barons, aristocrats, and brokers continue to maintain local order on behalf of the center. Regimes will not fear devolving power to trusted provincial allies.

Powersharing of this sort is not conducive to economic innovation, for this almost always destabilizes the relations of labor control and land access that underpin local notabilities. It is also not particularly open to expanded grassroots participation in local governance. The most noticeable effect of "democratic decentralization" in such cases, at least in the short run, is likely to be the further empowerment of the preexisting local elite. As Mamdani (1996:298) noted, central rulers are likely to be enthusiastic proponents of devolutions of political power that shore up conservative rural elites and thus work as a check on, and counterweight to, representative demands from

Conclusion

urban civil society.[13] If these predictions are valid, then they should hold in cases like the Wolof groundnut basin, the Upper and Middle Senegal River Valley, northern Cameroon and northern Nigeria, Chad, the Zerma and Hausa regions of Niger, and Morocco. In a study of politics in the old and hierarchical societies of northern Ghana, Ivor Wilks (1989:4) anticipated much the same in describing decentralizing reforms on the agenda for the 1990s (including inauguration of new, elected District Assemblies) as "similar in some respects to the indirect rule essayed in the colonial period."[14] In the Korhogo region of northern Côte d'Ivoire, where social hierarchy is present but more attenuated than it is in the cases just mentioned, we would expect changes in the same direction (i.e., the center devolves prerogative to the local state), if not to the same degree.[15]

Where rural areas have been governed via administrative occupation, the state apparatus is suspended above rural society (spatial concentration of the state apparatus, centralization of prerogative in the hands of the regime's direct agents). Central rulers will be reluctant to decentralize, either in the sense of building new state institutions at local levels or in the sense of actually devolving power, for the reasons that made them reluctant to do so in earlier periods. They will not want to create new political arenas that political entrepreneurs or opponents can capture and use as bases from which to launch demands on the center, or organize challenges to the center. Rulers' second-best option, if they are forced to take it, will be to try to engineer administrative deconcentrations that ensure that the regimes' direct agents retain control of new local institutions, as well as the old ones. When that happens, the central government moves closer to rural communities, but there is no increase in local participation or real political competition.

---

[13] On devolution of power as a strategy to insulate past political wins from new, democratic pressures, see also Frye 1997 and Boylan 1998. Devolution can thus be seen as a lock-in strategy, or as a preemptive strike on the part of elites who fear wider democratic forces. On the structural role of what O'Donnell 1993 called "brown areas" (nondemocratic political spaces within an otherwise democratic country) in the politics of transition, see also Gibson 1997 and Munro 2001.

[14] See also Ribot 1999.

[15] This seems consistent with what was happening until the end of 1999. The December 1999 coup in Côte d'Ivoire dealt the death blow to the regional geopolitical order built by Houphouet from 1950 to his death in 1993. By the late 1990s politics at the national level was structured along a stark north-south fault line. In the legislative elections of December 2000, presidential contender Alassane Ouattara sought the legislative seat for Korhogo, but was barred by the Supreme Court from contesting this seat. Ouattara, generally seen as the "North's candidate" for the Ivoirian presidency, was barred from competing in presidential elections. See Toungara 2001.

If devolution (or breakdown) should occur in cases that have known long histories of administrative occupation, there is potential for great political innovation, and also for great political volatility. One variable that will impact the outcome, as I argued above, is the presence or absence of local, nonstate institutions that can produce social cohesion and provide mechanisms for local governance. Where these *are* present, getting the center to lift its heavy boot is likely to have its most productive effects. This seems to be the kind of reform scenario envisioned by democratic decentralization's most avid proponents, the leftist communitarians who value local autonomy and liberals who hope to see more procedural democracy (and responsive government) at the local level. What the present study underscores, however, is that the rural social-structural conditions for this positive outcome are not uniformly present in Africa, or even within any given country. Of the cases encountered so far in this study, Lower Casamance and southeastern Nigeria are the cases that might fit in this category. In general, social equality is better for democracy *if* you have social organizations and institutions that allow you to transcend the collective action problem.

Where regimes pursued institutional strategies of usurpation aimed at displacement of a wealthy and influential local elite, institutions were spatially deconcentrated, but power was centralized. There were dense networks of state institutions at the local level, but the center's own direct agents retained control. What is the likelihood of institutional reform in these settings, and what are its likely effects? Here it is more difficult to answer in the abstract, for in many places the old rural elite was never truly destroyed by usurpation, and will hover in the political background as a "counterelite," eager to reassert its privileges. This is certainly what we see in the Asante region of Ghana and in analogous cases like the Buganda region of Uganda. We would expect parallels in the Abomey region of Benin, and perhaps echoes in the Chagga district of Tanzania.[16] The hypothesis that emerges from this study is that central rulers will continue to see these groups as competitors or antagonists. They will be reluctant to devolve power without instituting many safeguards to protect the center's capacity to redistribute wealth on a national scale and to preserve central politicians' direct access to local constituencies.

---

[16] Perhaps the most extreme case of usurpation in all of postcolonial Africa is the expulsion of the Tutsi in the "Rwandan Revolution" from 1959 to 1961. Their institutional power in the rural areas was destroyed. See Newbury and Newbury 2000.

Conclusion

With the dismantlement of institutions to control rural markets for credit, inputs, and commodities, however, it will be more difficult for the center to achieve the desired effect of constraining the power and influence of the provincial economic elite. State agents and direct representatives of central rulers (such as local politicians beholden to the center) are likely to find themselves in intensifying competition with more autonomous local notabilities for control over the institutions of the local state. In these contests, each side will surely try to enlist the support of ordinary farmers and town dwellers. Ethnic appeals, fights over who wields legitimate authority at the local level, and multisided struggles for control over extractable resources will probably figure prominently in these contests. A challenge for local elites will be to expand their bases of wealth accumulation without destroying the ideologies and economic relations that bind together their political clienteles. This is another scenario that could produce an expansion of democracy, although citizens may find their part in participatory government confined to their role as voters who are linked to local big-men and chiefs by economic and patron-client ties. It could also lead to forms of conflict between local elites and the center that cannot be contained in the institutions and procedures of electoral democracy.

In zones of non-incorporation, central rulers have governed minimally and from afar. Under these conditions, state reform delivered in the name of democratic decentralization is likely to amount to what one Senegalese Rural Council president called "an empty envelope" (O'Bannon 2000). In the geostrategic triages conducted by hard-pressed central rulers, zones that have been long neglected will probably be the first abandoned. This may be more or less what we can expect for large swaths of the Sahel, for example, where incorporation into the modern state has been minimal at best, and in vast reaches of the Congo where state decay has left entire regions on their own, with no presence or sign of the central government. Concrete changes may follow from rulers' decisions to *stop policing the boundaries* of regions that have not been deeply incorporated into the modern state. This leaves local populations even more vulnerable to invasions and predations by neighboring groups, as both farmers and herders in the West Africa savannah have found. Rural communities located near sources of extractable minerals in the Congo Basin have perhaps suffered the most from state withdrawals that open the door to predatory behavior on the part of opportunistic neighbors.

Expectations of the new wave of state reform in the 1990s were high. Because political and administrative decentralization was accompanied by moves to liberalize rural commerce, privatize the export trade, and disman-tle the institutions of state-led rural development, there were important ruptures with earlier patterns of regional incorporation and state building. To what extent do the expected patterns of change show up in the cases we studied?

A. 1990s Continuities in Local State Forms

In the core agricultural regions of West Africa – that is, in the traditional export-producing regions – what is striking about local trajectories in the 1990s is the *continuities* with earlier patterns of institutional development, rather than the ruptures. In part, this can reflect the fact that many of the de jure transformations of the local state – such as dismantling of statist producer cooperatives, the introduction of partisan electoral competition at the regional and village level, and expansion of the fiscal and legal powers of town governments – are fairly new, and their full consequences are not yet clear. Partly, however, the continuities reflect rulers' ongoing attempts to manage the kinds of regional threats and opportunities that are the focus of this book.

Senegal in the 1990s.   Many detailed local studies track the "democratic decentralization" that has been under way in Senegal since the mid-1980s. Most of them concentrate on the politically strategic Wolof groundnut basin, where state controls over the groundnut economy were dismantled in the 1980s and early 1990s, and where the administrative, political, and land-use prerogatives of elected Rural Councils and municipal government have gradually expanded.[17] As Diop and Diouf pointed out in 1992, these reforms and the many analyses of their possible effects raised the issues that had provoked the fight over Animation Rurale in the early 1960s: Could there be, and should there be, grassroots participation in politics and eco-nomic autonomy for small farmers, so that peasants are brought into direct contact with the state and the market? Should the institutions and pro-cesses of rural indirect rule be dismantled? Could they be? (Diop and Diouf 1992a).

---

[17] See Niang 1991; Diop and Diouf 1992a:86; Diop and Diouf 1992b; Dione 1992; Vengroff 1993; Kante 1994; Ribot 1996, 1999; Beck 1996, 1999; Patterson 1996, 1999; Blundo 1995, 1998b. After 1996 half of the seats on the Rural Councils were allocated on the basis of proportional representation. Suppression of the "winner takes all" voting rule intensified electoral competition in the localities. See also Villalon 1993, 1995.

Conclusion

Studies of reform's effects – that is, of outcomes to date of reforms that have been under way for more than a decade – reveal strong continuities with the earlier era of rural politics and administration in central Senegal. Contemporary analysts emphasize the continuing domination of decentralized institutions by the groundnut basin's long-standing rural elite, and the processes by which these local notables have captured control of the resources and prerogatives so distributed. There has been a stark deterioration of the regime's capacity to pump cash into rural outposts of the state, but local government and party institutions still function as purveyors of central resources and as sites that local elites capture in order to consolidate their personal clienteles and constituencies. Notables work to sustain some measure of legitimate authority by ensuring that some benefits trickle down to ordinary rural folk. Meanwhile, Senegal's long-time ruling party continued to rely on rural strongholds to assure its electoral victories through the 1990s, and many leading politicians count on hierarchically structured rural electoral constituencies to guarantee their places in the legislative and executive branches of government in Dakar. The institution-building strategy of powersharing still produces political pay-offs for the regime in Dakar. The opposition PDS, which won the presidency in 2000, courted Mouride leaders in the run-up to the 2000 elections and has cultivated these ties since taking power.

In Senegal, economic liberalization and the general decline of the agricultural export economy have promoted decay of some of the formal and informal institutions that structured relations between the peasants, the rural elite, and the state in the earlier period. Rural notables like the Mouride marabouts no longer derive personal profit and political resources from their control over groundnut cooperatives (which were dissolved in 1984). As the groundnut economy declined, the old land-based ties between marabouts and their followers eroded. The increasing competitiveness of rural politics in central Senegal is partly a result of these changes. Change has not been revolutionary, however: the kinds of community-level power relations that structured rural government and administration in the period from 1960 to 1985 are still very much in evidence. Local electoral competition, for example, usually revolves around rival factions within the established elite (as it did from the 1940s to the 1980s), rather than populist or popular challenges to the old aristocratic and religious leaders. As Mamadou Niang wrote in the early 1990s, decentralization and "disengagement of the state" should not have been expected to overturn the power structure of central Senegal: possibilities for real reform have been constrained by "the power of notables in the extremely stratified and hierarchical social system which is the peasant's universe. . . . These notables mediate relations between the state and the peasantry" (Niang 1991:8–9).

Southern Côte d'Ivoire. In southern Côte d'Ivoire, the politics of local state reform in the first half of the 1990s fit squarely into the center-periphery mold established in the period from 1960 to 1985. As Fauré (1993), and Crook and Manor (1998) have observed, in the Ivoirian south decentralization initiatives of the early- to mid-1990s were "reform" in name only, for virtually nothing by way of resources or administrative prerogative was devolved to newly created municipal governments and the councils elected to run them.[18] Even as the number, de jure mandates, and de facto responsibilities of municipal governments expanded in the 1990s, observers continued to stress the elected bodies' lack of connection to, or communication with, local constituencies. In the Ivoirian south, local government throughout the 1990s remained under the control of Abidjan-based politicians and administrators whose power derived from the center, rather than from the support or allegiance of local populations. Abidjan attempted to govern via top-down processes in the South. As before, rural localities did not "throw up" leaders who were then co-opted into the institutions and political processes of the regime.

The particular vulnerabilities of rural society in southern Côte d'Ivoire were much in evidence during the years of Bédié regime, which came to power with the death of Houphouet at the end of 1993 and was overthrown in a military coup d'etat at the end of 1999. Ruling-party and opposition politicians now needed rural constituencies to win elections: as fighting within the elite intensified, the PDCI split and many old-guard politicians competed by making direct ethnic appeals to rural voters. Dominant factions within the ruling party clung to power by espousing a naked xenophobia that pitted "real Ivoirians" – farmers from the South-center and Southeast – against immigrants, migrant workers, merchants, and northerners. Sporadic mobilizations of southern populations proved difficult to control or channel, given the absence of politically organized local communities and provincial notables who could have served as intermediaries for Abidjan-based politicians. The outbreaks of ethnic violence, violent land conflicts within villages, and mob justice in the core export-producing zones of the Southwest that marked the 1990s are manifestations of the problem.

---

[18] Bakary 1986; Diahou 1990; Fauré 1993; Crook and Manor 1998. See also N'Diaye 2000.

Conclusion

The state in southern Côte d'Ivoire is suspended above politically unstable rural societies, and so-called decentralizations of the early 1990s only served to accentuate this fact. Bitter struggle within the elite helped produce the 1998 Rural Property Law, which announced a plan to dispossess so-called non-native Ivoirians of their land rights and claims (Chauveau 2002). This played a key role in bringing ethnoregional tensions in Côte d'Ivoire to the breaking point in 2002.

Ghana under Rawlings. From about 1970 to the early 1980s Ghana endured a virtual collapse of the cocoa-export economy and the extensive decay of the state's rural institutional infrastructure.[19] The Rawlings regime undertook to rebuild the local state and rural economy in southern Ghana in the 1980s and 1990s. The politics of institutional choice have been remarkably similar to those observed during the Nkrumah period. Rawlings pursued a strategy aimed at consolidating a populist rural support base for the regime. By institutionalizing this constituency base, the regime hoped to bypass the old, partisan rural elite in the South and to offset the weight of its urban rivals, middle-class detractors, and Asante-based opponents (Green 1998).

In the rural areas of the South, Rawlings created "peoples committees," Committees for the Defense of the Revolution (CDRs), and District Assemblies to run local government.[20] In organizing local government, the regime sought to sideline the old partisan elite and bring "a whole new group of average citizens" to power.[21] Many teachers and ordinary farmers were indeed elected to seats in Ghana's new District Assemblies. Devolution of authority to localized instances of this newly deconcentrated state apparatus remained very limited, however. The CDRs and other rural youth brigades remained under tight central control, while in each District Assembly, one-third of all seats were filled by individuals appointed by Accra (as had been the case under Nkrumah). The regime retained a firm grip on the local state. Attempts to consolidate and institutionalize a populist rural base served Rawlings and the ruling Provisional National Defense Council

---

[19] See Beckman 1981; Mikell 1989b; Herbst 1993.

[20] On local-level administrative reforms and political mobilizations in Ghana under Rawlings, see Herbst (1993:84), who observed that in 1989 "most of the organizations that the Rawlings government [had] attempted to establish in the rural areas [were] disorganized and ineffective." See also Green 1998; Mikell 1989b; Crook and Manor 1998; and Crook and Sverrisson 2001.

[21] Green 1998:198.

(PNDC) well in the 1992 and 1996 elections. Asante was the only region of the country outside of Accra to deliver a majority vote against the regime.

The PNDC-Asante divide has usually been cast as ethnic rivalry. The reasoning laid out above, however, draws attention to long-standing economic and social-structural sources of tension between the regime and the rural elite in Ghana's cocoa belt. The Kumasi-based Asante elite along with ordinary farmers in the cocoa belt benefited disproportionately from Ghana's post-1983 economic reforms and economic upturn. As Herbst reported (1993:86–8), the Kumasi elite resented the transfer of wealth out of their region to fund state spending in other parts of the country. Not only did their long-standing economic grievances vis-à-vis the center carry over into the 1990s, but so too did some of their capacity to organize rural constituencies and to back candidates for national office. The seismic fault that had divided Nkrumah from the cocoa farmers of Asante remained active in the Rawlings era.[22] Nugent (1999) depicts the electoral battles of the 1990s as a battle between the Rawlings regime and the chiefly notables and bigwigs of the cocoa-producing core – Asante and the Eastern Region.[23] This tension shaped the character and effects of the decentralization initiatives of the Rawlings era. To read the Rawlings strategy as the politics of usurpation may be somewhat overdrawn, but something hinting of this dynamic persists in center-local politics in this region of Ghana.

Most of the literature on 1990s rounds of decentralization in Senegal, Côte d'Ivoire, and Ghana conveys a real sense of disappointment in the limited success of these reforms in promoting real democratic participation. By the argument advanced here, open-ended participation was far from what regimes were actually seeking to achieve with rural institutional reform in the 1990s, especially in the politically strategic rural zones we have just

---

[22] See Nugent 1999; Lentz and Nugent 2000. Crook and Sverrisson (1999:45) noted a general tension between the existing rural elite on the one hand, and local-level actors promoted by Rawlings' state-building initiatives on the other. Crook and Manor observe that where local leaders "such as the chiefs and the wealthy, professional often absentee elites (successful sons and daughters of the town)" are influential and active in well-established community development associations, local constituents defer to them and are less willing to go along with the state-building initiatives of the regime. Where the local elite is active and respected, local constituents are "less willing to pay [District] Assembly taxes or accord any legitimacy or usefulness to their activities."

[23] See also Berry (2002), who writes that Asante chiefs continue to compete with the Ghanaian state for shares of the economic rent generated by land transactions and/or productive forms of land use, and also for control over revenues generated through the extraction of timber and gold.

discussed. For all the weakening of the state (fiscal crisis, neoliberal reforms, institutional erosion, etc.) since the onset of economic decline, in the 1990s these regimes still possessed the incentive, some capacity, and the where-withal to sustain the basic institution-building strategies set in motion in core export-producing regions in the 1950s, if not before. Some of the most visible concessions to economic austerity and downsizing of the state came in a kind of geostrategic triage whereby the center withdrew from regions deemed to be politically and economically marginal in determining the fate of the center.

B. Embeddedness and Modes of Popular Action

State-building strategies from the 1920s to the 1980s produced clear differ-ences not only in how, but also in the *degree to which*, state institutions were implanted in rural localities. Today, state structures are far more embed-ded in rural political arenas in the Wolof groundnut basin (and the main cocoa-producing regions of Ghana) than in the cocoa-coffee region of Côte d'Ivoire. This basic difference helps explain variation in the staying power of state institutions in the rural areas, and also in their administrative ef-ficiency and malleability via top-down reform. As suggested above, it also helps explain differences in the character of local politics and modes of popular action in these regions.

The governing strategy of administrative occupation produced state institutions that were suspended above rural society. Under these condi-tions, state bureaucracy could function with less local-level entanglement. Grassroots agencies of the state were less numerous, more compact, and unlikely to be captured by local actors with their own agendas and in-terests. Rulers did not try to share power with local strongmen or build patron-client networks to co-opt and constrain the peasantry. State agen-cies appeared to have an unusually high degree of administrative capacity in the cocoa-coffee belt of southern Côte d'Ivoire in the 1960s through 1980s, and this was a reflection of these highly centralized structures of control.[24] The state did not become entangled at the grassroots. Darbon made sim-ilar observations about Senegalese administration in Lower Casamance, where the institutional profile was similar to southern Côte d'Ivoire's: in Lower Casamance through the end of the 1970s, provincial administration operated with less corruption, more hierarchy, and more responsiveness

[24] See Crook 1990. See also World Bank 1978; Gbetibouo and Delgado 1984.

341

to central directive than it did under the powersharing arrangements that prevailed in central Senegal.

What this meant, however, was that local political life, which was centered largely around land-tenure issues, was played out outside the formal structures of the state. This was true in Lower Casamance until the end of the 1970s, and has only been thrown into question in Côte d'Ivoire recently, with the placing of the new rural land law on the political agenda at the end of 1998. In Lower Casamance, there were modes of popular organization, leadership formation, and agenda setting that ultimately helped produce and sustain the guerrilla movement that emerged in 1982; this parallels in many ways the rural political mobilization that developed just across the border in Guinée Bissau. In southern Côte d'Ivoire, local political life is similarly unstructured by the state: it now takes the form of often-violent land conflicts in the towns, villages, and forests of the Southwest. State hegemony is less stable and secure in regions of administrative occupation. It is paradoxical that the more "efficient" bureaucratic apparatuses, which were less deeply rooted in localities, may be more brittle and ultimately less enduring. Perhaps this fate is common to all insulated, isolated authoritarian regimes: in these African cases, we are encountering it as a localized, rather than national-level, phenomenon. It is certainly not a problem that is universal throughout all of rural Africa.

Where rulers chose to build deconcentrated institutional apparatuses, states became more implanted in rural areas. The administrative order built from the 1950s on seems more stable (although still vulnerable to long-term change in social structure), and also more politicized. It is more buffeted by the push and pull of local factionalism, competition between influential local personalities and old families, and long-standing rivalries over land, chieftaincy, and so on that seem a permanent fixture of the provincial landscape. Machine politics is the predominant modus operandi in these settings. Administration is harnessed to the political machine at the cost of bureaucratic insulation and rationality.

What does embeddedness mean for the character of local politics? One general effect is that existing social alignments and conflicts are transported into the internal structures of government. The formal political arena is infused with an *intense localism* that often overrides national-level political issues and that stands in stark contrast to places where the state seems "irrelevant." In places like southern Ghana and the Wolof groundnut basin this kind of localism is unmistakable. Owusu (1970:248) wrote that in the 1950s Kwame Nkrumah himself was quite incidental to the electoral battles that were fought out in many rural localities of southern Ghana. Beckman (1976) argued that politics in the cocoa belt were animated in large part by the transportation of existing local conflicts into the deconcentrated instances of the party-state apparatus. The point is that in these settings, local politics is played out largely *within*, rather than almost exclusively outside, the institutions of the state (within political parties, in fights over government resources and office, etc.).

III. *The Fate of the Center*

In African studies by the mid-1960s, constitutional issues connected to the founding of new states seemed settled, and most political observers' interest in formal-legal issues of state structure waned anyway. Fights over federal versus unitary constitutions that lay at the founding crises of postcolonial states in Nigeria, Cameroon, Kenya, Uganda, Ghana, and Congo (Zaire), for example, seemed over and done with. Since the mid-1960s, "national integration" has been framed mostly as the ideological challenge of building national consciousness and identity. Almost everywhere, territorial control itself was more or less taken for granted. Rulers were assumed to be getting on with the tasks of consolidating and centralizing power at the top (and within the institutions of the central state), promoting development, and, in the most disillusioned formulations, advancing their own interests as individuals, families, or social classes.

This center-centric perspective on the African state – if I may put it that way – is now undergoing rethinking and revision. This comes in the wake of weakening of central states since the 1980s, the accumulated effects of decline in rural economies since about that time (felt intensely because of dramatic falls in world market prices for African commodities), and the development of new and highly uneven patterns of land (and labor) shortage that can spark sociopolitical change and conflict. As Bates wrote in an echo of Achebe and Keats, in many African countries the center does not hold. This is forcing analysts to return to questions of regional and local power, and to the problem of territorial integration (Reno 1998; Herbst 2000; Bates 2001; Callaghy, Kassimir, and Latham 2001).

A new territorial politics, or politics of regional competition and regionalist power plays, has flared in many countries across the African continent. Even of Ghana, a country facing no imminent threat of territorial disintegration, Lentz and Nugent (2000:23) say that "[t]he legacy of the Gold Coast as a federation of 'native states' is very obvious today." Price

(1984:191) reminds observers that in Ghana in 1957, "at the very moment of independence, two regions [Ashanti and Volta regions] were in virtual or actual revolt against central authority" and signs of opposition to the new national government in Ga itself [the region around the capital city of Accra] were evident. "Even 'national' control over the land occupied by greater Accra was contested." Senegal, with what is generally recognized as a democratic national government firmly rooted in the central ground-nut basin, has faced open rebellion in Lower Casamance and secessionist demands from that region for almost two decades. Côte d'Ivoire at the end of the 1990s was ripped along north-south lines, and torn also between the Southeast and Southwest. The Abidjan government lost control of the North in 2002 in what is widely described as a civil war.

The arguments presented in this text suggest that the challenge of territorial integration in these countries – and all three have been viewed as among the most politically developed and well integrated in sub-Saharan Africa – may have been far more determinant of state structure, national political trajectories, and even agricultural development strategy than most outsiders realized, or were inclined to theorize robustly given the prevailing social science agendas and analytic frameworks. The high levels of central state spending, and the real growth of rural economies, that took place at the heyday of the developmentalist era from 1960 to 1980 facilitated the political demobilization of the peasantry, smoothed over rural strains, and salved regional tensions.

Studies of the African state have gone far in showing how a "politics of distribution" promoted the political consolidation of postcolonial states. State spending permitted the co-optation of opposition politicians, union leaders, regional strongmen, and other potential rivals of those who captured control of the center. What was less studied, especially in understanding center-region ties, is the institutional mechanisms by which rural peripheries were tied to the center. This point has been stressed by Mamdani, who attributes the failure of democracy in most of Africa (and by implication, the staying power of various kinds of authoritarian regimes) not to distributive politics, machine politics, ethnic politics, or patron-clientelism per se, but rather to the institutional legacies of indirect rule in the countryside.

Institution building tied distinct rural peripheries, each posing distinctive risks threats and opportunities to the center, into the national space. This had consequences not only for the political character of the state (how democratic it could be), but also for its overall structure and integrity as an apparatus for controlling the national space. What was established in most places, as this text has tried to suggest, were patterns of segmented authority whereby regions and regional populations (different agrarian societies) were tied to the center, but at the same time separated from each other by the very institutions of the state (as under colonial rule). Central rulers cut different deals with regional powerbrokers depending on their political weight and willingness to participate in a state-building project orchestrated by the center. As in the former Soviet Union, where central rulers institutionalized "nationalities" and appointed native elites to represent them, these structures of political control can prove to be subversive of the territorial integration they were intended to promote (Bunce 1999). What appeared to be centralized political machines in Africa's one-party states, held together at the top by "fusions of elites" (Bayart 1985), can easily fracture along regional lines. Regionalist ideologies, institutions, constituencies, and forms of local authority can provide the basis for making new demands on a weakened center, including demands for renegotiation of center-periphery ties or the right to ignore "rules of the game" established by the center. At the extreme, regional groups can demand secession (de facto or de jure), make moves on their neighbors, or advance direct bids for control of the center.[25]

A point stressed here is that there is great unevenness in the topography of core-periphery linkages, and that this is as true today as it was at the height of developmentalism. This helps explain the wide variation we see in the political trajectories of African states since 1990, and also underscores the ongoing realities of political variation across space within any given country. Rulers in Senegal, with a firm stand in a stable, geostrategically central region, are in a position that can only be envied by rulers of Côte d'Ivoire, who have basically lost what always was a weak political foothold in the core export-producing zones of the Ivoirian south.

The geopolitics of the current era involves strategies of triage (abandonment of some regions) as well as institution-building strategies designed to shore up the center's hold via devolutions or direct occupation. The latter is most difficult now because, as Hechter (2000) argues, it involves the

---

[25] See Bunce 1999:188, who discusses Hechter 1992. Hechter (1992:276) writes that weakness of the center can encourage moves for regional autonomy "for two quite different reasons. On the one hand, it reduces the economic benefits of regional incorporation. On the other hand, it reduces the [center's] capacity to repress secessionist mobilization." This holds true not only for outright secession, but also for bids for greater regional autonomy (and also attempts to take over the center).

highest initial investment and high recurrent costs. Direct occupation of the regions (direct rule) is most difficult precisely where the fate of sitting central rulers hinges on its success – that is, where powerful regional elites pose a direct challenge to central rulers. Fiscal crises of the state and the end of state-led development make challenges of territorial integration hard for the center to resolve.

There are more everyday forms of regional or territorial politics, such as the rise of regional and hometown associations with both political and developmental agendas, and the strengthening of regionalist political parties. A widespread phenomenon is the heating up of land tenure politics as land scarcities become acute, urban dwellers "return to the land," and farmers shift from export crops to food crops that can be sold domestically.[26] There are forms of politics in the regions and localities that the center is less and less able to channel or control, but that will go far in determining prospects for the survival of the center, and the chances for economic and political progress for most Africans in coming decades.

IV. Rural Africa and the Failure of Developmentalism

Most observers of the African state have argued for some time that rulers' concerns for political survival, rather than developmentalist priorities, have animated economic policy choice. This argument can be extended to institutional choices as well. Rulers sought stable ways of taxing and governing rural producers. In doing so they were far more concerned with consolidating the political hegemony of new regimes and avoiding rural political challenge than with developmentalism. Rulers' biggest challenge in the early-postindependence decades lay in demobilizing the rural populations brought into the political arena by nationalist mobilizations of the 1950s. The solution lay in designing rural political institutions that could hinder or hamper forms of rural political organization (and economic accumulation) that rulers could not control. Strategies varied, as we have seen, but had the common effect of shoring up nonmarket controls over rural land and labor, and keeping producers out of export-crop marketing and processing. Regimes worked to tie *peasants* to the state as acquiescent subjects (either directly or indirectly) and, in the best circumstances for new rulers,

---

[26] See Woods 1994; Geschiere and Gugler 1998; Pélissier 2000; Berry 2002.

as generators of tax revenues. If taxing the peasants was too politically risky, rulers settled for political hegemony alone.[27] The net effect was to create or reinforce stagnationist tendencies in smallholder agriculture. As Keith Hart (1982:15) put it, "[t]hese preindustrial states restrict agricultural development in order to preserve their own material and social bases."

Transition from peasant farming to large-scale commercial farming through an evolutionary process of rural accumulation and class formation was, in general, an outcome that colonial and postcolonial rulers sought to avoid. There were several related reasons for this. First, such a process was a threat to the stability of the peasant farming sectors that postcolonial rulers' depended upon for political support. Second, it represented a potential challenge to rulers' ability to drain surpluses from the rural areas to finance the growth of the state. Third, it implied the "release of labor" from the rural areas and thus an acceleration of rural-to-urban migration (which rulers sought to limit). And fourth, it was associated with the rise of class and class-like tensions in the rural areas, and this is what colonial and postcolonial rulers feared above all else.[28] From the political perspective, therefore, new rulers had plenty of reason to stifle the development of rural capitalism, as the Nkrumah regime tried to do in the case of Asante. Analysts of "economic backwardness" in early-modern Europe such as Brenner (1982) would define this strategy as conservative, rather than as statist or radical as political analysts in African studies have tended to do. Yet given low productivity in peasant agriculture, African regimes, like their counterparts in France and Russia in the 1700s, had little choice but to "squeeze the peasantry" to extract resources for the state.[29] Once again, fear of peasant revolt or total rural decay placed absolute limits on this strategy. Governments like Senegal's in the 1970s and 1980s simply backed off from efforts to tax rural producers when the political risks of this seemed too high.

As Nicolas van de Walle (2001) has argued recently, African governments did, in the final analysis, have two alternatives to squeezing the peasantry.

---

[27] The preference ranking that can be inferred from the case studies here is: (1) political gain with economic gain; (2) political gain without economic gain; and (3) economic gain with political risk.

[28] See Phillips 1989.

[29] As Barrington Moore (1966:472) said of France and Russia in the eighteenth century, "the failure of commercial farming to take hold on any very wide scale meant that there was scarcely any alternative to squeezing the peasants."

In the short run they could rely on inflows of external resources to avoid too heavy a tax burden on domestic producers, as virtually all economic theory in the 1960s and 1970s advised them to do.[30] Just as Carlos V's influxes of silver from the New World delayed the buildup of internal extractive mechanisms in Spain, so too were African regimes able to get away with preserving a politically stable but economically stagnant rural base. When inflows of foreign capital began to dwindle in the 1980s, African regimes "deficit financed": they presided over the depreciation of the stock of economic and political infrastructure they had built up since the 1950s. Again, it was regimes' hold on the rural areas that made this politically possible: rural electoral support allowed regimes to counterbalance opposition in the cities, where urban populations – including African middle classes – paid a heavy price for economic decline in the 1980s and 1990s.

At just the same time, nature itself began to place dramatic limits (drought, soil exhaustion and erosion, nonexistence of new virgin land to exploit) on the capacity of rural producers in much of Africa to generate agricultural surpluses that could be appropriated by the state. Global overproduction, the rise of competitive new producers in Asia, and falling prices for most of Africa's agricultural commodities on world markets also conspired to erode the economic viability of much of the smallholder-based export-crop production in Africa.

Fifty years after independence, the entire question of "rural transformation" remains more or less as it stood in the early 1950s. It is striking that in the democratization and political reform initiatives of the early- to mid-1990s, there was little by way of national-level discussion of matters related to raising the productivity of smallholder agriculture, land tenure regimes and possible revisions thereof, or investment in rural processing of agricultural commodities. This may be because in the neoliberal era these matters are supposed to be left to the invisible hand of incremental and spontaneous social change. By the end of the 1990s it was the World Bank that began aggressively to push the land issue and to pressure governments to undertake institutional reform in this highly sensitive domain.

With downscaling of the state and liberalization of commodity and input markets in the 1990s, struggles over land tenure, communal membership

---

[30] Indeed, the whole point of Walter Rostow's *Stages of Growth: A Non-Communist Manifesto* (1960) was to encourage developing countries to mobilize investment resources on international markets in order to avoid the kinds of painful and politically disruptive methods of transforming the peasantry employed by Stalin and Mao.

and land claims, market access, and local political control were played out for the most part in the villages and small towns, rather than in courts, parliaments, and the presidency. This is what Schattschneider (1966) defined as the localization and privatization of conflict, and as such it remained below the radar of many outside political observers.[31] These processes, however, will go far in determining whether and how African farmers are able to respond to changing market opportunities, and whether the local state and, eventually, the central state will be able to create political and institutional conditions that are conducive to innovation and investment in farming.

Perhaps the core challenge for African rulers and political visionaries today is to find political formulae that can somehow generate political order (including the preservation of national states) while also allowing for economic changes that will relaunch agriculture. In confronting this problem, African state builders are not alone: to generate both political order and economic growth has been the central challenge of the modern state, and it is one that is never resolved definitively, as we in the United States can see. Samuel Huntington pointed out in 1968 that economic modernization can undermine political stability, and in the perspective of *longue durée* this is probably a truism. African rulers inherited this problem from the colonial states, which had been unable to resolve the political contradictions unleashed by postwar economic development – including rural political instability generated by growing economic inequality, over-taxation, and the coercive nature of the local state – within the framework of colonial rule. African states have remained pinned on the horns of this dilemma ever since. Economic transformation, including the land titling reforms (land privatization) that the World Bank has now placed on its development agenda for West Africa, can disrupt the rural social and political relations that underpin state control over the countryside. It can also unleash new local conflicts that the center cannot control.

---

[31] To the extent that they have been remarked upon, local and regional conflicts that have erupted in the last decade over land rights, over access to other natural resources, over citizenship, and even in partisan competition have often been described by African politicians and academic analysts alike as ethnic conflicts, ethnic rivalries, or "ethnic insurgencies." It is misleading to cast ethnicity as a purely cultural or ideational variable in these contexts, because virtually everywhere in sub-Saharan Africa, ethnic identity confers property rights in land (or denial thereof); citizenship in a local community, which must be understood as relation of coercion, property, and authority as well as one of cooperation and reciprocity (or again, exclusion from membership therein); and a political status vis-à-vis the state.

V. *Structure and Choice*

If theory is to avoid naive voluntarism, and yet not exclude choice and politics altogether, then one solution lies in models of "constrained choice." A large part of the challenge thus lies, as Tseblis (1990) and others have acknowledged, in conceptualizing *constraints*, or what some refer to more generically as "context." This can be pretty straightforward if you define context in terms of formal institutional rules, such as the rules of parliamentary procedure within a legislature. Political science has clearly gravitated toward micro and institutional theories in the last decade, and a good part of the explanation for this is the fact that this theoretical toolkit has been used to good effect in understanding political strategy and behavior in settings with fixed and clearly specified rules (such as well-institutionalized legislatures).

In confronting empirical issues having to do with institutional change and reform, however, we run up against the basic epistemological limitations inherent in any attempt to rely on this slim toolkit. If "institutional choice" (institutional design) is the outcome to be explained, then we are forced outside theories that take institutional structure as the fixed constraint within which choice operates. Rational choice gives us a micro-level theory, but rational choice itself cannot define the relevant actors; their goals, preferences, or options; the power balances; or the costs and benefits associated with various strategic possibilities.

Many political scientists have overcome some of these limitations by employing theoretically agnostic definitions of *social structure*, which involves selecting one of a range of possible conceptualizations thereof. Rogowski (1989) and Frieden (1991), for example, select "relative factor scarcity" (rather than class relationships or sectionalism) as the source of underlying social cleavages that are revealed in domestic debates over foreign trade policy. In the present analysis, I point to rural social hierarchy and rural elites' modes of surplus appropriation – rather than, for example, linguistic or cultural identity, or ethnic homogeneity or diversity, group size, or proximity to the center – as the decisive source of variation in rural societies' capacity to engage the postcolonial state. Most of these definitions of social cohesion and cleavage, conflict of interest, or power vis-à-vis the center are structuralist, and therefore can only be evaluated seriously through debate over the validity of the conceptualizations of social structure they employ. This leads directly to debate over the relative explanatory or descriptive power of competing models of social organization, and over the merits of alternative operationalizations. In a constrained-choice model, the definition of "social context" is the most fundamental source of possible theoretical bias and error. Political science cannot address this problem by relying only on individual-focused and institutionalist theories. Choice-theoretic analysis cannot separate itself completely from macrosociology.

There are practical reasons for scrutiny and innovation in theorizing about social structure. In constrained-choice models, definitions of social context are not only theories about how political settings differ and why outcomes vary across settings. These models also contain implicit propositions about how and why political outcomes can change over time. If social "givens" or constraints (such as actors' interests or the distribution of power among actors) change, then presumably the outcome we are interested in will change as well. A political science that forecloses explicit theorization of social structure is not only being disingenuous about the sources and possible arbitrariness of its assumptions and underlying models, but is also crippled in its basic analytic endeavors.

The model of institutional choice proposed here suggests that there are two basic sources of change in the institutional strategies rulers chose to govern a given region: one is a change in central rulers' basic goals or preferences, and the other is change in the region's social structure. If central rulers lost interest in supporting politically powerful regional allies, stifling provincial rivals, or even simply governing some parts of the previously incorporated rural periphery, then that would constitute a change in preferences. Although this book does not attempt to specify general conditions under which rulers' goals would change, it is clear that general weakening of the state, neoliberal reforms, and the unleashing of bitter intraelite competition have narrowed rulers' capacity and ambitions, and shortened their time horizons. Cases considered here do show, however, that there is more stability over time in African rulers' governing strategies than ideology-centered or voluntarist explanations of institutional choice would suggest.

Change in provincial social structure can also be expected to produce shifts in governing strategy, or institutional choice. Social-structural change could come in the form of significant modification of the extent (territorial scope, functional scope, or intensity) of rural social hierarchy. It could also be caused by, or manifest in, changes in how provincial notables get the material resources they need to reproduce their standing and influence in the regions, or whether they are able do so.

What produces change in rural social hierarchy and in notables' economic dependence on, or autonomy from, the center? Here the list of possibilities is very long indeed. It includes rural economic decay, out-migration and the inflow of remittances, environmental degradation, the debilitating effects of HIV-AIDS on population structure and production, arrival of resource-purveying nongovernmental institutions (NGOs), development of land markets and new regional trading patterns, technological innovation and investment in agriculture, and secularization. Transformations under way are extraordinarily complex, and highly uneven across space. It is a good time for debating theories about how rural African societies differ and change, and about the political and economic implications of this for democracy, development, and the territorial integrity of the state.

A Note on Sources, Evidence, and Measurement

I. Data and Sources

Data for this study were gathered in the course of my comparative studies of political control over rural and urban marketing circuits in Senegal and Côte d'Ivoire (Boone 1992, 1993, 1995a). Between 1984 and the mid-1990s I did field work, concentrating mostly on documentary sources, archival sources, and interviews in Côte d'Ivoire and Senegal (Abengourou, Korhogo, Man, Abidjan, Dakar, Thies, Saint-Louis, and Ziguinchor). Research was funded by grants from the Social Science Research Council, Fulbright, the McNamara scholarship of the World Bank Development Institute, and the Harvard Academy of International and Area Studies.

The present analysis expanded upon this work through a study of a wide variety of primary and secondary sources dealing with the countries concerned for the period from 1930 to 2000. Sources included studies by colonial administrators, anthropologists, historians, geographers, political scientists, and agricultural economists, and local-level studies of rural administration, development administration, electoral politics, migration patterns, and land tenure use. Valuable analyses were also written by university students in each of the countries studied, government agencies in all three countries, government-funded research institutes, aid-agency and nongovernmental-organization (NGO) monitoring teams, etc.

Many "gray" documents – unpublished studies, theses and dissertations, conference papers, and reports from governmental, nongovernmental, and academic sources – provided critical pieces of this study. Many of these I found in INADES-Documentation (the documentation center of the

Institut Africain pour le Devéloppement Economique et Social in Abidjan), the documentation center of the Centre Ivoirien de Recherche Economique et Sociale (CIRES) in Abidjan, the National Archives of the Republic of Senegal, the Centres de Documentation of the Chambres de Commerce in Abidjan and Dakar, the case-study data bank of the Centre des Etudes Supérieures en Gestion (CESAG) in Dakar, case studies and theses by students at the Université Nationale de Côte d'Ivoire's Faculté des Sciences Economiques and the Université Cheikh Anta Diop in Dakar, and the French colonial archives.

Most of this work is place and time specific (although some analysts do draw comparative assessments). One contribution of the present research is to bring hitherto unconnected material together into a unified analytic framework, which was deduced, in part, from macrosociological theories of state formation in agrarian societies.

II. Operationalization of the Dependent Variable

The dependent variable in this work is institutional structure, which is defined as having spatial and processural dimensions. How was it operationalized? What do we look for in the historical descriptive materials, reports on policy implementation and effects, and the secondary accounts of political scientists and administrators, to determine whether power/authority is centralized or devolved, and whether the state apparatus is spatially concentrated or deconcentrated at the local level? (See Lemieux 1996.) What are indicators of different values on the dependent variable? To operationalize the dependent variable and make a judgment about its value in different contexts, I pursued answers to the following questions:

A. Centralization versus Devolution of Authority

By what logic are administrative and political units demarcated (what is the strategy of *découpage administratif*)? (See Rajagopalan 1999.) Do units of territorial administration and political representation correspond with preexisting political jurisdictions and/or social collectivities, or not? Were preexisting political/administrative units deliberately dismembered by modern state builders? Do kinship and local collectivities have legal status?

Who provides/regulates access to local resources necessary for material reproduction of the household (land, labor, credit, seeds) – state agents or indigenous authorities (or neither)?

How large is the rural household and what is its internal structure? What are the political and economic prerogatives of the household head, and what does the state do to reinforce (erode) those powers?

Does anyone intermediate between the farmer (head of the farming household) and low-ranking state agents? If so, who is it, and how did she/he get this role or job? What does the intermediary gain from serving this role?

If the state appoints/selects agents to represent it at the local level, does real prerogative over the selection of these individuals lie with central authorities, or local notables? (Do local notables have veto power?) Are these local state agents outsiders or insiders to the locality? Who decides how long they get to stay in office or work in one particular locality?

Who controls the deployment of state resources (jobs, money, contracts, access to schools and health care, access to legal resources like identity papers) on the local level? To what extent do central authorities direct or supervise the local deployment of state resources?

Are state resources used to enhance the prestige and prerogatives of local notables, or to erode local notables' prestige?

Do the state's laws (e.g., land tenure law, family/inheritance law, administration of justice, laws governing local tributes and debts, and the appropriation of household surpluses) uphold or undermine the preexisting rights and privileges of the local elite? When laws bearing on these relations exist, is there enforcement (or not), and if so by whom? Are observed patterns uniform (or uneven) across space and social categories?

If there are local elections, who selects the candidates, how competitive are the elections, and who determines the outcomes? What local-level political/social considerations influence voters?

Do local big wigs have access to or influence over decisions taken at higher instances of the state apparatus? Do they hold formal offices in the local- or regional-level state apparatus? Do they hold office in higher instances of the central state?

Who controls the local-level implementation of state policy (e.g., national education policy, rural development, health policy including family planning)? (See Binder 1978; Alston and Ferrie 1999.)

What are the spheres of responsibility and range of decision of neotraditional actors, compared to those of state agents?

B. *Spatial Concentration and Deconcentration of the State Apparatus*

Are there local outposts of the party-state at the village level (e.g., official administrative offices, cells of the ruling party, agricultural cooperatives, or points of access to social services)? How resource rich (or poor) are these? How much does the central state invest in maintaining their viability and salience at the local level (for example, are offices actually staffed)? What is the de facto mandate, and functional and territorial scope of action, of these state outposts?

How many layers of administrative hierarchy are interposed between center and locality? For example, is state administration organized at the national, regional, district, and village level? What is the size and weight (importance) of each level in defining the overall character or output of political and administrative process?

How large are the "smallest" political and administrative jurisdictions: From the villagers' perspective, is the state distant or omnipresent?

Is the municipality an important political arena?

III. *Measurement*

There are many challenges to measurement of the kinds of empirical evidence considered here and to constructing quantitative measures that could be valid across space and time. With respect to comparability, there are obvious problems of collecting data across countries with different administrative and data-gathering traditions. Other problems arise in evaluating the validity of whatever numerical measures of, for example, rural administration, a government may provide. Equally daunting is the challenge of deciding what external factors to hold constant, or to somehow weight, in trying to generate data that is comparable across time and space (e.g., geographic size of the local administrative/political unit? population density? density of settlement? household size? quality of the roads and distance from the capital? quality of telecommunications?).

Future researchers will surely find ways to surmount some of these challenges. In this study, I have resorted to a logic by which evidence from one case is measured, as it were, against the standard set by the other cases. For example, the Wolof groundnut basin sets the standard for "extensive powersharing" (devolution of authority and spatial deconcentration of the state apparatus) by which the amount of powersharing in the other cases is assessed.

Appendix

By analyzing many observers' descriptions and assessments of the variables and relationships considered in a particular case, we gather data from different sources, triangulate, and gain confidence in the descriptions. One observer's anecdote, when it conforms to similar anecdotes recounted by several other observers and when it also fits with still *other* analysts' more abstract statements about general patterns and processes, becomes a data point. This method rarely gives us many numbers, and it generates still fewer that could be processed statistically. It does, however, generate a lot of footnotes.

In comparing "data" from cases arrayed cross-sectionally and/or logitudinally, other analysts' comparative assessments have been particularly useful. Pélissier (1966), Balans, Coulon, and Gastellu (1975), and Beck (1996), for example, all explicitly compare core-periphery relations across regions of Senegal. The role of local authorities in mediating land-tenure relations has been compared across regions in Côte d'Ivoire (Boutillier 1960; Hecht 1985; Gastellu 1989; Nguessan-Zoukou 1990). These works not only provide data points for the analysis, but also can be used to construct continua along which the various cases can be placed with respect to each other. This helps anchor the comparisons advanced here, and also provides them with intersubjective validity. Cases were deliberately selected in order to provide analytic leverage on hypotheses and rival hypotheses laid out in Chapter 2, as per the method of focused structured comparison (George and McKeown 1985; Snyder 2001b). This means that the cases were not selected randomly and are not presumed to represent the full range of possibility in sub-Saharan Africa. I hope the approach provides a starting point for richer and more subtle mappings of political variation in rural Africa, and for analyses of territorial politics as it is played out in different national contexts.

References

Adamolekun, L., D. Olowu, and M. Laleye. 1988. *Local Government in Africa since Independence*. Lagos: University of Lagos Press.

Adams, Adrian. 1977a. The Senegal River Valley: What Kind of Change? *Review of African Political Economy*, 10:33–59.

Adams, Adrian. 1977b. *Le Long Voyage des Gens du Fleuve*. Paris: Maspero.

Adams, Adrian. 1985. *La Terre et les Gens du Fleuve*. Paris: L'Harmattan.

Adams, Adrian, and Jaabe So. 1996. *A Claim to Land by the River: A Household in Senegal, 1720–1994*. Oxford: Oxford University Press.

Adedeji, Adebayo. 1994. An Alternative for Africa. *Journal of Democracy*, 5, 4 (October):119–32.

Africa Confidential. Periodical.

Africa South of the Sahara. Yearly. London: Europa Publications.

Agrawal, Arun, and Clark C. Gibson. 1991. Enchantment and Disenchantment: The Role of Community in Natural Resource Conservation. *World Development*, 27, 4:629–49.

Agrawal, Arun, and Jesse Ribot. 1999. Accountability in Decentralization: A Framework with South Asian and West African Cases. *Journal of Developing Areas*, 33, 4:473–502.

Agrawal, Arun. Forthcoming. *Environmentality: Technologies of Government and the Making of Subjects*. Durham, N.C.: Duke University Press.

Ake, Claude. 1993. The Unique Case of African Democracy. *International Affairs*, 69, 2:239–44.

Akpan, Ntieyong U. 1956. *Epitaph to Indirect Rule: A Discourse on Local Government in Africa*. London: Caswell and Co.

Alderfer, Harold F. 1964. *Local Government in Developing Countries*. New York: McGraw-Hill.

Allman, Jean Marie. 1993. *The Quills of the Porcupine: Asante Nationalism in an Emergent Ghana*. Madison: University of Wisconsin Press.

Allman, Jean Marie. 2001. Review of *Nkrumah and the Chiefs: The Politics of Chieftaincy in Ghana, 1951–60*, by Richard Rathbone. *African Studies Review*, 44, 3 (December):116–18.

Alston, Lee J., and Joseph P. Ferrie. 1999. *Southern Paternalism and the American Welfare State: Economics, Politics, and Institutions in the South, 1865–1965.* Cambridge: Cambridge University Press.

Amin, Samir. 1967. *Le Développement du Capitalisme en Côte d'Ivoire.* Paris: Editions de Minuit.

Amin, Samir. 1969. *Le Monde des Affaires Sénégalais.* Paris: Editions de Minuit.

Amin, Samir. 1973. *Neo-Colonialism in West Africa.* London: Monthly Review Press.

Amon d'Aby, F. J. 1958. *Le Problème des Chefferies Traditionelles en Côte d'Ivoire.* Abidjan: Institut d'Ethno-Sociologie, Université d'Abidjan.

Amondji, Marcel. 1986. Côte d'Ivoire, le PDCI, et la Vie Politique de 1944 à 1985. Paris: L'Harmattan.

Amondji, Marcel. 1988. *Côte d'Ivoire: La Dépendance et l'Épreuve des Faits.* Paris: L'Harmattan.

Anderson, Perry. 1974. *Lineages of the Absolutist State.* London: New Left Books.

Anyang' Nyong'o, Peter. 1987. "The Development of Agrarian Capitalist Classes in the Ivory Coast, 1945–75." In Paul Lubeck, ed., *The African Bourgeoisie,* 185–248. Boulder, Colo.: Lynne Rienner Press.

Aprin, Robert. 1980. Développement et Résistance Paysanne: Le Cas des Soninkés de Bakel. Memoire, Paris [S.1.:s.n], mimeo.

Apter, David E. 1968. *Ghana in Transition.* New York: Anetheneum. First published as *Gold Coast in Transition,* Princeton: Princeton University Press, 1955.

Apter, David E. 1972. *Ghana in Transition.* 2d ed. Princeton: Princeton University Press. First published as *Gold Coast in Transition,* Princeton: Princeton University Press, 1955.

Arrighi, Giovanni. 1970. "Labor Supplies in Historical Perspective: A Study of Proletarianization of the African Peasantry in Rhodesia." In Giovanni Arrighi and John S. Saul, eds., *Essays on the Political Economy of Africa,* 180–236. New York: Monthly Review Press.

Association Euro-Africaine pour l'Anthropologie du Changement Social et du Développement (APAD). 1998. Les Dimensions Sociales et Economiques du Développement Local et la Décentralisation en Afrique au Sud du Sahara. *APAD Bulletin,* 15 (May).

Atta, Noël Brou [Brou Noël]. 1991. "Analyse Économique de la Collecte Primaire de l'Igname dans le Nord de la Côte d'Ivoire: Etude de Cas dans la Région de Korhogo," Thése de doctorat 3ème cycle en Sciences Economiques (Economie Rurale), Université Nationale de Côte d'Ivoire, Faculté des Sciences Economiques, Centre Ivoirien de Recherches Economiques et Sociales (CIRES), Abijdan.

Atta, Brou Noël. 1992. Rapport de Synthèse sur la Filière Café-Cacao. Unpublished manuscript, Abidjan, 10 janvier.

Augé, Marc. 1973. L'illusion Villageoise: Limites Sociologiques et Politiques de "Développement" Villageois en Côte d'Ivoire. *Archives Internationale de Sociologie de la Coopération et du Développement,* 34 (juillet-décembre):240–51.

Austin, Dennis. 1964. *Politics in Ghana: 1946–1960.* London: Oxford University Press.

References

Austin, Dennis, and Robin Luckman, eds. 1975. *Politicians and Soldiers in Ghana, 1966–1972*. London: Frank Cass.

Austin, Gareth. 1987. The Emergence of Capitalist Relations in South Asante Cocoa-Farming, c. 1916–1933. *Journal of African History*, 28, 2:259–79.

Austin, Gareth. 1988. Capitalists and Chiefs in the Cocoa Hold-Ups in South Asante, 1927–38. *International Journal of African Historical Studies*, 21, 1:63–96.

Austin, Gareth. 1996. National Poverty and the 'Vampire State' in Ghana: A Review Article. *Journal of International Development*, 8, 4:553–73.

Bakary, Tessy D. 1985. Côte d'Ivoire: Logiques du Recrutement Politique et Eventuels Changements à la Tête de l'Etat. *Le Mois en Afrique*, 237–8 (octobre–novembre):3–32.

Bakary, Tessy D. 1986. Côte d'Ivoire: Une 'Décentralisation Politique Centralisée. *Géopolitique Africaine*, 2, 1 (juin):205–30, and 2, 2 (octobre):65–104.

Bakary, Tessy D. 1991. Côte d'Ivoire: l'Étatisation de l'Etat." In Jean-Francois Médard, ed., *Etats d'Afrique Noire: Formation, Mécanismes, et Crise*, 53–91. Paris: Karthala.

Balans, Jean-Louis, Christian Coulon, and Jean-Marc Gastellu. 1975. *Autonomie Locale et Intégration Nationale au Sénégal*. Paris: A. Pedone.

Barkan, Joel D., ed. 1984. *Politics and Public Policy in Kenya and Tanzania*. Rev. ed. New York: Praeger (first edition in 1979).

Barkan, Joel D., and Michael Chege. 1989. Decentralising the State: District Focus and the Politics of Reallocation in Kenya. *Journal of Modern African Studies*, 27, 3:431–53.

Barker, Jonathan. 1971. "The Paradox of Development: Reflections on a Study of Local-Central Political Relations in Senegal." In Michael F. Lofchie, ed., *The State of the Nations: Constraints on Development in Independent Africa*, 47–63. Berkeley and Los Angeles: University of California Press.

Barker, Jonathan. 1985. Gaps in the Debates about Agriculture in Senegal, Tanzania, and Mozambique. *World Development*, 13, 1:59–76.

Barker, Jonathan. 1987. Political Space and the Quality of Participation in Rural Africa: A Case from Senegal [Birkelane]. *Canadian Journal of African Studies*, 21, 1:1–16.

Barnes, Leonard. 1969. *African Renaissance*. London: Victor Gollancz.

Barreteau, Olivier. 1998. "Un Système Multi-Agent pour Explorer la Viabilité des Systèmes Irrigués: Dynamiques des Intéractions et Modes d'Organisation [Senegal River Valley]." Thèse presentée pour obtenir le grade de Docteur de l'ENGREF [Ecole Nationale du Génie Rural, des Eaux et des Forêts], Ecole Nationale du Génie Rural, des Eaux et des Forêts, Centre de Montpellier, Montpellier, France.

Bassett, Thomas J. 1984. "Food, Peasantry, and the State in Northern Ivory Coast, 1898–1982." Ph.D. diss., University of California, Berkeley, Department of Geography.

Bassett, Thomas J. 1988. The Development of Cotton in Northern Ivory Coast. *Journal of African History*, 29:267–84.

Bassett, Thomas J. 1993. "Land Use Conflicts in Pastoral Development in Northern Côte d'Ivoire." In Thomas J. Bassett and Donald E. Crummey, eds., *Land in African Agrarian Systems*, 131–56. Madison: University of Wisconsin Press.

Bassett, Thomas J. 2001. *The Peasant Cotton Revolution: Côte d'Ivoire, 1880–1995*. Cambridge: Cambridge University Press.

Bassett, Thomas J., and Donald E. Crummey, eds. 1993. *Land in African Agrarian Systems*. Madison: University of Wisconsin Press.

Bates, Robert H. 1981. *Markets and States in Tropical Africa*. Los Angeles and Berkeley: University of California Press.

Bates, Robert H. 1988. Contra Contractarianism: Some Reflections on the New Instituitonalism. *Politics and Society*, 16, 2–3:387–401.

Bates, Robert H. 1989. *Beyond the Miracle of the Market: The Political Economy of Agrarian Development in Kenya*. Cambridge: Cambridge University Press.

Bates, Robert H. 1990. Capital, Kinship, and Conflict: The Structuring Influence of Capital in Kinship Societies. *Canadian Journal of African Studies*, 24:151–64.

Bates, Robert H. 1991. "Agricultural Policy and the Study of Politics in Post-Independence Africa." In Douglas Rimmer, ed., *Africa 30 Years On*, 115–29. London: James Currey and Heinemann.

Bates, Robert H. 2001. *Prosperity and Violence: The Political Economy of Development*. New York: Norton.

Bates, Robert H., and William T. Bianco. 1990. "Comment: Applying Rational Choice Theory." In Karen Schweers Cook and Margaret Levi, eds., *The Limits of Rationality*, 349–58. Chicago: University of Chicago Press.

Bates, Robert H., Margaret Levi, Jean-Laurent Rosenthal, and Barry R. Weingast. 1998. *Analytic Narratives*. Princeton: Princeton University Press.

Baulin, Jacques. 1989. *La Succession d'Houphouët-Boigny*. Paris: Editions Eurafor Press.

Bayart, Jean-François. 1985. *L'Etat au Cameroun*. Paris: Presses de la Fondation Nationale des Sciences Politiques.

Bayart, Jean-François. 1989. *L'Etat en Afrique: La Politique du Ventre*. Paris: Fayard.

Bayart, Jean-François, ed. 1994. *La Réinvention du Capitalisme*. Paris: Karthala.

Beck, Linda J. 1996a. " 'Patrimonial Democrats' in a Culturally Plural Society: Democratization and Political Accommodation in the Patronage Politics of Senegal." Ph.D. diss., University of Wisconsin, Madison, Department of Political Science.

Beck, Linda J. 1996b. "Decentralization in Senegal: Political Reform or Rhetoric?" Paper presented at the annual meeting of the African Studies Association, San Francisco, Calif., November.

Beck, Linda J. 1998. Patrimonial Democrats: Incremental Reform and the Obstacles to Consolidating Democracy in Senegal. *Canadian Journal of African Studies*, 31, 1:1–31.

Beck, Linda J. 2001. Reining in the Marabouts? Democratization and Local Governance in Senegal. *African Affairs*, 100:601–21.

Beckman, Bjorn. 1976. *Organising the Farmers: Cocoa Politics and National Development in Ghana*. Uppsala: Scandinavian Institute of African Studies.

362

References

Beckman, Bjorn. 1981. "Ghana: 1951–78: Agrarian Basis of the Post-Colonial State." In Judith Heyer et al., eds., *Rural Development in Tropical Africa*, 143–67. New York: St. Martin's Press.

Behrman, Lucy C. 1970. *Muslim Brotherhoods and Politics in Senegal*. Cambridge: Harvard University Press.

Benveniste, C[orrine]. 1974. Le Boucle de Cacao, Côte d'Ivoire: Etude Regionale des Circuits de Transport. Paris: ORSTOM. Photocopy.

Bergmann, H. 1974. Les Notables Villageois: Chef de Village et Imam Face à la Coopérative Rurale dans une Région du Sénégal. *Bulletin de l'IFAN* [Dakar], 36, ser. B., n. 2:283–322.

Berman, Bruce. 1984. Structure and Process in the Bureaucratic States of Colonial Africa. *Development and Change*, 15:161–202.

Berman, Bruce, and John Lonsdale. 1992. *Unhappy Valley: Conflict in Kenya and Africa. Book One: State and Class*. London and Nairobi: James Currey and Heineman Kenya.

Bernstein, Henry, and Terence J. Byres. 2001. From Peasant Studies to Agrarian Change. *Journal of Agrarian Change*, 1, 1 (January):1–56.

Berry, Sara. 1985. *Fathers Work for Their Sons: Accumulation, Mobility, and Class Formation in an Extended Yorùbá Community*. Berkeley and Los Angeles: University of California Press.

Berry, Sara. 1993. *No Condition Is Permanent: The Social Dynamics of Agrarian Change in Sub-Saharan Africa*. Madison: University of Wisconsin Press.

Berry, Sara. 2001. *Chiefs Know Their Boundaries: Essays on Property, Power, and the Past in Asante, 1896–1996*. Portsmouth, NH, Oxford, and Cape Town: Heinemann, James Currey, and David Philip Publishers.

Berry, Sara. 2002. Debating the Land Question in Africa. *Comparative Studies in Society and History*, 44, 4(October):638–69.

Béthemont, Jacques, 1986. Acteurs et Stratégies de l'Eau dans la Vallée du Sénégal. *Revue de Géographie de Lyon*, 61, 1:63–78.

Beugre Owo Sero, Pierre, and Yaya D'Alepe. 1992. "L'Exemple des Commerçants-Planteurs du Sud-Est de la Côte d'Ivoire de 1930–1960." In Leonard Harding and Pierre Kipré, eds.,*Commerce et Commerçants en Afrique de I'Ouest: la Côte d'Ivoire*, 189–243. Paris: L'Harmattan.

Biebuyck, D., ed. 1963. *African Agrarian Systems*. Oxford: Oxford University Press.

Binder, Leonard. 1978. *In a Moment of Enthusiasm: Political Power and the Second Stratum in Egypt*. Chicago: University of Chicago Press.

Blair, Harry. 1996. "Supporting Democratic Local Governance: Lessons from International Donor Experience – Initial Concepts and Some Preliminary Findings." Paper prepared for the annual meeting of the American Political Science Association, San Francisco, Calif., 29 August–1 September.

Bloch, Peter C. 1991. "Des Aménagements Hydroagricoles pour Qui? L'Avenir de l'Irrigation dans la Vallée du Sénégal Vu d'une Zone Périphérique: Bakel." In Bernard Crousse, Paul Mathieu, and Sidy M. Seck, eds., *La Vallée du Fleuve Sénégal: Evaluations et Perspectives d'une Décennie d'Aménagements (1980–1990)*, 237–54. Paris: Karthala.

363

Bloch, Peter C. 1993. "An Egalitarian Development Project in a Stratified Society: Who Ends Up with the Land?" In Thomas J. Bassett and Donald E. Crummey, eds., *Land in African Agrarian Systems*, 222–46. Madison: University of Wisconsin Press.

Blundo, Giorgio. 1995. Les Courtiers du Développement en Milieu Rural Sénégalaise. *Cahiers d'Etudes Africaines*, 35–1, 137 (August):73–99.

Blundo, Giorgio. 1998a. "Decentralization, Participation, and Corruption in Senegal [SE groundnut basin]." Paper presented at the fourteenth International Congress of Anthropological and Ethnographical Sciences, 26 July–1 August, Williamsburg, Va.

Blundo, Giorgio. 1998b. Logiques de Gestion Publique dans la Décentralisation Sénégalaise: Participation Factionnelle et Ubiquité Réticulaire. *APAD [Association Euro-Africaine pour l'Anthropologie du Changement Social et du Développement] Bulletin* 15 (May):21–48.

Bogner, Arthur. 2000. "The 1994 Civil War in Northern Ghana: The Genesis and Escalation of a 'Tribal' Conflict." In Carola Lentz and Paul Nuent, eds., *Ethnicity in Ghana: The Limits of Invention*, 183–203. Houndmills and London: Macmillan.

Bonin, Hubert. 1987. *CFAO: Cent Ans de Compétition*. Paris: Economica.

Bonnal, A. 1986. L'Administration et le Parti Face aux Tensions [Côte d'Ivoire]. *Politique Africaine*, 24 (décembre):20–8.

Bonnefonds, Asté Léon. 1968. La Transformation du Commerce de Traite en Côte-d'Ivoire Depuis la Deuxième Guerre Mondiale et l'Indépendance. *Cahiers d'Outre Mer*, 84:395–413.

Boone, Catherine. 1992. *Merchant Capital and the Roots of State Power in Senegal, 1930–1985*. Cambridge: Cambridge University Press.

Boone, Catherine. 1993. Commerce in Côte d'Ivoire: Ivoirianization without Ivoirian Traders. *Journal of Modern African Studies*, 31, 1:67–92.

Boone, Catherine. 1994a. "States and Ruling Classes in Sub-Saharan Africa: The Enduring Contradictions of Power." In Joel Migdal, A. Kohli, and Vivienne Shue, eds., *State Power and Social Forces*, 108–42. Cambridge: Cambridge University Press.

Boone, Catherine. 1994b. Trade, Taxes, and Tribute: Market Liberalizations and the New Importers in West Africa. *World Development*, 22, 3:453–67.

Boone, Catherine. 1995a. The Social Origins of Ivoirian Exceptionalism: Rural Society and State Formation. *Comparative Politics*, 27, 4 (July):445–64.

Boone, Catherine. 1995b. Rural Interests and the Making of Modern African States. *Journal of African Economic History*, 23:1–36.

Boone, Catherine. 1998. State Building in the African Countryside: Structure and Process at the Grassroots. *Journal of Development Studies*, 34, 4 (April):1–33 (corrigenda in 35, 1, October).

Boone, Catherine, and Jake Batsell. 2001. Politics and AIDS in Africa: Research Agendas in Political Science and International Relations. *Africa Today*, 48, 2:3–34.

Botchway, Karl Quaye. 1998. "Interrogating 'Development' in Ghana: The Case of the Northern Region Rural Integrated Program (NORRIP)." Ph.D. diss.,

New York, New School for Social Research, Department of Political and Social Science.

Boumedouha, Said. 1987. "The Lebanese in Senegal: A History of Relationship between an Immigrant Community and its French and African Rulers." Ph.D. diss., Centre of West African Studies, University of Birmingham.

Boutillier, Jean-Louis 1960. *Bongouanou, Côte d'Ivoire: Etude Socio-Economique d'une Subdivision*. Paris: Editions Berger-Lavrault.

Boutillier, Jean-Louis. 1963. "Les Rapports du Système Foncier Toucouleur et de l'Organisation Social et Économique Traditionelle: Leur Évolution Actuelle." In Daniel Biebuych, ed., *African Agrarian Systems*, 116–36. London: Oxford University Press.

Boutillier, Jean-Louis, P. Cantrelle, J. Caussé, C. Laurent, and Th. N'Doye. 1962. *La Moyenne Vallée du Sénégal: Etude Socio-Économique*. Paris: République Française, Ministère de la Coopération and Presses Universitaires de France.

Boye, François. 1992. "Les Mécanismes Économiques en Perspective." In Momar Coumba Diop, ed., *Sénégal: Trajectoires d'un Etat*, 39–94. Paris and Dakar: Karthala and CODESRIA.

Boylan, Delia. 1998. Preeemptive Strike: Central Bank Reform in Chile's Transition from Authoritarian Rule. *Comparative Politics*, 30, 4 (July):443–62.

Bratton, Michael. 1987. The Comrades and the Countryside: The Politics of Agricultural Policy in Zimbabwe. *World Politics*, 39, 2 (January):174–202.

Bredeloup, Sylvie. 1989. *Négociants au Long Cours: Rôle Moteur du Commerce dans une Région de Côte-d'Ivoire en Declin (Dimbokro)*. Paris: L'Harmattan.

Brenner, Robert. 1976. Agrarian Class Structure and Economic Development in Pre-Industrial Europe. *Past and Present*, 70 (February):30–75.

Brenner, Robert. 1982. The Agrarian Roots of European Capitalism. *Past and Present*, 97 (November):16–113.

Brustein, William. 1989. *The Social Origins of Political Regionalism in France: 1849– 1981*. Berkeley and Los Angeles: University of California Press.

Buchanan, James, and Gordon Tullock. 1962. *The Calculus of Consent: Logical Foundations of Constitutional Democracy*. Ann Arbor: University of Michigan Press.

Bunce, Valerie. 1999. *Subversive Institutions: The Design and the Destruction of Socialism and the State*. Cambridge: Cambridge University Press.

Bunker, Stephen G. 1987. *Peasants against the State: The Politics of Market Control in Bugisu, Uganda, 1900–1983*. Urbana: University of Illinois Press.

Callaghy, Thomas, Ronald Kassimir, and Robert Latham, eds. 2001. *Intervention and Transnationalism in Africa: Global-Local Networks of Power*. Cambridge: Cambridge University Press.

Cammack, Paul. 1992. The New Institutionalism: Predatory Rule, Institutional Persistence, and Macrosocial Change. *Economy and Society*, 21, 4 (November):397– 429.

Campbell, Bonnie. 1973. "The Social, Political, and Economic Consequences of French Private Investment in the Ivory Coast." Ph.D. diss., University of Sussex, November.

Campbell, Bonnie. 1984. "Inside the Miracle: Cotton in the Ivory Coast." In Jonathan Barker, ed., *Politics of Agriculture in Tropical Africa*, 143–73. Beverly Hills: Sage Publications.

Campbell, Bonnie. 1985. "The Fiscal Crisis of the State: The Case of the Ivory Coast." In Henry Bernstein and Bonnie K. Campbell. eds., *Contradictions of Accumulation in Africa*, 267–310. Beverly Hills: Sage Publications.

Campbell, Bonnie. 1987. "The State and Capitalist Development in the Ivory Coast." In Paul Lubeck, ed., *The African Bourgeoisie*, 281–306. Boulder, Colo.: Lynne Rienner Press.

Casswell, N. 1984. Autopsie de l'ONCAD: La Politique Arachidière du Sénégal, 1966–1980. *Politique Africaine*, 14 (juin):39–73.

Caverivière, Monique, and Marc Debene. 1988. *Le Droit Foncier Sénégalais*. Paris: Berger-Levrault.

Chappell, David A. 1989. The Nation as Frontier: Ethnicity and Clientelism in Ivoirian History. *International Journal of African Historical Studies*, 22, 4:671–96.

Charbonneau, R. 1968. Les Libano-Syriens en Afrique Noire. *Le Mois en Afrique: Revue Française d'Etudes Politiques Africaines*, 26:56–71.

Chauveau, Jean-Pierre. 1980. "Agricultural Production and Social Formation: The Baule Region of Toumodi-Kokumbo in Historical Perspective." In Martin A. Klein, ed., *Peasants in Africa: Historical and Contemporary Perspectives*, 143–76. Beverly Hills: Sage Publications.

Chauveau, Jean-Pierre. 1982. "Le Status du Foncier dans l'Analyse de l'Économie de Plantation au Ghana." In E. Le Bris, E. Le Roy, and F. Leimdorfer, eds., *Enjeux Fonciers en Afrique Noire*, 45–56. Paris: Karthala.

Chauveau, Jean-Pierre. 2002. Une Lecture Sociologique de la Loi Ivoirienne de 1998 sur le Domaine Foncier. IRD [Institut de Recherche pour le Développement], Unité de Recherche 095: Régulations foncières, Document de Travail n. 6 (septembre). Montpellier, France.

Chauveau, Jean-Pierre, and Jean-Pierre Dozon. 1987. "Au Coeur des Éthnies Ivoiriennes ... L'État." In Emmanuel Terray, ed., *L'Etat Contemporain en Afrique*, 221–96. Paris: L'Harmattan.

Chauveau, Jean-Pierre, Jean-Pierre Dozon, and J. Richard. 1981. Histoires de Riz, Histoires d'Igname: Le cas de la Moyenne Côte d'Ivoire. *Africa*, 55, 2:621–58.

Chauveau, Jean-Pierre, and J. Richard. 1977. Une 'Périphérie Recentrée': À Propos d'un Système Local d'Économie de Plantation en Côte d'Ivoire. *Cahiers d'études Africaines*, 17:485–523.

Chege, Michael. 1988. "The African Economic Crisis and the Fate of Democracy in Sub-Saharan Africa." In Walter O. Oyugi et al., eds., *Democratic Theory and Practice in Africa*, 191–205. Portsmouth: Heinemann and Currey.

Chege, Michael. 1995. Between Africa's Extremes. *Journal of Democracy*, 6, 1:44–51.

Clapham, Christopher. 1982. "The Politics of Failure: Clientelism, Political Instability and National Integration in Liberia and Sierra Leone." In C. Clapham, ed., *Private Patronage and Public Power: Political Clientelism in the Modern State*, 75–92. London: Frances Pinter.

References

Cohen, Michael A. 1973. The Myth of the Expanding Centre: Politics in the Ivory Coast. *Journal of Modern African Studies*, 11, 2:227–40.

Cohen, Michael A. 1974. *Urban Policy and Political Conflict in Africa: A Study of the Ivory Coast*. Chicago: University of Chicago Press.

Cohen, John M., and Stephen B. Peterson. 1996. "Methodological Issues in the Analysis of Decentralization." Development Discussion Paper, no. 555 (October). Cambridge: Harvard Institute of International Development.

Cohen, John M., and Stephen B. Peterson. 1997. "Administrative Decentralization: A New Framework for Improved Governance, Accountability, and Performance." Development Discussion Paper, no. 582 (May). Cambridge: Harvard Institute for International Development.

Cohen, John M., and Stephen B. Peterson. 1999. *Administrative Decentralization: Strategies for Developing Countries*. West Hartford, Conn.: Kumarian Press.

Cohen, William B. 1971. *Rulers of Empire: The French Colonial Service in Africa*. Stanford: Stanford University Press.

Collier, David, and Deborah L. Norden. 1992. Strategic Choice Models of Political Change in Latin America. *Comparative Politics*, 24, 21 (January):229–43.

Colvin, Lucie Gallistel, ed. 1981. *The Uprooted of the Western Sahel: Migrants' Quest for Cash in the Senegambia*. New York: Praeger.

Commander, Simon, Ousseynou Ndoye, and Ismael Ouedrago. 1989. "Senegal, 1979–88." In Simon Commander, ed., *Structural Adjustment and Agriculture*, 145–74. London: Overseas Development Institute.

Compagnie d'Etudes Industrielles et d'Aménagement du Territoire et la Société d'Etudes et de Réalisations Economique et Sociales dans l'Agriculture (CINAM et SERESA). 1960. "Rapport Général sur les Perspectives de Développement du Sénégal. Archives Nationales de France, Section Outre-Mer, D3135 (janvier). Photocopy.

Contamin, Bernard, and Yves A. Fauré. 1990. *La Bataille des Entreprises Publiques en Côte d'Ivoire*. Paris: L'Harmattan.

Copans, Jean. 1988. *Les Marabouts de l'Arachide: La Confrérie Mouride et les Paysans du Sénégal*. Paris: L'Harmattan. First published in 1980 by Le Sycomore.

Cottingham, Clement. 1970. Political Consolidation and Centre-Local Relations in Senegal. *Canadian Journal of African Studies*, 4, 1 (Winter):101–120.

Coulibaly, Sinali. 1978. *Le Paysan Senoufo*. Abidjan and Dakar: Les Nouvelles Editions Africaines.

Coulon, Christian. 1981. *Le Marabout et le Prince: Islam et Pouvoir au Sénégal*. Paris: Editions A. Pedone.

Crook, Richard C. 1986. Decolonization, the Colonial State, and Chieftaincy in the Gold Coast. *African Affairs*, 85, 338:75–105.

Crook, Richard C. 1988. "Farmers and the State." In Douglas Rimmer, ed., *Rural Transformation in Tropical Africa*, 116–39. Athens: Ohio University Press.

Crook, Richard C. 1989. Patrimonialism, Administrative Effectiveness and Economic Development in Côte d'Ivoire. *African Affairs: The Journal of the Royal African Society*, 88, 351 (April):205–28.

Crook, Richard C. 1990. Politics, the Cocoa Crisis, and Administration in Côte d'Ivoire. *Journal of Modern African Studies*, 28, 4 (December):649–70.

Crook, Richard C. 1991. "State, Society and Political Institutions in Côte d'Ivoire and Ghana." In James Manor, ed., *Rethinking Third World Politics*, 213–42. London and New York: Longman.

Crook, Richard C., and James Manor. 1995. Democratic Decentralisation and Institutional Performance: Four Asian and African Experiences Compared. *Journal of Commonwealth and Comparative Politics*, 33, 3 (November):309–34.

Crook, Richard C., and James Manor. 1998. *Democracy and Decentralization in South Asia and West Africa*. Cambridge: Cambridge University Press.

Crook, Richard C., and A. S. Sverrisson. 1999. "To What Extent can Decentralised Forms of Government Enhance the Development of Pro-Poor Policies and Improve Poverty-Alleviation Outcomes?" Unpublished manuscript, Institute of Development Studies, University of Sussex, August.

Crook, Richard C., and A. S. Sverrisson. 2001. "Decentralisation and Poverty Alleviation in Developing Countries: A Comparative Analysis, OR, is West Bengal Unique?" University of Sussex, Institute of Development Studies Working Paper, n. 130.

Crousse, Bernard, E. Le Bris, and E. le Roy, eds. 1986. *Espaces Disputés en Afrique Noire: Pratiques Foncières Locales*. Paris: Karthala.

Crousse, Bernard, Paul Mathieu, and Sidy M. Seck, eds. 1991. *La Vallée du Fleuve Sénégal: Evaluations et Perspectives d'une Décennie d'Aménagements (1980–1990)*. Paris: Karthala.

Crowder, Michael. 1964. Indirect Rule – French and British Style. *Africa: Journal of the International African Institute*, 34, 3 (July):197–205.

Crowder, Michael. 1968. *West Africa Under Colonial Rule*. Evanston, Ill.: Northwestern University Press.

Crowder, Michael, and Obaro Ikime, eds. 1970. *West African Chiefs: Their Changing Status under Colonial Rule and Independence*. New York: Africana.

Cruise O'Brien, Donal B. 1967. Political Opposition in Senegal: 1960–67. *Government and Opposition*, 2, 4 (July–October):557–66.

Cruise O'Brien, Donal B. 1971a. *The Mourides of Senegal: Political and Economic Organisation of an Islamic Brotherhood*. Oxford: Oxford University Press.

Cruise O'Brien, Donal B. 1971b. Co-operators and Bureaucrats: Class Formation in a Senegalese Peasant Society. *Africa: Journal of the International African Institute*, 41, 4 (October):263–77.

Cruise O'Brien, Donal B. 1975. *Saints and Politicians: Essays in the Organisation of a Senegalese Peasant Society*. Cambridge: Cambridge University Press.

Cruise O'Brien, Donal B. 1979. "Ruling Class and Peasantry in Senegal: 1960–1976." In Rita Cruise O'Brien, ed., *The Political Economy of Underdevelopment: Dependence in Senegal*, 209–27. London: Sage Publications.

Cruise O'Brien, Donal B. 1984. Les Bienfaits de l'Inégalité: l'État et l'Économie Rurale au Sénégal. *Politique Africaine*, 14 (June):34–8.

Darbon, Dominique. 1988. *L'Administration et le Paysan en Casamance: Essai d'Anthropologie Administrative*. Paris: Pedone.

References

Davidson, Basil. 1992. "Africa: The Politics of Failure." In Ralph Miliband and Leo Panitch, eds., *Socialist Register 1992*, 212–26. London: Merlin Press.

de la Rochière, Jacqueline Dutheil. 1976. *L'Etat et le Développement Economique de la Côte d'Ivoire*. Paris: Editions A. Pedone.

Delavignette, Robert. 1950. *Freedom and Authority in French West Africa*. London: Oxford University Press.

de Miras, Claude. 1982. "L'entrepreneur Ivoirien ou une Bourgeoisie Privée de son État." In Yves A. Fauré and J.-F. Médard, eds., *Etat et Bourgeoisie en Côte-d'Ivoire*, 181–230. Paris: Karthala.

Deschamps, Hubert. 1963. Et Maintenant, Lord Lugard? *Africa: Journal of the International African Institute*, 33, 4 (October):293–306.

Dia, Ibrahima, and Boubacar Fall. 1991. "Dimensions Socio-Culturelles dans la Conception des Aménagements." In Bernard Crousse, Paul Mathieu, and Sidy M. Seck, eds., *La Vallée du Fleuve Sénégal: Evaluations et Perspectives d'une Décennie d'Aménagements (1980–1990)*, 141–60. Paris: Karthala.

Diahou, A. Y. 1990. L'Etat et les Municipalités en Côte d'Ivoire: Un Jeu de Cache-Cache? *Politique Africaine*, 40 (décembre):51–9.

Diallo, Youssouf. 1995. Les Peuls, les Sénoufo et l'Etat au Nord de la Côte d'Ivoire: Problèmes Fonciers et Gestion du Pastoralisme. *APAD Bulletin [Association Euro-Africaine pour l'Anthropologie du Changement Social et de Développement]*, 10 (décembre):35–46.

Dian, Boni. 1985. L'Economie de Plantation en Côte d'Ivoire Forestière. Abidjan-Dakar-Lomé: Nouvelles Editions Africaines.

Diarra, Samba. 1997. *Les Faux Complôts d'Houphouet-Boigny*. Paris: Karthala.

Diarrassouba, Valy Charles. 1968. *L'Evolution des Structures Agricoles du Sénégal: Destructuration et Restructuration de l'Économie Rurale*. Paris: Editions Cujas.

Diaw, Aminata, and Mamadou Diouf. 1992. "Ethnies et Nation au Miroir des Discourses Identitaires: Le cas Sénégalais [Casamance]." Paper presented at the CODESRIA seminiar on "Conflicts Ethniques en Afrique," Nairobi, Kenya, 16–18 November.

Dione, Samba. 1992. "Evolution des Politiques de Décentralisation au Sénégal." Dakar, Ecole Nationale d'Economie Appliquée (ENEA). Photocopy.

Diop, Abdoulaye[-Bara]. 1965. *Société Toucouleur et Migration: Enquéte sur la Migration Toucouler à Dakar*. Dakar: IFAN.

Diop, Abdoulaye-Bara. 1981. *La Société Wolof, Tradition et Changement: Les Systèmes d'Inegalité et de Domination*. Paris: Karthala.

Diop, M[omar] C[oumba]. 1981. Les Affaires Mourides à Dakar. *Politique Africaine*, 1, 4 (novembre):90–100.

Diop, Momar Coumba, ed. 2002. *Le Sénégal Contemporain*. Paris: Karthala.

Diop, Momar Coumba, and Mamadou Diouf. 1990. *Le Sénégal sous Abdou Diouf: Etat et Société*. Paris: Karthala.

Diop, Momar Coumba, and Mamadou Diouf. 1992a. L'administration Sénégalaise, les Confréries Religieuses, et les Paysanneries. *Africa Development*, 17, 2:65–87.

Diop, Momar Coumba, and Mamadou Diouf. 1992b. Enjeux et Contraintes Politiques de la Gestion Municipale au Sénégal [Dakar]. *Canadian Journal of African Studies*, 26, 1:1–23.

Doboscq, Pierre, and Patrick Quantin, eds. 1993. *Les Paysans du Monde: Électeurs sous Influence*. Paris: L'Harmattan.

Doornbos, M. 1986. "Incorporation and Cultural 'Receptivity' to Change." In van Binsbergen, Filip Reyntjens, and G. Hesseling, eds., *Etat et Communauté Locale en Afrique*, 349–68. Bruxelles: CEDAF.

Dozon, J. P. 1978. Logique des Développeurs/ Réalité des Développés: Bilan d'une Expérience de Développement Rizicole en Côte-d'Ivoire. *Mondes en Développement*, 24:909–34.

Dozon, J. P. 1982. "Epistémologie du 'Foncier' dans le Cadre des Économies de Planation Ivoiriennes." In E. Le Bris, Etienne Le Roy, et F. Leimdorfer, eds., *Enjeux Fonciers en Afrique Noire*, 56–60. Paris: Karthala.

Dubresson, Alain, and Claudine Vidal. 1991. "Loin d'Abidjan: Les Cadres, Urbanistes de l'Intérieur – La préfecture de Toumodi." Unpublished report. Abidjan: Institut Français de Recherche Scientifique pour le Développement en Coopération [ORSTOM], Centre ORSTOM de Petit-Bassam, Avril.

Due, Jean M. 1969. Agricultural Development in the Ivory Coast and Ghana. *Journal of Modern African Studies*, 7, 4:637–60.

Dumont, René. 1972. *Paysanneries aux Abois: Ceylan, Tunisie, Sénégal*. Paris: Editions du Seuil.

Dunn, John. 1975. "Politics in Asunafo." In Dennis Austin and Robin Luckham, eds., *Politicians and Soldiers in Ghana*, 164–213. London: Frank Cass.

Dunn, John, and A. F. Robertson. 1973. *Dependence and Opportunity: Political Change in Ahafo (Ghana)*. Cambridge: Cambridge University Press.

Dzisah, Melvis. 1998. "Rights – Côte d'Ivoire: Land Conflict Leaves a Trail of Blood." Interpress: Third World New Agency (IPS), worldwide web distribution via APC networks, received via email 28 May 1998.

Elkins, Catherine. 1995. "Property and Rights at the Microlevel: Rural Communities in the Middle Valley (Senegal)." Unpublished manuscript, Duke University, Department of Political Science, 25 October.

Engelhard, Philippe. 1991. "La Vallée 'Revisitée' ou les Enjeux de l'Après Barrage cinq ans Plus Tard." In Bernard Crousse, Paul Mathieu, and Sidy M. Seck, eds., 1991. *La Vallée du Fleuve Sénégal: Evaluations et Perspectives d'une Décennie d'Aménagements (1980–1990)*, 45–76. Paris: Karthala.

Ensminger, Jean. 1992. *Making a Market: The Institutional Transformation of an African Society*. Cambridge: Cambridge University Press.

Ensminger, Jean, and Andrew Rutten. 1990. "The Political Economy of Property Rights: Dismantling a Kenyan Commons." Political Economy working paper, Washington University in St. Louis, School of Business and Center in Political Economy, September.

Epstein, David, and Sharyn O'Halloran. 1999. *Delegating Powers: A Transaction Cost Politics Approach to Policy Making under Separate Powers*. Cambridge: Cambridge University Press.

References

Fauré, Yves A. 1982. "Le Complexe Politico-Économique." In Yves A. Fauré and J.-F. Médard, eds., *L'Etat et Bourgeoisie en Côte d'Ivoire*, 21–60. Paris: Karthala.

Fauré, Yves A. 1988. "Le Monde des Entreprises en Côte d'Ivoire: Sources Statistiques et Données de Structure." Abidjan: ORSTOM (novembre).

Fauré, Yves A. 1993. Democracy and Realism: Reflections on the Case of Côte d'Ivoire. *Africa: Journal of the International African Institute*, 63, 3:313– 29.

Fauré, Yves A. and J.-F. Médard, eds. 1982. *L'Etat et Bourgeoisie en Côte d'Ivoire*. Paris: Karthala.

Faye, Jacques. 1981. "Zonal Approach to Migration in the Senegalese Peanut Basin." In Lucie Gallistel Colvin, ed., *The Uprooted of the Western Sahel*, 136–60. New York: Praeger.

Fearon, James D., and David D. Laitin. 1996. Explaining Interethnic Cooperation. *American Political Science Review*, 90, 4 (December):715–35.

Ferguson, James. 1999. *Expectations of Modernity: Myths and Meanings of Urban Life on the Zambian Copperbelt*. Berkeley and Los Angeles: University of California Press.

Fieldhouse, D. K. 1986. *Black Africa, 1945–1980: Economic Decolonization and Arrested Development*. London: Allen and Unwin.

Firmin-Sellers, Kathryn. 1992. "The Concentration of Authority: Constitutional Creation in the Gold Coast, 1950." Paper presented at the annual convention of the Midwest Political Science Association, Chicago.

Firmin-Sellers, Kathryn. 1996. *The Transformation of Property Rights in the Gold Coast: An Empirical Analysis Applying Rational Choice Theory*. Cambridge: Cambridge University Press.

Firmin-Sellers, Kathryn. 1997. "Institutions and Outcomes: Explaining the Impact of European Colonial Rule in West Africa." Unpublished manuscript, Indiana University, Department of Political Science. Photocopy.

Firmin-Seller, Kathryn. 2000. Institutions, Context and Outcomes: Explaining French and British Rule in West Africa. *Comparative Politics*, 32, 3:253–72.

First, Ruth. 1970. *Power in Africa*. New York: Pantheon Books.

Fitch, Bob, and Mary Oppenheimer. 1966. *Ghana: End of an Illusion*. New York: Monthly Review Press.

Foltz, William J. 1977. "Social Structure and Political Behavior of Senegalese Elites." In Stetten W. Schmidt, James C. Scott, Carl Landé, and Laura Guasti, eds., *Friends, Followers, and Factions: A Reader in Political Clientelism*, 242–50. Los Angeles and Berkeley: University of California Press.

Forrest, Joshua. 1998. "The Colonial and Social Origins of Rural Power and Prospects for Democratic Decentralization." Paper presented to the annual meeting of the African Studies Association, Chicago, November.

Forrest, Joshua. 2002. "Guinea-Bissau." In Patrick Chabal, ed., *A History of Postcolonial Lusophone Africa*, 236–63. London: Hurst.

Forum Economique (Abidjan). Periodical.

Foster, Philip, and Aristide R. Zolberg, eds. 1971. *Ghana and the Ivory Coast: Perspectives on Modernization*. Chicago: University of Chicago Press.

Foucault, Michel. 1980. *Power/Knowledge: Selected Interviews and Other Writings, 1972–77*. Edited by Colin Gordon. New York: Pantheon Books.

Founou-Tchuigoua, Bernard. 1979. Quels Changements dans l'Agriculture Ivoirienne? *Africa Development*, 4, 1:71–8.

Fox, Jonathan. 1990. Editor's Introduction. Special Issue on "The Challenge of
Rural Democratization: Perspectives from Latin America and the Philippines."
Journal of Development Studies, 26, 4 (July):1–19.

Fox, Jonathan. 1984. The Difficult Transition from Clientelism to Citizenship:
Lessons from Mexico. *World Politics*, 46 (January):151–84.

Frankenberger, Timothy R., and Mark B. Lynham. 1993. "Household Food Security
and Coping Strategies along the Senegal River Valley." In Thomas K. Park, ed.,
*Risk and Tenure in Arid Lands: The Political Ecology of Development in the Senegal
River Basin*, 51–86. Tucson: University of Arizona Press.

Fraternité Edition. 1980. *Côte d'Ivoire, 20 Ans*. Abidjan.

Fraternité Matin (Abidjan). Periodical.

Fréchou, H. 1955. Les Plantations Européenes en Côte d'Ivoire. *Cahiers d'Outre
Mer*, 8, 29:56–83.

Frélastre, Georges. 1983. En Côte d'Ivoire: Prudente mise en Oeuvre de la Nouvelle Politique de Développement Rural Intégré. *Le Mois en Afrique*, 18, 213–4
(octobre–novembre):52–62.

Freund, Bill. 1998. *The Making of Contemporary Africa: The Development of African
Society since 1800*. 2d. ed. Boulder: Lynne Rienner Press (first edition published
by Indiana University Press, 1984).

Frieden, Jeffry A. 1991. *Debt, Development, and Democracy: Modern Political Economy
and Latin America, 1965–1985*. Princeton: Princeton University Press.

Frye, Timothy. 1997. "Delegation and Competition: Governing Emerging Markets
in the Post-Communist World." Paper presented at the annual meeting of the
American Political Science Association, Washington, D.C., 28– 31 August.

Furedi, Frank. 1989. *The Mau Mau War in Perspective*. London, Nairobi, and Athens,
Ohio: James Currey Ltd, Heinemann Kenya, and Ohio University Press.

Gal. See Le Gal.

Galvan, Dennis. 1995. "Commodification, Land Pawning, and Peasant Lore: Responses to the Standardization of Tenure in the Siin Region of Senegal." Paper
presented at the annual meeting of the African Studies Association, Orlando, Fla.

Galvan, Dennis. 1996. " 'The State Is Now the Master of Fire': Adapting Institutions
and Culture in Rural Senegal," Ph.D. diss., University of California, Berkeley,
Department of Political Science.

Galvan, Dennis. Forthcoming. *Crafting a Local Modernity: Institutional Syncretism
and Culturally Sustainable Development in Senegal*. Berkeley and Los Angeles: University of California Press.

Garnier, Maurice, et al. 1992. "The Experience in Ivory Coast with Decentralized
Approaches to Local Delivery of Primary Education and Primary Health Ser-
vices." Unpublished manuscript prepared by Associates in Rural Development
(ARD), Burlington, Vt., 20 January.

Gastellu, J[ean]-M[arc]. 1982. "Droit d'Usage et Propriété Privée." In E. Le Bris,
Etienne Le Roy, et F. Leimdorfer, eds., *Enjeux Fonciers en Afrique Noire*, 269–80.
Paris: Karthala.

References

Gastellu, Jean-Marc. 1989. *Riches Paysans de Côte-d'Ivoire*. Paris: L'Harmattan.

Gbagbo, Laurent. 1982. *Côte-d'Ivoire: Economie et Société à la Veille de l'Indépendance (1940–1960)*. Paris: L'Harmattan.

Gbetibouo, Mathurin, and Christopher L. Delgado. 1984. "Lessons and Constraints of Export Crop-Led Growth: Cocoa in Ivory Coast." In I. William Zartman and Christopher Delgado, eds., *The Political Economy of the Ivory Coast*, 115–47. New York: Praeger.

Geddes, Barbara. 1991. A Game Theoretic Model of Reform in Latin American Democracies. *American Political Science Review*, 85:371–92.

Geddes, Barbara. 1994. *Politician's Dilemma: Building State Capacity in Latin America*. Berkeley and Los Angeles: University of California Press.

Gellar, Sheldon. 1987. "Circulaire 32 Revisited: Prospects for Revitalizing the Senegalese Cooperative Movement in the 1980s." In John Waterbury and Mark Gersovitz, eds., *The Political Economy of Risk and Choice in Senegal*, 123–59. London: Frank Cass.

Gellar, Sheldon. 1990. "State Tutelage vs. Self-Governance: The Rhetoric and Reality of Decentralization in Senegal." In James S. Wunch and Dele Owolu, eds., *The Failure of the Centralized State*, 130–47. Boulder: Westview.

Gentil, Dominique. 1986. *Les Mouvements Coopératifs en Afrique de l'Ouest: Interventions de l'Etat ou Organisations Paysannes?* Paris: Editions L'Harmattan.

George, Alexander L., and Timothy J. McKeown. 1985. Case Studies and Theories of Organizational Decision Making. *Advances in Information Processing in Organizations*, 2:21–58.

Geschiere, Peter. 1982. *Village Communities and the State: Changing Relations among the Maka of Southern Cameroon since Colonial Conquest*. London: Kegan Paul International.

Geschiere, Peter. 1985. "Imposing Capitalist Dominance through the State: The Multifarious Role of the Colonial State in Africa." In Wim van Binsbergen and Peter Geschiere, eds., *Old Modes of Production and Capitalist Encroachment: Anthropological Explorations in Africa*, 94–143. London: Routledge and Kegan Paul.

Geschiere, Peter. 1986. "Hegemonic Regimes and Popular Protest – Bayart, Gramsci, and the State in Cameroon." In Wim van Binsbergen, Filip Reyntjens, and Gerti Hesseling, eds., *State and Local Community in Africa*, 309–400. Brussels: CEDAF [Centre d'Etude et de Documentation Africaines].

Geschiere, Peter. 1989. "Accumulation and Non-Accumulation in Agriculture: Regional Variations in South Cameroon." Paper presented at the African Social History Workshop, Columbia University, 31 October.

Geschiere, Peter. 1993. Chiefs and Colonial Rule in Cameroon: Inventing Chieftaincy, French and British. *Africa: Journal of the International African Institute*, 63, 2:151–75.

Geschiere, Peter, and Josef Gugler. 1998. The Urban-Rural Connection: Changing Issues of Belonging and Identification. *Africa: Journal of the International African Institute*, 68, 3 (Summer):309–19.

Geschiere, Peter, and J. van der Klei. 1987. "Le Rélation Etat-Paysans et ses Ambivalences: Modes Populaires d'Action Politique chez les Maka (Cameroun) et les

Diola (Casamance)." In E. Terray, ed., *L'Etat Contemporain en Afrique*, 297–340. Paris: L'Harmattan.

Gibson, Edward L. 1997. The Populist Road to Market Reform: Policy and Electoral Coalitions in Mexico and Argentina. *World Politics*, 49 (April):339–70.

Girard, Jean. 1963. "De la Communauté Traditionelle à la Collectivité Moderne en Casamance." In University of Dakar Faculté de Droit et des Sciences Economiques, *Annales Africaines*, 135–65. Paris: Pedone.

Goheen, Mitzi. 1992. Chiefs, Subchiefs, and Local Control: Negotiations over Land, Struggles over Meaning. *Africa: Journal of the International African Institute*, 62, 3:389–412.

Goody, Jack. 1980. Rice-Burning and the Green Revolution in Northern Ghana. *Journal of Development Studies*, 16, 2 (January):136–55.

Gourevitch, Peter Alexis. 1980. *Paris and the Provinces: The Politics of Local Government Reform in France*. Berkeley and Los Angeles: University of California Press.

Gramsci, Antonio. 1988. *An Antonio Gramsci Reader: Selected Writing, 1916–1935*. Edited by David Forgacs. New York: Schocken Books.

Green, Daniel. 1998. "Ghana: Structural Adjustment as State (Re)Formation." In Leonardo Villalon and Phillip Huxtable, eds., *The African State at a Critical Juncture*, 185–212. Boulder: Lynne Rienner.

Green, Reginald H. 1971. "Reflections on Economic Strategy, Structure, Implementation, and Necessity: Ghana and the Ivory Coast, 1957–67." In Philip Foster and Aristide R. Zolberg, ed., *Ghana and the Ivory Coast: Perspectives on Modernization*, 231–64. Chicago: University of Chicago Press.

Grier, Beverly. 1987. "Contradiction, Crisis, and Class Conflict: The State and Capitalist Development in Ghana Prior to 1948." In Irving Leonard Markovitz, ed., *Studies in Class and Power in Africa*, 27–49. New York: Oxford University Press.

Griffeth, Robert R. 1968. "The Islamic Theme in Senegalese Institution-Building: The Nineteenth Century." In Arnold Rivkin, ed., *Nations by Design: Institution-Building in Africa*, 184–92. Garden City, N.Y.: Anchor Books.

Gunderson, William Charles. 1975. "Village Elders and Regional Intermediaries: Differing Responses to Change in the Korhogo Region of the Ivory Coast." Ph.D. diss. Department of Political Science, Indiana University.

Guyer, David. 1970. *Ghana and the Ivory Coast: The Impact of Colonialism in an African Setting*. New York: Exposition Press.

Guyer, Jane. 1980. Head Tax, Social Structure, and Rural Incomes in Cameroun, 1922–37. *Cahiers d'Etudes Africaines*, 20, 3:305–29.

Guyer, Jane. 1981. Household and Community in African Studies. *African Studies Review*, 24, 2/3 (June/September):87–137.

Guyer, Jane. 1991. "Representation without Taxation: An Essay on Democracy in Rural Nigeria, 1952–1990." Boston University African Studies Center Working Paper, no. 152. (Published under same title in *African Studies Review*, 35, 1 (1992):41–79.)

Halpern, Jan. 1972. La Confrérie des Mourides et le Développement au Sénégal. *Cultures et Développement*, 3, 1:99–125.

References

Hamer, Alice. 1981. "Diola Women and Migration: A Case Study." In Lucie Gallistrel Colvin, ed., *The Uprooted of the Western Sahel: Migrants' Quest for Cash in the Senegambia*, 183–203. New York: Praeger.

Hansen, Emmanuel, and Kwame A. Ninsin, eds. 1989. *The State, Development, and Politics in Ghana*. London: CODESRIA Book Series.

Harbeson, John W. 1990. "Centralization and Development in Eastern Africa." In James S. Wunch and Dele Owolu, eds., *The Failure of the Centralized State*, 174–92. Boulder, Colo.: Westview.

Harbeson, John W., Donald Rothchild, and Naomi Chazan, eds. 1994. *Civil Society and the State in Africa*. Boulder, Colo.: Lynne Rienner Publishers.

Harms, Robert. 1987. *Games Against Nature: An Eco-Cultural History of the Nunu of Equatorial Africa*. Cambridge: Cambridge University Press.

Hart, Keith. 1982. *The Political Economy of West African Africulture*. Cambridge: Cambridge University Press.

Harvey, David. 2001. *Spaces of Capital: Towards a Critical Geography*. London: Routledge.

Hecht, Robert M. 1982. "Cocoa and the Dynamics of Socio-Economic Change in Southern Ivory Coast." Ph.D. diss., University of Cambridge, Department of Social Anthropology.

Hecht, Robert M. 1983. The Ivory Coast 'Miracle': What Benefits for Peasant Farmers? *Journal of Modern African Studies*, 21, 1:25–53.

Hecht, Robert M. 1984. The Transformation of Lineage Production in Southern Ivory Coast. *Ethnology: An International Journal of Cultural and Social Anthropology*, 23:261–77.

Hecht, Robert M. 1985. Immigration, Land Transfer, and Tenure Change in Divo, Ivory Coast: 1940–1980. *Africa*, 55, 3:319–36.

Hechter, Michael. 1983. "A Theory of Group Solidarity." In Michael Hechter, ed., *The Microfoundations of Macrosociology*, 16–51. Philadelphia: Temple University Press.

Hechter, Michael. 1987. *Principles of Group Solidarity*. Berkeley and Los Angeles: University of California Press.

Hechter, Michael. 1992. Dynamics of Secession. *Acta Sociologica* 35:267–83.

Hechter, Michael. 2000. *Containing Nationalism*. Oxford: Oxford University Press.

Hechter, Michael, and William Brustein. 1980. Regional Modes of Production and Patterns of State Formation in Western Europe. *American Journal of Sociology*, 85 (March):1061–94.

Herbst, Jeffrey. 1993. *The Politics of Reform in Ghana, 1982–1991*. Berkeley and Los Angeles: University of California Press.

Herbst, Jeffrey. 2000. *States and Power in Africa*. Princeton: Princeton University Press.

Hesseling, Gerti. 1986a. "La Réforme Foncière au Sénégal: Consensus entre Paysans et Pouvoirs Publics?" In Wim van Binsbergen, Filip Reyntjens, and G. Hesseling, eds., *Etat et Communauté Locale en Afrique*, 113–18. Bruxelles: CEDAF.

Hesseling, Gerti. 1986b. "Le Droit Foncière dans une Situation Semi-Urbaine: Le Cas de Ziguinchor." In Bernard Crousse et al., eds., *Espaces Disputées en Afrique Noire*, 113–32. Paris: Karthala.

Hesseling, Gerti. 1994. "La Terre: À Qui Est-Elle? Les Pratiques Foncières en Basse-Casamance." In F. G. Barbier-Wiesser, ed., *Comprendre la Casamance: Chronique d'une Intégration Contrastée*, 243–61. Paris: Karthala.

Hill, Polly. 1963. "Three types of southern Ghanian cocoa farmers." In D. Biebuyck, ed., *African Agrarian Systems*, 203–23. Oxford: Oxford University Press.

Hill, Polly. 1966. Landlords and Brokers: A West African Trading System (with a Note on Kumasi Butchers). *Cahiers d'Etudes Africaines*, 6, 23:349–66.

Hinderink, J., and G. J. Tempelman. 1978. Rural Change and Types of Migration in Northern Ivory Coast. *African Perspectives*, 1:93–108.

Hirschfeld, A. 1975. Histoire, Situation, et Perspectives du Mouvement Coopératif en RCI. *Informations Coopératives*, 3:51–73.

Howard, Rhoda. 1976. Differential Class Participation in an African Protest Movement: The Ghana Cocoa Boycott of 1937–38. *Canadian Journal of African Studies*, 10, 3:469–80.

Huntington, Samuel P. 1968. *Political Order in Changing Societies*. New Haven: Yale University Press.

Hyden, Goran. 1980. *Beyond Ujamaa in Tanzania: Underdevelopment and an Uncaptured Peasantry*. Berkeley and Los Angeles: University of California Press.

Hyden, Goran. 1983. *No Shortcuts to Progress: African Development and Management in Perspective*. Berkeley and Los Angeles: University of California Press.

Ihonvbere, Julius O. 1996. On the Threshold of Another False Start? A Critical Evaluation of Prodemocracy Movements in Africa. *Journal of Asian and African Studies*, 31, 1–2:140.

Institut de Développement Économique et Technique, Filiale de la Commission Générale d'Organisation Scientifique (IDET-CEGOS). 1963. *La Distribution en Côte-d'Ivoire*. Abidjan and Paris: IDET-GEGOS.

Institut de Développement Économique et Technique, Filiale de la Commission Générale d'Organisation Scientifique (IDET-CEGOS) and République de Côte d'Ivoire, Ministère des Affaires Economiques et Financières (RCI, MAEF). 1969. *Ensemble de Projets Devant Concourir à l'Amélioration et au Développement de la Distribution en Côte d'Ivoire: Mission d'Étude et de Mise en Place des Structures du Commerce et de la Distribution en Côte d'Ivoire*. Abidjan: MAEF and IDET-CEGOS (juin).

Issacman, Alan. 1990. Peasants and Rural Social Protest in Africa. *African Studies Review*, 33, 2 (September):1–120.

Jarrige, F., and F. Ruf. 1990. Understanding the Cocoa Crisis. *Café Cacao Thé*, 34, 3 (juillet–septembre):221–9.

Johnson, G. Wesley, Jr. 1971. *The Emergence of Black Politics in Senegal: The Struggle for Power in the Four Communes*. Stanford: Stanford University Press.

Kane, Papa Mamadou. 1988. "Administration Locale et Organisations Paysannes." In Cheikh Tidjane Sy, ed., *Crise du Développement Rural et Désengagement de l'Etat au Sénégal*, 23–45. Dakar: Nouvelles Editions Africaines.

References

Kante, Babacar. 1994. Senegal's Empty Elections. *Journal of Democracy*, 5, 1 (January):96–108.

Kay, G. B. 1972. *The Political Economy of Colonialism in Ghana: A Collection of Documents and Statistics, 1900–1960*. Cambridge: Cambridge University Press.

Kipré, Pierre. 1983. "Grandes Sociétés et Entreprises Individuelles dans la Ville Coloniale en Côte d'Ivoire à la Veille de la Seconde Guerre Mondiale." In Laboratoire 'Conaissance du Tiers-Monde,' ed., *Entreprises et Entrepreneurs en Afrique, XIXe et XXe Siècles, Tome II*, 229–40. Paris: L'Harmattan.

Kiser, Edgar. 1996. The Revival of Narrative in Historical Sociology: What Rational Choice Theory Can Contribute. *Politics and Society*, 24, 3 (September):249–71.

Kiwanuka, M. Semakula. 1970. Colonial Policies and Administrations in Africa: The Myths of the Contrasts. *African Historical Studies*, 3, 2:295–315.

Klein, Martin. 1968a. *Islam and Imperialism in Senegal: Sine-Saloum, 1847–1914*. Stanford: Stanford University Press.

Klein, Martin. 1968b. "The Evolution of the 'Chefferie' in Senegal." In Arnold Rivkin, ed., *Nations by Design: Institution-Building in Africa*, 192–207. Garden City, N.Y.: Anchor Books.

Klein, Martin. 1972. Social and Economic Factors in the Muslim Revolution in Senegambia. *Journal of African History*, 13, 3:419–41.

Knight, Jack. 1992. *Institutions and Social Conflict*. Cambridge: Cambridge University Press.

Köbben, A. J. F. 1963. "Land as an Object of Gain in a Non-Literate Society: Land Tenure among the Bété and Dida (Ivory Coast, West Africa)." In Daniel Biebuyck, ed., *African Agrarian Systems*, 245–66. Oxford: Oxford University Press.

Koffi Tèya, Pascal. 1985. *Côte d'Ivoire: Le Roi et Nu*. Paris: L'Harmattan.

Kouassi, Kouadio Jean-Baptiste. 1989. "L'apport des Travailleurs Immigrés dans l'Économie Ivoirienne: Le Cas des Syro-Libanais dans le Secteur Agro-Alimentaire." Thèse de doctorat de troisième cycle, Departement d'Ethno-Sociologie, Faculté des Lettres, Arts, et Sciences Humaines, Université Nationale de Côte d'Ivoire.

Kouassi, René. 1993. La Répartition des Moyens d'Incitation à la Production entre Cultures d'Exportation et Cultures Vivrières in Côte d'Ivoire. *Africa Development* (Dakar), 18, 1:67–86.

Labazée, Pascal. 1991. "Organisation Sociale et Stratégies Economiques des Réseaux Marchands Transfrontaliers: Le Case des Échanges entre le Mali, le Burkina Faso et le Nord de la Côte d'Ivoire." Abidjan: ORSTOM-CNRS, novembre.

Ladouceur, Paul André. 1979. *Chiefs and Politicians: The Politics of Regionalism in Northern Ghana*. London: Longman.

Lam, Aboubacry Moussa. 1992. Crise Agraire et Après-Barrages au Fuuta. *Sociétés, Espaces, Temps* (Dakar), 1, 1:116–24.

Launay, Robert. 1982. *Traders without Trade: Responses to Change in Two Dyula Communities*. Cambridge: Cambridge University Press.

Laurent, Pierre-Joseph, and Jean-Philippe Peemans. 1998. Les Dimensions Socio-Economiques du Développement Local en Afrique au Sud du Sahara: Quelles

Stratégies pour quels Acteurs? *APAD Bulletin* [Association Euro-Africaine pour l'Anthropologie du Changement Social et du Développement], 15 (May):9–20.

Lavigne Delville, Philippe. 1991. "Migration et Structuration Associative." In Bernard Crousse, Paul Mathieu, and Sidy M. Seck, eds., *La Vallée du Fleuve Sénégal: Evaluations et Perspectives d'une Décennie d'Aménagements (1980–1990)*, 117–40. Paris: Karthala.

Lawler, Nancy. 1990. Reform and Repression under the Free French: Economic and Political Transformation in the Côte d'Ivoire, 1942–45. *Africa: Journal of the International African Institute*, 60:88–110.

Lawler, Nancy. 1992. *Soldiers of Misfortune: Ivioirien Tirailleurs of World War II.* Athens: Ohio University Press.

Le Bulletin de l'Afrique Noire (BAN). Periodical.

Lee, Eddy. 1980. Export-Led Rural Development: The Ivory Coast. *Development and Change*, 11, 4:607–42.

Le Fichier Permanent de la Côte d'Ivoire. Periodical. Paris: La Documentation Française.

Le Gal, Pierre-Yves, and Ibrihima Dia. 1991. "Le Désengagement de l'Etat et ses Conséquences dans le Delta du Fleuve Sénégal." In Bernard Crousse, Paul Mathieu, and Sidy M. Seck, eds., *La Vallée du Fleuve Sénégal: Evaluations et Perspectives d'une Décennie d'Aménagements (1980–1990)*, 161–74. Paris: Karthala.

Lele, Uma, Nicolas van de Walle, and Mathurin Gbetibouo. 1989. *Cotton in Africa: An Analysis of Differences in Performance.* Managing Agricultural Development in Africa (MADIA) Discussion Paper 7. Washington, D.C.: The World Bank.

Lemarchand, René. 1977. "Political Clientelism and Ethnicity in Tropical Africa: Competing Solidarities in Nation-Building." In Steffen W. Schmidt et al., eds., *Friends, Followers, and Factions: A Reader in Political Clientelism*, 100–22. Berkeley and Los Angeles: University of California Press.

Le Meur, Pierre-Yves. 1998. Décentralisation par le Bas et Participation Clientéliste au Bénin. *APAD [Association Euro-Africaine pour l'Anthropologie du Changement Social et du Développement] Bulletin* 15 (May):49–64.

Lemieux, Vincent. 1996. L'Analyse Politique de la Décentralisation. *Canadian Journal of Political Science*, 29, 4 (December):661–80.

Le Monde. Periodical.

Le Nouvel Horizon (Abidjan). Periodical.

Lentz, Carola, and Paul Nugent, eds. 2000. *Ethnicity in Ghana: The Limits of Invention.* Houndmills and London: Macmillan.

Leonard, David K. 1991. *African Successes: Four Public Managers of Kenyan Rural Development.* Berkeley and Los Angeles: University of California Press.

Le Roy, Etienne. 1984. Enjeux, Contraintes, et Limites d'une Démocratisation d'une Administration Territoriale: Les Communautés Rurales Sénégalaises (1972–1980). *Annuaire du Tiers Monde*, 8:61–76.

Le Roy, Etienne. 1991. "Urbanisation et Agro-Industries." In Bernard Crousse, Paul Mathieu, and Sidy M. Seck, eds., *La Vallée du Fleuve Sénégal: Evaluations et Perspectives d'une Décennie d'Aménagements (1980–1990)*, 175–96. Paris: Karthala.

References

Le Soleil (Dakar). Periodical.

Leveau, Rémy. 1985. *Le Fellah Morocain: Défenseur du Trône*. 2d ed. Paris: Presses de la Fondation Nationale des Sciences Politiques. (First published in 1976.)

Levi, Margaret. 1988. *Of Rule and Revenue*. Berkeley and Los Angeles: University of California Press.

Lewis, Barbara. 1971. "The Dioula in the Ivory Coast." In Carleton T. Hodge, ed., *Papers on the Manding*, 273–307. Bloomington: Indiana University Press.

Lewis, Barbara. 1980. "Ethnicity and Occupation Specialization in the Ivory Coast: the Transporters' Association." In John N. Paden, ed., *Values, Identities, and National Integration*, 75–87, 381–2. Evanston, Ill.: Northwestern University Press.

Lewis, Barbara. 1991. "Land, Property, and Politics: Rural Divo at the *Fin de Régime*." Paper prepared for the annual meeting of the African Studies Association, St. Louis, Mo., 23–26 November.

Lewis, Barbara. 1992. "Political Liberalization, Economic Liberalization, and Obstacles to Rural Empowerment in Côte d'Ivoire." Paper prepared for the meeting of the African Studies Association, Seattle, Wash., 20–23 November.

Ley, A. 1982. "La Logique Foncière de l'Etat depuis la Colonisation: l'Expérience Ivoirienne." In E. Le Bris, Etienne Le Roy, and F. Leimdorfer, eds., *Enjeux Fonciers en Afrique Noire*, 135–40. Paris: Karthala.

Lichbach, Mark. 1994. What Makes Rational Peasants Revolutionary? Dilemma, Paradox, and Irony in Peasant Collective Action. *World Politics*, 46, 3 (April):383–418.

Lichbach, Mark. 1995. *The Rebel's Dilemma*. Ann Arbor: University of Michigan Press.

Linarès, Olga F. 1992. *Power, Prayer, and Production: The Jola of Casamance, Senegal*. Cambridge: Cambridge University Press.

Little, Daniel. 1989. *Understanding Peasant China: Case Studies in the Philosophy of Social Science*. New Haven and London: Yale University Press.

Lombard, Jacques. 1967. *Autorités Traditionelles et Pouvoirs Européens en Afrique*. Paris: Librarie Armand Colin.

Lonsdale, John. 1968. Some Origins of Nationalism in East Africa. *Journal of African History*, 9, 1:119–46.

Lonsdale, John. 1981. States and Social Processes in Africa: A Historiographical Survey. *African Studies Review*, 24, 2–3 (June–September):139–224.

Loucou, Jean-Noël. 1976. Les Premières Elections de 1945 en Côte d'Ivoire. *Annales d'Historie de l'Université d'Abidjan*, Série 1, vol. 4 (Histoire):5–33.

Loucou, Jean-Noël. 1977. Aux Origines du Parti Démocratique de la Côte d'Ivoire. *Annales de l'Université d'Abidjan*, Série 1, vol. 5 (Histoire):81–105.

Lubeck, Paul. 1987. "The African Bourgeoisie: Debates, Methods, and Units of Analysis." In Paul Lubeck, ed., *The African Bourgeoisie: Capitalist Development in Nigeria, Kenya, and the Ivory Coast*, 3–26. Boulder, Colo.: Lynne Rienner Publishers.

Lucier, Richard L. 1988. *The International Political Economy of Coffee: From Juan Valdez to Yank's Diner*. New York: Praeger.

Luckham, Robin. 1978. Imperialism, Law, and Structural Dependence: The Ghana Legal Profession. *Development and Change*, 9, 2:201–43.

Lugard, Frederick D. 1926. *The Dual Mandate in British Tropical Africa*. 3d ed. Edinburgh: William Blackwood and Sons.

Ly, Abdoulaye. 1958. *L'Etat et la Production Paysanne ou l'Etat et la Révolution au Sénégal*. Paris: Présence Africaine.

Ly, Abdoulaye. 1992. *Les Regroupements Politiques au Sénégal, 1956–1970*. Dakar: CODESRIA.

Machiavelli, Niccolo. 1966. *The Prince*. Edited by Daniel Donno. New York: Bantam Books.

Mafeje, Archie. 1991. *The Theory and Ethnography of African Social Formations: The Case of the Interlacustrine Kingdoms*. London: CODESRIA Book Series.

Magagna, Victor V. 1991. *Communities of Grain: Rural Rebellion in Comparative Perspective*. Ithaca: Cornell University Press.

Mahieu, F. R. 1984. "Stabilisation des Prix de Produits Agricoles d'Exportation: L'expérience de la Caisse de Stabilisation en Côte d'Ivoire." Unpublished manuscript. CIRES, Abidjan. Photocopy.

Mamdani, Mahmood. 1996. *Citizen and Subject: Contemporary Africa and the Legacy of Late Colonialism*. Princeton: Princeton University Press.

Manchuelle, François. 1997. *Willing Migrants: Soninke Labor Diasporas, 1848–1960*. Athens: Ohio University Press.

Manso, M. Eyi J. Marie. 1981. Le Mouvement Coopératif Ivoirien. *Cahiers du CIRES*, 28–9:147–77.

Marchés Tropicaux et Méditerranéens (MTM). Periodical.

Mark, Peter, Ferdinand de Jong, and Clémence Chupin. 1998. Ritual and Masking Traditions in Jola Men's Initiation. *African Arts*, 31, 1 (Winter):36–47.

Markovitz, Irving Leonard. 1970. Traditional Social Structure, the Islamic Brotherhoods, and Political Development in Senegal. *Journal of Modern African Studies*, 8, 1 (April):73–96.

Martin, Bradford. 1971. "Al-Haji 'Umar Tall, Samori Turé, and their Forerunners." In Carleton T. Hodge, ed., *Papers on the Manding*, 159–65. Bloomington: Indiana University Press.

Marx, Karl. [1852] 1963. *The Eighteenth Brumaire of Louis Bonaparte*. New York: International Publishers.

Massey, Rachel Ida. 1994. Impediments to Collective Action in a Small Community. *Politics and Society*, 22, 3 (September):421–34.

Mathieu, Paul. 1991. "Irrigation, Transformation Économique et Enjeux Fonciers." In Bernard Crousse, Paul Mathieu, and Sidy M. Seck, eds., *La Vallée du Fleuve Sénégal: Evaluations et Perspectives d'une Décennie d'Aménagements (1980–1990)*, 197–214. Paris: Karthala.

Mathieu, Paul, Madiodio Naisse, and Pierre-Pol Vincke. 1986. "Aménagement Hydro-Agricoles, Concurrence pour l'Espace et Pratiques Foncières Locales dans la Vallée du Fleuve Sénégal: Le Cas de la Zone du Lac de Guiers." In Bernard Crousse, E. Le Bris, and Etienne le Roy, eds., *Espaces Disputés en Afrique Noire: Pratiques Foncières Locales*, 217–37. Paris: Karthala.

References

McLaughlin, Fiona. 1997. Islam and Popular Music in Senegal. *Africa: Journal of the International African Institute*, 67, 4:560–81.

Médard, J.-F. 1982. "La Régulation Socio-Politique." In Yves A. Fauré and J.-F. Médard, eds., *L'Etat et Bourgeoisie en Côte d'Ivoire*, 61–88. Paris: Karthala.

Meillasoux, Claude. 1973. The Social Organization of the Peasantry. *Journal of Peasant Studies*, 1, 1:81–90.

Michel, Gilles, and Michel Noel. 1984. "The Ivoirian Economy and Alternative Trade Regimes." In I. William Zartman and Christopher Delgado, eds., *The Political Economy of Ivory Coast*, 77–144. New York: Praeger.

Migdal, Joel, Atul Kohli, and Vivienne Shue, eds. 1994. *State Power and Social Forces: Domination and Transformation in the Third World*. Cambridge: Cambridge University Press.

Mikell, Gwendolyn. 1989a. *Cocoa and Chaos in Ghana*. New York: Paragon House.

Mikell, Gwendolyn. 1989b. Peasant Politicization and Economic Recuperation in Ghana. *Journal of Modern African Studies*, 27, 3:455–78.

Miles, William. 1987. Partitioned Royalty: The Evolution of Hausa Chiefs in Nigeria and Niger. *Journal of Modern African Studies*, 25, 2:233–58.

Miles, William. 1994. *Hausaland Divided: Colonialism and Independence in Nigeria and Niger*. Ithaca: Cornell University Press.

Moore, Barrington Jr. 1966. *The Social Origins of Dictatorship and Democracy*. Boston: Beacon.

Morgenthau, Ruth Schachter. 1964. *Political Parties in French West Africa*. London: Oxford University Press.

Morgenthau, Ruth Schachter. 1979. "Strangers, Nationals, and Multinationals in Contemporary Africa." In William A. Shack and Elliott P. Skinner, eds., *Strangers in African Societies*, 105–20. Berkeley and Los Angeles: University of California Press.

Munro, William A. 1995. Building the Post-Colonial State: Villagization and Resource Management in Zimbabwe. *Politics and Society*, 23, 1 (March):107–40.

Munro, William A. 1998. *The Moral Economy of the State: Conservation, Community Development, and State Making in Zimbabwe*. Athens: Ohio University Press.

Munro, William A. 2001. The Political Consequences of Local Electoral Systems: Democratic Change and the Politics of Differential Citizenship in South Africa. *Comparative Politics*, 33, 3 (April):295–313.

Murray, Roger. 1967. Second Thoughts on Ghana. *New Left Review*, 42 (March–April):25–39.

N'Diaye, Boubacar. 2000. Ivory Coast's Civilian Control Strategies, 1961–1998: A Critical Assessment. *Journal of Political and Military Sociology*, 28, 2 (Winter):246–71.

Ndiaye, Birame. 1979. La Participation à la Gestion des Affaires Publiques: Les Communautés Rurales Sénégalaises. *Revue Française d'Administration Publique*, n. 11:539–72.

Newbury, David, and Catharine Newbury. 2000. Review Essay: Bringing the Peasants Back In: Agrarian Themes in the Construction and Corrosion of Statist Historiography in Rwanda. *American Historical Review*, 105, 3 (June):832–77.

Nguessan-Zoukou, L. 1990. *Régions et Régionalisation en Côte d'Ivoire.* Paris: L'Harmattan.

Niang, Mamadou. 1975. Réflexions sur le Régime des Terres au Sénégal. *Bulletin de l'IFAN [Dakar]*, Tome 37, Sér. B, n. 1 (janvier):137–53.

Niang, Mamadou. 1983. "Réflexions sur la Réforme Foncière Sénégalaise de 1964." In E. Le Bris, Etienne Le Roy, et F. Leimdorfer, eds., *Enjeux Fonciers en Afrique Noire*, 219–27. Paris: Karthala.

Niang, Mamadou. 1991. "La Réforme de l'Administration Territoriale et Local au Sénégal: Un Cadre Institutionnel pour l'Autopromotion Paysanne?" Paper prepared for the Centre d'Etudes d'Afrique Noire (Bordeaux)-Institute Fondamental d'Afrique Noire (CEAN-IFAN) colloquium on "Etat et Société au Sénégal," Bordeaux, 22–24 October.

Niasse, Madiodio. 1991. "Les Périmètres Irrigués Villageois Vieillissent Mal." In Bernard Crousse, Paul Mathieu, and Sidy M. Seck, eds., *La Vallée du Fleuve Sénégal: Evaluations et Perspectives d'une Décennie d'Aménagements (1980–1990)*, 97–116. Paris: Karthala.

Ninot, Olivier, Michel Lesourd, and Jérome Lombard. 2002. Nouveaux Espaces, Nouvelles Centralités: Echanges et Réseaux en Milieu Rural Sénégalais. *Historiens et Géographes*, 379 (juillet):235–45.

Ninsin, Kwame A. 1989. "The Land Question since the 1950s." In Emmanuel Hansen and Kwame A. Ninsin, eds., *The State, Development and Politics in Ghana*, 165–83. London: CODESRIA Book Series.

Noronha, Raymond. 1985. A Review of the Literature on Land Tenure Systems in Sub-Saharan Africa. Report n. ARU43 of the Research Unit of the World Bank Agriculture and Rural Development Department (19 July). Washington, D.C.: The World Bank.

North, Douglass. 1990. *Institutions, Institutional Change and Economic Performance.* Cambridge: Cambridge University Press.

Novicki, Margaret. 1997. Good Governance Key to Progress. *Africa Recovery*, 11, 1 (July):22–3.

Nugent, Paul. 1999. Living in the Past: Urban, Rural, and Ethnic Themes in the 1992 and 1996 Ghana Elections. *Journal of Modern African Studies*, 37, 2:287–320.

O'Bannon, Brett R. 1995. "Class and Gender in the Senegal River Valley: Institutions of Oppression." Paper presented at the annual meeting of the African Studies Association, Orlando, Fla., 3–6 November.

O'Bannon, Brett R. 2000. "Power and Resources in Herder-Farmer Conflict: Problems for Governance under Neo-liberal Reform in Rural Senegal." Paper presented at the African Studies Workshop, University of Chicago, 7 November.

O'Donnell, Guillermo. 1993. On the State, Democratization, and Some Conceptual Problems: A Latin American View with Glances at some Postcommunist Countries. *World Development*, 21, 8:1355–62.

Ostrom, Elinor. 1986. An Agenda for the Study of Institutions. *Public Choice*, 48:3–25.

Ostrom, Elinor. 1990. *Governing the Commons: The Evolution of Institutions for Collective Action.* Cambridge: Cambridge University Press.

References

Ottoway, Marina. 1997. African Democratization and the Leninist Option. *Journal of Modern African Studies*, 35, 1:1–15.

Owolu, Dele. 1990. "The Failure of Current Decentralization Programs in Africa." In James S. Wunch and Dele Owolu, eds., *The Failure of the Centralized State: Institutions and Self-Governance in Africa*, 74–99. Boulder, Colo.: Westview.

Owusu, Maxwell. 1970. *Uses and Abuses of Political Power*. Chicago: University of Chicago Press.

Owusu, Maxwell. 1992. Democracy and Africa – A View from the Village. *Journal of Modern African Studies*, 30, 3:369–96.

Paige, Jeffrey. 1975. *Agrarian Revolution: Social Movements and Export Agriculture in the Underdeveloped World*. New York: The Free Press.

Park, Thomas K. 1993. "Arid Lands and the Political Economy of Flood Recession in Fuuta Tooro." In Thomas K. Park, ed., *Risk and Tenure in Arid Lands: The Political Ecology of Development in the Senegal River Basin*, 1–30. Tucson: University of Arizona Press.

Patterson, Amy. 1996. "Participation and Democracy at the Grassroots: A Study of Development Associations in Rural Senegal." Ph.D. diss., Indiana University, Bloomington, Department of Political Science.

Patterson, Amy S. 1999. The Dynamic Nature of Citizenship and Participation: Lessons from Three Rural Senegalese Case Studies. *Africa Today*, 46, 1 (Winter):3–28.

Pélissier, Paul. 1966. *Les Paysans du Sénégal: Les Civilisations Agraires du Cayor à la Casamance*. Saint-Yrieix, Haute-Vienne: Imprimerie Fabrègue.

Pélissier, Paul. 2000. Les Intéractions Rurales-Urbaines en Afrique de l'Ouest et Central. *APAD [Association Euro-Africaine pour l'Anthropologie du Changement Social et Développement] Bulletin*, 19 (juin):7–19.

Person, Yves. 1981. Colonisation et Décolonisation en Côte d'Ivoire. *Le Mois en Afrique: Revue Française d'Études Politiques Africaines*, n. 188–9:15–30.

Person, Yves. 1982. Islam et Décolonisation et Côte d'Ivoire. *Le Mois en Afrique: Revue Française d'Études Politiques Africaines*, n. 198–9:14–30.

Phillips, Anne. 1989. *The Enigma of Colonialism: British Policy in West Africa*. London: James Currey.

Polanyi, Karl. 1944. *The Great Transformation: The Political and Economic Origins of Our Time*. Boston: Beacon Press.

Pontussen, Jonas. 1995. From Comparative Public Policy to Political Economy: Putting Political Institutions in Their Place and Taking Interests Seriously. *Comparative Political Studies*, 28, 1 (April):117–47.

Popkin, Samuel. 1979. *The Rational Peasant: The Political Economy of Rural Society in Vietnam*. Berkeley and Los Angeles: University of California Press.

Portères, Roland. 1952. "Aménagement de l' Economie Agricole et Rurale au Sénégal: Rapport de la Mission Roland Portères." Dakar: Gouvernement Général de l'AOF, Territoire du Sénégal (mars–avril). Archives Nationales du Sénégal, po I 4–208 (1, 2, 3).

Potholm, Christian. 1970. *Four African Political Systems*. Englewood Cliffs, N.J.: Prentice Hall.

Price, Robert. 1971. Military Officers and Political Leadership: The Ghanaian Case. *Comparative Politics*, 3, 3 (April):361–79.

Price, Robert M. 1984. Neo-Colonialism and Ghana's Economic Decline: A Critical Assessment. *Canadian Journal of African Studies*, 18, 1:163–93.

Programme des Nations Unies pour le Développement, Bureau International du Travail, Government of Ivory Coast (PNUD/BIT/IVC). 1990. "Recherches sur les Causes de la Prolifération de GVC dans un Même Village: Etude de Cas dans la Région d'Ayamé." Unpublished manuscript. Abidjan (August). Photocopy.

Programme des Nations Unies pour le Développement, Bureau International du Travail, Government of Ivory Coast (PNUD/BIT/IVC). 1991. "Project d'Appui à la Consolidation et la Réstructuration des Coopératives de Commercialisation: Quelques Éléments Sociologiques à Prendre en Considération Pendant la Promotion des Structures Faîtières au Niveau Régional Dans les Secteurs Coton et Café-Cacao." Unpublished manuscript. Abidjan (February). Photocopy.

Rajagopalan, Swarna. 1999. Internal Unit Demarcation and National Identity. *Nationalism and Ethnic Politics*, 5, 3–4 (Fall and Winter):191–211.

Rapley, John. 1990. "Class Formation in French West Africa: The Rise of an Ivoirien Bourgeoisie." Ph.D. diss., Queen's University at Kingston.

Rapley, John. 1993. *Ivoirien Capitalism: African Entrepreneurs in Côte d'Ivoire*. Boulder, Colo.: Lynne Rienner Publishers.

Rathbone, Richard. 1973. Businessmen in Politics: Party Struggle in Ghana. *Journal of Development Studies*, 9, 3:390–401.

Rathbone, Richard. 1993. *Murder and Politics in Colonial Ghana*. New Haven: Yale University Press.

Rathbone, Richard. 2000. *Nkrumah and the Chiefs: The Politics of Chieftaincy in Ghana, 1951–60*. Accra, Athens, and Oxford: F. Reimmer, Ohio University Press, and James Currey.

Reno, William. 1995. *Corruption and State Politics in Sierra Leone*. Cambridge: Cambridge University Press.

Reno, William. 1998. *Warlord Politics and African States*. Boulder, Colo.: Lynne Rienner Publishers.

République de Côte d'Ivoire, Caisse de Péréquation et de Stabilisation des Prix. 1995. "Riz: La Filière dans Toute sa Réalité." *Le Soleil*, 30 juin.

République de Côte d'Ivoire, Diréction Centrale des Grands Travaux (RCI, DCGTx). 1990a. "Etude de la Filière du Riz." Unpublished report (janvier).

République de Côte d'Ivoire, Ministère de l'Economie et des Finances (RCI, MEF). 1973. *Assises du Commerce: Recueil des Documents Établis par les Groupes de Travail, Tomes I–III*. Abidjan: MEF, Chambre du Commerce (mai).

République de Côte d'Ivoire, Ministère du Plan. 1976. *Projet de Plan Quinquennal de Développement Economique, Social, et Culturel, 1976–1980*. Abidjan: RCI (mai).

République de Côte d'Ivoire, Ministère du Plan. 1981. *Plan Quinquennal de Développement Economique, Social, et Culturel, 1981–1986*. Abidjan: RCI.

Ribot, Jesse C. 1996. "Participation without Representation: Chiefs, Councils and Forestry Law in the West African Sahel." *Cultural Survival Quarterly*, 20, 3 (Fall):40–4.

References

Ribot, Jesse C. 1999. Decentralization, Participation and Accountability in Sahelian Forestry: Legal Instruments of Political-Administrative Control. *Africa: Journal of the International African Institute*, 69, 1:23–43.

Ridler, Neil B. 1985. Comparative Advantage as a Development Model: The Ivory Coast. *Journal of Modern African Studies*, 23, 3:407–17.

Ridler, Neil B. 1988. The Caisse de Stabilisation in the Coffee Sector of the Ivory Coast. *World Development*, 16, 12:1521–6.

Rimmer, Douglas. 1984. *The Economies of West Africa*. London: Weidenfeld and Nicolson.

Rimmer, Karen, and Eric Wibbles. 2000. The Political Economy of Decentralization in Latin America. *APSA-CP: Newsletter of the Organized Section in Comparative Politics of the American Political Science Association*, 11, 1 (Winter): 28–32.

Rogowski, Ronald. 1989. *Commerce and Coalitions: How Trade Affects Domestic Political Alignments*. Princeton: Princeton University Press.

Root, Hilton. 1987. *Peasants and Kings in Burgundy: Agrarian Foundations of French Absolutism*. Berkeley and Los Angeles: University of California Press.

Rostow, Walter W. 1960. *Stages of Growth: A Non-Communist Manifesto*. Cambridge: Cambridge University Press.

Rouveroy van Nieuwaal, Emile A. B., ed. 1987. Chiefs and African States: Some Introductory Notes and an Extensive Bibliography on African Chieftaincy. *Journal of Legal Pluralism and Unofficial Law* (special issue on "Chieftaincy and the State in Africa"), 25–6:1–46.

Rubin, Jeffrey. 1996. Decentering the Regime: Culture and Regional Politics in Mexico. *Latin American Research Review*, 31, 3:85–126.

Sall, Ebrima. 1991. "Le Queue d'Aronde Sénégalo-gambienne." Paper presented at the Centre d'Etudes d'Afrique Noire (Bordeaux)-Institute Fondamental d'Afrique Noire (CEAN-IFAN) colloquium on "Etat et Société au Sénégal," Bordeaux, 22–24 October.

Samoff, Joel. 1990. Decentralization: The Politics of Interventionism. *Development and Change*, 21, 3 (July):513–30.

Sandler, Todd. 2001. *Economic Concepts for the Social Sciences*. Cambridge: Cambridge University Press.

Saul, John S. 1973. "On African Populism." In Giovanni Arrighi and John S. Saul, eds. *Essays on the Political Economy of Africa*, 152–79. New York: Monthly Review Press.

Saul, John S., and Roger Woods. 1971. "African Peasantries." In Teodor Shanin, ed., *Peasants and Peasant Societies*, 103–14. Baltimore: Penguin Books.

Savonnet-Guyot, Claudette. 1973. Espace Politique et Paysannat d'Afrique Noire. *L'Homme et la Société*, 27, 1 (jan–mars):149–68.

Schattschneider, E. E. 1960. *The Semi-Sovereign People: A Realist's View of Democracy in America*. Hinsdale, Ill.: Dryden Press.

Schiffer, Harriet. 1970. Local Administration and National Development: Fragmentation and Centralization in Ghana. *Canadian Journal of African Studies*, 4, 1:57–75.

Schmitz, Jean. 1991. "Problèmes Foncières ou Territorialité Politique dans la Vallée du Sénégal." Paper presented at the Centre d'Etudes d'Afrique Noire (Bordeaux) – Institute Fondamental d'Afrique Noire (CEAN-IFAN) colloquium on "Etat et Société au Sénégal: Crises et dynamiques sociales," Bordeaux, 22–24 October.

Schoonmaker-Freudenberger, Karen. 1991. Mbengue: The Disingenuous Destruction of a Sahelian Forest. *Development Anthropology Network*, 9, 2:2–12. Binghamton, N.Y.: Institute for Development Anthropology.

Schultz, Manfred. 1975. Rural Development Policy in the Ivory Coast. *Intereconomics*, 3:81–5.

Schumacher, Edward. 1975. *Politics, Bureaucracy, and Rural Development in Senegal.* Berkeley and Los Angeles: University of California Press.

Scott, James C. 1976. *The Moral Economy of the Peasant: Rebellion and Subsistence in Southeast Asia.* New Haven: Yale University Press.

Scott, James C. 1998. *Seeing Like a State: How Certain Schemes to Improve the Human Condition Have Failed.* New Haven: Yale University Press.

Seck, Sidy M. 1986. La Maîtrise de l'Eau et la Réstructuration Sociale Induite par l'Organisation de la Production Irriguée dans le Bassin du Fleuve Sénégal. *Les Cahiers de la Recherche Développement* [Montpellier], n. 12 (décembre):13–20.

Seck, Sidy M. 1991a. "La Dynamique de l'Irrigation dans la Vallée du Fleuve." In Bernard Crousse, Paul Mathieu, and Sidy M. Seck, eds., *La Vallée du Fleuve Sénégal: Evaluations et Perspectives d'une Décennie d'Aménagements (1980–1990)*, 17–42. Paris: Karthala.

Seck, Sidy M. 1991b. "Les Cultivateurs 'Transfrontaliers' de Décrue Face à la Question Foncière." In Bernard Crousse, Paul Mathieu, and Sidy M. Seck, eds., *La Vallée du Fleuve Sénégal: Evaluations et Perspectives d'une Décennie d'Aménagements (1980–1990)*, 297–320. Paris: Karthala.

Skinner, Elliott P. 1989. *The Mossi of Burkina Faso: Chiefs, Politicians and Soldiers.* Prospect Heights, Ill.: Waveland Press.

Skinner, G. William. 1964–5. Marketing and Social Structure in Rural China. 3 parts. *Journal of Asian Studies*, 24:3–43, 195–228, 363–99.

Skocpol, Theda. 1979. *States and Social Revolutions: A Comparative Analysis of France, Russia, and China.* Cambridge: Cambridge University Press.

Snyder, Francis G. 1978. Legal Innovation and Social Change in a Peasant Community: A Senegalese Village Police. *Africa*, 48, 3:231–47.

Snyder, Richard. 2001a. *Politics after Neoliberalism: Reregulation in Mexico.* Cambridge: Cambridge University Press.

Snyder, Richard. 2001b. Scaling Down: The Subnational Comparative Method. *Studies in Comparative International Development*, 36, 1:93–110.

Société Africaine d'Edition. 1982. *Les Elites Ivoiriennes.* Paris: Sté Africaine d'Edition.

Société d'Etudes pour le Développement Economique et Social (SEDES). 1985. Analyse Ex-Post de la Promotion des PME et de l'Artisanat en Côte d'Ivoire. Abidjan and Paris: Ministère des Relations Extérieures, Coopération et Développement, SEDES, CEGOF (décembre).

References

Société d'Etudes pour la Promotion de l'Industrie Caféière et la Société d'Etudes pour le Développement Economique et Social (SEPRIC/SEDES). 1970. Eléments pour une Réforme de la Commercialisation du Café en Côte d'Ivoire: Rapport Général et Annexes. Paris: SEDES (septembre).

Solnick, Steven Lee. 1998. *Stealing the State: Control and Collapse in Soviet Institutions.* Cambridge: Harvard University Press.

Southall, Roger J. 1978. Farmers, Traders, and Brokers in the Gold Coast Cocoa Economy. *Canadian Journal of African Studies*, 12, 2:185–211.

Sow, Aboubacar. 1988. "L'étude des Problèmes Organisationnels des Structures d'Encadrement dans l'Optique du Management: Le Cas des CER." In Cheikh Tidjane Sy, ed., *Crise du Développement Rural et Désengagement de l'Etat au Sénégal*, 79–100. Dakar: Nouvelles Editions Africaines.

Staniland, Martin. 1968. Local Administration in Ivory Coast: Part I. *West Africa*, 9 March, n. 2649, p. 273; Part II. *West Africa*, 16 March, n. 2650, p. 315.

Staniland, Martin. 1969. "Single-Party Systems and Political Change: The PDCI and Ivory Coast Politics." In Colin Leys, ed., *Politics and Change in Developing Countries*, 135–75. Cambridge: Cambridge University Press.

Staniland, Martin. 1970a. Colonial Government and Populist Reform: The Case of the Ivory Coast: Part I. *Journal of Administration Overseas* (*JAO*), 9, 1 (January): 33–43; Part II. *JAO*, 9, 4 (October):113–27.

Staniland, Martin. 1970b. "Nationalism and Communal Partnership: The Case of Bongouanou, Ivory Coast." In R. W. Johnson and C. H. Allen, eds., *African Perspectives: Papers in the History, Politics and Economics of Africa Presented to Thomas Hodgkin*, 371–91. Cambridge: Cambridge University Press.

Staniland, Martin. 1970c. The Rhetoric of Centre Periphery Relations. *Journal of Modern African Studies*, 8, 4:617–36.

Staniland, Martin. 1971. Colonial Government and Populist Reform: The Case of Ivory Coast: Part I. *Journal of Administration Overseas* (*JAO*), 10, 1 (January):33–42; Part II. *JAO*, 11, 2 (April):115–26.

Staniland, Martin. 1975. *The Lions of Dagbon: Political Change in Northern Ghana.* Cambridge: Cambridge University Press.

Stavenhagen, Rodolfo. 1975. *Social Classes in Agrarian Societies.* Garden City, N.Y.: Anchor Press/Doubleday.

Steinmo, Sven, Kathleen Thelen, and Frank Longstreth, eds. 1992. *Structuring Politics: Historical Institutionalism in Comparative Analysis.* Cambridge: Cambridge University Press.

Stier, Harald. 1972. Fertilizer Distribution in the Ivory Coast. Paris: Development Centre of the OECD (Organisation for Economic Cooperation and Development).

Stinchcombe, Arthur. 1961. Agricultural Enterprise and Rural Class Relations. *American Journal of Sociology*, 67, 2 (September):165–76.

Stoner-Weiss, Kathryn. 2001. "The Russian Central State in Crisis: Center and Periphery in the Post-Soviet Era." In Zoltan Barany and Robert G. Moser, eds., *Russian Politics: Challenges of Democratization*, 103–34. Cambridge: Cambridge University Press.

Stryker, Richard E. 1970. "Center and Locality: Linkage and Political Change in the Ivory Coast." Ph.D. diss., University of California at Los Angeles, Department of Political Science.

Stryker, Richard E. 1971a. "Political and Administrative Linkage in the Ivory Coast." In Philip Foster and Aristide R. Zolberg, eds., *Ghana and the Ivory Coast: Perspectives on Modernization*, 73–102. Chicago: University of Chicago Press.

Stryker, Richard E. 1971b. "A Local Perspective on Developmental Strategy in the Ivory Coast." In M. Lofchie, ed., *The State of the Nations*, 119–39. Berkeley and Los Angeles: University of California Press.

Suret-Canale, Jean. 1964. *Afrique Noire: L'ère Coloniale, 1900–1945*. Paris: Editions Sociales.

Suret-Canale, Jean. 1966. La Fin de la Chefferie en Guinée. *Journal of African History*, 7, 3:459–93.

Sy, Cheikh Tidjane, ed. 1988. *Crise du Développement Rural et Désengagement de l'Etat au Sénégal*. Dakar: Nouvelles Editions Africaines.

Syndicat Agricole Africain de la Côte d'Ivoire (SAA). 1947. Composition du bureau du SAA. Archives de la Chambre de Commerce d'Abidjan, dossier n. 51, 14 novembre. Abidjan. Photocopy.

Syndicat Agricole Africain de la Côte d'Ivoire (SAA). 1955. Procès verbal de la reunion du 31 mars 1955. Archives de la Chambre de Commerce d'Abidjan, dossier n. 51, 31 mars. Abidjan. Photocopy.

Taylor, Michael. 1989. "Rationality and Revolutionary Collective Action." In Michael Taylor, ed., *Rationality and Revolution*, 63–97. Cambridge: Cambridge University Press.

Tendler, Judith. 1997. *Good Government in the Tropics*. Baltimore: Johns Hopkins University Press.

Terpend, Marie-Noëlle. 1981. *La Filière Café: Production et Commercialisation du Café en Côte d'Ivoire*. Paris: Les Dossiers Faim/Développement; GRAAP, avril (reactualisé en nov. 1982).

Terpend, Marie-Noëlle. 1982. *La Filière Cacao: Filière Ivoirienne, Marché Mondial, Consommation Européenne*. Paris: Les Dossiers Faim/Développement; GRAAP-CCFD, juillet.

Tetlock, Philip, and Aaron Belkin. 1996. *Counterfactual Thought Experiments in World Politics*. Princeton: Princeton University Press.

Thelen, Kathleen, and Sven Steinmo. 1992. "Historical Institutionalism in Comparative Politics." In Sven Steinmo, Kathleen Thelen, and Frank Longstreth, eds., *Structuring Politics: Historical Institutionalism in Comparative Analysis*, 1–32. Cambridge: Cambridge University Press.

Thioub, Ibrahima. 1996. À Propos de la Plate-Forme Revendicative de l'UNACOIS. Unpublished manuscript. Université Cheikh Anta Diop (Dakar, Senegal). Photocopy.

Thioub, Ibrahima, Momar-Coumba Diop, and Catherine Boone. 1997. La Libéralisation de l'Économie et les Groupements Professionels au Sénégal. *Sociétés Africaines et Diaspora*, n. 5 (January):5–44.

References

Thompson, Virginia, and Richard Adloff. 1958. *French West Africa*. London: George Allen & Unwin.

Tice, Robert D. 1974. Administrative Structure, Ethnicity, and Nation-Building in the Ivory Coast. *Journal of Modern African Studies*, 12, 2:211–29.

Tignor, Robert. 1987. "Senegal's Cooperative Experience, 1907–1960." In John Waterbury and Mark Gersovitz, eds., *The Political Economy of Risk and Choice in Senegal*, 90–122. London: Frank Cass.

Tilly, Charles. 1964. *The Vendée*. Cambridge: Harvard University Press.

Tilly, Charles, ed. 1975. *The Formation of National States in Western Europe*. Princeton: Princeton University Press.

Tilly, Charles. 1990. *Coercion, Capital, and European States, AD 990–1900*. Cambridge, Mass.: Basil Backwell Publishers.

Toungara, Jeanne Maddox. 1996. "Kinship, Politics and Democratization among the Malinke in Northwestern Côte d'Ivoire." In Jan Jansen and Clemens Zobel, eds., *The Younger Brother in Mande: Selected Papers of the Third International Conference on Mande Studies, Leiden, 20–24 March 1995*, 48–60. Lieden: CNWS Publications.

Toungara, Jeanne Maddox. 2001. Ethnicity and Political Crisis in Côte d'Ivoire. *Journal of Democracy*, 12, 3 (July):63–72.

Touré, Mamoudou. 1985. Politique d'Ajustement Économique et Financier. Dakar: Communication au Conseil National du Parti Socialiste du 11 mai 1985.

Treisman, Daniel. 2001. *After the Deluge: Regional Crises and Political Consolidation in Russia*. Ann Arbor: University of Michigan Press.

Tricart, Jean. 1957. Le Café en Côte d'Ivoire. *Cahiers d'Outre Mer*, 10, 39:209–33.

Tsebelis, George. 1990. *Nested Games: Rational Choice in Comparative Politics*. Berkeley and Los Angeles: University of California Press.

Union Nationale des Commerçants et Industriels Sénégalais (UNACOIS). 1994. Place et Rôle du Secteur Informel dans l'Économie. Éléments de Diagnostic de Meilleure Performance et Perspectives. Note Contributive de l'UNACOIS au 25e anniversaire du Club Nation et Développement.

Vail, Leroy, ed. 1989. *The Creation of Tribalism in Southern Africa*. London: James Currey; Berkeley and Los Angeles: University of California Press.

van Binsbergen, Wim M. J., ed. 1984. *Old Modes of Production and Capitalist Encroachment: Anthropological Explorations in Africa*. London: Routledge and Kegan Paul.

van Binsbergen, Wim M. J., F. Reyntjens, and Gerti Hesseling, eds. 1986. "Aspects of Modern State Penetration in Africa." In Wim M. J. van Binsbergen et al., eds., *State and Local Community in Africa/Etat et Communauté Locale en Afrique*, 369–400. Brussels: Centre d'Etude et de Documentation Africaines.

van chi Bonnardel, Régine. 1978. *Vie de Relations au Sénégal: La Circulation des Biens*. Série Mémoires de l'IFAN, 90. Dakar: IFAN.

van de Walle, Nicolas. 2001. *African Economies and the Politics of Permanent Crisis, 1979–1999*. Cambridge: Cambridge University Press.

van der Klei, Jos. M. 1978. "Customary Land Tenure and Land Reform: The Rise of New Inequalities among the Diola of Senegal." In R. Buijtenhuijs and Peter Geschiere, *Stratification and Class Formation*, 35–44 (special issue of *African*

389

Perspectives 1978, no. 2) (Leiden, The Netherlands: Afrika-Studiecentrum/ African Studies Center):35–44.

van der Klei, Jos M. 1985. "Articulation of Modes of Production and the Beginning of Labor Migration among the Diola of Senegal." In Wim van Binsbergen and Peter Geschiere, eds., *Old Modes of Production and Capitalist Encroachment: Anthropological Explorations in Africa*. London: Kegan Paul International.

Varshney, Ashutosh. 1993. Urban Bias in Perspective. *Journal of Development Studies*, 29, 4 (July):3–24.

Vengroff, Richard. 1987. Decentralization and the Implementation of Rural Development in Senegal: The Role of the Rural Councils. *Public Administration and Development*, 7:273–88.

Vengroff, Richard. 1993. The Transition to Democracy in Senegal: The Role of Decentralization. *In Depth*, 3, 1 (Winter):23–52.

Vengroff, Richard, and Alan Johnson. 1989. *Decentralization and the Implementation of Rural Development in Senegal: The View from Below*. Lewiston, N.Y.: Edwin Mellen Press.

Vengroff, Richard, and Michael Magala. 2001. Democratic Reform, Transition and Consolidation: Evidence from Senegal's 2000 Presidential Election. *Journal of Modern African Studies*, 39, 1 (March):129–62.

Verdier, R. 1971. Evolution et Réformes Foncières de l'Afrique Noire Francophone. *Journal of African Law*, 15, 1:85–101.

Villalón, Leonardo A. 1993. Democratizing a (Quasi) Democracy: The Senegalese Elections of 1993. *African Affairs*, 93, 371 (April):163–94.

Villalón, Leonardo A. 1995. *Islamic Society and State Power in Senegal: Disciples and Citizens in Fatick*. Cambridge: Cambridge University Press.

Villalón, Leonardo A., and Phillip Huxtable, eds. 1998. *The African State at a Critical Juncture*. Boulder, Colo.: Lynne Rienner.

Wallerstein, Immanuel. 1964. *The Road to Independence: Ghana and the Ivory Coast*. Paris: Mouton.

Waterbury, John, and Mark Gersovitz, eds. 1987. *The Political Economy of Risk and Choice in Senegal*. London: Frank Cass.

Watts, Michael, and Thomas J. Bassett. 1985. Crisis and Change in African Agriculture: A Comparative Study of the Ivory Coast and Nigeria. *African Studies Review*, 28, 4 (December):3–27.

Weingast, Barry R. 1995. The Economic Role of Political Institutions: Market-Preserving Federalism and Economic Development. *Journal of Law, Economics, and Organization*, 11, 1:1–31.

Werlin, Herbert. 1972. The Roots of Corruption: The Ghanaian Inquiry. *Journal of Modern African Studies*, 10, 2 (July):247–67.

Widner, Jennifer. 1991. "The Origins of Agricultural Policy in Côte d'Ivoire, 1960–1986." Paper prepared for the annual meeting of the American Political Science Association, Washington, D.C.

Widner, Jennifer. 1993a. "'The Discovery of Politics': Smallholder Reactions to the Cocoa Crisis of 1988–1990 in Côte d'Ivoire." In Thomas M. Callaghy and John

References

Ravenhill, eds., *Hemmed In: Responses to Africa's Economic Decline*, 279–331. New York: Columbia University Press.

Widner, Jennifer. 1993b. The Origins of Agricultural Policy in Ivory Coast, 1960–86. *Journal of Development Studies*, 29, 4 (July):25–59.

Widner, Jennifer A. 1994. Single-Party States and Agricultural Policy Reform. *Comparative Politics*, 26, 2:127–48.

Widner, Jennifer. 1995. States and Statelessness in Late Twentieth Century Africa. *Daedalus*, 124, 3 (Summer):129–54.

Wilks, Ivor. 1989. *Wa and the Wala: Islam and Polity in Northwestern Ghana*. Cambridge: Cambridge University Press.

Williams, Gavan. 1981. "The World Bank and the Peasant Problem." In Judith Heyer, Gavan Williams, and Pepe Roberts, eds., *Rural Development in Tropical Africa*, 16–51. New York: St. Martin's Press.

Willis, Eliza, Christopher da C. B. Garman, and Stephan Haggard. 1999. The Politics of Decentralization in Latin America. *Latin American Research Review*, 34, 1:7–56.

Woods, Dwayne. 1989. Ethno-Regional Demands, Symbolic and Redistributive Politics: Sugar Complexes in the North of the Ivory Coast. *Ethnic and Racial Studies*, 12, 4:469–89.

Woods, Dwayne. 1994. Elites, Ethnicity, and "Home Town" Associations in the Côte d'Ivoire: An Historical Analysis of State-Society Links. *Africa*, 64, 4 (Winter):465–83.

Woods, Dwayne. 1999. The Politics of Organizing the Countryside: Rural Cooperatives in Côte d'Ivoire. *Journal of Modern African Studies*, 37, 3:489–506.

World Bank. 1978. *Ivory Coast: The Challenge of Success*. Washington, D.C.: The World Bank.

Woronoff, Jon. 1972. *West African Wager: Houphouet versus Nkrumah*. Metuchen, N.J.: Scarecrow Press.

Wunch, James S., and Dele Owolu, eds. 1990. *The Failure of the Centralized State*. Boulder, Colo.: Westview.

Yang, Dali L. 1996. *Calamity and Reform in China: State, Rural Society, and Institutional Change since the Great Leap Famine*. Stanford: Stanford University Press.

Youm, Prosper. 1991. "The Economy since Independence." In Christopher L. Delgado and Sidi Jammeh, eds., *The Political Economy of Senegal under Structural Adjustment*, 21–30. New York: Praeger.

Young, Crawford, Neal P. Sherman, and Tim H. Rose. 1981. *Cooperatives and Development: Agricultural Politics in Ghana and Uganda*. Madison: University of Wisconsin Press.

Zan, Semi-Bi. 1977. La Chambre de Commerce en Côte d'Ivoire: 1908–1940. *Godo Godo*, 3 (January):75–89.

Zan, Semi-Bi. 1996. *Ouezzin Coulibaly: Le Lion du RDA*. Abidjan: Presses Universitaires de Côte d'Ivoire.

Zartman, I. William, and Christopher Delgado. 1984. "Introduction: Stability, Growth, and Challenge." In I. William Zartman and Christopher Delgado, eds., *The Political Economy of the Ivory Coast*, 1–20. New York: Praeger.

Zolberg, Aristide R. 1964. *One-Party Government in the Ivory Coast*. Princeton: Princeton University Press.

Zolberg, Aristide. 1966. *Creating Political Order: The Party-States of West Africa*. Chicago: Rand McNally and Co.

Zolberg, Aristide R. 1971. "Political Development in the Ivory Coast since Independence." In Philip Foster and Aristide A. Zolberg, eds., *Ghana and the Ivory Coast: Perspectives on Modernization*, 9–32. Chicago: University of Chicago Press.

Zucarelli, François. 1966. L'arrondissement Sénégalais. *Annales Africaines* (University of Dakar Faculté de Droit et Sciences Economiques and Paris: Pédone): 261–80.

Zucarelli, François. 1970. *Un Parti Politique Africain: L'Union Progressiste Sénégalais*. Paris: R. Pichon and R. Durand-Auzias.

Zucarelli, François. 1973. De la Chefferie Traditionelle au Canton: Évolution du Canton Colonial au Sénégal, 1855–1960. *Cahiers d'Études Africaines*, 13, 50:213–38.

Index

Aboisso, *see* Sanwi
Acheampong regime (Ghana), 172 n65
administrative occupation, 35–7; in Lower
  Casamance, 97–8, 136–7; and 1990s
  decentralization, 333–4; in southern
  Côte d'Ivoire, 177–9, 213–6, 239;
  see also direct rule
African socialism, 14–5, 63, 66, 73, 114, 142
Afrique Occidentale Française (AOF), 50
age groups, 102; *see also poro* societies
Agni region: and Abengourou chieftaincy
  dispute, 199 n124; and collective
  action, 193–4; and colonial rule, 183–7;
  and commercial agriculture, 185–7, 192
  n103; and cotton, 276 n70; kingdoms,
  181 n76, 182–3, 188 n94; and planter
  bourgeoisie, 187, 190–7, 198, 204,
  231–2; political defeat of, 235–8;
  see also Côte d'Ivoire, southern; PP;
  Sanwi
AIDS, 352
Akim Abuakwa (Ghana), 148 n11, 149, 151,
  157, 161, 163 n44; *see also* Asante chiefs;
  Asante region
Anderson, Perry, 34, 321
animal traction, 274, 277, 310
Animation Rurale (Senegal), 65–6, 84–7, 89,
  302, 336
Aoulou, Kacou, 232
Asante chiefs: and British rule, 147–54, 316;
  as cocoa producers, 150–9, 173, 168;
  and collective action, 237–8, 340, 344;
  legitimacy, 154–5; and 1990s
  decentralization, 339–40; and the

PNDC, 340; political clout, 156–9,
  344; post-1966, 171–2, 340; resilience,
  177, 340; retraditionalization attempts,
  see chiefly authority; usurpation by
  CPP, 144–6, 162, 167, 171–6; *see also*
  Asante region; Ghana; NLM; planter
  bourgeoisie
Asante Confederacy, 146–8, 176, 181
Asante region: and Acheampong regime,
  172 n65; British rule, 147–54, 164–5,
  316; and Brong-Ahafo, 167, 175–6;
  community development association in,
  340 n22; land sales in, 150 n14, 151,
  153–4, 340 n23; land tenure in, 149–53,
  172 n64, 340 n23; landlord-stranger
  relations, 151–3; Local Councils, 164,
  166; Native Authorities in, 147–9, 154
  n26, 164–5; and NLC, 171–2; and
  Rawlings regime, 340; territorial
  administration and unit demarcation,
  163–7; *see also* Asante chiefs; cocoa
  economy (Ghana)
Ashanti Concessions Ordinance (1903), 150
Assalé family, 192 n102
associational life, 305 n138, 313–14, 326;
  autonomy of, 325; community
  development, 233, 340 n22, 346;
  cultural associations, 263; Diola, 101–4,
  110, 123–4, 129–30, 137; ethno-
  regional association, 112; militia, 137;
  minimization of, 206; *see also* civil
  society; collective action; political
  mobilization
Associations d'Intérêt Rural (AIRs), 129–30

393

Index

choice-theoretic analysis, *see* rational choice
 theory
citizenship, 325; in civil state, 177; and
 ethnicity, 349 n31; and land rights, 151,
 153, 155, 349 n31
civil society, 322, 325; *see also* associational
 life; "brown areas"; urban
 constituencies
class relations in rural Africa, 21, 23–4, 27–9,
 34–6, 149 n13, 163, 177; and class-like
 tensions, 163, 177, 207, 229, 347
cocoa and coffee economy (Côte d'Ivoire),
 184–91; and Caistab, 226 n197;
 class-like tensions in, 207; cooperatives
 in 225, 227–9, 230, 233 n211;
 credit/credit relations, 191–2, 201,
 222–4, 227; crisis of 1989–90, 234–5;
 European plantations, 184–5, 204 n41;
 fertilizers, 222–3; labor relations,
 185–6, 188, 191, 196–7, 199, 221; land
 conflicts, 201, 219–20; land tenure,
 182–9, 196, 218–21; landholding size,
 184, 195, 224; landlord-stranger
 relations, 185–9, 203 n137, 207,
 219–20, 229–30; marketing, 192,
 225–32; output, 217; and planter
 bourgeoisie, 187, 190–8, 204, 219–21,
 232, 235–8; prices, 104 n193, 216, 226
 n197, 231 n208, 234, 236; quality and
 yields, 217, 224–5; regeneration of,
 223; and rural development, 216–18;
 222–5; sharecropping, 186; *see also*
 labor, forced; planter bourgeoisie;
 SAA
cocoa economy (Ghana), 149–53; and
 Asante chiefs, 150–9, 168, 173; class
 relations, 149 n13, 150–4, 163, 177;
 cooperatives, 170–1; credit relations,
 152–3, 158, 167–70, 176; decline of,
 144, 172, 237; labor relations, 149–52;
 land tenure, 149–54, 164 n45, 169, 172
 n64; marketing and taxation, 156–62,
 167–70, 171; prices, 160–1, 171; and
 sharecropping, 149–50; *see also* Asante
 chiefs; Asante region; cocoa hold-ups
cocoa hold-ups (colonial Ghana), 156–8,
 161, 173, 234
Cocoa Marketing Board, 159–60, 172
Cocoa Purchasing Company, 167–70
coffee processing plants, 226

coffee production (Côte d'Ivoire), *see* cocoa
 and coffee economy
collective action, 23 n17, 326; and farmers,
 129–31, 154, 195, 234–5, 305; and rural
 elites, 65–6, 154, 156–9, 161, 193–4,
 234, 297–8, 337–8, 340; and social
 structure, 204–5, 206, 237–8, 330;
 see also associational life; political
 mobilization
colonial rule, *see* direct rule; indirect rule
communal solidarity, *see* communal
 structure; social cohesion
communal structure, 20, 21–7, 29, 34
Communautés Rurales (Senegal), *see* Rural
 Councils
community, rural: as a legal entity, 77, 218,
 219 n177
community leaders, 22 n15; *see also* chiefs;
 teachers and schooling
community resource management, 322
Compagnie Française de Développement
 des Fibres Textiles (CFDT), 264–7,
 273–80
Compagnie Ivoirienne de Développement
 des Fibres Textiles (CIDT), 273–80
Compagnie Sucrière Sénégalaise, 292, 299
 n118, 313
Congo, Democratic Republic of the, 343
Congo Basin, 335
Conseil Supérieur des Chefs Réligieux
 (Senegal), 65–6, 297
Conseils Ruraux (CRs) in Senegal, *see* Rural
 Councils
constitutional choice, 139–40, 329; and
 founding of African states, 343; in the
 United States, 139, 161 n41
core-periphery relations, *see* center-region
 relations
COSU (Coordination de la Opposition
 Sénégalaise Unie), and Mamadou Dia,
 86 n85
Côte d'Ivoire: African bourgeoisie in, 187,
 190–8, 204, 219–20, 235–8;
 Africanization, 205, 215; ethnic/land
 conflict in, 203 n137, 207, 220, 326,
 338; exports, 217; and liberalism,
 142–3, 218; multipartism, 211 n152;
 municipalities, 205–6, 211–13, 338;
 National Assembly, 209, 262, 270;
 national dialogues, 263; national

Index

Democratic Republic of the Congo, 335, 343
development, rural, *see* rural development
Dia, Mamadou, 61–2, 80 n75, 85–7, 88, 296
Diagne, Blaise, 61
Diallo, Ibou, 112
Diamacoune Senghor, Augustin, 112 n133
Diatta, Alinsitoué, 111
Diola society (Lower Casamance), 96; and colonial rule, 104–9; community institutions, 101–4, 110, 123, 129–30; compared to Sereer, 93; horizontal cohesion in, 103–4, 137, 325–6; and Islam, 109; labor, 102; land tenure, 102, 125–7, 133–5; militia, 104, 110, 137; out-migration, 108 n123, 110; social structure, 100, 105, 135–6; women, 110; youth, 110, 125; *see also* Casamance, Lower; groundnut economy, Lower Casamance; Senegal
Dioula (in Côte d'Ivoire), *see* Dyula
Diourbel (Senegal), 80, 80 n75, 86 n84
direct rule: and abolition of African slavery 253; and backlash, 138–40; costliness of, 35 n28, 138–40; by France in Lower Casamance, 97–8; as French doctrine, 15, 49, 178, 253; as vertical integration, 35 n28; *see also* administrative occupation; labor, forced; usurpation
distributive politics, 344
drought, Sahelian, 285, 304–6
Dyula traders and planter-traders, 188, 191–2, 191, 231, 248; as PDCI agents, 198, 201–2, 260, 262, 267; PDCI controls over, 231 n209

East Africa, 300, 320 n4, 327; *see also* settlement schemes
économie de plantation (Côte d'Ivoire), *see* cocoa and coffee economy (Côte d'Ivoire)
egalitarianism, 314, 325; and indirect rule, 99
environmental degradation, 47, 79, 86, 348; *see also* drought, Sahelian; Ferlo region; forest use; land pioneering
ethnicity: and ethnic politics, 229, 326, 335, 340; land rights, 151, 340, 349 n31; and modernization theory, 25–7; and

traditional culture, 26; *see also* landlord-stranger relations
Europe, 11; feudalism contrasted to Senoufoland's, 249 n12; and historical sociology, 321; and modes of production, 19, 20 n10, 21, 23, 321; and state building, 22–4, 347; *see also* Moore, Barrington Jr.
European plantations (Côte d'Ivoire), 184–5, 204 n141; *see also* labor, forced
export-crop marketing: in Asante, 156–62, 167–70, 171; in Côte d'Ivoire, 191, 225–32, 226 n197; 274, 280; in Senegal, 70–2, 81–3

Fadika family, 192
Fall, Médoune, 68
Farmers' Council (Ghana), 168 n55
Farmers' Unions (Ghana), 158–60
federalism, 319, 329; and founding crises, 343; in Ghana, 162, 167
Ferlo region, 54 n16, 55, 78 n72, 86, 292
fertilizers, 70, 86–8, 108 n124, 222–3, 274, 277–8, 309 n150
food crop production, 255, 264, 284, 286, 294, 309; in the 1990s, 346; *see also* millet; rice
forced labor, *see* labor, forced
forest use, 37, 79, 188–9, 218–21, 340 n23
forests, sacred, 268; *see also* Diola society
Fouta Toro, *see* Senegal River Valley
Foyer de Ronkh (Senegal), 313
France: local government, 35 n26; peasantry, 21, 347; *see also* Côte d'Ivoire; direct rule; Senegal
Franco-African Community, 66, 114, 203
French Assemblies, Constituent and National, 61, 196, 197 n117, 199–200, 259, 260, 295
French Communist Party (PCF), 200–3, 205
Fulani people, *see* Peul pastoralists
"fusion of elites" (Bayart), 60, 345

Gagnoa uprising, 202, 207; and party struggles, 220 n183
Gambia, 95, 131
gender, 22, 251, 257, 277–8, 323; *see also* labor, women's
gerontocracy, 101, 110, 251, 268, 278–9; and out-migration, 257 n28, 265–6

397

Index

Geschiere, Peter, xii, 122, 137
Ghana, 343–4; constitutions 162, 172 n64; elected District Assemblies, 333, 339–40; federalism in, 167, 343; Local Councils, 164–6; localism of politics, 343–4; military coups, 171–2; national land law, 150, 164 n45, 169, 172 n64; and the NLC, UP, and Acheampong, 171–2; under Rawlings, 339–40; Regional Assemblies in, 166; and usurpation, 238; *see also* Akim Abuakwa; Asante chiefs; Asante region; cocoa economy (Ghana); CPP; Ghana, northern; Ghana, southern; Gold Coast; Nkrumah, Kwame; NLM; usurpation
Ghana, northern, 148, 162, 172 n65, 174–5; 1990s local state reforms, 333; *see also* Dagomba
Ghana, southern: Ga, 344; Volta region, 344; *see also* Akim Abuakwa; Asante region; Gold Coast; Swedru
Ghana Commercial Bank, 172
Gold Coast, 146 n4, 163 n44; as a federation of "native states," 343–4; *see also* Ghana
Grand Nord (Côte d'Ivoire), 272–3, 281–2, 333 n15
Great Lakes region (Africa), 24 n18
green revolution, 86
groundnut basin (Senegal), 57, colonial chieftaincy, 50–1, 57, 61, 63; under colonial rule, 54–60; Diourbel, 68, 80, 80 n75, 86 n84, 89 n93; Kaolack, 83; Kebemer, 83 n82; land tenure, 73–9; landholding size, 77 n68; landlord-stranger relations, 73; Louga, 47 n4, 80 n74; municipalities, 83, 120; in the 1990s, 73, 76, 78, 81 n77, 90–2, 336–8; Nouvelle Politique Agricole, 311; and the PDS, 91; and the Petite Côte, 86 n84, 327; powersharing in, 67–83, 90–2, 281; regional-level, 80–2; Rural Councils (CRs), 73–9, 84, 89, 93; and Sine, 92–3; social structure, *see* Mouride confrérie, Tidjane confrérie; territorial administration, 84, 88 n90; territorial demarcation, 50, 58, 64, 80–3; Touba, 68, 77 n68; and the UPS/PS party-state, 64, 72, 80, 90 n95;

villages, 69–73; *see also* groundnut economy, central Senegal; Mouride confrérie; Sine; Tidjane confrérie; Wolof kingdoms and aristocrats
groundnut economy, central Senegal: cooperatives including SIPs, 55–7, 61, 70–2, 63; decline, 78, 86, 90–1, 99 n102, 132–3, 138, 337; expansion 53–6, 73–9; fertilizers, 70, 86–8; labor, 52–3; land pioneering, 53–4, 77–9, 132–4; land tenure, 73–9; marketing, 70–2, 81–3, 86 n85; marketing (parallel), 131; Mouride marabouts as producers, 79 n72, 87, 90; output, 128–9; price subsidy, 131; and rural development, 81 n77, 84, 86–8; *see also* Animation Rurale; groundnut economy, Lower Casamance
groundnut economy, Lower Casamance, 98–9, 128–9; cooperatives, 127–32; expansion of, 107–9; parallel markets, 131
groundnuts, as a wage good, 235
Guèye, Lamine, 61–3, 91, 113–14, 295–6
Guinée-Bissau, 137

head tax, 103, 189, 209, 255
Hechter, Michael, 11, 21 n13, 22 n15, 34; *Containing Nationalism*, 138–40, 319; on secessionism, 345 n25
historical sociology, *see* macrosociology
HIV/AIDS, 352
hometown associations, 210–11, 233, 246, 327, 340 n22, 346; *see also* associational life
Houphouet(-Boigny), Félix, 142–3, 281; and end of forced labor, 258; ideology, 142–3, 178, 218, 228; and the Moro Naba, 199–201; and rural bourgeoisie, 235–9; and SAA, 196–7; and Senoufo notables, 259–60; and western Burkina Faso, 259; *see also* Côte d'Ivoire; French Assemblies; PDCI
Huntington, Samuel, 349
Hyden, Goran, 11, 22 n14, 23 n17

ideology, 11, 14–15, 142–3, 146, 174, 178, 218; nativist, 229; populist, 244, 237, 331
India, 322

Index

SFIO (French Socialist Party): in Côte d'Ivoire, 202 n136; in Senegal, 61–4, 112–14; *see also* Guèye, Lamine
sharecropping, 149–52, 186, 286, 289, 303, 321 n4
Sine (Senegal), 75 n59, 92–3
SIPs (Sociétés Indigènes de Prévoyance): in Côte d'Ivoire, 227 n201, 257; in Senegal, 55–7, 61, 63, 70–1, 108–9, 293
So, Jaabe, 305 n136, 305 n138
social cohesion, 22–3; and ethnic identity, 26; horizontal form, 103–4, 137, 325–6
social structure: change in, 315–17, 351–2; and collective action, 237, 330; and democracy, 116, 324; and out-migration, 257 n28, 265–6, 273; and rational choice theory, 18–19, 350–1; and rural development, 286; and settlement schemes, 314; and state capacity, 276; variation in, 21, 24–30, 323–4; *see also* class relations; state building; territorial authority
SODEPRA (Société pour le Développement des Productions Animales), 279
SODERIZ (Société pour le Développement de la Riziculture), 265
SODEVA (Société de Développement et de Vulgarisation Agricole), 88
SODIFITEX (Société pour le Développement des Fibres Textiles), 188 n148
SOMIVAC (Société pour la Mise en Valeur de la Casamance), 148 n118
SONAR (Société Nationale d'Approvisionnement Rurale), 81 n77
Soninké society (Senegal River Valley), 286, 291, 305, 307
state, African, 5; capacity of, 276; and state autonomy, 16–17; 97, 119, 123, 216, 234, 329, 341
state building: and capitalist agriculture, 346; in Europe, 9–10, 19, 22–3, 34; highwater mark, 324; and territorial authority in Africa, 135–6, 138–40, 143, 148–9, 233–4, 238–9, 267, 280–2, 284–6, 323; *see also* local state
state retreat, 241, 320, 335; and the empty envelope, 317, 335

state-society relations literature, 5
Structural Adjustment Programs (SAPs), *see* neoliberal reforms; World Bank
subnational analysis, 39, 178
subnationalist opposition, 139–40, 319; *see also* regionalism
Sufi brotherhoods, *see* Mouride confrérie, Tidjane confrérie
sugar production, 273 n64, 282, 292
Swedru (southern Ghana), 163 n44, 165 n47, 166, 175 n70
swollen shoot fungus, 157
Sy, Abdou Aziz, 58 n30, 296
Sy, Malik, 58 n30, 59

Tall, Saidhou Nourou, 295–7, 303 n129
Tanzania, 300 n122, 327, 334; *see also* settlement schemes
taxation, 7, 28–9, 143; *see also* export-crop marketing; head tax; labor, forced
teachers and schooling, 76 n62, 89 n93, 113 n136, 119, 125, 198, 327, 339
territorial authority: scope of, 22, 34; and unit demarcation, 64, 80, 82–3; 107, 117, 165–6, 252–3, 270 n57, 293; *see also* chiefly authority; chiefs; land tenure; local state; state building
territorial politics, *see* center-region relations; regionalism
thought experiment, 86 n86
Tidjane confrérie, 52, 58 n30, 59, 296, 303 n129; and collective action, 65–6, 234, 297–8; electoral politics, 60–3; powersharing with UPS/PS, 67–83, 241–2, 337; *see also* groundnut basin; Mouride confrérie; Senegal
Tiembara chiefdom (Côte d'Ivoire), 246–51; *see also* Korhogo region
time horizons, 325, 351
topography, political, xi, 241, 320, 324, 345
Touconleur and Soninké notabilities, 284, 291, 294–5, 297–8, 302–3, 310–11; *see also* Senegal River Valley
Toucouleur society, 286–91; *see also* Senegal River Valley
Touré, Lamine, 197
Touré, Samory, *see* Samory empire
trade union leaders, 205; *see also* urban constituencies

Index

Continued from page iii

Roberto Franzosi, *The Puzzle of Strikes: Class and State Strategies in Postwar Italy*
Geoffrey Garrett, *Partisan Politics in the Global Economy*
Miriam Golden, *Heroic Defeats: The Politics of Job Loss*
Merilee Serrill Grindle, *Changing the State*
Anna Grzymala-Busse, *Redeeming the Communist Past: The Regeneration of Communist Parties in East Central Europe*
Frances Hagopian, *Traditional Politics and Regime Change in Brazil*
J. Rogers Hollingsworth and Robert Boyer, eds., *Contemporary Capitalism: The Embeddedness of Institutions*
Ellen Immergut, *Health Politics: Interests and Institutions in Western Europe*
Torben Iversen, *Contested Economic Institutions*
Torben Iversen, Jonas Pontusson, David Soskice, eds., *Unions, Employers, and Central Banks: Macroeconomic Coordination and Institutional Change in Social Market Economies*
Thomas Janoski and Alexander M. Hicks, eds., *The Comparative Political Economy of the Welfare State*
Pauline Jones Luong, *Institutional Change and Political Continuity in Post-Soviet Central Asia: Power, Perceptions and Pacts*
David C. Kang, *Crony Capitalism: Corruption and Development in South Korea and the Philippines*
Junko Kato, *Regressive Taxation and the Welfare State: Path Dependence and Policy Diffusion*
Robert O. Keohane and Helen B. Milner, eds., *Internationalization and Domestic Politics*
Herbert Kitschelt, *The Transformation of European Social Democracy*
Herbert Kitschelt, Peter Lange, Gary Marks, and John D. Stephens, eds., *Continuity and Change in Contemporary Capitalism*
Herbert Kitschelt, Zdenka Mansfeldova, Radek Markowski, and Gabor Toka, *Post-Communist Party Systems*
David Knoke, Franz Urban Pappi, Jeffrey Broadbent, and Yutaka Tsujinaka, eds., *Comparing Policy Networks*
Allan Kornberg and Harold D. Clarke, *Citizens and Community: Political Support in a Representative Democracy*
Amie Kreppel, *The European Parliament and Supranational Party Systems: A Study in Institutional Change*
David D. Laitin, *Language Repertoires and State Construction in Africa*
Fabrice Lehoucq and Ivan Molina, *Stuffing the Ballot Box: Fraud, Electoral Reform, and Democratization in Costa Rica*
Mark Irving Lichbach and Alan S. Zuckerman, eds., *Comparative Politics: Rationality, Culture, and Structure*
Doug McAdam, John McCarthy, and Mayer Zald, eds., *Comparative Perspectives on Social Movements*
Scott Mainwaring and Matthew Soberg Shugart, eds., *Presidentialism and Democracy in Latin America*